PRIVATE LIVES

Benita Eisler

Private Lives

MEN AND WOMEN OF THE FIFTIES

FRANKLIN WATTS
New York · London · Toronto · Sydney
1 9 8 6

The following songs are quoted with the kind permission of the publishers:

My Troubles Are Over by James V. Monaco & Edgar Leslie © 1928 Edwin H. Morris & Company, A Division of MPL Communications, Inc. © Renewed 1956 Edwin H. Morris, A Division of MPL Communications, Inc. International copyright secured. All rights reserved.

Rockin' Robin by Leon Rene (J. Thomas) Copyright 1958. Recordo Music Publishers—BMI.

The Chapel of Love by Jeff Barry, Philip Spector, and Ellie Greenwich. Copyright 1964 Trio Music Co., Inc. All rights reserved.

Prehistoric Man by Betty Comden, Adolph Green, and Roger Eden. Copyright 1949 (Renewed) Warner Bros, Inc. All rights reserved.

Portions of the interview with Martin Duberman in Chapter 7 appeared previously in *Salamagundi*, Fall 1982/Winter 1983. They are quoted with permission of the author.

The photograph *Longboat Key, Florida, 1958* by Joe Steinmetz is reproduced with the generous permission of the Photography Archive, Carpenter Center for the Visual Arts, Harvard University.

Library of Congress Cataloging-in-Publication Data

Eisler, Benita.
  Private lives.

  Bibliography: p.
  Includes index.
  1. United States—Social conditions—1945–
2. United States—Economic conditions—1945–
3. United States—Moral conditions. 4. United States—
Popular culture—History—20th century. I. Title.
HN58.E36 1986   973.92   85–29606
ISBN 0–531–15010–0

For Rachel

CONTENTS

A couple of cars,
A couple of kids
A couple in clover
Just picture us there,
Floating on air
My troubles are over.

from "My Troubles Are Over"
     James Monaco and Edgar Leslie

. . . one always remains a child of his age,
even in what one deems one's very own.

     Sigmund Freud to Wilhelm Fleiss
     November 5, 1897

1

"JUST PICTURE US THERE...."

The scene is a Florida beach with white sand and palm trees. The people are an attractive all-American middle-class family on vacation. Dad soberly tends the hot dogs on the grill. Mom, a wholesome blond Venus just emerged from the sea, smiles proudly at her three children. The year is 1958.

Does the picture* speak to you?

What does it say?

To anyone who came of age in the 1950s, this image of the ideal nuclear family on holiday evokes mixed emotions.

We laugh. There's something funny here, starting with the clothes. Mom's decorous bathing suit reminds us that we are ancient history. Barely had we begun to think of ourselves as adults when the fashions of our youth cornered the nostalgia market, somewhere between camp and serious revival. Fifties style— clothing, furniture, music, even the once-reviled gas-guzzler—is big business.

---

* Joe Steinmetz, *Longboat Key, Florida, 1958.* See jacket illustration and frontispiece.

My daughter, a college senior, and her friends favor a disco whose decor, described as "tacky fifties country club," features a stuffed marlin over the bar. How hilarious!

It began with high preppy in the seventies. After a decade of olive drab army surplus or denim worn by sixties campus guerrillas, the Brooks Brothers look was back, rendered a little less anemic than the original by adding an L. L. Bean down-filled vest.

Now trendy young people adopt witty send-ups of fifties sleaze —pointy-toed, stiletto-heeled pumps worn with leopard-patterned toreador pants and rhinestone-framed harlequin glasses. Young men with DAs or Marine "jughead" haircuts sport the Hawaiian shirts that once camouflaged the paunch of presidents. In chillier weather, they don "draped" one-button sharkskin jackets and outsize tweed overcoats that appear to be made entirely of lint.

For older trend setters, fifties home furnishings are the hottest item. Young Japanese industrialists are snapping up "complete chrome bars"; spun aluminum "tree lamps," molecular clocks, and biomorphic cocktail tables. Low kitsch has still more passionate devotees: collectors kill for harlequin-patterned or flocked wallpaper and sparkle-plenty Formica dinette sets. And recently I read of a chic Paris housewares shop whose entire stock consists of American blenders and mixers of "classic" fifties design: Warings, Osterizers, Sunbeams, and Mixmasters are worth a fortune in francs. *Our* wedding presents!

This vacationing family hasn't brought a blender to the beach. But if they left their kitchen at home, they appear to have carried the entire patio with them, starting with the fixture most emblematic of fifties family life—the backyard barbecue. Once the hunter, father has acquired a new role: he's now in charge of all grill work. While he tames the fire, the family unpacks a tidy checked tablecloth and other utensils designed to domesticate the barbarism of outdoor eating: a proper picnic basket complete with cutlery and sectioned plastic plates, each with its own fitted tumbler.

A Jane Powell look-alike, the mother who smiles benignly down at her three children has certainly bought the *Good Housekeeping* message. There is no holiday from good nutrition. They've brought their own (all-meat) frankfurters to grill, along with fresh fruit and milk for the kids—no soda pop, potato chips (of which 532 million pounds[1] would be sold to other Americans that same year), or packaged cookies. Even on the road, these parents are impervious to pleas for junk food.

Water safety rules are enforced, we can be sure. Even in the shallow waters of the Gulf, there is an inner tube for the non-swimmers. The children will have to wait an hour after eating before splashing back into the briny. At the end of the day, there will be no debris left on the beach by these good citizens: everything will disappear magically back into the car—the only member of the family not in the picture.

Indeed, without an automobile, our Florida vacationers, weighted down with kids, barbecue, and beach chairs, wouldn't be here. By 1958, the year this photograph was taken, the number of automobiles in the United States had doubled from the 25,500,000 registered at the end of World War II. In 1956, the National Defense Highway Act authorized the paving of the nation with a multibillion dollar interstate highway system. See America First became a slogan eagerly exploited by both public and private interests, and automobile tourism became big business. No day-trippers on the evidence of their freight, our family could have stayed at one of the more than 40,000 new motels or motor courts constructed by the end of the fifties.[2] And if Dad's credit rating was as solid as this picture suggests, he could have paid the bill with his Diner's Club card. By 1958 the eight year old credit company was billing over $90 million annually to some 750,000 members.

The invisible car (with a probable second one left at home in the garage) had more crucial functions than holiday transportation. As suburbanites—to judge from the number of youngsters and father's practiced crouch at the grill—their daily schedules depended on a car.

If father was a "junior executive" (a title that doesn't even exist anymore), he and his family would have joined the one out of three suburbanites who pulled up stakes every three years, adding up to 33 million moves made by Americans in 1958.

Indeed, willingness to relocate would be a key factor in father's success. The carefree family holiday he has provided, along with the visible consumer durables—all on one income—suggest that the executive suite is in sight. Clothing, feeding, and educating his three youngsters doesn't seem to worry him. Kids' indulgences will certainly be no problem; neither the hula hoops (which reached their peak of fad frenzy in 1958) and Barbie doll (with friends and extensive wardrobes) that his daughter will require by next year nor the allowances that all three children will soon need to buy records (70 percent of all those manufactured in 1958 were purchased by teenagers).[3]

As baby boom parents, moreover, our family may not stop at three. In 1957, the year before this picture was taken, the annual American birthrate reached an all-time peak.* In answer to a nosy census interviewer, asking this head of household how many children he wanted, our father might have echoed a graduate of the class of 1955: "I'd like six kids," he reported. "I don't know why I say that—it just seems like a minimum production goal."[5]

Looking at this picture, we would never guess that in 1958 the American economy was suffering a serious depression, largely the result of 1957 automobile overproduction (including Ford's disastrous Edsel). Unemployment that spring rose to 7.2 percent—the peak of the decade. Yet the optimistic, well-outfitted group here suggests an immunity to economic downturns, like that of middle-class America itself. By the end of the fifties, prosperity had acquired a momentum of its own: No culture so new and shiny

---

* Had the birthrate remained at the 1957 level, the average woman would have given birth to about four children.[4]

could ever rust. With interest rates at 4 percent to encourage more building, borrowing, and spending, we would ride out the bad times.

To compare the end of the decade with its beginnings is to see two Americas.

When the fifties began, John Chancellor observes in his introduction to an unforgettable collection of photographs of the period, "the look and feel of the countryside, of the big cities and the small towns was very much of the Thirties; America in the summertime was still a country of ceiling fans, pitchers of ice-water and dusty roads . . . where Sears Roebuck still did a brisk business in selling parts for Model T and Model A Fords."[6] By the end of the decade, everything was air-conditioned and automatic and self-service; there were TVs and transistors, credit cards and computers, long-playing records and king-size, filter-tipped cigarettes. Chrome, glass, steel, aluminum, shiny glazed brick, and baked enamel were everywhere. We had become a sleek, spiffy, big-spending country, where the accent was on youth—babies, teenagers, coeds, and "young marrieds."

In 1958, about to select the first astronauts, create a 49th state, and synthesize pencillin, we could afford to ignore the 200,000 Volkswagens sold that year, the founding of the John Birch Society, the stoning of Vice President Nixon in Peru, and the cost of subsidizing the South Vietnamese armed forces.

This was America when I graduated from college in 1958. If you had shown this picture to me and my classmates—then or earlier, when we were in high school—we would have seen it as a crystal ball. There we were in five or ten years. The wife and mother in the photograph was just "the kind of woman we thought we would become," described by Susan Allen Toth, who graduated from Smith three years later, as the woman her hometown of Ames, Iowa, regarded as the American ideal. There she

> rolled snowballs with two smiling red-cheeked children or unpacked a picnic lunch on emerald grass as an Irish setter lounged nearby, or led a cherubic toddler into the water. Her

tall handsome husband hovered close by. . . . Pretty and well-dressed, she laughed happily into the KodaColor sunshine that flooded her future."[7]

But something happened in the next twenty-five years. That "gleaming ideal," Toth points out, "had become tarnished, scratched and blackened as the copper bottoms on the shiny saucepans we got as wedding presents."

Some of what happened in the last two decades I hear in the reactions of my friends and contemporaries as they look at this picture. Those first giggles and guffaws or sighs of nostalgia stop abruptly.

"It makes me feel guilty," said a close friend, divorced, with three nearly grown daughters and a successful career. "My life was supposed to be just like that family—forever. The picture reminds me that I've failed."

But a friend who is a psychoanalyst saw that "wholesome blond family" as "Nazi propaganda." "That photograph spells 'Fascist' to me," he said. "During the Cold War, we *became* Nazi Germany, celebrating 'fake' family life, physical fitness, children's health, the sanctity of the home. It says, 'Be successful and mind your own business.' "

"I thought I was free of sexist rage," hissed the most ladylike of my friends, "until I saw that penis-oriented fantasy: the ghoulish middle-class male with his hot dogs at the ready, his umbrella erected, his palm trees erupted, having spawned three kids without ever removing his J. Press swim trunks!"

Another friend, a man who would have been my last candidate for a misogynist, peered at the mother, smiling fondly down at her children, and sneered, "Look at the silly way she's posturing for the photographer; at least the rest of the family is behaving naturally."

A usually tough feminist saw the wife as a figure of pathos. "No one," she said, "is paying any attention to that poor woman."

To a college classmate, divorced and remarried, the entire scene spelled "horror"—just because it's so real," she said. The reality it brought back to her was her youth as a time of "pretending, faking every reaction," in a period when "you couldn't express a frank thought or a real feeling. It's all those games we had to play—all the things I hated but did—from getting dressed up and going to dances to getting married."

"Did I ever tell you," she said, still looking at the picture, "I crossed my fingers when I repeated my wedding vows?"

She had never told me.

My "amusing" fifties outdoor portrait proved to be a TAT* of my age group. The "story behind the picture" was characterized by sadness, guilt, and anger—political as well as personal—directed at the "myths we bought" and included feelings that hadn't surfaced in years of conversation.

Private Lives is about the man and woman in this picture—about all of us who expected our lives to resemble this ideal of togetherness and some who were forced to pretend they did, differing from our own parents only in our greater prosperity and success.

How did we get from there to here? From our expectations about this image and our disillusionment with it? Strangely enough, the story of our generation, we who graduated into an America of unprecedented affluence and anxiety, has yet to be told. Maybe we preferred it that way. We were not so much a "silent" generation as a secretive, private one; a cohort of closet individualists, our "real" lives were lived underground. *The Subterraneans*, the title of Jack Kerouac's novel about a handful of Beats, is a description that would fit many of us. Outwardly conforming, "we dived into convention," a friend once said, seeking the protective coloration of wary creatures who scent danger everywhere.

Until the 1970s, I never thought of myself as part of any age, period, or generation.

In the mid-fifties, when I was an undergraduate, I was dimly aware that our age group was thought to suffer from some kind

---

* Thematic Apperception Test, in which the subject is asked to make up a story based on the figures in an intentionally ambiguous illustration.

of aphasia; we had been dubbed "silent," "quiet," or, in tribute to our bland, boring leader, the Eisenhower Generation.

We had earned these labels, we were told, by virtue of our collective "apathy." Politically "uninvolved," morally "uncommitted" (some of us even "alienated"), we lacked the fiery idealism of young people in other eras and in other countries, who were trying to change the world.*

Yawn. When I say I was but "dimly aware" of the editorial clucking that we inspired, I am offering myself as Exhibit A in apolitical apathy: "part of the problem," as a later generation would say.

Foreign affairs, the domestic economy, the Cold War and the struggle (then just beginning) for racial integration all seemed as remote as the possibility of life on Mars. The year I entered college—1954—saw the Army-McCarthy hearings; the fall of Dien Bien Phu; the Algerian revolt against French rule; a CIA-financed right-wing coup in Guatemala; the banning of Thoreau's *Walden* from U.S. Information Service libraries abroad, on the grounds that it was "downright Socialistic"; and the Supreme Court decision in *Brown* v. *Board of Education*, which made segregation in the public schools illegal.

I may have glanced at headlines or skimmed an occasional article on these events; certainly, the issues they represented were never the subject of even a few moments' discussion among my friends. The few who were exceptions to this ideological indifference were considered tediously "earnest types." To my shame, I recall a classmate trying to induce a group of us to come to a lecture on apartheid by a professor of government recently returned from South Africa. As I would do so often later in life, I paid my two dollars for a benefit ticket—in order not to "waste" an evening hearing about it.

However, if we were apathetic, we were anything but silent; we

---

* Needless to say, ten years later, when young people became the romantic revolutionaries our elders blamed us for not being, they were confronted by guns and tear gas.

talked all the time. But what we talked about was ourselves (taking care to say nothing revealing); sex, love, and the difference between the two; friendship; parents; clothes; books—but mostly boys. On every blind date we all hoped to meet the handsome, smart, witty young man—with shining prospects and a beautiful soul—we would marry. It never occurred to us that our expectations (if normal) were anything but individual. The notion that my friends and I could possibly have anything in common with other Americans who happened to have been born in 1937 would have suggested to us only extraordinary simplicity of mind. In the year following my graduation in 1958—the year of our vacationing family—almost all of my college friends were married. Three Junes later, I joined the ranks of the 96 percent of us wed within four years of receiving our B.A.* My relative lateness was revealed by the contents of the closet my husband-to-be helped me move. More than half the clothes were bridesmaids' dresses; a pastel spectrum of organza skirts, ranging from pistachio to pale peach, hung there like a headless corps de ballet.

As young marrieds and then parents, we marched in a phalanx through the early sixties. Flanked by my peers, I still saw only individuals. Most of them were women, friends from different phases of my life—college, graduate school, two years of employment, sandbox and nursery-school mothers. We exchanged recipes and books and invited each other to occasional dinner parties, where we eyed curiously the husbands we had long heard about but never met.

On timetables that varied only slightly, all of us were "phasing back" into the real world, returning to school or looking for work.** For many of my friends, the decision to seek careers grew

---

* The statistics of my college class are identical with the national figures. By 1957, 96 percent of Americans "of marriageable age" were indeed married.

** Harvard economist Victor Fuchs points out that women were already returning to the labor force by the early fifties: in 1951, the new peak of women workers—19,308,000—far exceeded the wartime records set by Rosie the Riveter. Betty Friedan's argument that only a job could save women from the feminine mystique was reasoning after the fact.[8]

out of an astonishing change—political engagement. The spring-
board had been volunteer work at the grass-roots level, in one
area or another of the New Politics. From canvassing for reform
candidates, tutoring in settlement houses, or starting neighborhood cooperative nursery schools, they started getting degrees in
social work, law, or education in order to become professionals in
Great Society programs.

After a decade of sitting peacefully in the library, translating
French, I was ready for full-time work. Marching against the war
in Vietnam and poverty at home, the shock of actually breaking
the law—through civil disobedience—and being maced on the
mall of our nation's capital convinced me that I, too, had changed.
But a few weeks of job hunting, and I began to feel like a historical relic of a period lost in the mists of time.

The formal, paternalistic manners of the men who had interviewed us for jobs when we were fresh out of college, had under-
gone a radical transformation—along with their office attire.
Jackets and ties had given way to torso-hugging turtlenecks and
even jeans. One executive interviewed me stretched out on a sofa
in his office. The president of a small publisher and his lieutenant
did manage to stay seated in upright positions, but after jocularly
discussing my qualifications as though I were not present, they
concluded the discussion by saying: "It's too bad you're married;
we only hire divorced or single women. But we want you to
know," the chief trumpeted in mock solemnity, followed by hoots
of laughter, "you have an irresistible smile."

In the elevator, my rage and humiliation were compounded by
confusion and self-hatred. I simply had not known how to behave.
To be sure, I no longer wore the hat and white gloves deemed
essential for job interviews a decade earlier. But my reactions to
what had happened placed me somewhere between Alice Roose-
velt Longworth and the young women who were beginning to
march in feminist parades, bearing placards that read: Don't Cook
Dinner. Starve a Rat Today.

My anger was not assuaged at home. My husband laughed. "You're overreacting," he said. "Where's your sense of humor?" I was not amused by his amusement.

Hearing my boiling wrath, a friend introduced me to her women's group. The narratives that unfolded at bimonthly meetings were harrowing. I heard accounts of seduction by fathers and gynecologists, stories of sexism and harassment in the workplace and in graduate school, and confessions of guilt about everything from spending an afternoon away from one's child to failure to give the lovely dinner parties that had inaugurated married life. The activity that was accompanied by the least guilt, it seemed, was adultery—occasional or habitual. (Had *everybody* crossed their fingers when repeating their wedding vows?)

Husbands, as they emerged from these accounts, were shadowy figures. Like those of my other friends, they worked tremendously long hours at professional occupations. At home they were weary, irritable, or preoccupied. Provided the household ran smoothly, they did not much care what their wives were up to, whether it was lovers or law school. Marriages were already dissolving; often, one or both partners were in psychotherapy.

The women in the group were all the same age and all college graduates. With one exception, we had all married within that magic four years after school. Most of us had children. Yet our puzzlement and problems struck no one as generational. The times were changing, but our difficulties in changing with them or staying the way we were rang no historical bells. As atypical urban dwellers, moreover, we appeared to have little in common with our classmates who now lived behind the wheels of station wagons in the suburbs. If "their" problem had no name, ours had many, and one cause—men: withdrawn, absentee, hectoring, or demanding; interested or insufficiently interested in only one thing; exploiting privileges unearned by either professional competence or contribution to domestic life. Yet no one ever thought to ask: Why *us*? Why had our expectations (the same, after all, as our mothers') fallen victim to such overwhelming disappointment? Surely women had not always felt the hatred, fear, and contempt for men that I heard all around me?

By the early 1970s I was employed full time; more often than not, at the public television station where I worked, that meant a twelve-hour day. My colleagues in production were representatives of an age group entirely foreign to me. These young men and women, at most ten years my junior, seemed to have grown up in another century.

Like us, most of them had married soon after college. But here all resemblance ended. Their unions, which had lasted on average no more than two years, left no issue, few scars—and almost no memories. One colleague said that the only thing he could remember about the young woman who had briefly been his wife were her bills from a boutique called Betsey Bunky Nini. But she had paid them herself, he added, honestly. Few of these thirty-plus young men had ever supported a family nor did they expect to do so. One exception was a coworker who was a father with custody of his two children. He was suing his former wife for child support. "She earns more than I do," he said, "and she wanted to be free to pursue her career. So she's going to pay," he announced. She did. "What ended your marriage?" I asked, as colleagues became close friends. The answers were most often conveyed in verbal shrugs: "Who-knows-we-just-seem-to-have-drifted-apart."

Many of our friends were getting divorced at this time. But the painful dramas of their dissolving marriages—"like surgery without anesthesia" was one description—made a study in contrasts. First, the couples we knew were almost all parents of young children. As yet, few wives were working full time and the realization of their economic dependence had just begun to dawn. But that was the least of it. Among our contemporaries, both spouses were overwhelmed by a sense of shame, failure, and defeat—a literal terror of telling parents, friends, even their children's teachers. The husbands—usually the ones to move out—added the disorientation of homelessness to their other griefs. But whether we spent an evening with "him" or "her," it was likely to become a long and tearful night, often with blood-chilling outpourings of rage and hatred toward the soon-to-be ex-spouse.

When I compared these sagas of suffering with the anecdotes of my associates—of the when-I-was-married-to-what's-her-name genre—it was clear that more was at issue than the duration of marriages or even the presence of children. The terrible grief, guilt, and especially the disappointment and betrayal I heard from my contemporaries bore witness to something larger. My friends and I shared an assumption that was not part of my younger colleagues' cultural baggage. We had expected to be married forever. We were the last of our kind.

Still, my consciousness, which had been "raised" on most issues concerning the relations between men and women, never focused on the question of generation.

At the end of the seventies, I came upon the writings of young women who left the farms of New England in the 1820s, to work in the cotton mills of Lowell, Massachusetts. Earning three dollars a week (less room and board), they were the highest-paid female work force in the world.

"My, don't it feel fine," one young woman wrote home to her sister, "to be dependent on no one."

Even as I wrote of their exultant sense of adventure and self-reliance, it never occurred to me how different they were from us. With our college and even graduate degrees, we were going to "feel fine" supported by men for the rest of our lives.

It was a man who finally introduced me to generational consciousness—precisely one of those men who expected to do the supporting and still does. I was interviewing him for a book about class in America. One of the richest self-made men in this country, he is a dramatic illustration of why the Horatio Alger myth lives. A grocer's son from a tiny Southern mountain hamlet, the first in his family to graduate from college, he created a multinational empire. Now, in the tradition of self-made fathers, he was complaining about his children. With all the advantages and options in the world, his sons were busy dropping in and out of college, postponing career decisions, moving in and out of cohabitation arrangements with women—definitely not "settling down."

"Those of us who came of age in the fifties," he said, "had no choice. You had to be a husband, a provider, and a success. Waal," he drawled, "you know how it was then. . . ."

But I *hadn't* known how it was then. Not for men. My men friends—*what* men friends? I didn't *have* any men friends my age. He had drawn me out of the class "frame" I was exploring into another perspective altogether.

A multimillionaire, corporate buccaneer, and political conservative—a man whom, moments before, I had felt to be as remote from my life (and sympathies) as a combination of Daniel Boone, Al Capone, and General William Westmoreland—was telling me that he and I had something important in common, that we shared some basic assumptions and beliefs because we were born a year apart. More astonishing still was to hear this "good ol' boy" take it for granted that our "subtext" of mutual understanding dissolved any gender gap and transcended social, professional, ethnic, and regional differences.

If anything, the substance of his remark was still more of a revelation. Did the men who were my contemporaries really feel they had had no choices—"back then"? White males who had gone to college? Who then chose from a challenging array of careers? For whom we had waited while they made up their minds whether or not to choose *us*? Such a provocative notion bore thinking about.

Like the good fifties' student I once was, incapable of thinking without reading, I read all the books about my generation I could find. What I found was startling. Books about the 1950s addressed themselves to men only. The "other sex" was either completely absent or a token presence.

To critic Paul Goodman, the oppressive cynicism and conformity of fifties culture was a problem for boys only; girls didn't even get to grow up absurd. They got married, which, in his view, was the natural order of things. In William H. Whyte's study of young men moving up the corporation, wives put in a cameo appearance at kaffeeklatches or wielding vacuum cleaners. Even so enlightened a scholar as David Riesman found his "lonely crowd" to be a mass of men. In the feminist books that began to appear in the early sixties, men had become the faceless enemy, abandoning women to suburban anomie during the day and turning into toddlers at twilight, when they demanded a cold martini instead of a warm bottle.

Jeremiads on the evils of suburbia began to be published in the early fifties. These studies did include men, women, and children, but their real subject was the deforming influence of a certain type of environment. With their first down payment on the subdivision ranch house,* individuals who had been loving couples became estranged from one another. Slavishly concerned with the opinion of neighbors and obsessed with their children "fitting in," they turned their young into well-adjusted robots.

No wonder the remark of my Southern entrepreneur had come as such a revelation. Among the many ironies of the Age of Togetherness, the only books suggesting that men and women were "in it" together turned us into families of laboratory mice! Watching us run about—ever more frantic or disconsolate—social scientists peeking through the picture window of a scale-model ranch house concluded that the behavior of an otherwise "normal" fifties mouse family had been modified by negative conditioning.

There was no objective book about our generation—men and women. Were we so silent and forgettable that we had actually been forgotten?

How had we gotten to where we were? And why did we end up choosing to marry younger and have children at younger ages than ever before in American history?

---

* The movie *No Down Payment* (1956), discussed in Chapter 10, is a gruesome morality tale of the malign influence of suburbia on young families.

I was still thinking about the books I hadn't found, when I came across the picture on the jacket. Its stylized "normalcy" seemed to say it all: the family-centeredness and separation of husband and wife and the "warning" contrast of the woman alone* with two children, seen slightly beyond our happy group. The intense and contradictory reactions of my friends to this fifties icon astonished me even more than the remarks of the Southern entrepreneur. They were us—this well-scrubbed, successful-looking family. They made up my mind for me: we had not been heard from in our common fate. What happened when we walked off that beach toward the car? Were we sunburnt and quarreling, joking and relaxed, sulking, or secretly relieved the holiday was over?

They were in my mind as I thought about who we were collectively. What is common about that "common fate?"

If Freud acknowledged that we are, all of us, children of our age, others have found the idea of any life as typical or representative to be reductive: a flattening-out of the richness of individual psychology and fate.

To the extent that any "frame analysis" necessarily excludes others, this is true: Marx's "economic man" would not recognize his Freudian self in any mirror. Still, I'm convinced that there exist what philosopher Karl Jaspers called "representative destinies." None of the men and women in this book—myself included —would be what they are had they come of age during any other decade. In no other period of American history could our expectations of "the good life," the way those expectations were realized, and the particular disappointments of our "answered prayers" have been the same.

---

* The figure of the "single mother" is in fact photographer Joe Steinmetz's daughter; far from being single, she was and is (according to her father) happily married, shown here with two of her five children. (Possibly her husband had to work too hard to afford a vacation!) Moreover, Ms. Steinmetz was one of those women who returned to work in advance of feminist exhortations. She soon took over the editorship of the popular *Ladies Home Journal* column: "Can This Marriage Be Saved?"

In important ways I am a classic fifties model. Starting with the most obvious, I am the first generation of my family to be college educated. At forty-eight, I have been married for twenty-four years: half my life and all my life as an adult.

By other measures, though, I once thought of myself as atypical: unlike almost all my friends, I have only one child, and I have never been divorced, had an abortion, or any psychotherapy. The absence of the last three experiences, which have marked most of my generation, point to aspects of my character of which I am not in the least proud: I am prudent and fearful, secretive about my personal life, and stuck with the lingering belief that, in adversity, I must exhaust all resources before I am "entitled" to help.

Yet these same qualities that made me a throwback (even a mutant) among my friends are still, I discovered, characteristic of many, many other contemporaries, especially once I crossed the Hudson River heading west.

Describing the picture of the vacationing family as "still my ideal—a dream which I made come true" (even to the handsome husband barbecuing hot dogs on the grill), Betts Saunders, former high-school homecoming queen, sorority belle, and wife of a successful doctor in a large Midwestern city, added soberly, "I was always very aware of the consequences of everything you do. And I was careful never, *never* to do anything which could harm me or damage my future."

Dan Ross, who has many times been tempted to give up his law practice for a career in photography and to leave his marriage for lovers with whom he glimpses the possibility of a "complete and passionate life," explains his refusal to do either in terms of an "inability to commit to anything fully."

"I'll go in up to my knees," he said, "but never over my head."

These are only two of the men and women in this book who, like the no-choice "husband, provider, and success," told me that particularly in the experiences I have refused, avoided, or missed, I stand revealed as a representative member of my generation.

At one point, I struggled to find categories for my sixteen contemporaries. A classically solid suburban householder and corporate manager was surely a "mainstreamer." Or was he? As I reread, yet again, his reflections on his life and times, I would decide that, like so many of us, he was an outsider who was successfully "passing." Finally, it dawned on me that my perplexity pointed to our most characteristic generational quality: *We are not what we seem.*

Is anyone? Men and women are mysterious and complicated creatures. From the Bible on, our hidden lives have been the stuff of novels and poetry. My great discovery seems to indicate only that those of us who came of age in the fifties (however zombie-like we may appear to those born a decade later) are simply more human than otherwise.

There is a difference, though, in our subterranean selves and hidden lives, that sets us apart from the generations immediately before and after us: a collective discrepancy between the way we are and our protective coloration; the willed blandness in style, speech, and dress; our propensity for and subsequent problems with role-playing; our need for "covers"—from gray flannel suits to marriages in which we could "disappear."

Pointing to the acceptance of authority as the stamp of our generation—the last for whom that will be true—a friend, who is also (as far as I know) a law-abiding lawyer, confessed: "I can be driving along, nowhere close to speeding. When a police car pulls up alongside me, I get that 'cold rush of shit to the heart.' "

As soon as he said that, I thought of the scene in the classic fifties *film noir*, repeated in many variations. The driver is stopped by a kind policeman, who informs him of a loose tire. Why is the motorist sweating profusely as the officer waves him on his way? He happens to have a corpse in the trunk of his car.

Real or imagined, many of us have a corpse in the trunk; in any case, the authorities are "right." But this attitude, indeed so characteristic of us, has another explanation: We did not take our acceptance in the America of the 1950s for granted.

"The story of American culture remains largely the story of our middle class," noted historian Warren M. Susman.[9] And of no period is that more true—perhaps oppressively so—than the fifties.

The sixteen men and women in this book are middle class, but at least one-third did not start there. The story of the fifties is also a history of upward mobility on a scale unprecedented in any industrial society. Thanks to the GI bill, passed in 1946, millions of American men—many first generation and from working-class families—became professionals and managers. Their wives enjoyed or suffered dramatic class change with them.

Because higher education is the crucible that most broadly shapes us as a generation, I have used college classes to date coming of age in the fifties.

Thus, the oldest respondent is Class of 1952—the first class not characterized by returning World War II veterans; the youngest is Class of 1962—one of the last years before the innocent goofiness of keg day contests, pinning ceremonies, and panty raids yielded to sit-ins, demonstrations, and killings.

Over half the men and women in this book are Midwesterners who grew up in small towns. One was raised on a farm; several came of age in the quiet residential neighborhoods of small cities—much smaller, of course, in the late forties and early fifties than now.

I found the majority through a process known as "snowball sampling"; every friend seemed to know a "typical fifties" man and woman I should talk to. Then, when I was a guest on a radio interview show in a large Midwestern city, the host suggested I mention my book, asking anyone who would like to talk about their life and times to call the station. As a measure of how little "we" have been heard from, the switchboard was swamped for two days. Housewives, executives, truckdrivers—even a former FBI agent—wanted to tell me their side of the fifties, and beyond.

When I finished interviewing, I found myself talking to another contemporary, a German sociologist who has been living and teaching here since the early sixties. "I hope you've found people who have changed their sexual orientation in midlife," Wolf Hildebrand said. In his view, ours is the first generation to share this experience in significant numbers. Indeed, two of the women in this book made such a change in their late thirties and early forties, respectively.

With one exception, the men and women who talked to me did not want their real names used. It should surprise no one that sexual adventures, divorce, psychotherapy, and children's problems are still not the stuff of community newsletters in many parts of America.

The exception is also the only respondent I knew before beginning the book. Speaking as a gay man, radical activist, and historian, Martin Duberman said: "I have not suffered all that I have since the fifties to revert to anonymity ever again." This remark is a source of my pride in "our generation." If I had to choose one image of the decade, I would say that the fifties were one big closet. Many men and women in this book have come a long way—in courage, self-acceptance and, not least, honesty.

It is commonly said that researchers share a strange tendency to find what they are looking for. Setting out to give voice to our silent generation, I heard myself in every story told.

We were lucky, they say. They don't want to sound boastful or attract the evil eye. We were born at the right time. They do a roll call of their high-school crowd: Hughie, Pat, Dom, Chick from down the block. A real estate tycoon, a judge, an anchorman. Every one a success story.

In the fifties, says Philip Catania, home builder and multimillionaire, "If you had a college diploma, a dark suit, and anything between the ears, it was like an escalator; you just stood there and you moved up."

Michael DiStefano is Philip's oldest and best friend. A dental surgeon, medical school dean, trustee of his alma mater, he isn't buying the escalator image.

"Come on!" he says, impatiently. "We worked harder than anybody else; we took advantage of every opportunity, every scholarship, every loan. We knew, being where we came from, we couldn't just walk into the bank or the law firm. We had the wrong accent, we went to the wrong schools, we knew we had to make our own way."

They keep score, these ex-basketball stars turned weekend sailors and skiers. Another high-school classmate is "the biggest success of all, with the largest number of franchises in the biggest fast food chain in America."

"He could buy out the rest of us, with his federal taxes alone," Mike DiStefano says proudly.

They keep up with each other, still sharing the all-male pleasures of the old days: beers after work, the big games on the tube or from box seats. But they socialize as couples and families, too.

They kid each other cruelly and ceaselessly, with pride and mutual admiration for "putting on the dog." None of them will let the others forget where they came from: before the silver Mercedes, the kids at Andover and Exeter, the architect-designed offices with travertine desks the color of angelskin coral.

Philip Catania comes in for the most ribbing. His house—its nobly proportioned rooms, eighteenth-century glass windowpanes, and molded plaster festoons delighting the visitor's eye— stands on a hill synonymous with Yankee dominance.

"He's very democratic; he doesn't ask us to use the back door," Mike DiStefano teases. His friends still find this patrician neighborhood daunting, unfriendly, but also too urban. For them, success is rolling green lawns and flowers. They all prefer the long commute and new brick colonial houses, with deck-tennis courts and picnic tables under their own trees.

After a ravioli supper prepared by Phil—Sunday is his wife
Pat's night off—they look at the photograph of the fifties vacationing family. Mike DiStefano's wife, Rowan, giggles at the
bathing suit: "My mom had one just like that"; then she turns
wistful.

"I was always the only kid in school whose parents were
divorced. I just hated it," she says. "I swore to myself, 'This was
how my family was going to be—forever.'"

Philip Catania sees the invisible family car. "There would be
a brand-new Chevrolet in the background. Because this picture
is a sales pitch," he explains. "It's selling success."

To all the men in this room—first-generation Americans, the
first in their families to graduate from college—this image is a
yardstick of how far they have come from the gritty, working-
class, immigrant city-within-a-city where they grew up. Now
sleek successful entrepreneurs and professionals, they are somewhat patronizing about the naive middle-class outing. They take
more luxurious vacations, usually without children. They charter
a sloop for a week of Caribbean cruising or head for Gstaad to ski.

White-coated and goggled technicians look up briefly from thousands of tiny microchips as Paul Michaelides leads a visitor
through the several stages of production in his semiconductor
plant. "I love showing off my new baby," he says proudly.

From the time he sold Hoover vacuum cleaners door-to-door
after high school, and then Robert Hall suits to put himself
through college, Paul Michaelides gave evidence of an all-
American form of genius—parting people from their money.

He is a supersalesman. Give him a product or a service and
he can sell it, position it, and reposition it for the market. These
were the skills that, in the early 1960s, catapulted ambitious
young men like him to the top of the organizational charts.

His career is the classic corporate success story for men of his
generation. The only difference between Paul and many of his
peers is that each of his moves up the ladder found him in another

company. He has been marketing manager of an automobile manufacturer, vice president for North America of a European electronics company, and president of the American subsidiary of a Japanese-owned corporation. "My jobs," he says, "seem to run in seven-year cycles."

In his present cycle, he has seized the dream of nearly 70 percent of his business school class of 1954. As chairman, president, and CEO of the semiconductor manufacturing company he founded with a partner, Paul Michaelides is his own boss.

But the way he first describes himself is neither corporate nor entrepreneurial.

"I'm a family man," he says. To know him at all, it's essential to meet his wife Elaine and those of his six children who happen to be visiting—from college, graduate school, or jobs. "I always bring people home for a meal," he says. "Clients, associates, foreign visitors. We love having them, and everybody seems to love meeting the family."

For Paul Michaelides, the measure of his success is his ability to take his wife and entire family on an Italian holiday, which includes a vacation from domestic chores.

"Neither parent should be preparing food," he says, with a disapproving look at the thermos and plastic plates spread out on the sand in the photograph. "They should be eating out at a café and relaxing together. I wouldn't want Elaine to be bothered with a picnic basket routine when we travel. She has too much of that at home."

Growing up in the Bronx, Dan Ross says, "We only had Orchard Beach, which I never went to. You might get polio swimming there." He, too, sees the Florida vacations as selling more than palm trees and uncrowded stretches of sand.

"That was sold to us as the good life," he says. "Comfort, family, plenty to eat, relaxed leisure time." But the image is also cautionary; it warns of the dangers of overreaching, of casting off into unknown foreign waters.

"This is not a yacht," he says. "This is not a mansion on a mountain. It's a family on a beach. It's a man with a pretty wife and healthy kids. It's about planning and organization and safety."

In the outer offices of Dan Ross's law firm, the only décor is a wilting philodendron. Between scarred filing cabinets, secretaries sit, tapping silently as they stare at the screens of their word processors.

But in Dan's corner inner sanctum rock lives! Blowups of his record jackets line the walls (photographs by Daniel Ross), flanked by Lucite-framed copies of a gold record won by the rock group he managed and the platinum record given to him by the beautiful folk-rock singer whose career he created. There are other, more recent portraits, familiar from trendy magazines— New Wave artists and glittering personalities, that curious substratum of New York life, famous for being famous, captured by Dan's camera as they gyrate at the "in" clubs.

The short corridor between Dan Ross's outer and inner offices is the distance between the fifties and the eighties, between his three careers and his many lives.

Unlike some of his contemporaries who "went through heavy changes" in the sixties and seventies, shedding old selves like so many shrunken skins, Dan Ross never gave up anything; instead he kept adding on.

He still has the same wife he married twenty-four years ago, the same house in Great Neck they bought when their second child was born, and the same partners he joined when he left a large firm in 1960 to go off with two other young tax lawyers.

In those same twenty-five years, Dan Ross has added (starting with the visible), a 1960s beard and steel granny glasses; a loft near Wall Street (variously referred to as a pad, pied-à-terre, or studio); two other careers: pop music promoter and photographer; a succession and sometimes simultaneity of lovers, ranging in age from teenage groupies to a sober psychotherapist of his own vintage; not forgetting the moral and emotional strains of a man who commutes between two worlds.

"I'll say one thing for that family on the beach," Dan Ross adds. "Nobody's suffering from hypertension."

"That's where we hoped we'd end up some day—on that beach," says Esteban Ortiz, whom his friends call Steve. From the day he was married at twenty, in 1953, to his seventeen-year-old high-school sweetheart, he has never held fewer than two jobs, essential to support three kids while going to school and paying off the mortgage on his first house.

Now a state educational administrator, he still moonlights evenings and weekends, selling real estate.

"Back then, it would have been the money. I couldn't imagine having the bread for a holiday like that," he says. "Now it's the time. I'm so conditioned to postpone gratification," he says. "I have a real problem with playing and leisure. I'm a classic workaholic."

Like many men and women who divorced in the late sixties only to remarry within a few years, Steve Ortiz also sees this fifties family image as measuring the worlds that separate his first and second marriages.

He and his second wife, Carrie Ortiz-Parker, a high-school Spanish teacher, leave their three children at home on their rare vacations. Not because they frequent jet-set resorts or "adults only" chartered cruises; Steve Ortiz and his wife both work so hard that "if we don't get away by ourselves, we never really talk," he says. "At home, it's all household management, chores, kids."

When Dick Robertson was married for the first time, right after graduation from the University of Oklahoma in 1956, "people like us only got to barbecue in their backyards," he recalls. Living in the Midwest, "a vacation at the beach would have been way beyond us—geographically and financially."

Later on, when he left his father-in-law's insurance company for a junior executive slot with a retail chain, he and his wife Barbara and their three children took occasional holidays at a nearby lake. "But always," he adds, "with two or three other couples and their kids."

In Dick Robertson's view of his life, his spectacular success as a commodities trader meshes with his happy second marriage. He can go anywhere, do anything. "Now, if I want to," he says, "I could go down to the plaza and find the best-looking young thing and say: "How would you like to go to Paris or Palm Springs for the weekend? If you want to play the sexual power game, it makes a big difference if you have a lot of money," he says. "But it's otiose if you're not with the person you want to be with. For me, success is the combination of economic freedom and living with the right woman."

Before she was married, Betts Saunders recalls, "I had one vacation in my entire life. My father was a druggist who was always working overtime. There was no Girl Scout camp, either. There just weren't any extras at all," she says. "Our kids had all been to Europe three times before they were fifteen."

"This picture was always the image in my head," she says. "To marry, have a family, and take trips. It was my dream and I made it come true. When the children were younger, we had lots of lovely holidays just like this—with Sam broiling hamburgers on the beach."

Success, for Betts Saunders, is not calculated in the distance traveled from backyard barbecues, beaches, and trips abroad.

"The family in that picture is still us," she says, "wherever we are."

2
THE ANXIOUS OBJECT: US

By the tranquil Gulf waters, in eternal Florida sunshine, we would barbecue our government-inspected hot dogs on a squeaky clean beach, not a mushroom cloud or the snout of a submarine on the horizon. With the perfect spouse (a doting, attractive mother or earnest young executive) and three (healthy, well-behaved) youngsters, we would enjoy the (paid) vacation from a (secure) job.

If our parents could have bought us a life—like one of the furnished model houses in the new suburban communities—this would have been its image. As young families, few of them had enjoyed such carefree idylls.

They were children of the depression. Whether they grew up on farms, in small towns or cities, "old stock" or first-generation Americans like my parents, immigrants or refugees—they entered adulthood in adversity. My mother and father married in 1929. When my older brother was born a year later, my father, a theater manager, was out of a job. By the mid-thirties, hard times had affected even the established middle class.

When prosperity arrived from "just around the corner," it exploded in the form of a wartime economy: 26,000 new fac-

tories were built in the two years following Pearl Harbor.
Materially, life improved for millions. But to the dislocations of
the depression were added another kind of uprootedness: 20
million people, many of them women, moved to take advantage
of new jobs in the defense plants of San Diego and Seattle, in
the offices of Washington, D. C., or near military bases to be
closer to men in training. The atomization of families, spinning
off the nuclear units characteristic of the fifties, began during
World War II.

Other fears replaced worries about the next paycheck. Some
of our fathers and older brothers saw active combat or, like the
hero of Saul Bellow's novel, *The Dangling Man*, they knew they
could be called up any day. Air raid warnings sounded in
blackout-darkened cities, enemy submarines were sighted, and
spies were revealed in the person of ordinary Americans.

The end of World War II ushered in the Atomic Age: the
devastation of Hiroshima and Nagasaki closed the last chapter
of the last "good war" we would ever fight. The Cold War was
ideology in high moral drag. Capitalism and the Protestant Ethic
versus Godless Communism. Good and evil became the arms
race: who could stockpile faster, get there first with the H-bomb,
win the space race. From wartime air raids to civil defense drills,
our parents had to debate new ethical questions, such as, should
neighbors be allowed into the family bomb shelter, stocked with
condensed milk and canned peas?

When I think of childhood in the late 1940s, the images that
come to my mind are those of Norman Rockwell's famous series
The Four Freedoms. On facing walls of the study hall in my
school (and thousands of others), kindly Grandpa, his eyes cast
down in subdued gratitude, prepared to carve the Thanksgiving
turkey, while across the rows of girls in blue serge uniforms, a
somber, unsmiling mother and father adjusted the covers over
their sleeping youngsters.

Literal embodiments of "Freedom from Want" and "Freedom
from Fear," these illustrations (along with "Freedom of Speech"

and "Freedom of Worship") were commissioned to explain why we fought World War II.* But, closer to home, they explained the anxieties of our families. Freedom—as defined by the two posters I remember—was always *from*, never *to*, as it came to mean in the sixties and seventies: "free to be you and me."

If our families were fearful, if they were worriers, they had good reason. For their generation, nothing could be taken for granted. There was a price for everything—especially mistakes. All parents want the best for their children. Ours seemed more determined that we avoid the worst: Don't get hurt, get pregnant, marry the "wrong" girl, get in with the "wrong" crowd, start your own business, try to make it in the arts or in sports. Stick with the union, the civil service, the corporation, the Navy. Uncertainty was the worst scenario. They knew. They had been there.

"Don't do that; it's dangerous," was probably the phrase we heard most often as children. A college friend invented a game called "Instant Death." The winner was the person who could think of the most activities held to be fatal by parents—touching lips to a public drinking fountain, getting out of bed with a fever, and of course, "talking to strangers."

Overprotective was a word first used to describe our parents. As children, those of us who came of age in the fifties withstood more surveillance and scrutiny than any cohort of kids born in the twentieth century. (Indeed, one of the selling points of the suburban communities we bought into when we became parents was that they were places where "youngsters could play without adult supervision.") Our families would have been mystified by sadistic posters needling: It's Ten O'Clock. Do You Know Where Your Children Are? Of course, they knew. Usually, they weren't

---

* Completed in 1943, the four posters were probably the most popular illustrations ever made. Millions of copies were printed and distributed by the government and by private agencies all over the world. The U.S. Treasury Department toured the originals to sixteen cities, where they were seen by 1,222,000 people and helped sell $132,999,537 worth of War Bonds.[1]

the only ones; nurses, teachers, coaches, scoutmasters, counselors, and later, housemothers and deans knew—or thought they did.

From the day I was born in 1937 to the day I went to college in 1954, there was at least one adult who knew where I was, what I was doing, and who I was doing it with every moment of every day in my life.

My mother grew up too poor for adult supervision. Her parents arrived here with the great wave of Eastern European Jews at the turn of the century. My grandfather was a ladies' custom tailor who preferred reading Kropotkin and other anarchist writers to cultivating a rich clientele. To support the family, my grandmother ran a boarding house and restaurant. Any of the three girls who didn't want to be pressed into hard labor had better stay out of sight. My uncle, as the only boy, was exempt.

My father's family was too rich to worry about what the children were doing. My paternal grandmother had a cook, maids, and a chauffeur to supervise, as well as an ancient mother-in-law in residence. Infants had nurses. As they got bigger the older of the six children were supposed to keep an eye on the younger—which meant out of the grown-ups' hair.

As depression babies, there were dramatically fewer of us. In 1933, the birthrate for women in the prime childbearing years had dropped to the lowest ever recorded in America. From the time we were born, we were easily outnumbered by adults. I had never heard the term *demography* when I arrived at college in 1954, but I was soon aware that, like me, most of my classmates had only one sibling. Before we had gotten this far from home, our health and safety, along with our manners, morals, and social and psychological "adjustment," had been intensely monitored by an assortment of caretakers.

Until I reached fourth grade, when I rebelled at the shame of being taken to school, I was looked after by a black nurse. My care was Angelina's sole responsibility. (To my daughter,

early entrusted to the charge of relays of college and even high-
school sitters, having a nurse situates my childhood squarely in
the Edwardian milieu of *Upstairs, Downstairs*. She was amazed
to learn that live-in help was commonplace in middle-class urban
households before World War II.

I once overheard my mother describe Angelina glowingly to
a friend. She never let me out of her sight, my mother said.
One reason for such prized watchfulness was surely the legacy
of the Lindbergh kidnapping in 1932. But her vigilance also
ensured that I would not drink from public fountains, play with
unmannerly children, or get overheated or overtired.

Concern about health wasn't just hysteria. We were also the
last generation of Americans to suffer the dread diseases of childhood—and to survive them without antibiotics, penicillin, or
even the sulfa drugs then needed for the "war effort." Every
family had its horror story of a young life cut short by meningitis
or polio. A cousin my age had died in early childhood of peritonitis
following a ruptured appendix. Anyone who was a child in the
1940s can recall the ill-disguised fear that greeted complaints of
a sore throat in summer, stomach cramps, a high fever, or even
a case of measles.

There is no trace today of the polio that attacked Martin Duberman in the summer of 1944, when he was thirteen, a recovery
he attributes to his mother's round-the-clock vigil of compresses
and exercise. To the severity of his case was added the symptoms
of irony. He was one of two victims at his boys' camp in the
Adirondacks, where fortunate kids were sent to keep them from
exposure to the dread disease. As soon as the first case was
diagnosed, the camp prepared to close.

"My parents didn't want me to come home on the train with
the other kids," Martin Duberman recalls. "They sent a taxi to
pick me up."

Only a few years before, at the very beginning of the war,

his father, a Russian immigrant whose first job on these shores
was as a cutter in a garment factory earning seven dollars a
week, started his own dress manufacturing company. When he
was awarded a government contract for uniforms "he made the
money that allowed us to move from a cramped apartment in
the city to Westchester. That led to the private schools, summer
camps, country clubs," what his son calls the "Everything-for-
the-Kids Syndrome."

Our health, safety, and happiness were the focus for more
free-floating anxiety and fear than those of any generation of
children in America. There was an almost voluptuous quality to
worrying about us. Now that "things were better," more secure
and prosperous, they could afford to let go. The only thing to
fear wasn't fear itself anymore, not the war or the economy, but
all the ills that could prevent us from enjoying the best of everything. Their fantasies seemed filled with car collisions, smashed
bones, concussions, flash fires; summer outings that ended in
death by drowning or diving into too-shallow water; blindings
and poisonings (remember Calvin Coolidge's son, I was warned,
dead of an untended cut; the dye from a sock entered his blood-
stream causing septicemia). I was lurid with iodine and mercuro-
chrome, plastered with freshly changed Band-Aids.

   With fury or forbearance, I always assumed this fearfulness to
be peculiarly Jewish. But on the first day of college, there were
Texan fathers demanding inspection tours of fire escapes and
sprinkler systems; an unmistakable Boston accent wanted to know
the temperature at which dishes were rinsed in the kitchen of our
dormitory.

   When my daughter first started to walk, the pediatrician announced to me: "If she hasn't broken a limb by adolescence,
you're overprotective." I turned my back on tree climbing, looked
the other way when her bicycle wobbled off into traffic, tried
not to say, "You'll get hurt." Still, I never earned the doctor's
merit badge. No plaster casts or crutches attested to my efforts

at "benign neglect." Imprinted with prudence, I could only produce a cautious child.

She is Dr. Diane Weikert. Before she was a psychotherapist, before she was divorced, before she was, for twenty-one years, a corporate wife, polisher of silver candlesticks, and mother of four children, even before she was runner-up for the title of state beauty queen and the first name on the rush list of her sorority, she was a farm girl. Diane Hoff, obsessed with horses.

She rode and trained and showed all over the state. By the time she was in junior high school in 1950, there was no more room on her shelves for cups and ribbons.

Still, her mother was terrified every time she got on a horse. "She was terrified that I would break my neck and be killed instantly. Or that I would break my back and be paralyzed for life," she says. "If anything ever happened to you, Diane," her mother said, "I just couldn't take it; I'd die."

When she broke two ribs, missing a jump, she was in agony for months. "But I never told anybody," she says.

Her father's family was from the East. She and her younger sister spent school vacations with their grandmother and aunt.

"They had money, nice manners, and education," she says. "My father would have been like them if he hadn't been an alcoholic and a gambler. He died when I was six."

Diane Hoff's mother was one of twelve children. Her father had come to this country from Austria. He was a coal miner and when he was disabled in an accident, her grandmother supported the family by cleaning houses.

"My mother was really scarred by the depression. Dropping back into poverty was always real to us, because it was my mother's deepest fear. She was also terrified of sex and men."

If we made it through childhood uneventfully, under the watchful gaze of a spectrum of "significant others," we also absorbed a profound message.

We were the luckiest kids in history.

Whether we were still reproachfully reminded of starving Armenians when we left food on our plates or, later, we saw for ourselves in the pages of *Life* magazine the faces, pinched and hollow-eyed, of children wandering the ruins of Europe, we could never doubt our good fortune.

Nor did our elders' concern for us stop with our physical health and safety—with shots, vitamins, and teeth straightening, fresh air and hot lunches. For the first time in history, the psychological (as opposed to spiritual) well-being of children became the responsibility of parents. Not just parents who were "opinion makers," intelligentsia, or the trendy rich, but ordinary middle-class Americans who read the *Readers' Digest*, the *Woman's Home Companion*, and *Parents'* magazine.

Beginning in the late 1930s, the Freudian gospel began to be disseminated by refugee psychoanalysts and popularized by the media. Child-rearing professionals and educators now underlined the crucial importance of the early years and the critical role of parents in preventing unhappy children from becoming neurotic adults. By the late 1940s, this influential intellectual import had taken on American coloration: a definition of mental health as social adjustment. Teachers routinely conducted sociometric surveys of grade-school classrooms. Parents who had produced an unpopular offspring got an F.

When William H. Whyte visited the families of his organization men in the new Chicago suburb of Oak Forest, one mother admitted to receiving worrying reports from school about her little boy. "The teacher explained to me," she told Whyte, "that he was doing fine on his lessons but that his social adjustment was not as good as it might be. He would pick just one or two friends to play with, and sometimes he was happy to remain by himself."[2]

At home, mothers and fathers were urged to be as watchful for signs of maladjustment as they would have been for symptoms of measles.

"When I was fourteen," Martin Duberman recalls, "I was so monosyllabic around the house, my parents sent me to a therapist. They assumed something was wrong with me. As soon as I sat down at the dinner table, I was grilled: 'Where were you? What were you doing?' Meals were the only times they could get to me with questions; otherwise, I was racing around with my friends or upstairs reading or studying. My mother worried about this too; she wanted me to 'play more,' to 'take it easy.' To this day," he adds, "I'm uncomfortable at meals."

Adult preoccupation with children—their inner lives as well as their social activities and games—was something new and peculiar to the postwar period in America. Concern intensified throughout the fifties.

In his 1957 best-seller, *"Where Did You Go?" "Out." "What Did You Do?" "Nothing,"* Robert Paul Smith poked fun at parents who meddled in childish pursuits or tried to control them through surrogates like Little League, Brownie and Cub Scout troops, and PTAs, which advised fathers on how to be a pal to a son. Waxing nostalgic for his own youth—when "kid stuff" was beneath adult attention, to say nothing of participation—Smith accused parents of "inventing a whole new perversion: child watching."[3]

True to his times, however, humorist Smith wasn't prone to look at the larger picture. Parents watched children fearfully because Big Brother was watching *them.* In the atmosphere of the Cold War, with witch-hunts and purges of suspected Communists or even fellow travellers from school faculties, trade unions, and the media, a child's wrong answer in a classroom could lead to suspicions of the wrong political atmosphere at home.

Sue Baker Hodges' family might have been Norman Rockwell's models. Both her parents had grown up in the small city on the Mississippi River where her father was vice president of the major industry, a leading manufacturer of farm equipment. "They always had the same friends, who all belonged to the same country club and church," she says.

One day, in 1950, when Sue Baker Hodges was in seventh grade, her junior-high-school assembly was shown a movie about Soviet children. The film was supposed to illustrate how terrible it was to grow up under Communism. But in the class discussion that followed, Sue raised her hand and said, "I don't see what's so awful about their lives. They just look like ordinary kids who go to a different kind of school than we do."

At dinner that evening, the telephone rang. It was the school principal, telling Fred Baker what his daughter had said in class that day and suggesting that he should find out "where she gets those ideas."

"My father said: "Let's forget it," she recalls, "but I could tell he was very upset."

"Say anything you want, fuck anything you want, but don't sign anything," Dan Ross's father told him when he was a student in a Bronx high school in the 1940s.

"Maybe it was the immigrant experience," Dan Ross says, "the fear that 'we' were here on sufferance and that 'they' could always throw us out if we did or said the wrong thing." His father may even have had radical alliances in his younger days that caused him sleepless nights in the postwar period. "He was always very close-mouthed about his early years in this country.

"When I got to college," he recalls, "there were petitions thrust at you constantly: the Stockholm Peace Appeal, the Scottsboro Boys." He would hear the speakers out. But no matter how tempted or even persuaded, he says, "I listened to my father. I never signed."

High-intensity hovering, or "overinvolvement" (as it would be called when we continued to do it with our children), was not voyeurism but anxious vigilance. As kids highly exposed to the scrutiny of neighbors, teachers, and scoutmasters, we were also unwitting fifth columnists.

Once upon a time, adults had been happy to forget about the young—if their tongues were pink, their foreheads cool, their manners "nice," if they weren't failing or in constant trouble at school. Now staying out of trouble took on new meaning. Ideally, a low political profile began in grade-school years; its most reassuring indicator was the ability to merge with the crowd, "be like the other kids."

Suddenly, in the America of the late 1940s, there was something "wrong" with a child who had only one or two playmates, with a teenager who was "moody and monosyllabic" or who liked solitude as much as "racing around with his friends."

"If there was anything that used to distinguish the period of youth from other times in the life of the human animal," wrote dissenting psychoanalyst Robert Lindner, "it was the privacy, the aloneness of those fretful years. Today, youth has abandoned solitude, it has relinquished privacy; instead, these are the days of pack-running."[4]

Solitude and solitary pursuits were not only worrisome in themselves; such preferences pointed to other, still more dangerous tendencies. The worst scenario—invoked darkly, but never described by the headmistress of my girls' school—was "going off the deep end."

It wasn't just sex that Mrs. Gillette was warning us against when she said she hoped we'd never do it. Going off the deep end was any loss of control, a plunge down the rabbit hole from which, unlike Alice, we might never return. To give yourself to impulse, intense interest, even to enthusiasm, was to risk losing yourself forever. Unlike the champion high divers, reversed in slow motion by my favorite *March of Time* newsreels, in real life, once you plunged, no miracle could return you—poised, dry, and smiling—to the diving board.

All discipline was geared to curbing spontaneity, irrationality, individualism of any kind. In girls especially, any hint of competitiveness was censured. Sportsmanship and teamwork were learned behaviors, designed to mask the murderous desire to win—and rage at losing. Ten years later, in the early 1960s, coach Vince Lombardi's famous dictum, "Winning isn't the main thing, it's the only thing," simply stated what we always knew but were forbidden to express. (The *real* court philosopher of Camelot, Lombardi also told us more about the Kennedy years as the end of the genteel fifties than all the progressive rhetoric of the New Politics.)

I was a prime "deep end" candidate, my parents were regularly warned. I was, first of all, "one-sided," the worrying antithesis of the "well-rounded" ideal. The implied geometry, though, was misleading. The "one" in "one-sided" didn't really refer to the number of one's interests so much as one's intensity. I was just as obsessed with basketball as with grades. I could have added ballet or horses or boys (if I had known any).

Fanatic, compulsive, romantic, I was destined to be one-sided forever. I didn't go off the deep end, though, then or ever. Instead, I went underground.

"Every father and mother trembles," noted psychoanalyst Lindner in 1952, "lest an offspring, in act or thought, should be different from his fellows; and the smallest display of uniqueness in a child becomes the signal for the application of drastic measures aimed at stamping out that small flame of noncompliance by which personal distinctness is expressed."[5]

A normal child was not "different" in any way. But were we normal? How could they be sure?

Legions of experts, armed with batteries of tests, stood ready to help parents find out. The fifties produced a mushroom cloud of "objective" personality evaluations that followed us from nursery school through the personnel manager's office.

Crucial to the definition of the "normal" child were early signs of "appropriate" sex-role identity. In the postwar period, observes historian Douglas Miller, America regressed to a "mock-Victorian family ideal,"[6] in which gender functions were rigidly prescribed. For what they tell us about Man the Provider, Woman the Nurturer, the husband and wife on the beach might be sporting swallow-tailed coat and bustle instead of bathing suits.

At the same time, the definition of masculinity itself was suffering an identity crisis. It's no accident, notes psychologist Joseph Pleck, that testing for "internal" characteristics of male-female roles became an obsession in America during the two periods in the twentieth century when external measures of what it means to be a man were most threatened.[7]

Sex and Personality, the first widely used study of sex roles, was published in 1936, in the depths of the Great Depression— the historical event, Pleck notes, "causing perhaps the greatest single crisis in the traditional institutional basis of the male role, that of economic provider. If holding a job to support a family could no longer be counted on to define manhood, a masculinity-femininity test could."

Then, just as American men had reestablished themselves as heroes, returning victorious from a just war, they experienced the shock of finding that wives and sweethearts were doing just fine without them. The girls they left behind had become psychologically independent, supporting themselves (and often their children) on assembly lines or in office jobs vacated by men. The job market itself, Pleck notes, had been transformed by the technological advances of wartime. Many kinds of work now required levels of training and education for which veterans were ill prepared, while postwar inflation made them still less adequate as providers.

Since the depression, a more sophisticated army of psychologists and educators had emerged, designing tests and devising measures and scales, all aimed at isolating the (reassuringly stable) psychological foundations of masculinity. These internal characteristics, properly developed from infancy, would make the American male's sexual self-image impervious to economic downturns or uppity women. From kindergarten on, real men tested right.

The preschool years, parents were warned, were none too early to see that boys gave evidence of gender-specific personality traits. In a longitudinal study of a group of children, begun in

the late 1940s when the subjects were very young, psychologists
Jerome Kagan and H. Moss compare excerpts from the case
histories of two boys, one rated "masculine" by the researchers
and the other classified as "nonmasculine."

When first observed at age seven, S (for *subject*) is described
as a "well-built, attractive-looking youngster; a real little boy,"
note the authors approvingly. After S constructed a barracks
with blocks, another classmate built a torpedo. "This quite
naturally led to war play. In a very short time," the observers
report, "all the children in the room were machine-gunning each
other," with our "real little boy" yelling, "All guns turn this way!"

In sad comparison, the nonmasculine lad is a "pale, bleached-
out-looking child." At age six, the researchers describe him as
"pasty-skinned, skinny; a loiterer [and] a slumper" who "did not
seem to quite fit into the group. In contrast to the interests of
most boys in athletics or construction, [this] S became interested
in flowers. He was very careful as he picked them so that the
stems wouldn't be hurt," note the psychologists, "sorting out
those of the most beautiful contrasting colors and making up
names for them." By age eleven, we are not surprised to learn,
this boy manifests other signs of pathology: "Teachers often find
him in the schoolroom when he should be out on the playground
with his peers."*⁸

For parents who wanted early warning signals to help them
raise a future Green Beret instead of a pasty-skinned flower
picker, there were tests designed to weed out the preschooler
who might be "passing":

The *"It" Scale for Children* (1956) showed very young subjects
drawings of a child named It (drawn to be ambiguous as to sex)
and asked them to indicate It's choice in types of toy (dump

---

* When we realize that the coauthor of the study is Jerome Kagan, one of the
leading researchers in child development in America, we understand the perva-
siveness of sex-role stereotyping (and terror of effeminacy) in this country at midcentury. If Kagan could describe six-year-old boys in these terms, it's useful to
contemplate the probable biases of less "enlightened" contemporaries.

truck or doll buggy) and "dress up" clothes (Indian chief or princess). The child's masculinity score is the sum of the "right" choices on these, along with a third task. Explaining his inspired idea of asking children for It's choices rather than their own, psychologist D. Brown, who designed the test, vaunted its usefulness in smoking out precocious kindergartners already adept at "faking it." These he defined as children whose answers "would reflect their conformity to social expectations rather than their real preferences."

Boys who slipped through the testers' net in elementary school found masculinity measures waiting for them at the more advanced levels of education as well. Designed for high-school and college students, the *Gough Femininity Scale* (1952), its author proudly announced, was an "instrument which is brief, easy to administer, relatively subtle and unthreatening in content, and which will, at the same time, differentiate men from women and sexual deviates from normals [*sic*]." Among the fifty-eight "relatively subtle and unthreatening" statements and questions Dr. H. Gough found to define masculinity, as indicated by the answer F, were:

"I think I would like the work of a building contractor." (F)
"I prefer a shower to a bathtub." (F)
"I get excited very easily." (T)

Significantly, there were no tests to "positively" define femininity in girls. Presumably, it was whatever didn't look good on boys—getting dressed up, getting "excited," wheeling doll buggies. Femininity was fallout. Whatever male children had early to be trained to repress in themselves and repudiate in other boys would be nurtured and cultivated by "maternal example" in girls.

In the most obvious sense, testing for masculinity but not its feminine counterpart clearly reveals the unimportance of women. In a male-controlled society, unmanly men were a threat to social order at home and to American dominance abroad. In the wake of *Sputnik*, there were no best-sellers to explain why Jane—as opposed to Johnny—couldn't read. And the responsibility of parents and schools was clear in both cases. Masculinity, like literacy, had to be learned. No longer doing what came naturally, it required diagnosis of weak spots, setting of goals, planning by objective, rewards and sanctions, discipline and training. And, most important, it needed the collaboration of women as never before. Thus the real definition of femininity— the real reason it couldn't be tested "objectively"—lay in those qualities that made a man feel more masculine!

"I talked back a lot," Carol Cornwell remembers. "I was bratty and obnoxious, my parents said. I was not demure and soft-spoken. I was abrasive. I argued all the time. It was wrong, they told me. It was unfeminine. A 'nice' boy wouldn't care for that sort of girl."

"Pert, trim and smartly dressed" was the way a reporter for her high-school newspaper described Carol Ruhe Cornwell in 1953 when, as vice president of student government, she brought down her gavel to open a meeting—in the absence of the boy who was president. Following her to the journalism office where "she is trying to write four articles at once," the awed underclassman barely finds space to enumerate her other activities—the clubs and service organizations, dance committees and hall patrol —the offices that attest to her "popularity" and "reputation as a leader." No wonder, he reports, that Carol finds little time for the knitting, sewing, and reading that she lists as hobbies. Her plans for the future, she tells the scribbling sophomore, "are not quite definite": an English or psychology major, Smith or Vassar for college. Her "ultimate goal, though, is altogether clear; to get married, settle down and have five children."

At forty-eight Carol Cornwell is still "pert, trim and smartly dressed," still favoring the pleated skirts, loafers, and yellow slicker of her college wardrobe. Her short red curls could be a poodle cut, once the resort of hair too unruly for a perfect page boy or even a ponytail. She still exudes the competence of the "well-organized" campus leader. She still giggles, too. (Girlish and ladylike, by our giggles and our good manners will you know us.) She did marry and settle down—exactly three weeks after graduation from college. But instead of five children, she is the mother of three—a daughter and two sons, ranging in age from eighteen to twenty-five—born thirteen months apart.

Until her divorce three years ago, Carol Cornwell was a corporate wife in the traditional fifties mold. She moved households alone, with very young children, four times in the course of a twenty-year marriage, starting over each time in another suburban community filled with young families like hers.

For two years she has been an ordained Unitarian minister. She has preached from the same pulpit as Emerson and Channing. A feminist, she scrutinizes Scripture for sexist or patriarchal language. She regularly sees a woman psychotherapist and a male astrologer.

She loves sex. She cannot stop seeing a married man who will never leave his wife. But she also has several men friends with whom she has sexual relations based on pleasure and affection. Or just pleasure. She is not averse, she says, to more casual encounters, as long as she doesn't feel used.

" 'Boys will want to take advantage of you; always be on your guard.' My mother spelled that out," Carol Cornwell says. The family who lived next door to her grandparents had two daughters a little older than Carol and her sister, Nancy. The younger one got pregnant. "Mother didn't have to say an awful lot; the message was loud and clear."

Both messages were loud and clear. There was nothing worse than an "unfeminine" girl, one who risked repelling a man by making him feel unmasculine, except a girl who, in Carol's mother's words, "did something stupid"—like yielding to masculine demands.

Femininity without sexuality was the name of the high-wire

act. Parental anxiety had focused breathlessly on its outcome since the origin of middle-class marriage. In postwar America, however, the traditional task of ensuring that nothing went wrong until a daughter could be safely delivered into the arms of the right man posed new problems. Young women were no longer courted in the parlor or on the front-porch swing. There was no place for a chaperone in Dad's '49 Chevy, borrowed for Saturday night. Years of parental vigilance could be undone in moments in the back seat of a car or even the balcony of a movie theater.

When Diane Weikert was fourteen and a high-school freshman, she arranged to meet a date at the movies. As the theater darkened and the feature began, "I remember he touched me," she says. "I don't remember how or where, but it was certainly not intimate. I just happened to turn around, and there was my mother in the row behind us.

Sex was "beautiful," Betts Saunders' mother told her. "At the same time, I was told if I did *that*, I was not to come home. I was not her daughter anymore."

Even if they knew *you* would never do it, undesirable friends could still cast doubt on a girl's "reputation." By the first year of high school, the social and sexual marketplace was in full swing. Guilt by association could cause a young woman's stock to sink, placing at risk the secure future of marriage.

"If my parents worried about anything," says Sue Hodges, "it was the wrong friends. They weren't from the right families. They didn't look right. They were greasers, sort of. I didn't have many of the wrong friends, just a few.

"There was a group of girls I really wasn't allowed to be with. They smoked. That was all I knew about them. I don't even know that they drank. And I never got close enough to know anything about their sexual behavior. They seemed pretty straight to me," she says. "But it was made clear at home they were un-acceptable. Our mothers heard things about certain kids that made them taboo."

In my family, two forms of parental anxiety came into head-on conflict. My father was obsessed with physical injury. He worried about automobile accidents and airplane crashes. The instant after deplaning I had to rush to the nearest telephone to announce my safe arrival. I had to promise him I would never ski or moun-tain climb. Dates involving boys with cars were not to be men-tioned at home.

My mother had only one fear—that I would never get married. From the time I taught myself to read at the age of three, a de facto only child with a much older brother, every book was con-sidered another nail in the coffin of spinsterhood.

In adolescence I was cold and unfriendly when not actually arrogant and surly. If intellectual interests didn't suffice to repel masculine attention, my personality would take care of the rest. The resolution of the conflict was the password of a familiar conspiracy: "Don't tell Daddy." My mother was so relieved when I received an invitation from a young man that any questions of danger, propriety, or expense were easily argued away. She would gladly have outfitted me to climb the north face of Everest.

"Don't tell Daddy" wasn't invented in America in 1950. In Jane Austen's novels the air is thick with just such mother-daughter conspiracies. This age-old feminine collusion reflects the burden, largely maternal, of the marriageable female child. (We never thought to explain such one-sided worry in oedipal terms. We just knew that Daddy didn't care if we languished in the library every Saturday night or if we wore the same dress to every party.)

Eagerly exploited by all middle-class girls, the historical con-spiracy gained peculiar intensity in postwar America. Like society itself, the marriage market was increasingly fluid and com-petitive. The "big game" was likely to be played on campuses far from home. To prevent getting lost in the shuffle and to neutralize the effect of overeducation, alluring packaging and lots of exposure were crucial factors. It was a mother's duty to aid and abet both.

To the millions of Americans in our generation who, for better or worse, met their mates in college, my mother's fear that higher education guaranteed the single state for women may seem strange. Until the 1950s, however, statistically speaking, she was right. In 1952 *Time* magazine made a study of U.S. college graduates. "For many co-eds," they found, "college amounts to an education for spinsterhood." Of all adult women at the time of the survey, only 13 out of 100 were unmarried. But of their sample of college graduates, 31 out of 100 were single. Thus, "while college men were actually more prone to marry than the average," *Time* reported, "the college woman was avoiding marriage—or being cheated out of it—in almost record numbers." Ten years later, our decade of college women would make these statistics dramatically obsolete.[9]

If we were first-generation daughters to attend college— higher education might be seen as a mixed blessing, for sons the worry was, would they make it? Parental dreams, immigrant or depression-deferred, focused on boys, as indeed they always had. But now they did so with greater intensity on the part of larger numbers of families than ever before. Unless they had older brothers who, as World War II veterans, qualified for the GI bill, young men in the 1950s graduating classes were likely to be the first in their families to earn degrees. That sheepskin (as it was known before being demoted to "piece of paper") spelled security in the marketplace and confidence at home as the male bread-winner. As high schoolers, nothing must be allowed to deflect brand-new opportunity—neither the wrong friends, girls, or career choice.

Paul Michaelides' grandfather came to America from Greece to seek his fortune and found work in the steel mills of Pittsburgh. His son, Paul's father, was a printer and typographer who lost his job during the depression.

"Those were rough times for the family," Paul recalls. "There were three of us kids. My mother had to go to work. She was Russian Jewish. I'm usually the only person anyone has ever met who was baptized and Bar Mitzvahed."

During the war, Paul's father bought a hardware store with his father's parents. Business was so good that soon the whole family could move from the grim mill city to a pleasant suburb, where Paul began high school and his mother began worrying.

"She was not happy with my associations," he says. "I just wasn't a very motivated kid at that point. In school, I felt much more comfortable with a mixed crowd—our group had a good representation of leather jackets, working-class kids. There were no motorcycle gangs or real delinquency. We did a lot of hanging out, drinking beer, cruising, a little sex with 'designated' girls— the ones who put out. My mother really objected to my friends' lack of ambition. She was very anxious that I go to college, become a successful mainstream American. I was smart. I was the oldest. I was going places. I heard that from everybody—including my grandmother."

Even those fathers who had made it in business, big or small, were less likely to have gone to college. They were the last generation of American men to reach the top without the benefit of higher education. They weren't going to allow their own efforts, which now permitted the luxury of university training for a son, to be denied by fickle career choices.

"My father was a typical self-made big executive," Dick Robertson says. "He worked for the same corporation all his life. He started out as a carryout boy in a grocery in Oklahoma; he ended as one of the five top executives in the company. If he hadn't become disabled and died relatively young, he certainly would have been president," adds his son, now president of his own commodity brokerage firm.

"During the depression, my father worked in a CCC camp. He took whatever jobs he could get after that. Then my dad leapfrogged out of his class. In 1946 he was running a grocery store in rural Oklahoma. In 1956, he was an executive in New York, in charge of the whole northeast operation."

Dick Robertson went through a period in high school when he wanted to be a professional golfer. "I was really very good," he says, "but my dad talked me out of it. At that time, there was no money in golf. Not like today. In 1955, if you won the Phoenix Open, the first prize was only $2000. Arnold Palmer was the leading money winner in the pro golf tournament in 1956, and he earned about $20,000. My father was real crafty. He found a guy who was a pro golfer. His specialty was a pseudo-science that measured your body: what percentage your trunk was of your legs. These measurements were supposed to correspond to personality traits. Pure hokum! But together my dad and his sidekick convinced me I wouldn't have the physical stamina, that I really didn't have that much natural ability. They claimed the reason I was so good was just because of stubbornness and practice. I would be much better off being a businessman."

He will not indulge any resentment of his father's duplicity. "My dad felt he was acting in my best interests," he says.

Our best interest was maximum security, no matter how imprisoning. Nightly battles raged when my brother determined not to go to college. It was open warfare when he announced his intention of becoming a jazz clarinetist. To my father that career spelled drugs in neon letters, bad black companions, probably prison. But worse than all these was another, more basic fear.

"You can't earn a living that way" was our parents' reaction to careers outside the mainstream of traditional men's work. Earning a living assumed supporting a family. Once his professional education was completed, no self-respecting man would allow his wife to work. She would be home raising the children.

Still more unimaginable was the possibility that he might never have a wife or family at all.

From starring in school plays, Martin Duberman toured New England for several months when he was sixteen, playing George in *Our Town.* "I came home determined to go to acting school. There were no family debates. My parents must have been subtle about imposing their demands in such a way that I never felt them. All I know is that instead of going to Carnegie Tech, I ended up as a freshman at Yale."

Later, there was more heavy-handed opposition to his studying history. "Both my parents wanted me to take over the family business, which was then flourishing. My father kept insisting, "Why would you want to go to graduate school? There's no money in teaching."

To Dan Ross's father, all risk was bad. Too many people depended on him. The big thing for that immigrant generation, Dan says, was that they had parents to support. They dreaded becoming that same burden to us. In his family's Bronx apartment, Dan recalls, "the *bubbameiser** stories were always about the brother-in-law who had the heart attack, the sister whose husband left her. It was always my father who had to take over. So first you had to have money in the bank—a good bank," Dan says, "even if the interest was small."

"His biggest concern for us, my brother and I, was that we have the chance he never had for a college education. It's the classic immigrant story," Dan says. "Otherwise, they expected me to support their system—marry a nice woman and raise a nice family. I panicked them constantly because I used to date all these crazy artist- and actress-types. But in my heart of hearts, I knew I was going to end up with somebody I could tolerate and whom they would feel comfortable with. For better or for

* Family gossip

worse, that's the way they programmed my head. I never wanted to jump where I felt I was free-falling, where I didn't know whether the parachute was going to open or not."

In 1953, when Dan Ross returned to Brooklyn College from three years in Alaska with Air Force Intelligence ("better than two as cannon fodder in Korea," he says), he had to decide what to do with his life.

"Ever since I saw *The Bicycle Thief*, what I wanted to do was make movies," he says. "I'd taken film courses and written criticism for the college magazine. But when I thought about it, I didn't see myself going to Hollywood without contacts. It would be like falling off the edge of the world. I had visions of starving to death. I decided it was a crazy idea.

"Then, I thought about being a psychotherapist. I did very well in psychology. I loved it, and my professor, who was also a lay analyst, encouraged me to go on. Then one time I was visiting him, and I had this flash: Law school is the only safe place to be. It's the only place I'm sure of making a few dollars and going on to that 'imaged world' that's in my head from the movies."

"I saw myself," Dan says with an ironic smile, "riding the commuter train to Long Island, settling down in the nice house with the white picket fence, far from the turmoil of the Bronx, with the nice wife, who just happens to look like Jeanne Crain, waiting for me."

"I wanted all the goodies in that picture of the family on the beach," Dan says. "That was what the culture told us to want. If that's what nice middle-class people do, I thought to myself, that's what I think I should do. Even though part of me was saying: Hey, go to Hollywood, make movies. Or become a therapist; help people who are really in trouble. But I didn't do either of those things," Dan says. "I took the safe course. Because the safe course was the one that was patrolled by my parents. My program had been laid out in advance. It was all set."

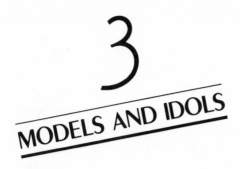

3

MODELS AND IDOLS

The fifties were an unheroic decade. There were no young conquerers. Old soldiers didn't die. One, General Douglas MacArthur, lived to be publicly humiliated by his commander-in-chief; the other, General Dwight D. Eisenhower, became president. Political leaders weren't father figures; they were grandfathers.

Young men who were the stuff of legend were hitting record numbers of home runs out of ballparks—Ted Williams, Stan Musial, Joe DiMaggio. But most of our larger-than-life idols were on the big screen, playing ordinary, middle-class, small-town or suburban Americans.

When they were in military uniforms, they were corporals like Prewitt (Montgomery Clift) in *From Here to Eternity* (1953), or officers, like the Navy pilot killed in Korea, played by William Holden in *The Bridges at Toko-Ri* (1955), both films based on best-selling novels. Men became leaders by heroic example and democratic consensus. They were first among equals.

In rumpled business suit, James Stewart continued his depression-inspired portrayals of the hero as Everyman: virtue incarnate and often inarticulate. Even when playing a Peeping Tom of ambiguous sexuality in Alfred Hitchcock's *Rear Window* (1954),

51

he was manfully resisting temptation close to hand, in the form of Grace Kelly. Whether he was a banker, journalist, or congressman, his real ambition was always revealed to be the protection of his fellow citizens. Working for principle, not profit, he was the hero as low-key crusader, making the "contribution to society" urged on all young men in the postwar period.

An older friend determined to become a doctor when, as an adolescent moviegoer in the late 1930s, he dreamed of becoming a hero of medicine like Paul Muni. But in fifties films there is no Pasteur. Whether hunting down pod people (Kevin McCarthy in *The Invasion of the Body Snatchers*, 1956) or isolating cholera carriers (Richard Widmark in *Panic in the Streets*, 1950), men in white were anonymous healers or government scientists; professionals who "worked with the community," not lone geniuses.

Philip Catania's father, a dentist, was one of the few professionals in their working-class community. "We had sheets on our bed and ate better than anyone else." His own early heroes, though, were not doctors or anyone like the multimillionaire entrepreneur he has since become. At sixteen, he recalls, "I wanted to be like Harry Truman." But in the movies "it was Jack Hawkins. He was always an officer and a leader," he says of the British actor. It wasn't his military roles that Philip Catania sought to emulate, though. "I did everything possible to stay out of the army," he confesses. "It was the man and the way he carried himself. He was a strong person who always did the right thing."

In the world of the Western, a man was assumed to do the right thing when he wore the symbol of authority. The marshal's star or sheriff's badge assured us that law and order would be upheld by physical courage. Before the West was won, leadership still had to be earned; it could not be automatically guaranteed by faraway bureaucrats.

"Since there was no one in the movies with a Spanish name," Steve Ortiz says, "I took John Wayne as my hero. He shot pretty straight. Then they changed the rules of the game so they didn't shoot straight anymore. In the Duke's heyday, it was real clear to me who the good guys and the villains were.

"I can't relate to androgynous males," Steve Ortiz says. "You don't know where they stand. Like James Dean. He was always just too mixed-up to be a bona fide hero.* The name of the game is to play to win. That's what was wrong with Vietnam. In Wayne's day it was a moral thing. They weren't looking for the big contract: cocaine after the game."

Steve Ortiz dropped out of college in 1952 to go into construction work. "I think I was following Wayne's macho image. It was a rough business; that appealed to me," he says. "When Wayne died, it seemed like the end of honesty and directness in male roles."

Masculinity in the movies separated the men from the boys. The most popular male stars of the 1950s had a strangely middle-aged quality, even when they were young men playing young men. More reliable than romantic, they exuded sincerity—that other highly prized fifties attribute—rather than sexuality.

"I would have liked to be William Holden," Martin Duberman says. "It was his easy masculinity, the way he inhabited his body."

William Holden was the most consistently employed actor of the 1950s** and one of the most enduringly popular. The constant in the characters he played was a man who inspires confidence. He was the low-key hero who doesn't need to do any heavy breathing to convince us of his competence as a journalist, executive, or lover. Never winning by intimidation, he got the girl because he had the goods.

---

* Sensitive "androgynous" stars like Dean and Montgomery Clift, more boy than man, were always far more popular with female than with male audiences.

** In 1956 he became the highest-earning male star in America, forging ahead of John Wayne, Jimmy Stewart, and Burt Lancaster.[1]

In *Executive Suite* (1954), whose plot hinges on the presidential succession of a furniture company, Holden plays a design engineer—the dark horse for the top post. But, as one critic noted, "as soon as we see that he's played by William Holden, we know he's the right man for the job."[2]

As a drifter in *Picnic* (1956), Holden still suggested masculine authority. Even playing a socially marginal man, he was always a mainstream American.

Classlessly middle class, with a regionless radio announcer's voice, Holden embodied the ideal male style of the period: relaxed, understated and somewhat anonymous. Attractive—that ultimate fifties accolade—more than handsome or sexually compelling, Holden's faintly ironic manner and crow's feet suggested wisdom and feelings held in reserve. He was a man you wanted to get to know.

If we had gotten to know him we would have discovered what a great actor William Holden really was. Like that other American icon of masculinity, Ernest Hemingway, Holden, by recent accounts, suffered from recurring potency problems. He was a life-long alcoholic (the cause of his accidental death), and terrifyingly erratic even when sober.[3]

More plausibly than any actor of the period, Holden portrayed the entire spectrum of culturally approved male roles: citizen, corporate manager, uniformed defender of democracy, suburban householder, husband, and father. He was American "man at his best," fifties style. Holden's skill at role-playing may have been his deepest bond with his audience. Like many of his fans, his real talent lay in passing: Holden made normalcy into a great performance. In this, he was truly a man of his time.

"We saw ourselves in terms of the movies," Diane Weikert says. "That's where we learned what men and women were supposed to be." From fifties movies, we learned that girls turned into wives. They traded in the ingenue's crinolined skirt, the smart hat of the career woman, the sex kitten's off-the-shoulder blouse for the homemaker's Peter Pan collar. No matter the convolutions of the plot, the outcome was never in doubt. We would become what we beheld.

Tall for her age and tawny-haired, Diane Hoff, at twelve wanted desperately to become Debbie Reynolds. "She was little, cute, and feminine. I wasn't any of those things. So I felt like a failure. I wore her shade of bright red lipstick but it didn't help."

More competent than any other girl in her farm community, Diane excelled at unfeminine skills—showing horses and getting A's. "Debbie Reynolds made me aware," she says, "that I couldn't be *too* good." Being too good was a dangerous diversion from a woman's real vocation: finding a man. No such detours ever deflected Debbie as she single-mindedly stalked husband material.

In *The Tender Trap* (1955) Reynolds plays an aspiring actress who gets the big part on her first audition. But she dismisses the congratulations of theatrical agent Frank Sinatra by announcing, "The theater's all right, but only temporarily." Marriage is the only permanent profession, she tells him, besides being "the most important thing in the world. A woman isn't really a woman until she's been married and had children."

With the crass guilelessness that was Reynolds's screen persona, she unveils her life plan, from finding Mr. Right ("I know everything about him except his blood type") to marrying on the same day as her parents did, to one baby in the city and two more after their move to suburbia, culminating in the graduation of their youngest from Scarsdale high school. "A person just can't go on ad-libbing their way through life," she explains.

Ad-libbing ended when we found and cast our life scripts. The big message that movies gave women, Diane Weikert says, was that at a certain point everything was fixed: "Once you were married, that would be all you ever had to do."

The walk into the sunset was our freeze-frame, the permanence that cast everything that came before in a provisional light. Within that fixity, our movie heroines assured us, we became our real selves. Morally transformed, the conniving little tease, the innocent waif, and the "wild" girl turned into perfect wives and mothers.

Before I found a movie idol, Madison Avenue defined my ideal of glamour. The moment I saw her, in my local drugstore at fourteen, I was hooked. Revlon's "Fire and Ice" girl became my fantasy self. She was everything I wanted to be. Swathed in chinchilla to match her silver-streaked halo of ebony hair, she gazed, as haughty and passionate as her product's name, from fashionable doe eyes. (Hours of practice proved that the look didn't work if you were nearsighted and astigmatic. The result of all my efforts suggested a cross between Ophelia and Jerry Lewis.)

Only a few years ago, I realized that my adolescent alter ego had captured me forever. When I worked as an on-camera reporter for public television, a colleague of professed feminist views advised me to dye my hair. "You'd look so much younger without the gray," she said.

"I was astonished. Young! Who wanted to look young?*

Under my now-much-grayer hair, I am still fourteen in my hated blue serge uniform, trying on lipsticks with my friend Isabel. We check the effect hopefully against the Revlon display. Would we ever look exotic, mysterious, as "unforgettable"—in the words of the Tony Bennett song we loved—as the fabulous silver-haired creature of fire and ice?

Consumer fantasies found fertile ground in the psyches of fifties' adolescents like me—those of us who would now be called "preppies." There was no name for us then because our existence aroused no envy and little interest. Unlike today's model—affluent teenagers, who lead more exciting lives than most adults (complete with their very own discos and drug dealers), we were

---

* With her masklike makeup and lacquered hair, Dorian Leigh, the "Fire and Ice" girl—like all the models of the 1950s and early 1960s—looked at least a decade older than her actual age.

sequestered in single-gender schools, fantasizing an (unknown) opposite sex in glamorous scenarios starring our adult selves.

I knew from my weekly devouring of *Life* magazine that elsewhere in America real life had already begun for kids my age. Out there, in Crestwood High, there were sock hops, homecoming games, fraternity queens, even drive-in movies where no one in the borrowed family car would have been able to give a synopsis of the plot.

But we were used to life in the slow lane. The realm of the promissory had its pleasures, too; the future was a perpetual growth stock, an IOU steadily earning interest. Life would be wonderful and exciting when—when *what*? *When* you were in college, *when* you found out what sex was like, *when* you were married.

Our highly developed skill in deferring pleasure had its price. A characteristic passivity has pursued our generation into present middle age. "Your day will come, dear," a friend's mother used to tell her, to soften the disappointment of the moment—the part she didn't get, the party she wasn't invited to.

"I'm still waiting," she says.

Audrey Hepburn was the patron saint of nice girls who waited. Clad in her very own Givenchy wardrobe, Andrey was glamorous but girlish, cultured but no bluestocking. In her screen roles, if she was not an orphan, she enjoyed enviably irregular family arrangements which gave her total freedom. Yet Audrey was never compromised either by lack of parental protection or by the ambiguity of her situation. Whether she was the butler's daughter (*Sabrina*, 1954), the last of a long line of courtesans (*Gigi*, on the Broadway stage in 1950), a poor waif working in a Greenwich Village book store (*Funny Face*, 1957), even a call girl (*Breakfast at Tiffany's*, 1961), she was always saved—for Mr. Right—by her aristocratic innocence. Men longed only to protect, never to exploit her. The snobbery implicit in her patrician Cinderella roles beamed an important signal. With the right style, you could get away with anything. A lady, as the Edwardians said, is never wrong. Which explains why our mothers, observes film historian Nora Sayre,[4] found Hepburn to be such a reassuring model.

If her innocence was really asexuality,[5] Audrey's enormous popularity was telling us something about our male contemporaries. Women as adult sexual beings aroused more dread than desire. Men could safely lust for Marilyn Monroe or Jayne Mansfield because these stars had been diminished to the "appalling innocence"[6] of wayward children—all mammaries with no moral or psychological complications. *The Girl Can't Help It*—the sniggering title of one of Mansfield's movies—said it all.

Audrey Hepburn did not "make bosoms obsolete," as screenwriter-director Billy Wilder supposedly predicted she would. Yet this inviolable creature, in nun's habit or buttoned up to the ears in a Givenchy suit, was clearly the (unthreatening) stuff of dreams. She might sell books rather than read them; her appeal suggested that the right mix of education and culture could be a secondary sexual characteristic.

Recalling his "enormous attraction to Audrey Hepburn, which still continues," sociologist David Riesman described her as "surely the ideal Bryn Mawr graduate."[7] In real life, the combination of a scholarship to study ballet and World War II ended her formal schooling early. Audrey never went beyond the equivalent of eighth grade. But as the thinking man's kind of woman, she gave hope to those of us who would.

When Carol Cornwell was "pert, trim" Carol Ruhe and a senior in her suburban New Jersey high school in 1953, her "feminine ideal was June Allyson," she says, "sweet and lovely; the girl next door who became the wife and mother next door. That was one part of it," she says. But as student council vice president and prizewinning journalist who was usually writing four articles at once, "I also had a hankering to be very brilliant, to be bright and beautiful, glamorous and talented, sought after by men *and* intelligent. I always had to have that part, too, even in my fantasies."

June Allyson was the easy part. Her career blossomed in the movies of the late 1940s where, as a transition figure, she ushered out that brief period of on-screen "career women"—Rosalind Russell, Ida Lupino, Katherine Hepburn—dressed for success in suits and hats. Later, in her Peter Pan collar and shining blond page boy, June Allyson was the archetypal yearbook picture. She was everybody's Mom—and us, before we became everybody's Mom (indeed, Allyson was frequently if discreetly pregnant). Her husky voice huskier with emotion, eyes brimming with all-purpose tears (pride, worry, relief, joy), Allyson watched her man take off in a fighter bomber or overcome polio to become a baseball star. Her tears provided the flow between the women's movies of the late 1940s—dubbed "weepies"[8] by an English critic —to the family films of the fifties.

The other part of Carol's fantasy self—the "talented and brilliant" half—didn't, significantly, find a real-life focus.

"In our community," Carol Cornwell says, "all our mothers bought the 1950s *Good Housekeeping* message. I saw only one kind of woman's role. It was acceptable for a woman to work *only* if she was widowed or divorced.

"I had three friends whose mothers worked. Two of them were widows and they just had 'jobs.' But the other had a real career, the only woman we knew who did. She was a social worker. My mother and her friends constantly put down Janet's mom for that reason. She *chose* to work! 'That was awful,' they said. 'What will it do to the children? Such a shame!' "

All those "advantages" provided by parents for their daughters plugged into conflicting fantasies—playing house and playing to a grandstand waiting to applaud our brilliance and beauty. "It was 'achieve, but don't do anything with it,' " Carol Cornwell says. "I was absolutely expected to do well in school. Then there were the *lessons*! Piano, of course, and private art lessons, ballet, and ballroom dancing. But, it was all in view of being a good wife and mother."

The youngest of Rowan DiStefano's four children began high school this September, and Rowan herself is back in her white nurse's smock. But she no longer wears the starched winged cap with its red cockade, pride of a famous teaching hospital, that once perched above her shiny black bangs. Four days a week, she works as an unpaid secretary for one of her husband's two dental practices.

She is looking for a "real" job in her old field, pediatric nursing. But it's hard to find part-time work that will get her home before the children arrive from school and leave her available for family vacations—the two summer months in New Hampshire with the kids and the spur-of-the-moment long weekends south that her busy husband will indulge in the winter. Meanwhile, the interaction with people is "better than nothing," she says. "And I save Mike a bunch of money."

Rowan Walsh DiStefano spent her first year of high school living with her father, a career officer in the Air Force, stationed at Pensacola, Florida. A Navy doctor gave her the first and only vocational guidance she ever received. He suggested that fourteen-year-old Rowan study nursing.

"It will help you become a better mother," he said.

"Anything that would make me a better mother, I was all for it," she says. "What did we know then? It was either teaching or nursing. That's how I got done out of a liberal arts education."

Three years after the doctor's advice, she was in a junior college nursing program. Three years after she received her R.N., Rowan Walsh DiStefano was married with two babies. "The best mother in the world," her husband says.

The only career counseling I ever received was "subliminal, like the new fifties advertising technique that flashed messages from the TV screen to the unconscious part of the brain.* Its content was distinctly "antivocational." Other than my teachers, the only women I knew who worked might as well have carried the palms of the martyrs into the subway. Closest to home, since she lived with us, was my aunt. Beautiful, clever, and charming, my mother's widowed younger sister was also an object lesson in how the "wrong" choice of man could condemn you to hard labor, as my mother always added solemnly, *"for your entire life."* A death sentence, in other words. The other working women I knew had a still more tragic aura. Refugees from Nazi-occupied Europe, they aroused unqualified compassion. (Sympathy for my aunt was always tinged with disapproval; she bore some responsibility for her fate.) Not least of Hitler's crimes was that he had forced friends like Lily and Gerda—cultured, refined, "sensitive" women —to work. Instead of their ordained lives—days filled with shopping, matinees, and bridge—they had jobs as secretaries or sold couture clothes. Every Sunday over tea and cake, I listened to their sufferings: how they were browbeaten by exploitive male executives or, worse, overworked and humiliated by denatured members of their own sex: women buyers or shop owners.

My mother's pity seemed more than justified. Her friends were very unhappy women. But it never occurred to me that their jobs were only one of the griefs and burdens of their uprooted lives. Labor for them was miserable both as an unexpected necessity and as a harsh reminder of the distance between past privilege and present need. Whether performed by refugees or widows, I saw work as the wages of dislocation or the wrong life decisions— loss of freedom, lack of choice, and worst of all, being unloved and uncared for by a man.

"Be good, darlings," my friend Litzy's mother would trill, as she disappeared for the afternoon, in a flash of silver fox tails and a cloud of Tabu. She was my first live role model.

---

* After objections by protest groups, subliminal commercials were withdrawn as "brainwashing."

Sitting at the kitchen table, with our cookies and algebra books, Litzy and I stared after her enviously. When would we be transformed from uniformed schoolgirls, in shapeless serge jumpers and middy blouses, to elegant creatures who wore veiled hats and cocktail rings? (In revenge, we tried to squeeze our large feet into her tiny custom-made Italian shoes.)

Later, when I met, in the pages of Betty Friedan and Nancy Friday, the women who were supposed to be our mothers—1940s career girls turned frustrated, frumpy hausfraus—I didn't recognize anyone I knew.

They toiled not, neither did they spin, our mothers. As far as we knew, they didn't hanker for earlier lives as Rosie the Riveter or Marie Curie. Looking and smelling as delicious as Marcel Proust remembered his mother, they were models of paradox—economically dependent women whose daily lives were characterized by a freedom few of their daughters enjoy.

"Why are you girls so discontented?" my mother would invariably ask, when, beginning in the mid-1960s, I would add still another divorce statistic to the mounting toll of school and college friends. She had the same puzzled response to anecdotes of our efforts to juggle jobs, law school exams, children's birthday parties: "Why do you make your lives so difficult?"

I never managed to answer that question to her satisfaction— or mine. Except to acknowledge that we changed, some of us. And that she was right to see these changes as making our lives harder.

Gail Feldstein grew up with two models at home—"my aunt who lived with us was a registrar at the rabbinical college and my mother, who was a housewife. My aunt who was outgoing, my mother who was submissive. My aunt, who had my father's ear; my mother, who did not. My aunt who had been very pretty. My mother who had a distinctly Jewish nose and always felt herself to be ugly. So I also learned early what it meant to be attractive and unattractive in our society. Both these women molded me. I had both and I am both," she says.

Home was a classic Midwestern suburb, where the streets had big houses with lawns just a driveway apart. The Feldstein house was ruled by her father, the rabbi. "Because he was blind," his daughter says, "my father never had a congregation. He served as chaplain to the American Legion, the Veterans of Foreign Wars, the V.A. Hospital." (He had been blinded in action, in the First World War, rescuing a buddy.) "The family myths were incredible," she says, "and they were perpetuated by everyone in town: 'your father the rabbi and war hero.'" The household revolved around him, his visitors, his food preferences, his study hours.

"My mother had a wonderful career before she was married. She was chief obstetrics nurse in a famous Boston hospital. Then my father came along and wooed her. She married him and became a housewife. A very unhappy woman and a very familiar story," Gail says. "She was happy in us—my brother and me—but she longed to go back to the hospital. She did not want to be a wife to my father and his sister."

Gail Feldstein's home now is the first floor of an airy Victorian farmhouse, whose long windows face the Berkshire hills. To support herself, her young son, and her chosen life near a Grandma Moses New England town, she has three jobs. Mornings, she is a cleaning woman; two afternoons a week, she teaches womens' studies at the local community college; the other two, she tutors prisoners as part of a federally sponsored adult literacy program.

For her, as for other burnouts from the days of rage, the peace of rural New England acted as a vast recovery room from Freedom Summers and winters of picketing ghetto schools in Bedford-Stuyvesant. She has lived in several houses in these hills since her second marriage and divorce three years ago. She has unlearned most of the lessons of her childhood and youth, taught her by the rabbi's wife and sister. She will never again be dependent—sexually, economically, emotionally—on a man.

Many of us had no conflicting models in our heads of the men or women we wanted to be: they were our fathers and mothers.

Even those who, like me, wouldn't have admitted it, fully expected to live as our parents lived, the last generation of American men and women to accept the traditional roles and family model as inevitable. (There were no alternatives to consider, as our juniors would later urge us to do.) Hollywood saw to it that our fantasy selves led straight from that walk into the sunset to settling down as home-loving, God-fearing, hard-working Americans, respecting authority and our neighbors' property, just like the solid citizens who reared us.

To be sure, we would have more and be more. We would be more educated and sophisticated and "casual" in our way of life. We would have more fun, more travel, more kids (and enjoy them more.)

But we didn't see ourselves as different, especially if our parents were successful, mainstream Americans, pleased with their own lives and admired by others. Unlike the children of the Jazz Age, rebelling against parents who were the "last Victorians," we were the neo-Victorians of the fifties, outwardly more conventional than our progenitors, the ex-flappers and college cut-ups, had been at our age. It certainly wouldn't have occurred to us that dear old Republican Pops was "part of the problem"—a contributor to social or economic blight. Or that mother the homemaker, if she appeared pleased with her life, was a "victim of false consciousness," as feminists would later claim, comparing her lot to that of a Peruvian peasant woman walking behind her husband on his donkey, unaware that she, too, is a beast of burden.

Some of us would not recognize our mothers or ourselves in Betty Friedan's description of any woman content to be "just a housewife." Like "prisoners in Nazi concentration camps," she wrote, "such women were 'walking corpses,' who surrendered their human identity and went almost indifferently to their deaths."[9]

Sue Hodges doesn't see anything about her mother's busy life as the wife of an executive in a small Midwestern city that suggested a corpselike prisoner. "She always seemed so happy with what she was doing," her daughter recalls. Her mother had been a dental technician before her marriage and she continued to work until Sue and her sister were born. "I never had the slightest sense of my mother's life as 'unfulfilled,' the way feminists describe women like her. I just wondered how she did it," she says wistfully.

She thought her life would be just like her mother's. "It was certainly what I wanted. My parents were always so loving with each other—and still are," she says.

How did they do it? Start out happy and stay that way.

Like her parents, Sue Baker Hodges and the prelaw student who would be her husband met when they were both sophomores at the state university, the year after she had pledged her mother's sorority.

On a page headed "Revels" in the Pledge Handbook of 1955, young women grin from grainy candid snapshots as they eat popcorn, piled four to a twin bed. Sue is easy to spot. Dark-framed harlequins give her plump face a quizzical look. In contrast to the mirth rocking the other girls in their plaid flannel nightgowns, she smiles wryly.

The harlequins have been replaced by round horn-rims, but the same smile plays across Sue Hodges' face, thinner now, as she describes her divorce, after seventeen years of marriage and three adopted children, and her move here, to a stucco house behind a scraggly privet hedge in a "borderline" part of the city.

"I just love this house," she says. "Bob was always trading up. None of the places we ever lived in felt like home to me." Her present block and neighborhood remind her of where she grew up, of where her parents and grandparents used to live.

"My family was always my model," she says. I wanted to be like them. I wanted to live the way we lived then."

"From the age of eight I wanted to be just like my father," Dick Robertson says. "I would get on a streetcar downtown and people would stop me and say, 'Are you Evan Robertson's boy? You look just like him.'" The tone in their voices told Dick Robertson that his father was already a local legend and the embodiment of the American dream—a carryout boy who had become a top executive in a national food corporation.

His awe for his father was magnified by the distance between them. "We weren't intimate, not the way we use that word today. Right through the late fifties, I think most boys had a relationship with their fathers that was more like the British. You called your dad 'Sir.' At dinner he'd ask: 'How are you today, Son?' And that was about it," he recalls.

For many American fathers and sons, what couldn't be expressed in words was conveyed in the satisfying sound of a ball caught in a worn leather mitt or, later, the hole in one, applauded by both.

From the time he was very young, Dick recalls, "My father and I did things together. First, there was baseball. Then we played a lot of golf. Dad was a pretty good player. Still, I could beat him fairly early on. I would come home from college just to play with him and his friends." At the same time, just after his freshman year at the university, Dick began to be included in more of his father's activities—with business associates as well as friends.

"In those days," he recalls, "if you were an executive of a national food chain, the brokers would do anything to get a product in your stores. We were constantly being entertained. At twenty, I was going to dinners at the Latin Quarter with my dad, where the bill was five hundred dollars!"

"They'd come for us in a limo, take Dad and me to play golf at the Westchester Country Club. They'd fly us to private islands in the St. Lawrence. We'd be shooting dice on the plane; it was a drinking, carousing, 'good ol' boy' man's world. Here I was, a kid, whooping it up with all these big businessmen! I definitely got the idea of what a man's life should be like from my father. I just took it for granted, mine would be the same."

Dick Robertson's mother was never present on these outings.

"The last fifteen years of my parents' marriage was not happy," he says. "Dad's class leap was just too dramatic. My mother sat home in her fancy Connecticut suburb, mad because she hated Northerners and didn't know anybody. He blamed her for being an uneducated farm girl who was holding back his career." That wasn't very fair, he admits. "After all, what do you want to be? Eventually, he asked to be transferred out of the East. Then he blamed her for that, too. They definitely would have been divorced had their time in history been advanced twenty years."

He is aware that his admired father was not an admirable husband; he is not certain that he was an admirable human being. At the same time, though, his father made sure his oldest son got a heady whiff of what it means to be a successful man in America —the perks and the power, the recognition and the deference. In the real world, he learned, a man's private failings don't count. (The private, after all, was women's sphere.)

The script was well-thumbed. The roles were all there to be learned by us, if not in private planes then in the kitchen, the "family room," or the car (where Daddy always did the driving). A man was a husband, father, provider, and winner.

Postwar prosperity left many communities untouched. For most of the Irish and Italian families in Mike DiStefano's neighborhood, nothing had changed since the depression, when most fathers barely managed to feed their families. For first-generation American sons, images of masculine competence and success came from elsewhere. If examples were close to home, the competitive juices started flowing early.

"Everyone needs role models," Mike DiStefano says. "For me they were my two older brothers. There were seven of us, six boys and a girl. My father was a shoemaker. My mother baby-sat during the day. At night she cleaned office buildings. She was determined that the American dream was going to come true for us, and it did.

"My oldest brother was the best student. He went to engineer-

ing school, graduated with honors. He worked all the time he
was in college. In 1948, he paid fifteen dollars a week room and
board to live at home. My other brother was captain of the college basketball team, a famous one in our day.

"I decided I had to be better than each of them in whatever
they were good at. So that's what I did. In college I was selected
the outstanding athlete *and* student in my class."

Somewhere between fandom, fantasy, and possession by spirits
stands cultism. In the fifties, the decade least tolerant of extremes,
certain fantasies of young people became apparent. Instead of
remaining underground along with other deviant behavior, they
went public. The cultist is a public fantasist. And in the fifties, an
era of joiners and organizations, public fantasists proliferated into
movements. Thus the hipster, with his dark shades and cool slang,
acolyte of black jazzmen; and the Beatnik, follower of pied pipers
whose song of the open road was most alluring to children of the
recently settled urban middle class.

Norman Mailer daydreamed himself a "white Negro,"[10] as far
as he could flee from being a nice Jewish boy from Brooklyn who
had gone to Harvard.

Joyce Johnson, a Barnard undergraduate, was initiated into real
life as a "minor character"—the title of her autobiography—one
of the many chicks in the all-male wanderings of Jack Kerouac
and his friends.

"In 1957," Johnson writes, "in the excitement and hope of that
moment, in what was real and strongly believed and truly lived
out—there seemed the possibilities of enormous transforma-
tions."[*][11]

Never had the ways of being a man or woman, an American,
seemed more restricted or the dreams of young people more

* Another measure of the inescapable "closed system of gender" in the 1950s: that
the marginal and exploited role of women in the Beat movement could be taken
for liberation. As Jack Kerouac proclaimed all over national television in the 1960s,
he was as antifeminist, antihippie, antiblack, and pro–Vietnam War as any hard hat.

standardized. A movement like the Beats, a sound like rock and roll, held out the promise of something else.

Until they become dress rehearsals, all fantasies are escape hatches. In the Wonder Bread decade—the most middle-class era in American history—our fantasies were a flight from the inevitable. In our heads we jumped the track of race or class, the burden of parental expectations, the "right" boy or girl, and we stopped inching up the ladder of (white-collar) success.

Not surprisingly, ours was the era that launched the first teen cult, rock and roll, complete with shamans (new young stars like Little Richard and Elvis); elders like disk jockey Alan Freed, who dictated the leisure activities and articulated the yearnings of seventeen million teenagers; and even a religion based on a teen martyr, James Dean.[12] For the first time, idols our own age embodied cool, glamour, sex; more radical still, they showed us that rebellion and defiance were rewarded with fame and glory.

In 1953, to a Southern boy with "all the advantages," Elvis Presley promised all this and more.

"Before there was Elvis," Cass Hunnicutt says, "I started going crazy for 'race music.' It had a beat. I loved it. I listened to it whenever and wherever I could, first on the local black stations. I loved to dance to it. This got me into big trouble with my parents and the schools, because we were not allowed to listen to this music openly.

"When I went off to prep school in 1953," Cass recalls, "we were not allowed to have a radio in our room. I had four radios confiscated, one after the other. I'd keep them hidden and bring them out at night. I used to listen to a station in Nashville, WLAC, that broadcast race music. It had a tremendous beam. You could hear those sounds all across the hills of Tennessee, across the Southern plateau. I was driving to Mexico in 1962, and I picked up this station. Suddenly, I recognized the DJ's voice. I've never been so excited. You stop to think: There's been no interruption between then and now, between Nashville and Mexico."

Between then and now spans a longer arc of time—thirty years exactly since Cass Hunnicutt sat in the same garden of his parents' house where he lounges today, on a similarly tropical May day, huddled on the same slightly rusted white wrought-iron bench, a "forlorn" fifteen-year-old, to hear that he was going off that fall to his father's old boarding school. There, his mother had said, they both so hoped he would buckle down" and "live up to his potential." And, she concluded significantly, he had all summer to let his peroxided surfer's hair grow out to its natural tar black color. His present drooping mustache, of the same shade, Cass cherishes as the only physical reminder of two decades of California life, lived at the febrile intensity of the sixties and seventies.

Cass Hunnicutt's "potential"—invoked by headmasters and deans, girlfriends and gurus, psychotherapists and business associates, along with his wife of twenty years—carried the charge of the past as much as the future. He is the vulnerable second son in a family where the burden of expectation, of achievement and distinction, harks back to the antebellum South. "My parents sure would have liked for me to excel in school," he says. "Dad graduated first in his class from my same prep school. He finished the university in three years. He was *some* scholar," Cass says. Today, ask most men downtown to name a law firm and chances are they will mention the one founded by Cass Hunnicutt's father just after World War II.

By this city's standards, Cass says, his father's family were latecomers. They arrived here in the early nineteenth century. His mother's people are what is meant by "old family." They had a plantation upriver since the state was settled. Cass's maternal great-grandfather was mayor, and there are enough Confederate heroes on both sides to fill a war museum handily.

"People still come up to me and say, 'Your mother has done so much for this city.' She's been Woman of the Year, president or vice president of just about every civic and cultural organization in town. She was way ahead of her time," Cass says, "for women speaking out in politics. What she said didn't always sit well, either."

"Before integration became the law," Cass says, "my mother recognized that black people were not getting a fair shake. In the schools they would get the outdated textbooks. When they published a new edition, the black schools got the used ones. My mother was on the Board of Education, and she would have groups of black ladies over to the house to discuss what should be done. I must have been about twelve, then. I would come home from school and see my mother serving iced tea and cookies to groups of black ladies in the living room. In the early 1950s that was just unheard of in this city, *just unheard of.*"

Pasty-faced, pure white-trash Elvis, in ghoul-green eye makeup and pink flash—was Cass Hunnicutt's great escape from tradition and expectation. "I loved Elvis's songs before I ever saw Elvis," Cass says. "I was right there when he started. Right in the rocket days. I bought all those first records on Sun label. I just about wore them out. I loved the beat, the rhythm. One of my favorites still, to this day, is 'Mystery Train.' When I saw and heard him sing it, right here in our local theater, I went wild. He didn't just just stand up there and sing a song. *He let her go!*"

Cass started to dance to the same sexual rhythm. "That was real taboo. I was always getting into trouble at school proms for 'suggestive dancing.' It all came from Elvis—all of his hip wiggling, pelvis gyrating. I'll never forget watching his first appearance on TV. They couldn't even show him from the waist down. But in the South, we had already seen him do all that in person— right here in town. I took my girlfriend to see him when he came here in 1955. He was just doing the south then. He hadn't gone on national TV yet; he hadn't been in the movies. He was our little local guy.

"Elvis was a Southern institution," Cass says. "He belonged to us, to the people down here. We were the ones who really knew his music.

"Oh man! Did I ever want to be like Elvis! I wanted to jump up on that stage, wiggle, and have all the girls scream and squeal.

"He had all the stuff," Cass says. "He was known by everybody —all over the world. If you wanted fame and fortune, if you wanted to be a household word, he was it. Great, educated statesmen didn't have that kind of renown. Plus, we all felt the rebelliousness, too; the way we did with James Dean. Our parents were scared that Elvis encouraged sexuality. But to the degree they disliked him, they emphasized the forbidden fruit aspect of both sex and Elvis. They were just telling us, if they thought it was so bad, it must be something great."

At the same time that Elvis inspired fear and loathing in the adult America of the decade, obsessed, as Albert Goldman noted, with its "menaces: the Commie menace, the Beat menace, the Hipster menace, the Teenage menace—by everything that did not conform to the constricting canons of 'normalcy' in that most abnormal age,"[13] the king of rock and roll was too popular to be ignored.

Looking back, Cass sees clearly that Elvis and his own coming of age are historically linked, representing the last moment of a uniquely regional culture and its heroes, the last era before the great leveler—television—changed American culture forever.

The fifties saw the final flowering of local talent, where you could follow your boy as he moved from dinky one-night stands at juke joints and carnivals to sellout concerts with thousands of screaming pubescent girls. (Can any adolescent today stake a claim to Prince or Madonna? Thrill to their shared origins? They belong to the media, to MTV and *People* magazine.) Elvis, Cass Hunnicutt knows, was part of growing up in a place as lost in time as the South of his great-grandfather—whose statue stands in one of the city squares.

"I'll never forget the year 1954," Cass says. "I was sixteen and I just got my driver's license. Then I was free, and with the greatest freedom of all time. We would go to black nightclubs.

At that time there was no racial hostility. The guys that owned the clubs made a place for us. It was real friendly. It was always, 'Y'all come on in and sit down.' Our dates would dance with the black guys there. Looking back," Cass says, "it had to be financial, too. We came in groups, spent some dollars. But you don't think of it that way when you're fifteen. We just knew we felt welcome, perfectly at ease. Our parents sure would have been distressed if they'd known. It wasn't just the black clubs. The drinking age was twenty-one, so to be found in any nightclub—black or white—when you were in high school, just wasn't where you wanted to be."

As far back as Cass Hunnicutt can remember, "I was stamped rebellious.

"I was constantly at odds and in trouble with my parents and with the administration of every school I went to. First my public school at home, then the monastery in Virginia where I got sent. Afterwards, it took me five years, four colleges, and three summer schools just to get through. You might say," Cass says, not without pride, "I was way ahead in rebelliousness.

"I was an early James Dean fan. I related completely to *Rebel Without a Cause*. I was convinced my mother and father didn't understand me.

"In the Fifties," Cass says, "you weren't intimate with parents. Not like I am with my kids. In the South, especially among well-to-do families, a lot of our upbringing was assigned to the servants. They potty-trained you; they were there in the afternoon when you came home from school.

"I'll never forget," Cass says, "when one of my friends went to Lawrenceville. They found out he was reading at second- or third-grade level. His black maid had been doing all his homework.

"We're in a great period now for people expressing their emotions," Cass says. "This sure wasn't the case when we were growing up. To admit to psychological problems—even ordinary troubles—was a *big* no-no. Nobody talked about stress or anxiety the way we do now. Tears for a man, men embracing men, in the Fifties you just didn't see that. You put a cap on your emotions— or else! So for Elvis to be this wild, wiggling, gyrating person, to moan and sob and howl—that was really something for me!

"Sure, I had some real good buddies. It was us against them." But even with his friends, Cass says, "I had the distinct feeling they wouldn't understand me, no matter what. Our conversations dealt with what girl did it; who didn't do it. Did you see the movie? Hear the record? Was it true that James Dean had gotten into a coffin a week before he died? Lots of speculation about the private lives of stars. I don't ever recall talking about our own feelings. The words just weren't there." Cass didn't need to risk closeness with his friends. Elvis provided intimacy by proxy, blowing off that "cap on the emotions."

"The lid was on so tightly," Martin Duberman says, "we didn't even know there was a lid." Through Elvis, Cass could experience what it would be like to abandon yourself out loud and in public to raw feeling: loss, pain, desire, sneering contempt—everything "you didn't dare show or else!"

The teen idols of the fifties were the first wave of the dominant youth culture to come. Glamorous young politicians and rock stars were followed by sixteen-year-old movie idols and fashion models. Never Trust Anyone Over Thirty became the slogan of a generation of middle-class young Americans who found it "sick" that anyone could ever have aspired to follow the example of a corporate father, a war hero brother, a housewife mother. Ten years later, the innocuous "generation gap" of the fifties had become a no-man's-land, ignited sporadically by guerrilla warfare, with a measure of class struggle to further fuel the hostilities. Elders whose credentials included a record of dissent from the earlier ethos of conformity, repression, and profit—Allen Ginsberg, Paul Goodman, Herbert Marcuse—became gurus of the new generation.

Elvis's mystery train chugged out of the gray fifties into a psychedelic landscape. The happy ending to boy-meets-girl was no longer the clinch followed by a walk into a postcard sunset, but a chemically enhanced embrace by "Lucy in the Sky with Diamonds." Together they would choose an alternate life-style where they could make love, not war, question authority, avoid the system, and hope "to die before they grew up."[14]

4

FOR ME TO KNOW, YOU TO FIND OUT

Dissimulation was our answer to adult anxiety and expectation. We learned not to show passion, enthusiasm, intense feelings of any kind. We became particularly skilled at covering negative emotions: anger, jealousy, fear, or grief.

"I would *never* have told my mother about any real problems," Rowan DiStefano says. "Being divorced, I felt she had enough troubles. I didn't think I should be a little thorn in her side. I didn't want to worry her. I told her what she wanted to hear."

Susan Allen Toth of Ames, Iowa, spent most of her first semester at Smith College in 1957 physically ill from homesickness. Yet she was afraid to tell her mother.

"I did not want to admit that I was not making what was called 'a good adjustment,'" she writes in *Ivy Days*. "I carried the weight, I thought, of many expectations: my own, my mother's, my friends', relatives', teachers' and well-wishers'. How could I confess I was scared? How dare I be homesick?"[1]

We cringed at the thought of disappointing our parents—whatever bold assertions we made to the contrary. Disappoinment did not only mean doing wrong. Being troubled was even worse. It was as though our families had exacted from us the unspoken promise that we would be happy all the time.

Even though grown-up, middle-aged, how deeply we dreaded telling our parents—even more than our children—of impending divorce. They would be so "disappointed," friends explained. They always assumed we were happily married. Why should they have thought otherwise? From an early age, we learned not to worry our parents, not to be a "little thorn" in their sides. We had lied to them for so long.

We lied in the interests of not "hurting" them, of being trusted, of being left alone.

"I had a big temper when I was young," Rowan says. "I learned to control it very early. The same with talking back, voicing my opinion. I learned very quickly that I didn't get anywhere that way. It was easier to go along with what they wanted. So I always did what they told me. I always came in on time, for example. Eventually, I built up such a good trust I could do almost anything I wanted. So there was no need to be defiant. As long as I was 'honest,' my mom said. I was dishonest about some things— things I knew she wouldn't like. But if I didn't tell her, she couldn't know and it wouldn't matter. So it wasn't really lying."

"I became a liar very early on," says Carol Cornwell. "I always lied. In school and to my parents. Not just failing to mention the sexual things I was doing, but lying about where I was and when.

"I felt awful about it. My parents are both very honest people. I knew that I would just disappoint them terribly if they know how much I lied."

We learned early; we got smart. We became compliant, "good" children—good sports, good all-around students, good citizens. (What had once been "Conduct" on the report card of my girls' school became known in the 1950s as "Citizenship.") We became

especially good at "psyching out"—in the phrase of the period—
those in authority.

I was, and still am, reliable, responsible, tidy, and well-groomed.
For sitting up straighter than anyone else in study hall period
all through tenth grade, I was made Posture Girl of the Year—
the only award I have ever won. I was polite, considerate, and
respectful. I also lied and broke rules all the time. Almost all the
time, I got away with it.

Part of this behavior is classic kid stuff: exploring the extremes,
the thrills-and-chills department. As Cass Hunnicutt says nostalgically, "There was always some excitement in bending the rules,
seeing what you could get away with; testing our wits against
'theirs.'"

Would we get caught if, like Cass, we sneaked out of the house
at night, not to return until dawn? Would I be discovered, a
model of deportment and a chain-smoker from the age of eleven,
puffing away in bathrooms or in the conveniently overgrown
school garden? I envied my brother's skillful and intrepid forging
of parental signatures; armed with "excuses" for doctor or dentist,
he was off to hear the big bands at the Paramount.

There was a special twist to our attitude to truth in the fifties,
to cheating and rule-breaking, that is the mark of our period. *We
had the right to lie.* For some, lying became a moral imperative.
Like Holden Caulfield, hero of *The Catcher in the Rye*, we lied
on principle. Like Holden, if we were going out for a pack of
cigarettes, we said we were going to the opera. We lied to protect
our privacy, to cover our tracks.

We felt only slightly less vulnerable with our peers. They posed
a different threat: Self-exposure would cause us to be laughed at.
I still recognize my contemporaries by our shared horror of appearing ridiculous, a horror no post-fifties form of therapy ever
manages to eradicate. This wholesome creature—the Ideal Boy
and Girl of the period—friendly, open, popular, uncomplicated,
well-rounded, and well-adjusted—made any deviation suspect. It

was safer to assume that everything about ourselves should be disguised. "For me to know and you to find out" was our retort to the nosy.

The truth was privileged information, imparted—or more often exchanged (as a safety measure)—among intimates who, as it happens, were rarely of the opposite sex.

Secrets, lies, evasions, and role-playing: As adolescents we created a precocious public persona, acceptable and accepted, in order to be left alone.

Most middle-class kids weren't risking any "life chances" by taking to the road with thumb or motorcycle, or rocking around the clock. Caught between an unquestioning acceptance of authority and our instinctive sense that the way this authority acted upon our lives was often hypocritical, corrupt, and senseless, we worked the system. What might have been deviance became inner resistance. In adolescence, many of us began lifelong careers as fifth columnists. Our elders were only too well aware of the threat to order we presented; never caught breaking a single rule, we were master strategists of a new type of germ warfare.

"Negative attitude" was the name of the contagious disease we spread. At fourteen, in tenth grade, I was a committed "carrier," certifiably state-of-the-art in decorous, smiling subversion. Give me one lunch period, and I could turn a tableful of hearty, gung-ho types into twisted cynics. Nobody could ever pin a rap on me; that was the infuriating part. (In fact, I was careful out of cowardice, craving adult approval too much to be an honest troublemaker.)

Cass Hunnicutt was braver. In his Virginia "monastery," he managed open rebellion and negative attitude at the same time. But even the demerits earned by listening to race music on his four forbidden radios were not as serious as the Dread Disease.

"We had a prefect system," Cass says, "guys who were the student leaders. I was always called in to see the prefect about

my 'attitude.' I needed to cooperate; to be more gung-ho for the
school, to fit in. That was my real problem, the prefect said. I
wasn't making an effort to fit in."

In frequent command performances in the headmistress's office,
my negative attitude was the subject of each lecture. More in
sorrow than in anger, she would wonder aloud why I didn't use
my "God-given gifts" and "leadership potential constructively."

There was nothing worse, she said, "than obeying the letter of
the law while sneering at the spirit." In Latin class, when we
read in Cicero of perfidious Catiline, his intelligence wasted
through lack of character, our teacher stared mournfully at me.

"I didn't have much rebelliousness as a teenager," recalls Sue
Hodges. "That came later." Along with rebellion, negative attitude
went underground but, like the radioactive waste that had begun
to be buried everywhere in the 1950s, its destructive capabilities
were far from dead. In smoldering half-life, we stockpiled resentment, rebellion, and rage. Negative attitude would prove particularly indestructible; it reemerged as passive aggression, a favored
weapon in marriage.

As adolescents, we were easily co-opted. Prizes for parodying
adult behavior were alluringly apparent and easily won. At fifteen
I traded in my negative attitude for "maturity." Instead of sub-
verting my peers, I set about seducing my elders. My, how I'd
grown. A middle-aged preemie, I was deemed responsible and
trustworthy at last. I was senior class president, editor of the
literary magazine, captain of the basketball team, and recipient
of a host of lesser offices and honors—all of which (even those
purporting to be democratically elected) were, of course, rigged
by the administration.

In the late spring of senior year, I indulged in one last lapse
into my old ways. With two sidekicks (one the head of student
government) I sneaked into the headmistress's office. A quick

forage in the files produced what we were looking for. Lolling on her worn brown leather sofa, sipping Cokes and exhaling smoke rings from our Pall Malls, we read aloud our college recommendations. "An outstanding all-around student . . . a natural leader," I read about myself. "An exceptionally mature young woman . . ." We shrieked with laughter.

Maturity was the ultimate fifties virtue, particularly admired in the young. If we had belonged to African tribes instead of American middle-class ones, our coming-of-age ceremony would have consisted of donning the masks of village elders. That we were travesties of adults worried no one. Like being "skipped" in the early grades (which many of us were), precocious maturity and its prizes suggested that adolescence, like second grade, might not be necessary for apt learners. Stuffed with vitamins, we were taller, healthier, smarter than any generation preceding us. Why shouldn't we also be the youngest specimens ever of caution, sobriety, and foresight? It never occurred to our elders that we were all style, camping what Norman Podhoretz called an "unearned maturity almost wholly divorced from experience . . . a generation that willed itself from childhood directly into adulthood, with our adolescence dangerously postponed."[2] But the children behind the middle-aged masks didn't willfully skip adolescence. It was made clear to us that we had no time to waste on such silliness.

In *Growing Up Absurd* (1956) Paul Goodman mourned the irrationality of coming of age in the 1950s, when "bright, lively children with the potentiality for knowledge, noble ideals, honest effort, and some kind of worthwhile achievement, [were] transformed into useless and cynical bipeds"[3] by the pressure to conform.

College was the finishing school for this process. In loco parentis, the role of residential institutions of higher learning, was an object lesson in collusion and hypocrisy. They knew that their promise to "take care of my little girl [and boy]" was Mission Impossible. For our part, we had even fewer qualms deceiving surrogate parents than real ones.

"I found out very early how to falsify the attendance sheet for required chapel," Carol Cornwell says. "After I did it the first time, I never went again. But they must have known. Because if everyone had gone who forged their names on those cards, the building would have been filled to overflowing."

"Liquor couldn't be served in any sorority or fraternity house at the university," Cass Hunnicutt recalls. "It was the state law as well as the college rules. The chaperones knew what was going down at all the parties. Just as long as we drank the martinis from malted milk containers, we were fine."

"My feeling was," Carol says, "there was nothing wrong with what I was doing. Therefore, I would lie to protect myself. They had no right to tell you sex or drinking was off limits. So I did all those things and lied about them. Even when you really didn't like it, you had to keep liquor in your room and drink because it was against the rules. That was more important than anything else: to break the rules. As much as you dared, as often as you could get away with it."

They knew why the chapel never overflowed, that nobody was getting blind drunk on malted milk. As long as we didn't blatantly confront authority, challenge the rules, defy them. The reward of our maturity was collusion.

At sixteen I arrived at Smith College, a creditable knockoff of a forty-year-old. To my advance billing of "exceptional maturity" and "leadership potential" I added a lacquered supercool manner that occasionally inspired fear, but never suspicion. I smoked and drank in my room, cut anything compulsory, and regularly falsified information on the blue cards on which students' weekend addresses at mens' colleges were to be recorded.

Infraction of this rule—the keystone of *in loco parentis*—was supposed to mean instant expulsion. Where sex was concerned, the consequences of truth were much more dangerous than lying; moral blackmail was the backup measure.

Known as the Fin for her sharklike ways, Mrs. Finley, our housemother, had a wicked spin to that ball. "Just imagine how you would feel," she drawled, in an accent not acquired in her native Buffalo, "if one of *your* parents [pause] became *seriously* ill and you had *deliberately* put the wrong address on your card!" Not even the dimmest debutante could have missed the cause-and-effect message. If you were "doing it" (and why else would you lie?), you were literally killing a mother or father. ("There is no statistical evidence," whispered a friend, fresh from the unexpected triumph of having passed Statistics, "that a single parent ever died while their daughter was in the middle of the sexual act in Amherst, Cambridge, or New Haven." Reassured, we continued to forge, falsify, perjure ourselves, and "cover" for friends.) "Rules were made to be broken," was the moral philosophy of our coming of age. Lying was the tunnel we dug between public compliance and private revolt. From our subterranean scurryings, we emerged with a sour and cynical individualism.

As young people, we had no "rights" whatsoever. Freedom and privacy were to be seized, the rewards of the wily and daring. I had no idea that these were the prizes of privilege, that "getting away with it" was a bribe. "They" would look the other way if "we" didn't rock the boat. If we broke the bargain, openly challenged authority, reprisal was swift and harsh. Exploits that in others eras were treated as youthful high jinks, in the fifties became close to capital crimes.

"Nobody rebelled when I was in high school, or in college, either," Dick Robertson says. "At the university I was with a group of guys that hung the dean of students in effigy. Heavy duty stuff. . . . They held a campuswide search for evidence. Had we been caught, we would have been expelled. That's what happened to other friends of mine who spray-painted the fraternity insignia on an overpass. In 1954 they called that rebellion. Everybody accepted authority. It probably wasn't right, but it took me fifteen years to realize it."

Our complicity with authority, with those in power, atrophied our sense of social justice, making collective action difficult for us later on. Trained in stealth, we knew that as individuals we had more to gain from breaking rules than from changing them. Institutions had absolute power. Confronting them was unthinkable. Negotiating with their representatives was a boring waste of time. (I was contemptuous of the earnest types who grooved on student government and honor board offices. Had they nothing more important on their minds than sober lectures to others on the evils of smoking in "undesignated areas"? In those days, it wasn't lung cancer or even immolation of their fellow students that worried them. In case of fire, we were warned, insurance premiums of the college would rise precipitously.)

We knew the deal we cut was far more to our advantage. They made insane, arbitrary rules impossible to police. We broke them without a twinge of conscience. I never questioned the legitimacy of authority, I merely determined it would never govern *my* life.

We were exceptional if we suspected that a repressive climate existed "out there." Otherwise, we might have understood the hysteria of our elders at the least hint of rebelliousness on our part.

"I'm always appalled at how unpolitical I was," Martin Duberman says. "Right through college, all through the McCarthy period, I really believed this country was fine. I was a New Dealer, just like my parents, a good patriotic American boy. I thought our system was the best in the world. Any social or ethical problems were essentially minor. They could be fixed with a little tinkering around the edges."

Those few who were politically aware tended to have good reason: their parents were either Cold War vigilantes or victims.*

Gail Feldstein, the rabbi's daughter, describes her family as "very, very political. They read the paper every day. They hated the Democrats. McCarthy was the hero. McCarthy had been vilified. My father didn't have his own congregation. What he had was the American Legion. He was a McCarthyite for the same reason he was anti-Zionist. If Jews made a thing of themselves, we would get into trouble—like the Rosenbergs. That's what I went to college believing, because that's all I heard at home."

"Church was the center of my parents' lives," Carol Cornwell recalls. "When I was ten, I didn't want to go to Sunday school any more. But I had to. It was absolutely required. My parents were shocked that I even *said* I didn't want to go.

"At sixteen, I went home and told my parents that I didn't believe in God. I had already told our minister. I will never forget my father's response. He said: 'As long as you live in this house, you will believe what I tell you to believe.'

"The members of my family were far-right conservative. I never agreed with them. From the beginning of McCarthy's campaign, I knew it was wrong. I watched the Army-McCarthy hearings on television every day after school. I was very upset.

"I don't know where my views came from. I must have absorbed the ethical teachings of the church. That wasn't what my parents wanted me to get out of religion. When I joined the youth service club at our church, they said, 'That's so nice, you'll do something for others. You'll be less selfish.' They were upset when I came back believing not only in service but in justice."

In the context of the times, even Carol Cornwell felt powerless

---

* Only years later did I meet a contemporary who had been directly affected by McCarthyism—a young man who spent his youth in Mexico, where his parents were members of the expatriate colony of blacklisted screenwriters.

to act on her impulse to dissent. "In college," she says, "I remember being very angry about some of the unjust rules, and yet I never challenged them. I wanted to speak out, but I was afraid. . . . I was afraid of what would happen if I publicly protested. . . ."

In 1956, the same year that Carol Cornwell graduated with honors in Physics from a New England women's college and three weeks later married an executive trainee with a large corporation, an influential book appeared.

The Organization Man, by *Fortune* editor William H. Whyte, Jr., painted a fearful picture of individualism at bay. Whether they worked for corporations, big government, or law firms, younger Americans were in the process of being subverted by the social ethic, "that contemporary body of thought which makes morally legitimate the pressures of society against the individual."[4]

At brainstorming sessions on the job or kaffeeklatsches in the new planned developments of suburbia, the organization threatened to transform American men and women into well-adjusted robots, capable of only "groupthink," team spirit, and togetherness. In board rooms, and at backyard barbecues, dissent was stifled and deviation from group norms punished.

"Imprisoned in brotherhood" by the "beneficence of his employer"—the organization man (along with his wife and children) was the future citizen of Orwell's *1984*.

Concluding his chilling study, Whyte (Princeton, Class of 1939) exhorted his younger contemporaries—namely us—to "fight the organization." We had nothing to lose but our pensions. And the strategy of his holy war sounded strangely familiar. There was no licking them without joining them. Step one was getting through Big Brother's net. Whyte's advice? Dissimulate.

In a helpful appendix, "How to Cheat on Personality Tests," the author provided detailed advice on "passing"—how to answer the questions designed to weed out weirdos, such as, "Have you enjoyed reading books as much as having company in?" Faking normalcy was the name of the game. The good fight would only be won by the fifth columnists—by skillful liars and con artists, role-players and gamesmen—by men and women who could be counted on to carry their closets with them wherever they went.

An essential element in our protective smokescreen was a sincere manner. Sincerity was the social mantle of maturity: the style of candor and openness without the substance. A famous article of menswear in the fifties was the "sincere" knitted tie. Among the many jokes on the subject, most focused on the work done by those who wore it. The sincere knitted tie* was the favorite of advertising executives, those professionals most highly paid to lie. But the real subject of the jokes went deeper—the assumption that in a sane society, no one—even those who were not Madison Avenue hucksters—could seriously be sincere.

Don't blow your cover, Whyte urged. Conceal everything, reveal nothing. Truth in any form would be held against you—by bosses, coworkers, neighbors; therefore, "they" didn't deserve your honesty. (Just who *did* would become a tricky question.) Above all, evade, never confront.

Guarding our individual privacy, we were happily absolved from acting on behalf of others. As inner resisters, we would remain pure-hearted and clear-headed. We could never be corrupted or even confused by our own lies.

"I was involved in a deception," the witness told a hushed House caucus room in 1959, as he began his testimony before a congressional subcommittee.[5] A historical understatement, as it turned out.

As the quiz show scandal unfolded, Charles Lincoln Van Doren, an English instructor at Columbia University and star of NBC's *Twenty-One*, was proved to have been on the take for three years. Along with other contestants, he had been fed information beforehand. Agreeing when to win or lose, he was even coached in the

---

* The sincere knitted tie also had the slightly arty, populist raffishness later associated with wearing workshirts to the office.

most dramatic on-air technique (eyes squeezed shut to suggest intense concentration before "remembering" the correct answer).

In 1957 Van Doren's first big win of $129,000 landed him on the cover of *Life* magazine, a $50,000-a-year job as consultant to the television station (where, as he later noted, nobody ever consulted him about anything), and a pundit's corner on Dave Garroway's *Today* show.

One year of ugly rumors later and the lid blew off. Every sordid chapter of quiz show corruption was revealed. Van Doren himself was fingered by another star contestant. Gravel-voiced Herbert Staempel of Brooklyn, an "unpopular" winner, had accepted a bonus for losing to the young, clean-cut, all-American teacher. Staempel had second thoughts that he shared with New York District Attorney Frank Hogan.

Even when all around him there was a rush to confession—or rationalization—by producers, sponsors, and other contestants (including celebrities like Xavier Cugat)—Van Doren still lied. He lied on the *Today* show. He lied again under oath before a New York grand jury, denying any knowledge that the show was fixed, along with any personal wrongdoing.

Exposure of the rigged quiz shows rocked the nation, focusing attention for months on what the *New York Times* called a "shocking state of rottenness within the radio-television world and in the get-rich-quick schemes through which so many people were corrupted and so many millions deceived."[6]

But the strongest tidal waves of shock were caused by Van Doren himself. Bearer of one of the most distinguished literary and academic names in the nation, Van Doren had seemed the "finest product of American education, character, family background, and native intelligence. Could it be," *Time* magazine mourned, "that all or much of that picture had been a sham?"[7]

In 1959 I was a graduate student in Cambridge, Massachusetts. Every young man I met who hadn't been born similarly well-connected would have liked to be Charles Van Doren—before the fall. Handsome (if a trifle toothy), he was the preppy-as-prodigy;

mathematician and humanist, gifted musician and popular teacher. Shortly after his first *Twenty-One* jackpot, Van Doren acquired a pretty wife (in reply to an ad for a secretary to answer his TV fan mail) and, as soon as possible, a baby daughter.

Following the family tradition, it seemed, had worked well for him. He now shared an office with his father, Mark Van Doren, poet, biographer, and chairman of the Columbia University English Department. The son appeared to be an enviable example of privilege leading to achievement, of parental expectations happily fulfilled. What had gone wrong?

Neither greed nor even an acquired taste for fame could fully explain this strange betrayal. Aside from a sports car for himself and a Christmas shopping spree during which he spent five-thousand dollars—significantly, on presents for his family—Van Doren showed no signs of changing his modest, rising-young-academic way of life.

Nor did his famous confession clarify matters greatly. "I've learned a lot about myself," Van Doren began, "and about the responsibilities man has to his fellow man. I've learned a lot about good and evil." The rapt legislators might have been listening to Dr. Norman Vincent Peale holding forth at the Marble Collegiate Church. To be sure, the witness conceded, his head had been turned by national celebrity, by "more money than I ever dreamed of having." He had continued to lie because "so many school-children and students had expressed their faith in me, their dedication to knowledge. I could not bear to betray that faith and hope. I felt that I carried the whole burden of the honor of my profession," he concluded.

Still, those who managed to stay to the end of this performance —"a tasteless exercise in guile and unction,"[8] as one editorial described it—might have picked up a few clues. Not only about the witness but about his era. He had been running, Van Doren said, away from himself. And he had been doing it for a long time. At thirty-three he was "just beginning to realize that the truth is always the best way."

What was the self this promising young man with "all the advantages" was fleeing? ("I was angry all the time," says Gail Feldstein. "I wanted someone to pay attention to the real me, not the one who was getting A's in school.")

"He was getting his innings," said a friend, a first-year law student. He put a strangely savage spin on the words. No one present needed to ask what he meant. We knew. Like Van Doren, we had toed the line. We had done all the right things. And so far we had avoided getting caught doing the wrong ones. More of the same was expected of us.

Like the law student, the other young people sitting around my scruffy furnished apartment had been raised on Charles Van Doren's mixed signals. You couldn't be greedy or sincerely want to get rich (or marry money); that was vulgar or "very unattractive"—the ultimate fifties put-down. *But* you had better be a success. In all its God-and-country pieties, Van Doren's confession was a perfect pastiche of every commencement address we had ever heard, of the valedictorian speeches many of us had given. Ambition was only acceptable when you made a contribution to society! (If you harbored any other kind of ambition, you kept it under your hat.)

As captive audiences, how often we had listened to lectures on the "responsibilities" of privilege or education, enjoining us to be a credit to our families, our college, our country, and admonishing us to set a good example to uncommitted nations or younger Americans (the excuse Van Doren gave for continuing to lie).

Indeed, many fifties graduates were not waiting for a president to urge them to ask what they could do for their country. Direct from college—with new law degrees or credentialed by revitalized schools of public administration and by new area studies programs in Russian and Chinese—young people were flocking to work for the government, especially in more glamorous areas like the foreign service.

Profit-making enterprises were required to justify their existence as local benefactors. Organizations like the Jaycees burgeoned in every town and city as showcases for young businessmen to outdo one another in conspicuous displays of "community service."

Doing good and doing well—the claim made by one Ivy League university of its alumni—did not acknowledge that these goals might frequently conflict. In the fifties, *image* began to be exploited on a scale undreamed of in the earlier days of advertising and public relations. Whatever discrepancy existed between the real conduct of life's business and its public dimension was papered over by the right publicist or PR man. The Age of Television—and the billions of dollars riding on its sales potential—was required to exploit Van Doren's sincere dishonesty.

Surrounded by pious hypocrisies, we had turned lying into a basic reflex: for many of us it became the key to survival. Like Van Doren, we had little experience in telling the truth. (Often, we had even more trouble recognizing it.) Later, many of us could be honest only with professionals whose discretion and "fee for service" were crucial to their trustworthiness. "There are only three people I never lie to," said a male contemporary a few years later, "my shrink, my lawyer, and my accountant."

There might be only one difference between me and my friends and Charles Van Doren. No one had tempted us to lie and cheat for profit. Not yet. He was, "after all, one of us."

5

IN-CROWDS AND OUTSIDERS

Before he coached young Americans on how to fight the system by boring from within, the author of *The Organization Man* had interviewed prospective recruits on campus. They did not suggest the stuff of inner resistance or heroic sabotage. Eager to conform before they were paid to do so, as Whyte noted sadly, the middle-aged college seniors he observed in the early 1950s did not seem about to graduate so much as "transfer" into the real world.[1] How did they get that way—so old, so soon—he wondered?

To have emerged such good gray specimens by the end of bright college years required a head start. Tryouts for middle age began in high school, where we auditioned for roles as the organization boy and girl.

Therein seems to lie the wildest paradox, the craziest contradiction about the decade in which we came of age. Forty-year-old senior citizens of twenty-one, judiciously weighing retirement benefits before graduation, were products of the same period that brought us—the American teenager.

A unique postwar phenomenon, the American teenager had no counterpart anywhere in the "Free World," as it was then known. Ken- and Barbie-doll prototypes, they came complete with all the artifacts of their own teen culture—clothes and hairstyles, music and dances, special cars and movie stars, foods and fads. "Fun, fun, fun . . ." the Beach Boys would sing at the end of the decade—that was the only responsibility of middle-class American teens.

Dancing and more dancing is what Betts Saunders remembers. "In school, after lunch, and during lunch, too, you could go to the gym and dance to records: jitterbug and slow dances." Academics were "incredibly important" to Betts in junior high. "Then when I got to high school, in ninth grade," she says, "I became breath-takingly shallow. Revlon had just come out with 'Cherries in the Snow' lipstick. That was the high point; next came clothes and dancing."

As soon as it got warm, Cass Hunnicutt and his friends cut school and went to the beach. "It was cool to have a tan and blond hair; we bleached it with peroxide for the surfer look."
    "In the South, the biggest influence on our culture as kids was the heat," Cass says. "Everybody forgets that now. The houses weren't air-conditioned. The cars weren't air-conditioned. The summer nights were hotter than hell. So, you did not sit around and swelter; you went out," Cass says. The beach and those ocean breezes were the biggest attraction. You swam at night. There was lots of skinny-dipping. Next to water, the only other way to sur-vive," Cass says, was to keep moving. "You rode and rode around. You drank lots of Cokes and iced drinks while you were driving. You just never wanted to be indoors."

"We had lots of parties," Rowan DiStefano recalls. "Parties with boys and dancing and pajama parties with just girls—silly, silly, silly parties where we just stayed up all night and talked about boys, parties where we ran around the streets in our nighties. We did all sorts of crazy stuff."
    We were wild and wacky kids, indulged in four years of pursuits so trivial most adults couldn't even understand them. Or we were

cases of arrested development, still behaving like children at sixteen instead of "mature," "responsible" young people. As the first
generation since the 1920s whose adolescence coincided with
peace and prosperity, we were given license to be goofier than
any kids had ever been in the history of the human race.

In fact, the "frenzied youth culture of the fifties" observed by
one critic[2] was only a brief parole between our policed childhood
and premature middle age. Our elders recognized that blowing off
steam as teenagers was a safety measure: we could be counted
upon to chug along nicely thereafter, tracked for life.

Even our appearance as carefree cutups was deceiving. A closer
look, if we can bear it, at our high-school yearbooks dissolves the
distance between our "crazy" teenage personae and the sober,
old-at-heart collegians we became. Both the professional photographer's camera and our own snapshots reveal in Mister and Miss
Teenage America our middle-aged selves (older by far than we
are now)—"his" earnest, responsible gaze, framed by bristly crew
cut and sprouting outsized ears, "her" jam-colored lipstick high-
lighting an anxious, I-aim-to-please Ipana smile.

Cruising, drag racing, jitterbugging, screaming for Elvis, or
running around the streets in our nighties, we never forgot the
expectations that weighed upon us—to be well-liked, well-
adjusted, well-educated, and well-married; to do good and do well
in careers.

There we are, dressed for success, in felt circle skirts or pleated
reversible ones; saddle shoes and penny loafers, tinkling charm
bracelets or IDs, letter sweaters, chinos or rolled dungarees—even
blue serge uniforms.

Success started with another name; it was called popularity.

We would have killed for it or made any pact with the Devil.
What was an immortal soul, compared with popularity's incan-
descent aura? Breathed there an adolescent in the America of the
fifties who did not know its every permutation and calibration?
We had learned by heart its objective criteria, as exemplified by

Supremely Popular Beings; its measurements in feet (height of males), inches (bust, waist, and hips of girls), in decimals (grade-point averages), whole numbers (varsity letters), and finally, those all-important elective proofs, the titles: cheerleaders and class officers. We knew our own rank and everyone else's, what they had and we didn't, along with shifts up- or downward that took place mysteriously from year to year.

In her rural Michigan high school, recalls Diane Weikert, "I was not all *that* popular. More than anything else, that's what I would have liked to be. I was part of a good group, but not one of the most popular girls in it. My best friend was, though. She was more outgoing. She made clever conversation. She was a leader; she managed our whole senior class. Since she was a girl, she could only be elected vice president. But she was a cheerleader every year."

"If I could have been anybody I wanted," says Rowan DiStefano wistfully, "I would have been a cheerleader. That was automatic popularity. You had to be real pretty, with lots of personality. I never even tried out."

For girls, the cheerleader's pom-pom was a literal and symbolic mark of election, proof of a state of grace that could only be conferred by the votes of your peers. Voting for such elusive and subjective qualities as "most personality" and "best looking" established a norm—the version of these attributes that appealed to the majority.

"Whatever the typically popular girl was," Sue Hodges says, "I sure wasn't it. They were always short,* thin, and blond. I was dark and plump, though maybe not as plump as I thought I was. I was also flat-chested."

---

* In fifties popular songs, the word *girl* is always accompanied by the adjective *little*, and a frequent form of address by the (male) vocalist is "little girl."

"You had to have personality," says Betts Saunders. "But it was personality of a very managed, created kind. We worked at it; we learned everybody's name. We'd go down the hall: 'Hi, John; Hi, Karen, Hi. Hi. How ya' been.'"

The qualities we admired and rewarded, envied and voted for were those with short maturity but high future yield. Cute 'n' perky (like Debbie Reynolds), chosen for "pep" and "personality," expected to whip up high enthusiasm and higher morale for her winning team, the varsity cheerleader was the junior varsity corporate wife.

Elected positions—varsity captain, class president, or cheer-leader—suggested attributes that were "outstanding" but not off-scale. Always team players, the "most likely to succeed" of both sexes remained first among equals.

Even a homecoming queen ascended her throne through a democratic process of consensus, the political ideal of the fifties.

"When I was elected Homecoming Queen," Betts Saunders recalls, "I said to myself, Betts, enjoy every minute of this, because it will be one of the few times—except maybe when you get married—that you will ever have this kind of attention. It's going to last two hours. So make the most of it."

When we became brides, after all, it was only by a vote of two.

Good-looking, good student, good athlete that he was, the B[ig]M[an]O[n]C[ampus] still acquired his envied acronym through elective office or popular acclaim, meaning the assent of lesser lights. Distinction existed only because the group said it did.

As teenagers, our social radar registered every blip of the collective will; prepubescents, we were perfect examples in embryo of the "other-directed" adults that David Riesman charted as a new American social type. Barely past grade school, we were past experts in guiding our behavior by the expectations of others, desperate for acceptance and approval, longing only to fit in.

"Baby, it's cold outside," singer Rosemary Clooney warned us. Not that we needed to be reminded. The crowd may have been lonely, but the alternative was worse: to become a species of non-person known as the Outsider.

Growing up in the fifties, the Outsider's spectral presence haunted us, lurking (like the Shadow) everywhere. The Outsider was the *un* in *unpopular*. With our lies and secrets, all the things we could never tell anyone, the ugly monster lay coiled inside us. Pariah status nibbled at our nightmares. Even those most likely to succeed harbored a secret identity—they were Outsiders who were passing.

It was no coincidence that the exciting new fiction of the fifties took as its subject the excluded: those outside that magic but elusive mainstream where we all wanted to be. Marginals, deviants, and subterraneans were the heros and heroines of all my high-school nonrequired reading. I identified with the deformed and obese outcasts of Carson McCullers' small-town South; Bernard Malamud's elderly Jews, left behind as their assimilated children fled the ghettos for the suburbs; Saul Bellow's Augie March, the outsider as con artist getting his innings on straight society; Ralph Ellison's invisible man, the black in white America who survives by going underground into the sewers of Harlem.

The humiliation and rage of rejection, the yearning to belong (along with its "cover," an all-too-familiar arrogance and moral superiority) were expressed for me by literary surrogates—the alienated adolescents of fifties fiction.

"All other people," thinks Frankie, the twelve-year-old heroine of Carson McCullers' *The Member of the Wedding,* "had a *we* to claim, all other except her. When Bernice, the black house-keeper, said *we,* she meant Honey and Big Mama, her lodge or her church. The *we* of her father was the store. All members of clubs have a *we* to belong to and talk about. The soldiers in the army can say *we* and even the criminals on chain gangs."[3]

One book remains the definitive portrait of the adolescent in revolt against the cynicism of his peers and the hypocrisies of his elders. In J. D. Salinger's *The Catcher in the Rye,* Holden

Caulfield came to personify the miseries of privileged youth in midcentury America. Neglected or manipulated by adults, repulsed by the crassness of his contemporaries, Holden is a preppy double of James Dean, teen martyr. An Outsider by choice, in his heroic refusals and purity of heart he flattered and consoled us.

"I was the Holden Caulfield of the South," Cass Hunnicutt says with some pride. "I remember every word of *The Catcher in the Rye*, because every description in it was true for me: the wimps down the hall, the smell of the jock's room. Most of all, it was that feeling of isolation. The idea of getting away, of getting back to civilization, was constantly in my head.

"I just hated being apart from everybody that counted for me," Cass says. "My grandfather, whom I was very fond of and who I was named after, died when I was up there in school. My parents didn't think it was very important for me to be at his funeral. But it was for me. I felt real forlorn a lot of the time," says Cass. "Just like Holden. And I was in trouble a whole lot, too."

Unlike Holden, though, we weren't incorruptible. We had a choice: it was the organized system (Paul Goodman's phrase) or a life sentence as an Outsider. There was nothing absurd about that message. It merely echoed what we all knew about in-crowds and those who were "out of it"; that you had to "go along to get along" (or do a convincing imitation shuffle). Few of us resisted the blandishments of belonging; we were easily coaxed in from the cold.

In his final two years at school, Cass did more than shape up and fit in. As a wrestler and football player he became something of a star. Once he started participating, "joining all the clubs," Cass says, "I ended up as the guy in the yearbook who had the most things written after his name."

At the university, Cass was president of his fraternity. "I look on that period of my life as a real high point," he says. "I was very popular on campus. It was the first time in my life I'd actually been elected to any honor like that. I just loved it. In fact, nothing has quite come close to that in later life.

"When you live in a house with a wife and two children, it's not like living in a house with fifteen other guys that you see every day; you joke with, drink with, party with, go to class with, play touch football with. It's such a good tight bond," Cass says, echoing millions of American men who, if not as popular as he was, still recall with nostalgia those times. "Some of my best friends today are the guys in my fraternity. And some of the best memories I'll ever have are of those years."

Like Cass, we usually got busy joining. "Lots of organizations and clubs," says Sue Hodges of her Missouri high school. "Of course, certain clubs had more prestige than others: School Service, for example."

In her Catholic girls' high school, Pat Brewster Catania recalls, "You had to do all the *right* things. You had to play on the *right* teams, sing in the singing group, be in the school play. Those were all marks in the popularity contest."

It was the same in her Catholic women's college: "If you could get on the dance committee," she says, "you were assumed to be a person who would attract the right boys to come to the dances. Because, if you were perceived to be popular with boys, that made you automatically popular with girls. Then you'd be put on other really good social events. Everybody would look up to you. That was the crucial thing in those days."

Everybody looked up to Pat. First, because they could look down on her. Just under five feet two inches and blond—not "mouse" or "dirty" blond, either. She was crowned with a shimmer of golden pageboy so silky it seemed a solid shaft of light, making her cornflower-blue eyes look even larger.

The nuns adored her. ("Academics don't come easy to our Patricia," they wrote, "but she triumphs through effort.") Her classmates loved her ("A friend in need" was the inscription repeated in flowing script on the slick pastel-colored pages of the autograph books passed around each June). Newly deepened voices of boys from their brother school tied up the family telephone to the point where Pat became the first of her crowd to have her own separate number. At sixteen she was so "responsible," her parents judged, that they went to Europe for the summer leaving her the household checkbook.

"I was a perfect little windup doll," she says.

Carol Cornwell wasn't small, blond, or conventionally pretty. She had curly red hair and freckles instead of the glossy dark brown pageboy her boyfriend was always admiring on another girl. She was also "very shy in new situations," she says. But she was still popular in her suburban New Jersey high school. "I became very involved in activities," she says. "I was elected to class offices. In our school, that moved you straight to the top."

Elective popularity still had a Catch-22. Individuals didn't make it on their own. "It only happened," Carol says, "because I was part of the in-group."

Before we ever heard the word *conformity*, and long before we knew there was any such thing as individualism or "doing your own thing," when there wasn't a different drummer to be heard throughout the land, the right (or wrong) crowd was an early warning signal of the company you would probably keep—forever. We knew what it took to become part of a favored social group, the precise weight given to looks and smarts, elective offices, "neat" clothes, or your own car.

"An aristocracy of brains, brawn, and beauty," is the way Martin Duberman describes his in-group, the elite of a private boys' school in a New York City suburb. "We were a strange overlap of high-powered jocks and intellectuals," he says. "We were also the physically attractive ones.

"We were scornful of wimps; a prototype of someone who was unacceptable was a former mayor's son," Martin says. "He just didn't have it—which is significant because it shows that distinguished heritage or money didn't equal acceptance. "The cliché describes it best. The world was our oyster. We owned it. We belonged. We were entitled to everything. We dated constantly. I was the star of the tennis team, the lead in all the plays. We were smug and happy, convinced of the 'rightness' of our superior status in life, sure of the inevitability of a contented future."

In Betts Saunders' "wrong-side-of-the-tracks" high school in a small Midwestern city, white-collar parents like hers were in the minority. "Families were mostly black, blue-collar whites, and farmers," she says. "Ours was the in-crowd, first of all because we were largely white and middle class."

"We were the Big Its," she says. "But I'm not sure why we were drawn together as a group. Maybe it was ambition. We were the people who were going places."

Even though Steve Ortiz's Arizona high school was "mixed Hispanic and Anglo, the class president and cheerleaders were always white," he says. "As Mexican Americans, we were held to a stereotype of the C student and athlete," he recalls. Dumb jocks, in other words. Not even a football or basketball star would be accepted if he had a Hispanic surname.

"The Anglos would play one or two sports just to be 'well-rounded' for Ivy League colleges," he says. "We went into sports for macho reasons. To win. To prove our manhood."

About his group of friends in a working-class New England high school, Phil Catania says, "We were a crowd that just never got into trouble. We were all sports-minded, and almost without exception, academic-minded. We knew that was the ticket out. It was expected of us. We were going to be given a privilege—college—that our parents didn't have. And we knew you had to get those grades or you could easily see how you'd end up: like the kids hanging out at the corner."

Membership might be based on sex appeal or mature motivation; the right crowd was the star vehicle for success in the real world. In the newly fluid, mobile society of postwar America, the parental investment in "successful" children was high.

"My mother was a fierce disciplinarian," Betts Saunders says. "I was switched, sent to my room, harangued for the least little thing. But interestingly enough, I was never grounded. That would have been the worst punishment. Mom never even threatened to do it." There was no crime so heinous as to deserve the worst punishment. Being grounded, forbidden to go out—even at the age of thirteen—would have removed Betts from the competition, defeating mother's ambitions for her daughter's success.

Deprived themselves, for so long, of consumer durables and just plain frivolities, parents who could afford to indulge themselves and their kids were playing catch-up. In the postwar period, families were easily persuaded that popularity and belonging derived not only from what you *were* and *did* but what you *absolutely had to have.* Social pressure and new prosperity combined to create another fifties phenomenon—teen consumerism.

"The time is past," *Life* magazine noted in 1959, "when a boy's chief possession was his bike and a girl's party wardrobe consisted of a fancy dress worn with a string of dime-store pearls. What Depression-bred parents may think of as luxuries are looked on as necessities by their offspring." Indeed, these necessities totted up to tens of billions of dollars spent on or by kids, a billion more than the total annual sales of General Motors of that same year.[4]

"You had to have lots and lots of clothes," Carol Cornwell says. "What mattered was variety; the more you had the better. The things that were very 'in' were just what poorer parents couldn't come up with, like cashmere sweaters. My family still didn't have much money; they were also very frugal. I was put on a clothing allowance when I started high school. It had to pay for everything except a winter coat and formal. So I did a lot of baby-sitting and sewing because I wanted a big wardrobe more than anything."

To provide the "lots and lots of clothes" that Betts Saunders also says she needed, her mother made almost all of them. "Except for the pink strapless tulle formal I had when I was Homecoming Queen. That was one of the few things I ever bought from a department store; they had to order it especially for me.

"I probably had the nicest clothes, as nice as anyone's. We wore full corduroy skirts with layers of crinoline petticoats underneath; wide elastic cinch belts and short-sleeved Ship'N Shore blouses. They cost $2.98, so they were one of the few things I could afford to buy. We wore them with little scarves knotted at the neck; you had to have lots and lots of little scarves."

It wasn't just what you wore but how you wore it that was subject to the most rigid and detailed rules.

"In Illinois you rolled the socks down to the anklebone," Carol Cornwell recalls. "Then, when I moved to New Jersey, one of the first things I learned is that you wore your socks up. The bad thing was the long skirts dug into the socks and pushed the tops down. But you just kept pulling them up: You had to, because you can't do these things wrong."

Adolescents have always been "insecure"—as we used to say back then; more vulnerable to fad and fashion than their elders. But the fifties saw peer-enforced dress codes that were paramilitary in their exigence. Rules governing the minutiae of how every article of clothing must be worn made the mandarin courts of China and the Versailles of Louis XIV seem lax in comparison. Social acceptance—even sex appeal—lay in the details. And sanctions cast a long shadow. A friend, long past sexual barriers of race and gender, insists she can never be attracted to a man who buttons the second button of a sport shirt, a habit associated with terminal nerd-dom in her high school in 1953.

Grooming was the single largest item in the teen budget by the late 1950s: 39 percent (including razors and lots of "greasy kid stuff" for boys). Of the 25 million deodorants sold, one-fifth ended up on the shelves of high schoolers. As consumers-in-training (with larger appetites and even bigger discretionary incomes to come), we were shamelessly wooed by advertisers. In 1958, one shampoo manufacturer invited all the girls of an entire Newport, Rhode Island, high school back to the gym on Saturday for a mass hair washing. Breck-Off preceded bake-off in women's spending patterns.

Beyond the 25 million Elvis singles, beyond the 145 million gallons of ice cream gobbled by teenagers in 1958, beyond even the 10 million phonographs, 13 million cameras, and 1 million TV sets of our own—all of which would surely need replacement— advertisers knew this was only the beginning. For our serious spending habits, they looked eagerly to the future.

A "seller's dream," seventeen-year-old Suzie Slattery of Van Nuys, California, was chosen by *Life* magazine as a typical, if well-off, teen consumer. But it's not just Suzie's soda fountain, her seven bathing suits, or even her brand-new set of matching luggage—Daddy's gift for an upcoming graduation trip to Hawaii— that made the "leggy blond" high-school senior representative of a new consuming class. The finale of Suzie's round of shopping sprees planted her squarely in her adult role: "On summer days," we learn, "she loves to wander with her mother through fashionable department stores picking out frocks or furnishings for her room or silver and expensive crockery for the hope chest she has already started."[5]

As a champion consumer, Suzie Slattery's gender was no accident. By the time we met her, she was in the final stages of apprenticeship for her future as the biggest spender of all time: the affluent American housewife, practicing (with Mom's help) in the fifties to boost the GNP of the early sixties to undreamed-of heights. While Suzie was stocking her hope chest and less-indulged girls were working and sewing to get the "lots and lots of clothes" they had to have, another great consumer romance was well under way: that of the American male and his car.

It happened in the fifties—as songs, verses, jokes, and every other form of our folklore tell us: jalopies, hot rods, junk boxes, GTOs, T-Birds, or sweet little deuce coupes. In Rangoon Ruby, Bali Hai Blue or Campus Cream.

Providing couples with a privacy that was the nightmare of parents, these "movable bedrooms" helped conceive babies and spawned a new mode of entertainment: the drive-in. But no high-tech gene-splicing genius will ever rival Detroit's effect on male neurobiology: More than a means of conveyance or even a status symbol, the automobile became a secondary sexual characteristic for an entire generation of American men. Girls, and the households they would manage as women, would continue to need lots of everything. In the fifties, a boy needed only one thing to feel like a man: his own car.

"The instant we got our driver's license at sixteen, we did a lot of drag racing," says Cass Hunnicutt. "You kept your arm hanging out of the car window so your muscles looked bigger."

"In Tulsa, Oklahoma, in 1953," says Dick Robertson, "if you couldn't get behind the wheel you were dead, socially. I was a year younger than my classmates. Not being able to drive until November of junior year, I couldn't date. Were your parents supposed to drive you to proms? You really couldn't do anything, except sports. It was awful! I couldn't wait to be sixteen."

In Steve Ortiz's high school, a boy's race, class, and social status were measured precisely by his relation to car ownership: "The Anglos," he says, "all had their own cars. Hispanics at the bottom of the heap took the school bus. I was in the middle; I had friends with cars."

It was a big thing if somebody had a car in Philip Catania's blue-collar New England high school. "Couldn't have been more than 5 percent of the guys owned one," he says. "Some of my friends had the classic junk boxes. I remember '36 Plymouths were big. They all cost under $200 and they were always being repaired. A couple of my pals were handy with their hands.

"It wasn't because they were fashionable," Phil says. "These guys needed cars because of their after-school jobs. Then, we had something you never hear of any more: gas pools. You wanted a ride to the football game twenty miles away, you had to cough up a quarter for gas money. Your pal who owned the car didn't have the money for gas; we all shared it. You got into somebody's car, you got in with a quarter. I only got my first car when I started college in 1952. It was a '39 Dodge; I paid $175 for it."

Borrowing the family car was still the norm, even for boys from wealthier households. In most schools, anyone who drove his own was automatically a big wheel.

"Peter was one of the few seniors who had a car," Sue Hodges says of her first steady boyfriend. "I was a junior then and that was a big attraction, at least equal to his being a BMOC, smart, and kind of a jock."

Betts Saunders' boyfriend had already graduated and worked as a produce manager in a supermarket. By junior year, Betts was voicing some doubts about Donny; college was not part of his plans. "My friends thought I was crazy. Everyone said, 'My God, his car's so neat.' It was a red-and-white '53 Chevy."

In the driver's seat of the cars they now borrowed but would soon own, and in our assigned places next to them, alone together or in multiples of two, double-dating, we rolled off. Destination? That "contented future" that loomed inevitable *if* we belonged— if we had the right clothes, the right clubs, the right crowd, the right boy; if we were elected cheerleader, class president, "best personality."

Cars and rings and everything. We were ready to join the grown-ups.

6
THE GREAT SATURDAY NIGHT TERROR

A pretty little raven at the bird bandstand
Taught him how to do the bop and it was grand
They started goin' steady and bless my soul
He out bopped the buzzard and the oriole

—from "Rockin' Robin"

Birds did it and their bop style took off. Even debutantes were doing it, as sociologist David Riesman noted with surprise.[1] Once the courtship pattern of rural or working-class kids, in the 1950s going steady moved up in status and down in age, sweeping high schools and even junior highs throughout the country.

In grade school, party games like Post Office and Spin the Bottle were no longer just promiscuous osculation. When the bottle stopped, when the letter was delivered, the lucky couple was likely to be this semester's item. By the first year of high school, millions of American teenagers were launched on a lifetime of serial monogamy.

"Usually," Carol Cornwell recalls, "you latched onto a boyfriend and started to go steady in ninth grade. It was the security thing."

A woman's security, at age fourteen, was also the first install-
ment on a lifetime package of financial support. As high-school
freshmen, boys began a long career of paying the bills. They
needed lots of cash to take out the girls with lots and lots of
clothes (all of which they would soon be expected to pay for).
Meanwhile, going steady, like marriage, was cheaper than outings
involving a variety of young women.

In Carol's suburban New Jersey high school, going steady was
the rule, not the exception. Events that included casually dating
pairs were so rare as to be memorable—thirty years later.

"One of the big things to do," Carol recalls, "was to drive in
a group up to New York State, where the drinking age was lower.
On these outings there would be a mix: people who were going
steady and others who were just out for the night. But that was
unusual," Carol says. "Generally, we only went out with people
who were going steady. In fact, we almost always double-dated
with the same other twosome. Just like old married couples!"

By junior year, in Sue Hodges's Missouri high school, "there
wasn't a lot of dating around," she says. "If you went out with
someone, then pretty soon you were going steady."

Far from disapproving, adult opinion generally applauded the
wisdom of settling down early. Going steady, as in a "steady"
job, a "steady" character, was reassuring and much to be preferred over going wild—as in "wild oats," "going off the deep
end"—or, in the whispered phrase of an earlier era, "going
wrong."

"Teen Sweethearts," as hit tunes of the fifties enshrined them,
were seen as trainees in the institution of marriage. "Steady
dating," noted a psychologist in 1951, after studying the phenomenon, "is an educational process, one in which the partners
gain poise, learn to adjust to each other and obtain the training
and experience needed for sensible selection of mates."[2]

After school in Gail Feldstein's junior high in a prosperous
Ohio suburb, there was a ballroom dancing class. "It was just

like a singles bar," she recalls. "Then in high school the dance classes became fraternities and sororities. We met at different kids' houses for parties. There was dancing to records, girls got pinned. There was a Sigma sweetheart: every sorority put up a candidate. That was a big thing. It was just like college.

"There were Gentile fraternities and sororities and Jewish ones, and a very sharp distinction between the two," Gail says. "Then, within the Jewish ones, there were the rich and the nonrich."

In her first two years of high school, Gail didn't date. "I was very lonely and very upset about it. Then I met Alex, and Alex and I started going steady because that was what people did. We were very compatible, both very academic. We would stay on the phone for hours doing our math problems.

"Alex would come over to my house, but I was not very welcome at his because he was Episcopalian and from a socially prominent family. As far as his parents were concerned, I was all wrong, being Jewish and being poor—not poor the way we know it today, but lower middle class.

"I used to sit in class pushing my nose up, trying not to have a Jewish nose," Gail says, "wishing I had blue eyes, wishing I had straight hair.

"Of course, we never talked about these things. We talked about math."

If neither set of parents disapproved too much, going steady, like marriage, promised upward mobility as well as security.

Despite her involvement in school activities and election to class offices, Carol Cornwell says she still felt "on the edge. Part of it was me. I was very shy in new situations. I was always afraid my clothes weren't right. I didn't want to bring people home because we lived in a smallish development compared to the 'gracious living' style of lots of my classmates. I had opportunities that I couldn't take, to move into the top group. I'd get invitations, then I'd back out, because I felt 'now I'm going to have to reciprocate.'"

When Carol started dating Don Cornwell in her junior year,

everything changed. "He was not only a member of the in-group," Carol says, "he was probably the most popular boy in our class. That was because he was tall, handsome, and athletic.

"For a girl, there was no surer way to popularity, to being at the absolute center of the in-crowd, than dating the right boy."

As soon as she started going steady with Don, Carol's parents forgave her for talking back, for not wanting to go to church, for arguing about McCarthy at the dinner table. "They were so happy when Don and I started going out. He was such a 'nice' boy, they said, so 'ambitious.' That meant," Carol adds ironically, "that Don was headed for an Ivy League school. As it turns out, he wasn't ambitious at all. But his parents were rich. His mother came from a 'fine old family.' Suddenly I was doing everything right."

Not all parents applauded going steady. Mothers who had been Jazz Age belles, frivolous flappers, or even late marriers were mystified by the premature monogamy of their children.

When she was a girl growing up in Kentucky, the "icebox was so full of flowers," a friend's mother recalls, "there was just no room for food." Popularity in those days was the number of a young lady's gentlemen callers and the lavishness of their floral tributes. Pat Carroll's mother, who had married on her thirtieth birthday, even disapproved of the one-night, one-date principle. "Coming home with the same boy who took you to the party," she told her daughter, "has to be the most boring thing to happen to a girl!"

Anxious children of prosperity and the Bomb, we preferred boredom to insecurity. Postwar America was a society with Stop-Go lights flashing everywhere we looked. Sex, its magic spell everywhere, was accompanied by the stern warning: Don't do it!

Atomic stalemate told us that the world could be blown up at any minute. Exposure of spies, foreign and homegrown, signaled "subversion from within." But munching our tasty

"Uranium burgers" (45 cents, as advertised by a Salt Lake City fast-food stand in 1952)[3] wondering whether we would always be too flat-chested or "chicken" to wear the new bikinis, it was not to worry. Weren't we well drilled in civil defense procedures? (When the siren sounded, we dropped under our school desks, right hand covering the "nerve center" at the nape of the neck.)

It was an unsteady world out there, over which we could look forward to having no control. The promise: "I'll be his and he'll be mine/We'll love until the end of time/and we'll never be lonely anymore," might be the only certainty.

By adolescence, millions of American teenagers were eager to forsake all others for the OAO: the one-and-only, once-and-forever love. Observing the rush to commitment, listening to songs bewailing "faithless love" beamed at fifteen-year-olds, an anthropologist could imagine that America was the only industrial society whose mating rituals had regressed to the primitive agrarian stage, its youth encouraged to find a permanent partner by the onset of puberty.

"There were dances at school all the time," says Carol Cornwell. "They were the most 'in' thing to do. Everybody went to the dances. *But* you had to have a date. So people who didn't date were really out of it."

The stag line, too, had gone the way of the Stutz Bearcat* and other relics of the frivolous twenties. Just as "dating around" was beginning to carry the same suggestion of promiscuity as "sleeping around," so "playing the field"—a traditional male prerogative—had started to take on overtones of the polymorphously perverse.

By the time I was a college freshman, not only had the stag line disappeared but cutting in—once an accepted way of mixing, mingling, and flirting—had become a frowned-upon practice. A

---

* The stag line lingered vestigially through the fifties at coming-out parties, where debutantes continued the tradition of inviting two escorts, thereby increasing the male talent pool.

man's date was as sacred a form of personal property as his wife
(and was likely to be the same young woman). "Bird-dogging"
was the disapproving description of unattached male behavior—
indicating an unseemly interest in other men's consorts.

High-school and college proms beckoned with all the excitement and sense of adventure of a country club "young marrieds"
evening. In the article "American Youth Goes Monogamous,"
Charles Cole, president of Amherst during the 1950s, noted that
dances ended much earlier and were far more casual in attire
than such festivities had been in his undergraduate days in the
depths of the depression. Dr. Cole swiftly put his finger on the
reason for change: "Were you going to get all dressed up and
stay out until dawn, just to dance every dance with "good old
George?"[4]

Boys might not be passive victims of the telephone that never
rang, but there was increasingly little place for the "naked
nomad," as a later writer would describe the undomesticated
male,[5] except grunting around the locker room or grinding at
home over his books. In high school as well as college, a boy
who didn't have a girl to call his own was no longer that alluring
"extra man" but a social misfit. Late-blooming lads were definitely,
in the automotive lingo of the day, a "fifth wheel."

A year younger than his high school classmates, Dick Robertson
was not only carless but physically slow to develop. "I was real
small—even for my age," he says. "Plus my ears stuck out. I
just wasn't ready for the boy-girl thing. I don't think I worried
about it too much then. I figured it would happen to me eventually." But after a moment's reflection, he changes his mind.
"I take that back. I felt pretty awful about being left out."

Dick Robertson has extracted the full measure of revenge on
his days as the Alfred E. Newman of his high-school class. A
growth spurt in the spring and summer of senior year pushed
him comfortably to that required American male height: six feet.

With his present year-round tan, aviator glasses, and bespoke English tailoring, he is the image of the sleek, successful executive. The once prominent ears are all but invisible, hidden under layers of expensively cut hair. He owns a full array of cars, from family station wagon to a Jaguar two-seater, and he hasn't felt left out of the "boy-girl thing" for fifteen years.

Another late bloomer, Dan Ross didn't date in high school. "I never went out with a girl once," he says. Too young, sexually and emotionally, his innocence made him the butt of every joke. "One girl was obviously after me," he recalls. "I remember being teased by my friends: 'She's crazy about you; she's coming on to you.' But I would say: 'What do you do with it?' I didn't have a clue."

Steve Ortiz started going out with a girl who lived down the street in his senior year of high school. "That's when everybody started dating seriously," he says. "But it wasn't like kids today. We went out seriously but we never talked seriously. There was a big difference between Hispanic and Anglo steady dating," he recalls. "The white kids broke up when they went off to college. My friends joined the Marines and got married the June after graduation."

Before he went away to boarding school in the tenth grade, Cass Hunnicutt found that "all the kids in my class had paired off. The girls were all wearing their boyfriends' rings and letter jackets." A lifelong romantic, Cass had already fixed on the unattainable. "The way I set it up," Cass says, "I picked on this girl who was a real dream. But she thought of me just like a brother. She would tell me all her troubles with other boys. That was a real crusher, because I was so enamored of her." Still Cass was lucky: With two brothers and two sisters, all close in age, there were lots of kids around to divert him from unrequited passion.

For many adolescents, casual coed occasions were becoming obsolete. Social life in most high schools was based on the couple

—as it would be in the real world—henceforth and forever more. Once pairing off began, the price of failing to latch on to a boy or girl was high: being left with no one, being left out.

Thus was born in the America of the fifties the Great Saturday Night Terror. More than fear of the Bomb, aging—certainly more than love or lust—the GSNT has coaxed many women (and not a few men) of our generation into the wrong beds and even the wrong marriages.

"The dread of not having a date on Saturday night will haunt me until I die," says a twice-divorced Texan friend. For a girl to be dateless on Saturday night in River Oaks in 1950 was wrist-slashing time. Crooning from every radio came reminders that it was the loneliest night of the week and the still more unnecessary intelligence that "one was the loneliest number."

The Great Saturday Night Terror passed me by completely. In my all-girls school, I never had a date on Saturday or any other night of the week. I didn't know any boys to ask me out or not to. Neither did my friends.

Spring, 1954, though, brought an end to innocence. We had barely survived the agony of waiting to hear from the college of our choice when another burning question absorbed us totally: Who to ask to the senior prom? My friend Marion had a priceless resource. Her brother Eric, a Princeton freshman, was pressed into service on my behalf.

For once my mother had no need to issue judgments of "too old" or "unsuitable" about my choice of costume. I yearned only for the ballerina-length "formal" of five million other teenage girls' dreams. Waiting for me at the now-defunct Best's, there it was: the skirt, layers of tulle ranging from deep blue to palest opaline; the bodice, with its sweetheart decolletage, so heavily boned there would be no need of the torso-length Merry Widow bras my friends were wearing under less rigidly autonomous creations. Under the top layer of gauzy stuff, a sapphire velvet sash floated, just like the costume of my favorite Balanchine ballet.

For this one enchanted evening, home restrictions on makeup were lifted. To carefully painted doe eyes and iridescent blue eye shadow, I added Maybelline's "Midnight Azure" mascara. A parental gift completed the costume—the traditional single strand of cultured pearls that circled the throat of every graduate, débutante, fiancée, and bride until the mid-1960s.

Duly bearing his white orchid, enshrined in a plastic box, Eric appeared promptly. As advertised, he was exceedingly tall and skinny—like my own brother, who was mercifully spared the role of escort by the U. S. Army. From behind pre–Annie Hall pink plastic-framed glasses, I could see him blinking as I made my entrance—dazzled, I hoped, by the vision in blue before him.

Eric seemed strangely impervious to the transformation of our school gym, where a revolving mirrored ball floated chips of light over unrecognizably glamorous classmates—all with their early graduation presents of pearls, and dramatically made-up faces like mine.

Conversationally, he was something of a disappointment. After a whole year at Princeton, where was the witty and smooth repartée my readings of F. Scott Fitzgerald had led me to expect? My attempts to "draw him out," as endless articles in *Seventeen* magazine advised, were unsuccessful. Pressed as to what courses a premed student took, Eric dutifully recited his class schedule, including labs and gym periods. That proved to be his longest speech of the evening. I refused to be daunted by his scanty supply of small talk. My conversational capital, accumulated for so long, was not going to waste.

Between dances I regaled him with anecdotes and stories, with opinions of plays and movies I had seen, about my passion for ballet and my favorite books, where I was going to college and why. He listened with an air of mild astonishment. On the dance floor, Eric's silence mattered little. I could finally display my expert Charleston and in the slow dances, stare up at a man while wearing three-inch heels! Afterward we went to Jimmy Ryan's, a place favored by collegians and preppies for drinking and listening to jazz. By now even I had run out of verbal steam. Silently we both sipped Scotch on the rocks. Eric concentrated on keeping his pipe lit while I smoked one Parliament after another, exhaling smoke through my nose—a recently acquired skill.

Leaving me at the door, Eric knew something was expected of him—if not a kiss then certainly a compliment. For the first time that evening he smiled. (Could it have been relief?) "Well," he said, peering down into my blue-fringed eyes, "you certainly have a large vocabulary."

I was devastated. No layers of blue tulle or mascara could disguise the bluestocking within. Still, the blow of having been found so wanting—in looks, charm, and sex appeal—was softened by another subliminal message: I had been lucky to have the bad news deferred for so long. In an all-girls' school, the "fatties," the "four-eyes," those with too-large vocabularies or whose tongues stuck to the roofs of their mouths on all social occasions, had breathing space—until, as my mother said soothingly the next day, we would "meet our own sort."

In my little all-female cocoon, I had been spared knowledge of the stigma that attached to bookish interests in the real teenage world and of the necessity of faking it, of acquiring a ready-made personality that would appeal to adolescent boys. (A close friend possessed of a larger vocabulary and sharper tongue than mine was afflicted by such pariah status in her big Midwestern high school that her pretty, popular sister was loath to acknowledge their relationship.)

It took no longer than my first hour at Smith College to realize that I had everything to learn. Allison, a fellow freshman with a long black ponytail, told me she had been pinned four times since ninth grade. In the sororities and fraternities of her famous high school, pride of a rich Chicago suburb, all the collegiate social and mating rituals had been mastered. Wasn't it painful, I asked, from the depths of my ignorance, breaking up with a boy, then seeing him in classes and at football games? "Oh, you learn how to handle it," said the seventeen-year-old worldling. But that was all practice scrimmage. Now the plays were for real.

The first fraternity pins I ever saw rose and fell on the cashmere-covered breasts of Texan classmates. Sent East to "attend"—as their engagement announcements would soon declare—"a New England women's college," they spent the year pining for boyfriends back home at S.M.U. or UT/Austin. (Interestingly, their young men stayed home. They didn't need Harvard Business School to help them increase their worldly goods.)

My friend Dixie Ann was not only lovesick, she also suffered, as did her fellow Texans, from the endless cold and damp of the Connecticut Valley. Snuffling and wheezing through the long winter, they spent teary hours on the phone to Dallas and Fort Worth. By the fall of sophomore year, they were mostly gone—home to warmer climes and lavish weddings. Before she left, Dixie Ann gave me the best advice I received in college: "Always wear your pearls twenty-four hours before a big date. They get a really great glow from your body's natural oils."

Even if they weren't pinned four times in high school or presently 'engaged to be engaged' to the boy back home, most of my classmates arrived with expertise as great as their expectations. Skilled dealers in futures, they knew the worth of every point in the rating and dating game. "If I marry Tom," said the Grosse Pointe Princess down the hall, about an admirer who planned to teach secondary school, "It'll be life in the 'lower-priced three.'" (Since my family didn't own a car, I needed a translation of this automotive purgatory.)

Knowledge of the cost and status of cars was only the beginning. Along with the worn, one-eyed stuffed animals of childhood, many of my new friends arrived at college with elaborate social Baedekers, designed to help them find Mr. Right.

They knew the relative prestige of neighborhoods and summer communities the length and breadth of the Americas; they knew the ranked order of schools, broken down into separate categories (prep schools, country day, and those few public high schools located in suburban enclaves so upscale as to constitute private academies). Otherwise incurious young women could analyze—with a sense of nuance so exquisite as to shame Proust or Henry James—the social resonance of every Princeton eating club, Harvard house, Yale secret society, and Amherst fraternity. From the answers to that inevitable conversational opener: "Do you know . . . ?" most of my classmates could produce faster than any computer the social profile of a blind date or dance partner at a mixer.

I sopped up all this data with a fascination made more intense by nibbles of shame. I knew this was nasty, snobbish stuff—anti-Semitic and unquestionably (had the term existed) racist. I also knew that people got hurt, marked for life—even—like Jeanne Crain in *Take Care of My Little Girl*—pushed to suicide by the failure of rejection.

Still, like my earlier readings of sex and sadism in Mickey Spillane, the very cruelty of this social sorting process was titillating. It seemed, moreover, a safe enough spectator sport; first, because women's colleges, unlike male institutions, permitted no social organizations or clubs. "We" were not morally implicated in this system. Then, being Jewish, I enjoyed an officially marginal role, a "protected" status, like exotic wildlife. As an outsider, information could be shared freely with me. I had no stake, it was assumed, in the intricacies of these games or their outcome. In the meantime, I enjoyed the role of social voyeur, a repository of arcane lore on which I would never be tested.

Graduates of large public schools, like my classmate who had been pinned four times, were not snobs so much as social Darwinists. They had a keen sense of the market value of their looks, personality, virginity—even that mysterious quality known as sex appeal. Honed by elections for cheerleader and sweetheart, practiced in "trading up" boyfriends, they had a sharp instinct for winners and champions. Trained to look for early warning signals of success, they reeled off attributes of boys they had just met like yearbook copy editors: Scott, last night's blind date, was varsity hockey, in the top third of his class, and president-elect of his fraternity. Like the personnel managers who would soon be interviewing these same young men, they had an ideal C.V. on file: the object of the dating game was to match the prototype to that unknown stranger in the night.

In the East, clothes were crucial to this process of social location. The right "look" of a date had an intensely reassuring function that will never be true to the same degree again. "When you didn't know anything about a girl," a male friend once explained, "you felt more comfortable if she was wearing a Peck & Peck suit."

We didn't know the acronym then, but in the East, the look in question was the Dominant WASP Ethos made visible. It was in the English fabrics and their neutral or dark colors: in tweeds, flannels, and camelhair. (Bright shades were acceptable only in the form of tartans.)

Asexuality in style and fit was a key element of this look, an asexuality having nothing in common with today's androgyny. None of us ever thought to question why, as girls entering young womanhood, we wore largely "little boy" clothes: Bermuda shorts, Shetland sweaters, button-down shirts, kilts, and Macintosh raincoats. Nor why, coincidentally, this borrowed menswear camouflaged hips and hid breasts; while the high socks we wore with shorts turned a classroom of leggy girls, as one older professor noted with disgust, into a sea of knobby knees.

Even when the sexes stayed in gender-specific garb, the WASP Ethos of the fifties held that the body beneath must be disguised. The Brooks Brothers three-button, "natural"-shoulder jacket, designed to droop and bag on the male torso, made sure that no one confused the wearer with Marlon Brando as Stanley Kowalski in *A Streetcar Named Desire*. Old and out of shape was even better than new and shapeless. Ideally, the same garment should graduate with the wearer, from prep school and college, to become the gray flannel suit of the Organization Man.

For women, especially, the WASP dress code stipulated that secondary sexual characteristics must be disguised or distorted. In Carol Cornwell's high school, all the girls wore the same sweaters. But, she says, "as the upper-middle-class, mostly WASP, college-bound group, we wore ours two or three sizes larger than the girls in the leather jacket crowd. Because anything sexual, like tight sweaters, toreador pants, or makeup was *out*. They were the signs of a 'fallen woman.'"

When breasts could be displayed, their shape had to be re-molded by stitching or boning into a standard form: widely separated and standing out from the rib cage, like filled-to-the-brim coffee filters. Foundation manufacturers flourished (I know because I modeled girdles one summer on Seventh Avenue) as the slightest suggestion of a behind became unladylike. In order to wear the sheath dresses of the fifties without a bulge, we sweltered in Playtex tubes and zipped and hooked ourselves into iron virgins that would have daunted any Victorian maiden. (I can still see the red welts and grooves on the willowy torso of my roommate—and hear her sighing with the relief of the circus fat lady as she liberated herself from one of these undergarments.)

Many of the basics of this wardrobe had been undergraduate fashion since the 1920s. But their increasingly symbolic importance in the 1950s pointed to new constituencies of students sporting old school ties. "Do you belong?" was the question the right clothes, like dirty (old) white bucks, were supposed to answer.

WASP style was the wrapping that promised a quality product within. As social reassurance, the girl in the Peck & Peck suit and her male counterpart became inseparable from a romantic and sexual ideal.* Like love, its magic spell was everywhere—in

---

* Blond and blue-eyed, Marilyn Monroe and Jayne Mansfield fused sex goddess and WASP princess roles, explaining why they overshadowed sexy "exotics" like Ava Gardner, Jane Russell, and Jennifer Jones.

every Ipana smile, Pond's fiancée, Woodbury bride (and handsome groom), Pontiac owner, and finally, every large, healthy, blond family bouncing on Beautyrest mattresses.

When Philip Catania left his working-class high school for a liberal arts college nearby, he saw the girls of his dreams made flesh: "WASP princesses right out of the movies," he says. Neither Phil nor most of his friends had steady girls in high school. "We were going to college and most of our female classmates definitely were not. We knew we should avoid any entangling alliances with the girls who were at school with us. They weren't supposed to be our future wives.

"I started dating as soon as I got to college. The girls were so much better looking. They were better dressed and took better care of themselves. It's funny, I don't remember two blonds in my entire high-school class of 647 students. It looked like we were so poor, we couldn't afford blonds."

Phil's classmate, Mike DiStefano, did go steady in high school. Barbara wasn't blond, but she was one of the few Methodists in a mostly Roman Catholic student body.

"Her mother wouldn't let me see her," Mike says. "So for three years we dated secretly. Her brother knew that I saw her. Everybody knew. But when I took her to senior prom, I couldn't pick her up at her home. Someone from her church called for her and brought her to my house."

Without secrecy and parental sanction, romance languished. "We were much closer when we weren't supposed to be together."

At Dick Robertson's Big Ten university in 1953, just about everybody was blond. "There wouldn't have been one student in ten," he says, "who could have told you what WASP meant. Because with the exception of the one black fraternity, that's what we all were.

"The campus was totally dominated by the Greek thing. Twenty percent of the student body was in a fraternity or sorority, but we held ninety-nine percent of the offices. The other eighty percent were 'barbs'—barbarians," he explains. "They were completely out of it."

Before Dick Robertson got to the university he "didn't know a fraternity from fried rice," he says. But they knew about him because of his junior tournament golf trophies. "I had my pick of the best," Dick says. "So I picked the most famous. It had big colonial pillars in front and tennis courts in the back—just like in the movies."

The fifties saw a resurgence of fraternity life on campuses that recalled the carefree twenties. Languishing during the depression, deprived of men during World War II, of little interest to older GI bill veterans, the Greek letter societies spoke to a new postwar college generation that was, finally, ready for playtime: panty raids and keg contests, queens and sweethearts, pinning ceremonies and gracious living.

Rushing fraternities and sororities perfectly expressed the rush to belong, to join, and to be accepted that characterized our coming of age. Besides competing for campus leaders, jocks, and beauty queens, Greek letter societies fulfilled a crucial social need. On vast campuses of more than 50,000 undergraduates, they took the guesswork out of finding Miss or Mr. Right, presorting both sexes according to the qualities deemed most desirable in a mate.

"As far as dating," Dick says, "almost any sorority girl would do, but it was definitely preferable if she was a Kappa or a Theta. You could almost go out with a bad-looking girl if she was in a good sorority. But if you got seen in public with some bad-looking girl who was also a 'barb,' you'd really hear about it. That's just the way it was."

Like fraternities, sororities tried to rush the high-school "stars"— ideally, queens and sweethearts, but at least pretty, potentially popular girls, those with "lots of personality" who already dressed well and possessed as many of the social graces as possible. But the women's organizations also served as finishing schools for their pledges: They provided training designed, as one historian noted,[6] "to mold an attractive co-ed into an ideal wife-companion." Practice was offered in serving as hostess, playing bridge, dancing, smoking, drinking—even applying cosmetics and styling hair. They also provided the all-important peer standards of sexual permissiveness: how far to go to interest a man—without going too far.

In turn, the sorority expected members to act as magnets. Pledges should attract a talent pool of the most desirable boys and be seen at all the right fraternity parties. At her Southern university, Cass Hunnicutt's wife, Betsey, recalls the wrath unleashed upon her sisters when their president discovered that she was the sole Kappa present at a Sigma Chi dance. "We are going to have to do better than that!" she stormed at Sunday brunch.

House rules underlined the importance of the sorority as a showcase for Ideal Womanhood. At the University of Texas in 1956, reported Willie Morris, his girl's sorority fined members who were seen carrying laundry bags out the front door.[7] Domestic drudgery might lie just ahead, but in order to qualify, a romantic image was essential. No lifting that bale before the ring was on the finger.

In the fall of 1952, Diane Hoff had to skip rush week at the denominational college she was to attend near her farming community. A finalist in the state beauty contest, every night that week found her parading slowly across the huge stage of the Capitol auditorium, "first in a bathing suit, then in a long evening gown, just like Miss America," she says.

"I was so dumb. I didn't know you were supposed to go to all the rush parties or explain your absence." But when Diane placed third for the state beauty queen title, nobody cared. She got bids from every sorority, pledging one of the two nationals "that everybody was dying to join. It had the neatest

girls," Diane says, "and we had our meals served in the dining
room by busboys. It was the elegant way I'd always wanted to
live and I really loved it." For the first month of freshman year,
Diane went out with different boys from approved fraternities.
Then she met Tom Weikert, a junior, who had returned from
two years in Korea.

"We started dating," Diane says, "and we kept on dating
until we got married my junior year. In between we did the
whole bit. First, Tommy gave me his class ring, then the lavalier—
the necklace with the letters of his fraternity. Next came the
fraternity pin, until finally, da-dum, the engagement ring."

Diane tries to remember what it was about Tom Weikert that
attracted her. "It was his datability," she says. "He was very nice
looking. He was president of his pledge class. From freshman
year on he had been chairman of everything on campus. So I
was in a position of some importance just dating him.

"I knew that he wanted to go into business and be very successful," Diane says of her husband of nearly thirty years. "That
was the most intimate thing I knew about him.

"He was attracted to me because I was a Theta. That made up
for my being a farm girl. All his friends from high school and
college came from well-off suburban families.

"I have no idea how we ended up getting pinned, engaged,
and married. It was just something that happened. You went to
parties. You liked each other. You had a good time. You were
part of a group. But you were also a twosome. So you said,
'okay, let's get pinned.'

"It's the most phenomenal thing, what we did," she says, "when
I think about it now."

Sue Hodges is just as mystified about how she and her former
husband ended up married in 1958, in her junior year at the state
university.

"I don't know how Bob and I really got together. We started
going out sophomore year. Then we weren't going out with

other people any more. There hadn't been any agreement or anything. Then he asked me to become pinned. Foolish person that I was," Sue says with a laugh, "I said yes."

Sue Baker Hodges' high-school yearbook predicted that she would be a "famous lady reporter." She was editor of the school newspaper and she chose the university nearby because of its famous journalism program.

As soon as she arrived on campus as a freshman, "I did what I was supposed to do, just the way I had always done. I went through rush, made my grades, and was initiated into a really good sorority." She was surprised to find many girls pinned and engaged by the middle of the first year. "But I really didn't want to do that as a freshman."

When Sue met Bob Hodges, she had just dropped out of the journalism program. "The courses really terrified me. There were lots of requirements like economics and business, but it was also the time. People in the J-school really had to devote a lot of hours to the department." Sue switched to social work where, it seemed to her, she would get to learn about people in a way that was "more comfortable" to her than "going out as a reporter asking questions."

In Bob Hodges, Sue saw "possibilities." But they were possibilities of a particular kind. "It was his potential for financial success that struck me. Even then he seemed to have a lot of drive. At the time I also thought that he was pretty humorous. It turned out that he wasn't humorous at all, but he was very successful."

The more intimate moments of courtship: when he proposed, gave you the engagement ring; weddings, and especially wedding nights tend to recede into a blur of nervousness and alcohol. But no woman ever seems to forget a detail of the ceremony that accompanied being pinned.

"While he was putting the pin on," Sue Hodges recalls, "Bob's fraternity brothers stood in a semicircle on either side of us.

Once you were pinned, they sang the song. Then each of them got to kiss you."

Another woman recalls that when her boyfriend's fraternity came to serenade her on the big night, they brought with them an entire chicken wire fence. As the brothers burst into song, tissue paper stuck into the squares was set ablaze. "I looked outside the window," she remembers, "and there, in huge letters of fire, was my name, SANDRA.

If they weren't already pinned, the boys who took turns kissing Sue Hodges or holding up Sandra's name in flame, were doing their best to get there.

The cliché of the period suggests that it was young women who, by guile and plotting, contrived to earn their MRS. degree. But the mores of the fifties (and earlier) should remind us that the girl had to wait to be asked. Most young men, it turned out, couldn't wait to do the asking. In fact, as one observer of her class of 1954 noted, "their fraternity pins were burning holes in their lapels."[8] Male undergraduates seemed, if anything, more relieved than their female counterparts to know that the Saturday Night Terror was over. Junior Prom and Winter Carnival were taken care of, along with the rest of life.

By senior year, recalls Dick Robertson, every single member of his fraternity pledge class was engaged.

"What I did," Dick says, "was what everybody did—get married to the last girl I went steady with. It was like the time clock in a basketball game, ticking down to graduation. Everybody got married when they graduated and started to work for General Motors. For men *and* women, it was a sense of the inevitable."

7
IS SEX DIRTY?

"Is sex dirty?" Woody Allen is asked in *Play It Again, Sam.*
"It is if you're doing it right," he answers.

Together, the question and the answer framed the short sexual
catechism of the fifties. Incessantly, we grappled with the conflicting signals of sex as forbidden, dirty, dangerous, to be denied
and lied about but also romantic, exciting, and glamorous—the
message from ever-more-suggestive advertisements, movies, and
popular songs. Then, just as we were about to marry, sex became
sanctified, sublime, beautiful, but suddenly difficult to do "right."

When Cass Hunnicutt's father decided it was time for a man-
to-man talk about the facts of life, his son recalls, "Dad took me
into the bathroom. It would have been hard to miss what he was
really telling me: where sex belonged."

Even if the earliest associations weren't quite that explicit, there
was nothing subliminal about the equation of sex and shit, rot,
and filth that informed every kind of erotic activity, starting with
the human body itself.

"Don't use the word 'naked,'" practiced seducer and literary
agent Bradley Holmes warns Allison Mackenzie, heroine of *Peyton*

Place (1956) just after deflowering her at his Connecticut farmhouse. Even the steamiest popular novel of the decade wasn't
ready for the joy of sex, or even the body beautiful. "Naked,"
Holmes explains, "has the sound of a rock being turned over to
expose maggots."[1]

When I was a college freshman in 1954, a required hygiene
course devoted an entire lecture to the dangers of heavy petting.*
Unmodified since the heyday of Victorianism, the embrace of Eros
by Hygeia, still clinging clammily together in postwar America,
left no doubt that the task of the latter was to sanitize the former.
Indeed, the 1950s in this country were a decade far more obsessed
with the horrors of bodily secretions and smells than the nineteenth century. Given a new license to go public with once unmentionable personal concerns, manufacturers and advertisers
seized upon the most profound terror of the period in ads warning
of the social perils of "halitosis," sweat, and menstrual odors.
Marriage manuals (as we shall see) hectored readers with reminders that good sex began with scrubbing and bathing (not
with one's partner, of course). In the fifties—hard as it may be to
recall in the era of the organic—*natural* was a dirty word.

Once cleanliness and sex had more profound and honorable
connections than the selling of personal hygiene. Symbolized by
the white bridal gown, the ideal of purity and ceremony of ritual
bathing are part of the religious traditions of both East and West.
From ancient times, assurance of the virginity of the bride was a
crucial clause in marriage contracts. The contribution of a secular and consumer society was to complete the transformation
from the religious into the economic. The last generation to place
any value on female virginity, we assigned it the value of a market
commodity.

"Respect," as in the famous fifties query "Will you still respect
me [if I sleep with you]?" really sought a promise of guaranteed

* The identical course, with the same heavy petting lecture, was still required of
Columbia College freshmen in 1962.

worth, somewhat akin to farm price supports. If the man was to be believed, his pledge of undiminished respect assured a girl that her stock as a marriageable young woman would not begin to drop with loss of virginity. "That's what we always heard," says Carol Cornwell. "If you go all the way with someone, he'll leave you and marry a 'nice' girl." At the other end of the scale, a reputation of promiscuity was the equivalent of inciting a panic —or wholesale dumping of shares.

In any market situation, value is always the *perception* of value. The worth of a commodity is as high or low as most people think it is and are willing to pay. Heroic independence of mind was required to escape a market psychology that described a woman's sexual favors in terms of "giving it away" or "saving it" (as in what-are-you-saving-it-for?). And this was only the realm of perception. The real danger—getting pregnant—was both public proof of and punishment for the nasty stuff you had been up to.

"Everybody was doing it," Cass Hunnicutt says. "But it was the Big Lie that nobody was." Of all the secrets of coming of age in the fifties, sex was the darkest and dirtiest. As sexual beings, people became underground men and women. For some, leading a double life was no metaphor.

In his third year of medical school, Mike DiStefano became engaged.

"Terry came from a rich family. She was very spoiled and a terrible student, but she really enjoyed life. I was attracted to her because she was all the things I wasn't. She was attracted to me because I was all the things she wasn't: disciplined, serious, hardworking. We were infatuated with each other.

"On Valentine's Day in my senior year, I went to her apartment with my little two-dollar packet of violets. Her roommate let me in. There were a dozen red roses on the table with a card. The card was from the married man she had been seeing. He was a 42-year-old pediatrician with three children.

"For a guy like me, who was so naive and inexperienced," Mike says, "it was like the whole world had ended. We were only lovers in the emotional sense. There was never any consummated sex. At that time, I was one of those idealistic sort of males who was still a virgin.

"I realize now that Terry had been involved sexually with all kinds of men. But because we were planning to get married and because of the way I was, she had to let me believe she was a virgin."

Young people from immigrant cultures had sanctions coming from all directions—religious and social, the old world and the new.

"It wasn't so much that I consciously believed in virginity for its own sake," Mike says. "It was a combination of other factors: the fear of pregnancy was a big one. But also respecting a woman's view that if she were not a virgin, she wouldn't be respected. That was the basic thing.

"I felt that if I were sexual with someone, that indicated that I didn't respect them. I could be sexual with someone I didn't care for, but not with someone I did care for. The fact that I was never sexual with anyone is because I never dated anyone I didn't care for."

Diane Weikert met Carl Anderson when she was thirteen and in seventh grade. Carl was seventeen, a high-school dropout and a horse trader.

"Our sexual relations were entirely between us," Diane says. "That was our secret. I would never have told anyone. Not my sister or even my best friend. In those days, no one did.

"We went together until I left for college. Every afternoon he came and picked me up a few blocks from school. I was crazy about horses then. We showed together and did other stuff, besides sex, that was separate from the rest of my life.

"I would never have taken Carl to parties or school dances. When I had to have a date, there was another boy I invited to those events.

"Sexually I never really had very much satisfaction," Diane says. "Circumstances were so limiting—where we could go and how long I could be away. Anyway, I felt so guilt-ridden I could never relax.

"It wasn't just the fear of doing something wrong. It was the certainty. Then there was the terror of getting pregnant. The terror was so great we clutched onto the myths, the myths that explained why it couldn't happen.

"Myth number one: Carl said that if you didn't have an orgasm at the same time, you couldn't get pregnant. I still can't believe that I ever believed that one!" Diane says, with a rare laugh. "Myth number two: that coitus interruptus always worked. When I think of the number of times—most of them, in fact—that we did not use prophylactics, the wonder is that I never got pregnant."

Of the many magical properties of the simultaneous orgasm, I had never heard this particular one—that beyond a measure of sexual compatibility, it was also the only opportunity for conception. The number one myth when I was in college held that you couldn't get pregnant the first time. This particular piece of folk wisdom was responsible for more pregnancies among my friends than all the other areas of our ignorance combined. Whether the first time was also apt to be the least planned of all sexual encounters or that defenses were weakest and desire most intense at the most fertile moment on the chart, that initial experience set conception records. I still hear the whispered shock and disbelief: "I can't believe it—that one time."

Diane says she doesn't know what she would have done if she had gotten pregnant. She and Carl "totally avoided the subject." But in the end, they were forced to confront a worse possibility. When Carl was drafted he was told he had gonorrhea.

"Since I had obviously been exposed," Diane says, "he wanted me to go to a doctor with him at home. I refused. The only doctor in town was a friend of the family. I was terrified that he might tell my mother. So I wouldn't go. Even though I knew I might have V.D. This was in tenth grade, when I was fourteen. That year, I lived through the most brutal terror of my life."

Diane knew her relationship with Carl would end with high-school graduation. "He said that if I went to college, it was all over. He wanted me to stay home and marry him." But Diane was never even tempted. "One of the reasons I was determined to go to college," she says, "was to change everything about my life, starting with Carl.

"I didn't appreciate him for what he was. He was really a noble savage—very, very intelligent. He had no schooling but more real self-esteem than any man I've ever met. And he was a very good person. But I wanted more. I wanted somebody who wore a suit and worked in an office."

Diane would never have told Tom Weikert about Carl, any more than she would have slept with Tom before they were married.

Some kinds of sex counted and other kinds didn't. An adolescent sexual past stayed home with high-school pennants and one-eyed dolls. Until she got to college, Diane thought she was the only one. "We all did. It was the secrecy," she says. "Then, when you picked up the clues, you realized that other girls, including my sorority sisters, had been sexually active in high school and even before."

When Cass Hunnicutt arrived at the university in a large southern city, he met a girl who was a high-school senior.

"She was big and blond and fun," he says. "She loved to dance and she liked to party. She was with a real good crew of people there in town. They all knew their way around. Coming from a much smaller city, it was exciting for me. The nightlife, the bars, the parties. And it was just so fine having a girl. She was the first woman I slept with. I just loved sex. I couldn't get enough of it. She felt the same way. We were like a couple of young animals. It was just great!"

Even though Cass told her he loved her, "when it came to discussing marriage, that was where the relationship ended. After you went together for a while, you got pinned, you got engaged, the next thing you did was to get married. It looked like that was coming. And I got cold feet," he says. "I just didn't want the responsibility of being married when I was still in college. So I bowed out right there."

For our generation, sexual experience didn't seem to result in greater biological knowledge. Even though, as Cass says, echoing every contemporary, "fear of pregnancy was the biggest thing, so that clumsy as they were" he used condoms all the time. He still admits, "I just wasn't very knowledgeable about how girls got pregnant." He attributes all of our ignorance to "the Big Lie: if nobody was doing it," Cass says, "nobody had any responsibility to instruct us.

"You just never discussed it, except for the little bit of bragging typical of the male. You didn't get much information from other guys either." The much-vaunted masculine bull sessions, a friend explained, "were just that: occasions for strutting your stuff, not for revealing innocence or asking for the real facts of life."

Secrecy perpetuated ignorance, fear, and guilt. But the unspeakable also soldered an intimacy based on collusion—often the only kind of intimacy young people experienced. In a period when everyone talked incessantly but took care to say nothing, the "sweet conversations of the flesh" were the more powerful.. Words were used more often to disguise than to reveal feelings. Without sex, communications between wary lovers were more cryptic than the Morse code. Collusion and conspiracy—us against them—were also powerful aphrodisiacs. Sexual partners were also partners in crime.

"Before we were married, sex was the big thing between us— probably the only thing," Carol Cornwell says about herself and the boy she dated for the last two years of high school and all of college, the boy to whom she was pinned, engaged, and married for twenty years.

By her parents' standards, Carol knew "what we were doing was awful. I remember the first time Don put his hand on my breast, under my clothes. It happened in my own home with my parents right upstairs.

"We both drew apart—as if in shock. And we gave serious thought as to whether we should see each other any more. He promised this wouldn't happen again—until next week, of course.

"Lots of times we'd come in after my parents had gone up to bed. It was really dumb because they probably weren't asleep. Anybody could have come downstairs and found us.

"I worried a lot about that. But at the same time, it made sex more exciting, more desirable. Because it was forbidden, because you might get caught."

Terror and titillation went together. What seemed to be an undercurrent of exhibitionism was also the need to know other people were around: parents, fraternity brothers, double dates. The real dread was being left alone together—as in marriage.

From the tie on the doorknob (to alert roommates) to "four on the floor"*—the rule governing the posture of those receiving visits from the opposite sex in dormitory rooms (which referred to feet), not forgetting the door half-open (Smith College regulations stipulated six inches—wide enough to peer inside and only on Sundays), the conventions surrounding sexual intimacy reflected not only the hypocrisies of authority but a powerful ambivalence on our part. How much privacy did we really want? Was our oft-stated fear of imminent discovery a hyperactive superego or a thinly disguised yearning for rescue?

Motels—40,000 new ones in the course of the decade—were sprouting at every intersection and on every back road. But when you were twenty in 1955, Dick Robertson says, "you had to have an awful lot of guts to check into one of those places with a girl.

---

* "Four on the floor" invites further speculation: Was anything other than the missionary position unimaginable to our elders or was this rule a test of their ingenuity?

"I did it once," Dick says. As soon as we got inside the room I thought, My God, the manager is calling my folks right now. Somehow he had gotten the number from Greenwich, Connecticut, information. I couldn't get that image out of my head. And of course, the girl was thinking the same thing. With so much fear it wasn't a great experience."

Even if they had access to cars and cash, most fearful twenty-year-olds didn't stray far from home or dormitory.

At colleges twelve miles apart, Carol Ruhe and Don Cornwell continued to date each other. "We really didn't decide to have sexual relations. It just sort of happened in the spring of freshman year," Carol says. "We were in the woods, right on campus. After that it was usually in the car, because it was still too cold to be outside. Then when Don was a junior, we used to use the Psych lab on Saturday night. But before we could go up there and fool around, I used to have to type his papers. That really appalls me, when I think of it now.

"We never used any contraception. That was the awful thing. Don was still too embarrassed to ask for condoms and, don't forget, it was illegal for doctors in New England to give information about any other methods.*

"We used coitus interruptus, which was horrible and not safe at all. It didn't presage well for the rest of our sexual lives together. I worried about getting pregnant all the time. It never stopped me from doing it, though.

"When you got your period, it was so wonderful. Thank God! You were lucky—one more time. I'll never forget that feeling of relief."

Luck was still the preferred method of birth control. Russian roulette was more acceptable to us than contraception; the terror of a missed period less frightening than confronting ourselves as adult women, planning on sex but not parenthood.

---

* Until 1965 the famous Comstock Laws made it a felony for a doctor to provide contraceptive information to a patient. No actual substance or object was needed to constitute a crime.

In Philip Roth's novella *Goodbye, Columbus* (1955),[2] the issue
of contraception becomes a test that both lovers fail. "I just don't
feel old enough for all that equipment," Brenda Patimkin objects,
in reply to Neil Klugman's demand that she go to the Sanger
clinic and get fitted for a diaphragm. "It's not age," the Radcliffe
junior explains, "it's so conscious a thing to do." For Neil, that,
of course, is the point. Her conscious act will prove that she is
his, not her parents' little girl. He wins but he loses. Brenda re-
lents, only to use this proof of adult sexuality to sabotage their
affair. When she goes back to college in the fall, she leaves the
diaphragm at home for her mother to find.

The summer between her junior and senior year at an Eastern
woman's college, Gail Feldstein went to California.

"Out of the blue, a guy I'd known in high school wrote me a
letter. He said he thought we ought to get married and I should
come out there to 'test our togetherness.'

"I don't know why my parents let me go," Gail says. "Probably
they were desperate because I hadn't found a man. I was a miserable failure on the blind date circuit at college. Somehow no one
ever clicked. My parents kept asking: What's wrong with all the
boys you meet? Here you are eighteen, twenty and you're not engaged yet.

"While I was out in San Francisco, I met someone else—actually, there were two guys. I met Joe at my waitress job. He was
working class and real macho. When we had sex, he put a sock
over his penis.

"The other guy, Eric, was a poet. He was marvelous, very gentle.
He got me into real genital sex. And that was very nice. I got
hooked on him and I wanted to get married. Of course, if you
were having regular sex with someone then, you had to marry
them. But he was just out for an affair. When he came East, he
visited me in college. And I got pregnant. That was my first abortion," Gail says. "May, 1959.

"I remember the abortionist played Nancy Sinatra, "These

Boots Are Made for Walking." He played it real loud in case I screamed. I've never been so frightened in my life. It was the combination of terror and the pain. The second time wasn't anything as bad."

When Gail Feldstein went back to her twenty-fifth high school reunion, she and her old boyfriend, Alex, had their own celebration. "We made out in the car; we even parked in exactly the same place we used to—down the street from my house.

"After that, he kept calling me from California. He was very unhappy with his wife, he told me. Sex was never, ever, as good as it had been back then, he said. As it still was in the car at reunion."

Nostalgia for sex in the back seat was more than mourning lost youth. As forbidden teenage gropings were left behind, erotic fulfillment required social justification: bona fides—literal or symbolic.

If you weren't pinned or engaged then you had to be certifiably in love. Among my college friends, all more emancipated than I was, sex without the probability of marriage expressed the outermost limits of existential heroism; a "relationship that wasn't going anywhere" was the tragically romantic phrase used to describe these detours from the inevitable.

Unbound by pin, ring, or even hopeless passion, there was one last excuse: sex as the solvent for the elaborate defense systems men had constructed. (None of us admitted to our own self-protective disappearing acts. We decided that camouflage, the flight from feelings, was a "male problem." And its severity justified sex as a means of flushing out our hidden quarry.)

Women have always tended to see men in an "agricultural light," Dorothy L. Sayers observed, as unclaimed land crying for cultivation. In the repressive fifties, sexual activity for women could be rationalized by turning agriculture into altruism. As long as it was for their own good—and not ours—we were all right. In this enterprise, my friends divided into archaeologists and theologians. The archaeologists claimed that only sex could unwrap the mummy in the Brooks Brothers suit, revealing a living, breathing male inside. My best friend was a theologian. Vigorously engaged in redeeming base lust, she quoted Fromm on *eros* and *agape*, Tillich on the "transcendental margin" that elevated the sexual to a spiritual act.

Justifiable by a promissory pin or solitaire, hopeless passion, or the saving of souls, the one absolutely forbidden, always proscribed carnal encounter was something called Meaningless Sex. In the fifties, for a young woman, meaningless sex was worse than doing it for money (which suggested rational need). Sex without (other) meaning held the same scary anarchic threat as motiveless crime.

Countless early marriages foundered on the discovery of all the meaningless sex we had missed. PTA mommies, and solid suburban householders freaked on a truth well hidden in the fifties: The real meaning was in the act itself. And the worst people made the best partners; men and women who had no "potential" for anything other than fucking.

Along with the belated discovery of meaningless sex came powerful feelings of resentment towards our benighted youth. We'd been had and "they" owed us one—or lots. That was the "excuse" for otherwise hard-to-excuse carryings-on in the late sixties and seventies. We'd been told that sex was dirty, dangerous, and powerful stuff. That nothing could touch it for pleasure and fun (a completely unknown word as applied to sexual congress in our youth) was the best-kept secret of our coming of age.

For the heterosexual majority, moral fig leaves were available to cloak sexual need as yet unsanctified by marriage; it didn't "count" yet; you had found the once-and-forever love—or almost. Or lust, like the lethal atom, had been harnessed to peaceful ends; placed in the service of higher psychological or spiritual communion, with procreation to follow as soon as legally possible.

If you grew up gay in the fifties, all sexual encounters were forbidden games. More than anarchic or antisoical, dirty, or even dangerous, homosexuals were emotionally arrested, abnormal, "sick," if not criminal. As sexual beings, they were Underground Men and Women.

"I didn't have real sex until I was twenty-two," Martin Duberman says. "Before that it was furtive episodes involving pickups on the New Haven Green. They were incomplete, full of tension and horror around the edges. The first time was when I was an undergraduate in 1951.

"I followed some stocky, drunk twenty-year-old out-of-towner into the park and (I think he encouraged me) groped at him. He reacted in a rage, swung at me drunkenly, got half of the collar of my jacket and ripped it down my back as I struggled out of reach and raced down the street. I told my roommates I'd gotten into a fight with some 'townie.' With my torn jacket as proof, I was treated like a hero. I trembled inside for days."

Soon after this episode, a classmate casually mentioned to Martin Duberman that he should stay away from the Green at night. It's a hangout for fairies, he was told. "I was shocked—and overjoyed. At last a place to meet someone.

"That same night I got drunk, reeled down to the Green, and sat on a bench opposite the only other person I could see in the area, a very fat, middle-aged black man. He whistled tantalizingly in my direction. I got up, reeled over and stood boldly in front of him. He started playing with my cock, then took it out of my pants. Wildly excited, I started to fondle him.

" 'Do you have any place we can go?' I whispered.

" 'Nope. No place.'

"Suddenly I heard laughter and noise coming in our direction. I was sure it was some undergraduates, and equally sure we'd been seen. Zipping up my fly, I ran out of the park, ran without stopping, panicked, hysterical, ran for my life back to my dorm room. I stayed in the shower for hours, cleaning, cleansing. I actually washed my mouth out with soap, though I hadn't used my mouth—other than to make a prayerful pact with the Divinity

that if He let me off this time, I'd never, never go near the Green
again. The panic lasted for days. By the end of the week I was
back on the Green, drunk again. I met a dancer. We had sex in his
car—that is, I let him blow me.

"I was aware of lust—an attraction to people of my own sex—
always," he says, " 'always' being as far back as I can remember.
But not until much later to the exclusion of the opposite gender.

"Within our in-group at school, several of us began serious
sexual experimentation in fellatio. Like all kids, we stayed over at
each other's houses. The first time it was at my house. I didn't
initiate it. The most macho of the three of us was the leader. We
didn't do it as a threesome; we took turns. As I recall, I pulled
away farthest, fastest," he says. "But that may have been my
terror at recognizing how much I really enjoyed it. The other guys
(both of whom have gone on to marry and lead completely
heterosexual lives) liked it. They wanted to go on. I didn't.

"We shared the same degree of unease. It was furtive, secret,
and disturbing. But the guilt came later, with my sense of isolation in college. Then I no longer had 'our crowd' for reassurance.

"Because, at the same time we were experimenting with fellatio, we all dated, constantly, all through high school. Going
steady, or at least having a girlfriend, was essential. That was true
for most of us in the fifties. Even a traditional boys' school became
more like the typical American high school. If anything, I was
the sexual superstar. The night of senior prom, I was the one
chosen by my classmates to lose my virginity—for all of us!

"I was seventeen and I had been dating a "wild girl" named
Rachel for a long time. We had promised ourselves and announced
to our friends that we would "consummate our love" that night.
After the prom our crowd went to a classmate's apartment: very
fancy, a fit setting for the big event. Everyone lay around on the
living room floor, drinking and making out—and waiting for the
moment when Rachel and I would go into the back bedroom. The
whole group was vicariously losing its virginity through us. In
the bedroom Rachel and I got undressed and lay together on the
huge bed. As with my ritual visit with friends to a whorehouse,

I was impotent. But this time, desperate, crazed, 'The doctor warned me that I've been making out too much. He said this would happen if I didn't cut down!' I told her.

"I had another lie for our friends. This time the excuse (agreed to by Rachel—I was lucky in my choice of women) was that we hadn't been able to do it because she was having her period.

"I was celibate from then until my pickups on the New Haven Green."

Fraught with all the terror and turn-on of Russian roulette, the chills and thrills of the furtive and forbidden, of getting "caught" (pregnant or arrested), consummated sex was too momentous an act to be concerned with skills.

As long as you were wrong to be doing it, there was no such thing as doing it wrong.

If we weren't too sure how babies got made, we were still less aware that there were levels of the game. As an unregulated, off-the-books activity, the erotic in the Age of Eisenhower could still be regarded as instinctual. Alone together, every couple invented sex for themselves. In its repressed way, the Fifties were the last days of the Garden of Eden—after the Fall, to be sure, but before Masters and Johnson, before Ruth Westheimer and *Good Sex* on cable TV. Ignorance may not have been bliss, but with little experience, few expectations, and no sense of the entitlement that would come a decade later, invidious comparisons had to be rare.

What little sexual activity Dick Robertson recalls from his undergraduate days was confined to couples who were pinned. And in retrospect, he admits, "it was probably pretty crude. Now, you can learn a lot of sexual intricacies just by going to the movies. There weren't those kinds of movies then, and there was very little casual sex to learn from.

"If I had had any great expectations about the earth moving," Carol Cornwell says, "I would have been sadly disappointed by what we did. Partly, it was the mystique that the man was supposed to know everything. If you suspected different, you didn't talk about it. Whatever the guy was able to do, that was supposed to be terrific. And at that point," Carol says, "whatever it was, I was all for it."

"Whatever it was" was something of a mystery to Betts Saunders until her marriage to an equally innocent young medical student. During her premarital examination, the doctor explained to her what was supposed to happen during sexual intercourse. "He asked me if I knew about the orgasm," she recalls. I'd heard of it, but I wanted to know what you were supposed to feel. "It feels," the doctor told her, "like a huge, giant sneeze." Concentrating on the nasal passages, the gynecologist never mentioned male sexuality.

"I just assumed men could keep doing it—twenty or thirty times at least," she says. "I was certainly surprised to learn that a normal man had definite limitations."

An age-old sexual injustice, the male burden of performance, with all its attendant ego risk, was literally muted in the fifties by the silence that surrounded illicit sex. Whatever wasn't happening wasn't discussed.

It takes Marjorie Morningstar, the first and most famous of Jewish princesses, two years and 417 pages of Herman Wouk's 1955 best-seller to lose her virginity to Noel Airman, glamorous composer and reputed ladykiller. But this event, eagerly awaited by heroine and reader, is far from Marjorie's fantasies of how it would be:

> She tried to seem pleasant and loving, but she was uncomfortable and unhappy. It became rougher and more awkward. It became horrible. There were shocks, ugly uncoverings, pain, incredible humiliation, shock, shock and it was over.

As Marjorie lies sobbing, her face buried in the pillow, Noel says to her crossly: "You're a big girl. It could have been more fun and it will be, I promise you."[3] (Marjorie doesn't pick up the raincheck.)

Today's reader may wonder about the basis for this lout's reputation as a great lover. From our one glimpse through the bedroom door, Noel Airman would seem to have all the finesse of a fourteen-year-old drugstore cowboy. But as long as he remained a seducer and not a spouse, he could rely on the discretion of his companions, stifling any disappointment with promises of "next time."

His problems would begin when sex became legal. As a bridegroom, Noel Airman wouldn't get off so easily.* Stripped of the fig leaves of the forbidden, the silence of sin, marital sex—from the wedding night on—would be open to the prying eyes of sexologists, psychologists, marriage counselors, ministers, and even employers. Once married, Noel Airman and every other American male, starting with the postwar generation, was expected to acquire skills not unlike those needed in the factory, office, or classroom.

Addressed almost exclusively to men, the marriage manuals of the fifties assumed the role of the husband as teacher. In *Love Without Fear: How to Achieve Sex Happiness in Marriage*,** author Eustace Chesser charges both partners with "frankly aspiring to become perfect lovers." The burden, though, is on the man to function as instructor, to "educate his wife, one step at a time, in the art of joyous mating." Pitiless toward any anxiety about performance or pedagogical skills, Chesser notes smugly, a "strange intuition of woman warns her against the nervous lover and her instinct is sound. He is among the enemies of women."[4]

Reflecting the beliefs of the most profamily era in American history, marriage manuals of the decade share a basic assumption: Since sex is the cornerstone of a happy marriage, failure in this area is no private affair. Sexual inadequacy constitutes a threat to social order.

"In a world of chaos," begins *Sex: Methods and Manners*, "and in an era in which national and international integrity have fallen

---

* His creator spares him this fate. But without wife and family, Airman is conspicuously unsuccessful in his career—a perfect antihero of the Fifties.

** *Love Without Fear*, first published in England in 1941, went into 39 editions, selling over three million copies by 1966.

to a low level, there remains only the solid structure of the home
to form the basis for the re-establishment of the ancient standards
of virtue." The author's purpose is to relieve "one of the major
threats to the stability of the home: sexual incompatibility."[5]

Other writers saw this threat as akin to any other public health
menace, proposing that "premarriage clinics should become as
common as clinics for the prevention and control of tuberculosis,
since a bad marriage is an equally tremendous liability to the
community."[6]

Lest any male think he can leave substandard sex at home,
Chesser reminds him that the Organization is keeping an eye on
his performance in the bedroom. "Those firms which ask appli-
cants for posts as salesmen and other positions whether they are
happily married, do so," the author notes approvingly, "because
they know from experience that a man must be happy in his sex
life before he can give of his best in his workaday life."[7]

In the fifties a husband who was an inadequate sexual partner
became a social subversive, undermining the primary institution
of society—the family. But help was at hand, provided the nervous or inept read their manuals carefully and took copious notes.
In an effort to demystify the sexual act, the doctors and psychologists who wrote these guides addressed their male readers in the
soothingly familiar language of the corporate training program.
In Love Without Fear the nuts-and-bolts chapter is entitled "How
to Manage the Sexual Act," while Sex Questions and Answers
responds affirmatively to the query "Is intercourse necessary the
first night of marriage?" by reminding the bridegroom who would
remain in control that "the proper management of the first night
of marriage often sets the pattern for future marital adjustments."[8]

Beyond executive skills, some instructions seemed to call for an
engineering degree (a popular major in the fifties). "Before at-
tempting intercourse," caution doctors Berg and Street, authors
of Sex: Methods and Manners, "the husband should thoroughly
acquaint himself with the genital region of his wife . . . directing
his attention especially to the construction of the vaginal canal

and the location of the hymen."[9] The authors were aware of the gaps in technical training that might leave some of their readers at a disadvantage. "It is probable that not one man in ten," they lament, "prior to marriage or subsequent to it, can draw a simple sketch of the cross section of a woman's genitals to include the uterus, the outer lips, the clitoris, the urethra, the inner lip . . . just eight small parts and seven of them all-important to an adequate understanding of what is involved in proper sexual indulgence." But for those nine men who never took mechanical drawing, an on-site crash course is provided, in the form of a detailed sketch, which, they urge, "should be studied on the bridal night; instead of making a determined effort to rupture the hymen at all costs, the husband should compare the diagram with his wife's genital region, as determined by actual examination."

In the anxious post-Sputnik era, a rational scientific approach was always to be preferred over instinct. To be avoided at all costs, warn the same authors, was "giving the bride the impression that this investigation arises from pure physical lust and to avoid arousing the suspicion that the husband may be unconventional in his habits."

At least, once the reader had mastered the sketch by comparing it with his wife's anatomy and doing a few practice drawings of his own, he was on the right track. Other experts seemed determined to program for failure. In a perfect example of poor pedagogy, Dr. G. Lombard Kelly, author of *Sexual Feeling in Married Men and Women*, provides a diagram (see page 146) of how *not* to do it.[10] (Be sure to forget you ever saw this, or you'll never get it right.)

When the style didn't ape the corporate trainee handbook, the typical marriage manual echoed the brisk, directive voice of *Popular Mechanics*. The fifties were a boom period in do-it-yourself hobbies of every type. From assembling model airplanes and souping up cars, most male readers had graduated to kits of material with detailed instructions on how to make your own camera or build an A-frame house. What terror should confound

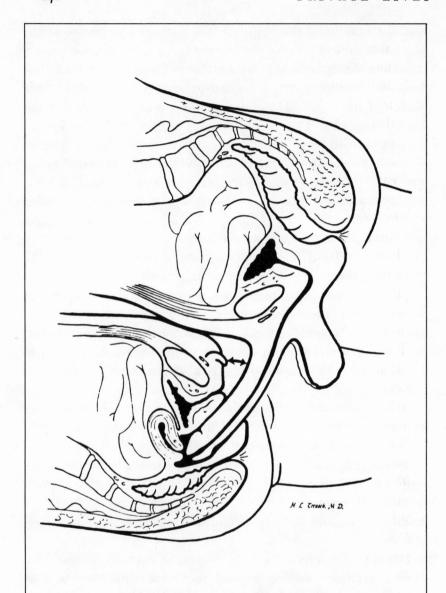

Wrong way to perform coitus. Double arrow shows distance separating penis from clitoris. (Figure 9 from *Sexual Feeling in Married Men and Women* by Dr. G. Lombard Kelly)

them, then, at the prospect of "Ten Easy Steps to Better Sex"? Both men and women, moreover, were equally used to being pro- grammed—at school, at play, and on the job. It was no accident, a friend reminded me, that the *Kama Sutra*, the eighteenth- century Hindu guide to lovemaking, was unofficial required read- ing when we were in college.

"For the first three days of marriage," we read, "the girl and her husband should sleep on the floor, abstain from sexual pleasure and eat their food without seasoning it with alkali or salt. For the next seven days they should bathe amidst the sounds of auspicious musical instruments. . . . On the tenth day, the man should begin in a lonely place, with soft words. . . ."[11]

There was something reassuring about the canonical rigidity prescribed for lovemaking. The *Kama Sutra* was the erotic in the familiar form of a semester schedule, as handed to us on large index cards. Taken literally, moreover, its fixed progression of in- timacies could end the arguments that accompanied grappling with garter belts as house lights flashed curfew. (If tonight was the fifth date and a Wednesday, the left inner thigh was *it!*)

Less reassuring was the central article of faith shared by all marriage manuals of the decade and by such meager sexual lore as we could obtain: the mystique of the simultaneous orgasm.

"In almost every activity of life, success comes to those who consciously and deliberately will to achieve," the author of *Love Without Fear* exhorts his readers—men *and* women for a change. There was no doubt as to the direction this triumph of the will should take. "Both partners should, in coitus, concentrate their full attention on one thing: the attainment of simultaneous orgasm."[12]

As the decade that elevated trust in testing to new heights, from IQ to vocational aptitude, the fifties made the achievement of simultaneous orgasm an "evaluative tool," as test designers put it, of sexual compatibility. Both a working goal and a production plan, this discrete event translated into an objective measure of success. If you were doing it right, you ended together, on the beat, like the Radio City Music Hall Rockettes.

More seriously, the tyranny of the simultaneous orgasm had moral dimensions. Failure was a measure of selfishness, "immaturity," frigidity, and the inability to submerge one's own needs or desires to those of the "team." "Faking it" suddenly emerged as a classic female defensive strategy. Who wanted to be found wanting, by measures human as well as sexual? If you couldn't do it right, then perhaps you were the wrong kind of person.

In a famous article, "I'm Sorry, Dear,"[13] psychoanalyst Leslie Farber launched a full-scale attack against the erotic ideal of the fifties. The quest for the simultaneous orgasm was, he wrote, nothing less than the "degradation of sex."

Introducing us to a hypothetical married couple, Farber chronicles their estrangement from one another as they frantically pursue the goal of sexual synchronization. "Making liars out of normally truthful people," the doctor's unhappy pair, when they are not trying desperately to achieve simultaneity through drugs or drink, are "continually tempted by deception; he may try to conceal his moment, she to simulate hers—as they stalk their equalitarian ideal."

This mechanistic travesty of passion, however, did not come about by accident. In Farber's scenario, the villain of the piece is the wife, as she joins her voice to the demands for equal (sexual) rights by women who now saw themselves as "entitled to an orgasm equal to the male, just as they were entitled to the vote."

Farber's polemic was occasioned by the first article by Dr. William H. Masters,* outlining his research-in-progress in new laboratory techniques of curing sexual problems, "complete with use of electrodes and color videotapes of the spreading orgasmic rash."

Through their misguided claims for equality of sexual pleasure, women had become brides of Frankenstein; responsible for moving sex from the bedroom to the laboratory, replacing romantic

---

* Dr. Masters would soon be joined by fellow researcher Virginia Johnson, coauthor of *Human Sexual Response*.

love with "organ grinding,"[14] as observed by white-coated technicians.

The good old days, when only one sex was assumed to number sexual beings, were indeed over. Even as Dr. Farber wrote in 1964, history had passed him by.

In 1960, the first year of the new decade, the FDA announced its approval of the first contraceptive pill, Enovid. Divorced from procreation, the sexual act no longer required the marriage bed as its testing ground. Entitlement was to more and better sex. Anything that felt good *was* good, in the phrase of the day; and by extension, anyone it felt good with was the right partner.

A minor casualty of changing times was the demise of the marriage manual as a primer for sexual self-help. Traditional experts tried to keep up with the sexual revolution. In 1960 the sober and respected psychologist and clinician Dr. Albert Ellis published *The Art and Science of Love,* a classic of advice to the newly married. In 1961, seizing on the "big" new word of the period, he produced *Creative Marriage.* In 1967 Dr. Ellis and *The Art of Erotic Seduction* skirted the question of who was using his instructions on whom. By 1972 there was no longer any pretense that sexual expression could be contained by marriage. In *The Civilized Couple's Guide to Extramarital Adventures,* Ellis showed that adultery need not mean anarchy—or even guilt.

Making no assumptions about the relationship of consenting adult readers, new guides like Dr. Alex Comfort offered instruction in masturbation and even safe bondage techniques. ("Don't ever leave a partner tied up," he advised.)[15]

Those of us still dragging around the sexual baggage of the fifties and earlier—the superiority of the simultaneous or vaginal orgasm and of genital sex; moral obstacles to pleasure like beliefs in monogamy, fidelity, heterosexuality, or even love—were advised to get rid of all such "hang-ups."

Nothing was dirty, dangerous, or forbidden. And there was no one right way to do it. Henceforth, we were limited only by imagination and anatomy.

———————————————— *Detours* ————————————————

When we were young, imagination, like meaningless sex, was a risky exercise. Indulging in either could deflect a young woman from her primary purpose of finding a marriageable young man. Most of my friends were in no danger of getting sidetracked. With Mr. Right's résumé in hand, they had their lives squared away. From their conversations topographical maps, like U.S. Army serial photographs, took shape. The future unfolded to the farthest horizons. They knew every rise and meander of the terrain—towel monograms and silver patterns, houses, cars, numbers of children and kinds of communities they would live in—forever. More incredible to me, they had approved it all in advance. The blueprint was their parents' way of life. The future was the past.

When I looked down from my reconnaissance plane at the dark future unrolling below, I got airsick. The thought of knowing it all right now seemed worse than the worst uncertainty, worse than never having a date on Saturday night.

"Detour . . . there's a muddy road ahead," Frankie Laine sang. I suspected that detours were my destiny. I wanted to act out all my fantasies of romance, adventure, passion; meetings of minds, souls, and bodies. More than anything, I wanted to fall in love. In the meantime, I was happy to settle for fun. I had acquired a boyfriend who took fun seriously.

Tyler came from Alabama, as did his three roommates. They all spoke in accents I had heard only in the movies. A Confederate flag hung from the window of their college suite, where life was a perpetual party. Dixieland jazz played endlessly and the Bourbon flowed at all hours of the day and night.

This was my first experience of the feverish social pace that Southerners take for granted. When their rooms weren't jammed rib-to-rib with all the students who hailed from below the Mason-Dixon line, we went out. We went to football games and Masters' teas, to cocktail parties at friends' suites, to informal fraternity dances, and to formal college proms. Just as his mother had taught him, Tyler telephoned on Wednesdays with a schedule of the weekend's strenuous social calendar so that I would know what clothes to bring.

My God, the clothes! When I think of college weekends in the fifties, I remember the suitcases we dragged from trains (sitting on them until they finally shut) to be shouldered manfully by our waiting dates. Outfits for two days could hardly be squeezed into an enormous valise whose capacity could now keep me clothed for a year of wintry travels.

The question asked about any event was: How dressy is it? In order of dressiness, we packed a wardrobe that might include Bermuda shorts, woolen dress, and "semiformal"—a street-length silk or taffeta requiring a waist-cincher and masses of crinolines (unless it was a sheath, necessitating just the opposite in undergarments)—or formal gown, not forgetting the spectrum of shoes needed for these changes of costume. "Can I get away with black suede pumps and my navy cocktail dress?" was a frequently debated issue on my floor.

Dazed by this sudden whirl, I was also relieved by what it told me. I was a "fun date," a social asset. My large vocabulary didn't seem to daunt Tyler and his friends. Perhaps it was the high noise level of their surroundings or the fact that, from Friday lunch on, they were not altogether sober. Possibly any unfamiliar words were attributed to my Yankee accent and speeded-up New York delivery. Besides, Southern girls were expected to have a ready stream of chatter. No one listened too hard to what they said. Thanks to Texan wisdom, my pearls shone. Bobby-pinned and hairnetted for two days, my page boy was reasonably sleek. Under layers of Revlon's "Touch and Glow," my skin, like that of all my friends, was a flawless beige. I had traded in "Fire and Ice" for Elizabeth Arden's "Silver Rose" lipstick, midnight blue mascara for medium brown—just to cover the invisible tips of the lashes. Balancing a cigarette in one hand and, depending on the hour of the day—a Bloody Mary, tea cup, sherry, or martini in the other—my social radar became attuned to giving the right beeps: adjusting to rowdy fraternity brothers, visiting parents, earnest young faculty, and genteel Masters' wives, grateful to girls who didn't arrive drunk and smash their best china.

Late Sunday afternoon, wan, haggard, and hung over, I tottered, along with hordes of similarly peaked young women, into the dining car of the New York, New Haven, and Hartford Railroad. I put my glasses on and stopped smiling. Over as many cups of coffee as could be swallowed before Springfield, I peered at index cards for my seminar report on the Aesthetics of Walter Pater. It was a relief to shed Scarlett O'Hara for another week.

At the very end of each evening (the only time we were ever alone), Tyler planted a chaste kiss on my lips. True, when dancing he held me in a pelvis-crunching grip, but otherwise he never "took liberties," as our mothers said. Hearing of the swinish lust friends were constantly obliged to fend off, I was disappointed. What Tyler wanted, as did many other young men I was to meet, was a presentable date. In the absence of passion or common interests, the parties began to pale. And I met someone else.

My friends called him the Perfect Person. Everyone else's male visitors appeared in chino trousers, sweaters, a tweed jacket if they were staying for dinner. The Perfect Person always wore dark suits of suspiciously foreign cut, a foulard tie and matching silk handkerchief sprouting negligently from his jacket pocket. His black hair was just a few millimeters shorter than a DA. Two New England prep schools had not modified his strange Anglo-European accent.

Nothing about my present self found much favor with the Perfect Person. Our uniform college weekend arrival attire—an oatmeal sweater, pearls, and a gray flannel skirt—he pronounced "banal." My A paper on Joyce was "superficial." But I was given to understand that I had potential.

Gone were the genial Southerners and their alcoholic gallantries. The Perfect Person's circle were aesthetes. One friend played the harpsichord, another collected Japanese prints. They all held strong opinions on a dizzying range of subjects—Armenian art historians and Cambridge literary theorists, early Purcell anthems, late Pound cantos. They expressed their views with a declamatory conviction I had never heard before. Having rarely heard of the subjects under discussion either, I felt doubtly disqualified.

His ex-girlfriend from Sarah Lawrence had such a bold, aphoristic—even outrageous—way of talking, he said, along with a dramatically individual style of dress. (How could such an exciting and original person ever become an "ex"? I wondered) I tried. I banished the banal wardrobe, at least on weekends. I bought an expensive, stark black dress, sending it home COD to my outraged parents. I wore jade beads and matching eyeshadow. My roommate contributed a jade cigarette holder to what she sympathetically called "the cause."

In this costume, I noticed, even the most unremarkable opinions sounded bolder, more aphoristic; occasionally, even outrageous. I knew when I was batting high; the Perfect Person would unknit his heavy brows and nod slowly at me, with just the suggestion of a smile. "If you have style, you can get away with anything," he said.

What he also wanted me to get away with was sex. During the week, I sat in the library in a constant state of sexual arousal, parts of his body floating between my eyes and the page. (Like most nearsighted girls of the period, I refused to wear glasses in the presence of any man, except in the darkness of a movie theater. For years, male anatomy would always be segmented—seen and recalled in small close-up sections, as though prepared for surgery.)

When we were together, a mulish anger and dread dissolved desire. It wasn't fear of physical violation or even of getting pregnant. Like everyone else, I was sure that couldn't happen to me. I was terrified by my passion for him. I had become his creation. I was completely in his thrall—in every way but one. If I lost that last hold over him, I would have nothing of my own. I would cease to exist.

"What do you *want?*" he would hiss angrily. "Do you want me to marry you?"

No, I shook my head stubbornly. That wasn't what I wanted. I wanted him to love me for a self I didn't have.

My resentful efforts to please men were cosmetic and cowardly. I had friends who took real risks, exuberantly trying on temporary selves.

Diana, a six-foot-tall Minnesotan with fox-red hair, was managing to forestall the future right in Northampton. Drinking stingers every afternoon in Rahar's—a vast, crumbling, firetrap of a bar by the railroad tracks—she became the mascot of a group of Beats, "townies" who shared a ramshackle apartment above the local Peck & Peck!

Somewhere between drifters and part-time students, these young men were in flight from their working-class fate and the upwardly mobile aspirations they were told to acquire. Supporting themselves with odd jobs, they spent the rest of the time listening to jazz, drinking beer, and smoking hash.

She talked me into one evening with her new friends. But I was too conventional and snobbish and middle class to find them or their life in the least appealing. Prim and bored, I sat stiffly on the dirty pillows spread over the floor, made queasy (then and ever after) by the smell of pot. For Diana, Jerry, Rick, and Phil meant more than sex that "didn't count," learning to smoke joints, and reading dog-eared copies of Kerouac and paperbacks on Zen. They offered a brief detour from destiny: the clean-cut all-American boy she would duly marry one week after graduation (and divorce a decade later) in the fanciest wedding of the Wayzata season.

The terror that her forays into the lower depths aroused in the administration was a measure of the times. Convoking the entire student body, the dean warned against "dangerous associations" and the depravity to which these inexorably led. Lest her remarks prove insufficiently discouraging, the college was turned into an army base for the duration of the semester, with the city of Northampton declared off limits after dark.

I thought of that lecture, and the far-off spring of 1955, a few years ago. On another glorious May afternoon, I stood on the steps of the college library watching a "Smith is for Lovers" celebration on the grassy oval outside. The considerable lesbian population of the college (dressed in lavender with matching balloons) was dancing, to the music of many different "boxes" and transistors. A strong smell of pot wafted on the balmy air.

"I'd do anything to get out of this place for a year," hissed my adviser, fresh from signing an oath promising not to overthrow the Commonwealth of Massachusetts "by force or violence." It was unclear whether he meant the college or the country, but I was glad to take his advice.

Junior Year Abroad was finishing school in role-playing. We were instructed in how to disappear into a foreign culture, with lessons and pointers for all occasions. Mirrors and tongue depressors were used to erase the accents of Memphis or New York, and there was a long list of social injunctions ("Never ask for milk at mealtimes, or of Frenchmen, what work they do.")

The family I lived with was my first experience of the extreme Right. During endless meals, with their rituals of the removal and replacement of perfectly clean plates, they raved on about the saintliness of Pétain, the perfidy of Jewish bankers, the vileness of Communists. Here were real fascists—the genuine article—and not wearing jackboots with swastika armbands but dressed in prewar Dior and Charvet, surrounded by threadbare Louis Quinze furniture. I practiced peeling my peach in a perfect spiral.

With my unerring instinct for the unlikely, I found a devout left-wing Catholic admirer. He belonged to a student group whose members were ascetic-looking young men like him, and pale un-lipsticked girls. They were brilliant, austere, and kind, and I loved them all. On weekends their respite from studies were walking pilgrimages to Chartres or Saint-Denis.

They lent me mystical writings—Péguy and Simone Weil—which they encouraged me to discuss with them, undaunted by my halting French. In their subdued, dignified way, these young men and women seemed so happy. Unlike me and my friends, oblivious to politics or the privations of others, they grieved for the poor, oppressed, godless.

That was the problem. Slowly, it dawned on me that my value to Xavier and his friends was impersonal. I was a soul ripe for conversion. I felt betrayed. This time I was a spiritual instead of a social asset: Scarlett O'Hara, Zuleika Dobson, St. Theresa, it was always someone else's script. Possibly, there was no "me" at all—only an apt learner who conveyed infinite suggestibility.

Once, I would have said this was purely female: a passive waiting until a husband and children would confer identity upon our unformed selves. Recently though, I have come to wonder if it is not generational. A contemporary, the writer Paul Zweig, spoke of his "suspicion of personal emptiness which all my talking and my anxious attempts at charm surround and decorate, but don't penetrate or even come close to."[1] And I have observed many of us who came of age in the fifties exhibit symptoms of what the psychoanalyst Helene Deutsch calls the "as if" personality, characterized by "a highly plastic readiness to pick up signals from the outer world and to mold oneself and one's behavior accordingly."[2] Certainly, there have been few periods in which young people were rewarded for just such aptitude.

Many of us, men and women, got over it. That "core of blandness," of which Zweig speaks, filled. We acquired feelings, maybe even character—that quaint, pre-Freudian notion. We took risks, went off the deep end, were able to say, I hurt, therefore I am.

For a brief period, between student days and real life, I lived with a young man.

Everything about him fascinated me, including qualities I found distasteful in others—the sure symptom of passion. He had what I later learned to recognize as the voluptuous thrift of the very rich. He would return from the rare shopping trip with an ecstatic litany of items he had decided not to buy. The unbecoming brown suits he wore reflected the dramatic and frequent markdowns of this unpopular color.

I should have known from our ritual exchanges of presents that we had no future together.

His gifts to me were as useful—even pleasurable—as they were impersonal and unromantic: a red flannel nightshirt, more suggestive of dormitory life than of "living in sin," and a recording of *Don Giovanni* I still enjoy—even the scratched parts. My presents to him were so unmemorable I'm unable to recall them. With one disastrous exception. Aimlessly window shopping, I succumbed to the perfect birthday gift, a Victorian seal that matched in style and color his grandfather's gold watch and chain. It was received stiffly and banished with dispatch to the depths of a bureau drawer.

When his college friends and their wives came to his apartment for dinner, sometimes accompanied by brand-new babies, the fiction was that I was just a date. When guests were due to arrive we did a militarily thorough check beforehand, to make sure that hair spray and perfume bottles were out of sight. I did not know whether to attribute these strategems to a gentlemanly code of "protecting my reputation" or to guilt. He was a believing Christian, a regular and solitary churchgoer—the only contemporary I knew who was more than formally observant. Either way, I felt vaguely humiliated. But I had no words to express my sense of diminishment. Anymore than I knew what to say to the Polish superintendent who stopped me on my way to work one morning and said, "This is none of my business, Miss, but a nice young lady like you shouldn't be living with a man. What would your parents think?"

I knew what my parents would think. To my own astonishment,

I felt no guilt about sex—then or ever. But everyone, including my lover, suggested I was morally deficient.

In the fifties, the only thing worse than sleeping with a man was telephoning him. On the infrequent occasions when I called him at the office, the receptionist would answer, her voice brimming with contempt: "Well . . . I'll be *sure* and tell him you called." (Why any man would return the call of a woman who had sunk so low, she obviously couldn't imagine.)

I became fearful, falling back on a familiar defensive tactic: sabotage. I sulked over trivia, played the arrogant intellectual with his clubby friends, and "made scenes," crying in restaurants.

"You don't love me, do you?" I asked, when I was sure of the answer.

"No," he said, "I don't."

What a relief, finally, to hear what I most dreaded.

Six months later, I was married.

8
A DIAMOND IS FOREVER

Solitaire was the name of the setting, and it was easily the ugliest piece of jewelry ever designed. Looking like a pulled tooth, the most popular style of engagement ring of the 1950s featured a naked "emerald cut" diamond propped high on a scaffolding of prongs, atop a platinum band. Whether a big sparkler or barely a chip, the point was maximum visibility. No fraction of a carat should be lost to view.

Even before it was found to be a girl's best friend, few girls have ever said no to a nice diamond. In earlier periods, though, many young women said yes to suitors bearing less costly gems, including semiprecious stones whose metal setting was meant to be admired for craftsmanship, not weight as measured in carats. More modest still, Victorian engagement rings were sometimes clasped hands or two golden hearts.

In postwar America, every young man, middle class in fact or aspiration, had to plight his troth with the purchase of this single diamond. Blue-white and free standing, paid for by parents or bought on time, the ring promised permanence in a world of Cold War chaos or delivered a down payment on the donor's success

("Baby, this is just the beginning!"). Sometimes even enduring love.

Whatever its value in carats or symbolism, the solitaire was the last in a sequence of gifts from men to women that marked the stages of dating and courtship in midcentury America. The way from junior high school to the altar was measured in class rings, ID bracelets, letter sweaters, lavaliers, and fraternity pins, until finally the diamond that was supposed to be forever.

The route might be leisurely or brief—high-school sweethearts, pinned in college or a "whirlwind romance" in the real world— but in most instances the diamond solitaire was given by young men and eagerly accepted by young women who were complete strangers to one another.

We were hardly the first to marry strangers. But earlier generations had better reasons. Then, young people were carefully chaperoned. A bride left her father's house only for a home of her own. We were the first men and women in history to be allowed so much time alone together, with so little intimacy to show for it.

Contemplating her unhappy husband, their unhappy marriage, their three unhappy children, Betsy Rath, wife of *The Man in the Grey Flannel Suit*, the best-selling 1955 portrait of the suburban good life gone sour, recalls their courtship. For three years

> they had gone to movies and football games and college dances and nightclubs and performed the whole ritual of entertainment preparatory to marriage. . . . They had kissed. At the time, they had known much less about each other than any personnel man knows about a prospective stenographer, but almost casually, certainly without anything which could be described as thought, on the strength of a kiss, she had agreed to marry him and had not considered it strange at all.[1]

"I was a Theta; that made up for being a farm girl. . . ." "It was his datability; he was a leader of everything on campus. . . ." "She was a nice girl; medium smart, medium pretty. . . ." "He had lots of ambition and drive. . . ." "She was a traditional-type woman; I knew she would go down well with my parents. . . ." "The most intimate thing I knew about him was that he wanted to be a big success. . . ."

To be sure, nothing resists our efforts more than trying to put love into words. (Why else do we need poets to help us count the ways?) Even harder to express is love that must be recalled, sometimes long after the fact. What has happened since then often colors memories with irony or bitterness. Still, the answers to the question, What attracted you to him or her? are too consistent to be ignored.

For those who felt betrayed or frightened by sex, marriage promised a refuge from unruly passion.

"Tom was never sexually attractive to me," Diane Weikert says of the man she married. "In fact, there was very little sexual attraction on either side. That was one of the reasons I wanted to marry him. I associated sexual magnetism with the wrong guys, like Carl, my high-school boyfriend."

When Mike DiStefano met Rowan Walsh on a blind date, he had finished medical school and was about to begin his internship. "It wasn't really a physical attraction," Mike says.

"After what I had been through: the terrible feelings of being taken and a very bad year of depression that followed, I was attracted to Rowan because she seemed like a very honest, genuine person. You knew where you were with her at all times. From the beginning, I couldn't imagine her being deceptive or deceitful. That was the initial attraction.

"I also knew that I had built up such a barrier that I couldn't ever have a relationship with a woman in which I could get as emotionally involved as I was with Terry, in which I had felt so vulnerable.

"With Rowan," Mike says, "I felt in control all the time. And that was very comfortable for me. I also perceived her to be a good person, and that she would be a good mother—both of which proved to be true. She was also a very classy woman. She had all the social graces that I lacked and wanted to learn.

"I was twenty-eight," Mike recalls. "I felt like I was getting old, that I should be getting married. I was about to start my practice, so I knew I would be in a financial situation shortly where a family wouldn't be a worry."

For three years before she met Mike DiStefano, Rowan Walsh had gone out with a young man who seemed to be an eternal student.

"I was really in love with him," Rowan says, "but I just thought he was getting nowhere. I was afraid I'd be working as a nurse for the rest of my life to support us.

"I didn't see nursing as a lifelong career, no way. I wanted to quit and get on with my life. Have babies. That was really the reason I'd gone into nursing anyway.

"When I met Mike, I was immediately attracted to his stability. That was the main thing, he was solid. And ambitious. Boy, was he ambitious!"

We described our mate (real or ideal) in the voice and language not of the lover, but of the marriage broker.

"I had a combination ideal woman in mind," Dan Ross says. "One part was an image created by the movies. She would be a Jeanne Crain type, the girl next door, but more attractive— WASPy—that whole thing. I also wanted someone who would devote herself entirely to my needs and interests.

"When I was in college, I thought I should try to get away from tradition-bound women. But the creative ones I crossed were very neurotic. The effort to escape their own cultural bonds was driving them crazy. They didn't give me the sense of security I got from more conventional women.

The spring of Dan Ross' first year in law school, he and a friend went down to Fort Lauderdale. "The minute we arrived," Dan recalls, "the motelkeeper says, 'If you guys promise to behave, I have two nice Jewish girls for you. I promised their parents I would introduce them to some nice boys, so you've got to promise to be nice.' So we promised," Dan says. "It turned out they were in the room next door. Two girls from Barnard."

"One of the girls was my wife's roommate. It never got serious with us. So, one weekend when she went home for a wedding, she fixed me up with Joan.

"That's one of my wife's favorite jokes. No Barnard girl ever threw away a good man. He always got passed along to a friend.

"Joan wasn't from a wealthy family, but coming from Westchester she was the right image for me. We started going out the summer after her sophomore year. I was kind of an exotic figure to her. I was a veteran. I was interested in ballet, theater, and art. The kinds of Columbia guys she had been dating didn't take her to museums. She also thought I was very experienced sexually, which I definitely wasn't.

"The role developments were excellent on both sides. In fact, I knew on the second date I was going to marry her. It was obvious she'd made up her mind. She wanted to marry me. I had already decided we would wait until she had finished college and I was through with law school. My schedule matched her family's expectation of when she should be married, so it was very traditional in this way, too.

"I felt that Joan would go down very well with my parents. I was sure they would love her and they did. She's a terrific person. I've had very good luck in that regard.

"Well, maybe it wasn't entirely luck," Dan concedes. "What got through my filtering system were the things I felt to be acceptable about Joan on a long-term basis. I knew that she would be a good adjunct to the life of a tax lawyer in New York commuting to suburbia. That was the life she had grown up with. It was the life she wanted to replicate. In terms of my domestic ideal woman, as opposed to my artistic one, I found the right person."

The Found Generation was the way David Riesman ironically described the reasonable, unromantic young men who emerged,

in their own words, from a national sample of the class of 1955.[2]
In marked contrast to his own depression class of 1931, ambitious, adventurous, and unsettled, for these younger men, Riesman noted, "the girl they are to marry is already picked out in
fact or fancy, and the style of life the family will lead is fore-
shadowed with equal clarity." Appearing to "highlight a norm,"
a future lawyer from Princeton declares:

> "I'll belong to all the associations you can think of—Elks,
> VFWs, Boy Scouts, and Boys Clubs, YMCA, American Legion,
> etc. It will keep me away from home a lot. But my wife [a
> 'purely hypothetical wife,' Riesman reminds us] won't mind.
> She'll be vivacious and easy with people and she will belong to
> everything in sight, too—especially the League of Women
> Voters."

And a classmate of this organization man-to-be harbored a
still clearer image of the sort of girl he wanted:

> "She will be the Grace Kelly, camel's hair coat type. Feet on
> the ground and not an empty shell or fake. Although an Ivy
> League type, she will also be centered in the home, a house-
> wife. Perhaps at forty-five, with the children grown up, she
> will go in for hospital work. . . . And improving herself cul-
> turally and thus bringing a deeper sense of culture into our
> home will be one of her main interests in fifteen years."

Will girls that "good," Riesman wondered, be satisfied with dul-
lards like these? (After all, Grace Kelly had a career and married
a prince.)

AWOL from prep school, Holden Caulfield in *The Catcher in
the Rye* has similar thoughts as he watches "millions of girls"
waiting for their dates under the clock at the Biltmore:

> "You kept wondering what the hell would *happen* to all of
> them. When they got out of school and college, I mean. You
> figured most of them would marry dopey guys. Guys that al-
> ways talk about how many miles they get to a gallon in their
> goddamn cars. Guys that get sore and childish as hell if you

beat them at golf, or even just some stupid game like ping pong. Guys that are very mean. Guys that never read books. Guys that are very boring.[3]

The fictional Holden Caulfield and the real David Riesman were both right and both wrong. As other surveys showed,[4] most girls wanted to marry lads just like these, along with the lives they had neatly planned—right down to knowing how many miles to the gallon he got in his new car. And no effort was spared to conform to his image of the ideal woman.

In earlier centuries, marriages were arranged by families, often with the help of a go-between. Marriage brokers negotiated with the economic and social counters of both parties: the dowry of the bride, the social standing of her suitor. As bourgeois society became more mobile and young people were expected to "make their own way in the world," "his" prospects, "her" beauty or household arts were factored in with greater weight.

In America by the middle of the twentieth century, parents as well as marriage brokers had all but disappeared from this process. Young people themselves assumed both roles. As a popular ad of the period promised, we eliminated the middle man, becoming expert packagers of the self, artful designers of our own desirability, and astute analysts of "mate potential." Like the brokers of old, we took it for granted that marriage was a serious business in which irrational passion had no place. We internalized our elders' expectations and values (along with their anxieties) perfectly. Surveying the (first) marriages of my friends and of the men and women in this book, I found that none made "unsuitable" matches. A difference in religion was the most daring declaration of independence in our choice of spouse. As such, it was the one guarantee of parental distress. Depending on the class and religion of the elders concerned, the reactions ranged from stiff upper lip to nervous breakdown.

"The one thing I could never have faced telling my parents," Carol Cornwell says, "is that I was going to marry a Catholic or a Jew."

When Sue Baker told her parents, the summer after sophomore year in college, that she and Bob Hodges were planning to be married at Christmas, they were even more unhappy than she thought they would be.

"They were distressed about my getting married before I finished school," Sue recalls. "They were afraid I wouldn't graduate. But that was nothing compared to the way they reacted to my marrying a Catholic—and converting! I'd never seen either of them so upset. There was very strong anti-Catholic feeling in the Midwest when I was growing up.

The difference in religion that parents predicted ominously would "cause troubles" later, sometimes did. But most of the dissolved marriages of my contemporaries didn't need institutional solvents. (Indeed, young people who married outside their religion were probably better armed against potential problems than other couples.) The marriage broker's ideal listing would prove to have low trade-in value by the time the self-fulfillment ethos of the sixties and seventies—christened the Culture of Narcissism—arrived. Our juniors, the "me generation," caused many of us to ask, What am I doing with you?

About his first wife Dick Robertson says, "I was going with her, I was pinned to her, and I married her. She was medium pretty, medium smart, and she came from a nice family. I think it impressed me that even her grandparents had been to college."

It's hard for Dick to talk about his first wife in a more personal way, "because we weren't at all intimate—ever, not sexually or emotionally. Not the way I am with my present wife or even the way I've been with other women in between.

"We never talked about anything personal. Not even everyday kinds of feelings." Dick doesn't hesitate to blame this on the fifties male of the species. "That's the way we all were then and mostly still are," he admits.

"It was pretty much me Tarzan, you Jane."

In her marriage-broker days, Pat Carroll Brewster Catania says, she would never even have considered Philip Catania, now her husband of one year. An Italian-American boy from a nondescript college? Out of the question. In 1953, at her proper Catholic women's college, "every single girl" may not have been as "blond and pretty" as Pat remembers her classmates, but almost every single girl wanted to marry an Ivy League WASP or a Kennedy.

After spending her junior year in Paris, Pat never went back to school. "It was just too boring." Instead, she went to secretarial school at home for six months, moved to New York "with a friend my parents thought was a safe roommate," and found the "dreamy" job filled by a rapid turnover of thousands of our contemporaries—editorial secretary at a weekly news magazine with "the promise of promotion to researcher."

"I had a wonderful year," Pat says. "I went out with lots of people. Then I met Lane. We were married six months later."

T. Lane Brewster III narrowed the choices, Pat says. "He was only thirty and already a vice president of his company. He'd gone to Yale, he'd been in the Navy. The whole education and career-path thing was all-important to me then. Especially the stable corporate track. Daddy's business had been so volatile, I didn't ever want to marry anyone who worked for himself. A job with a big concern was a 'must' for me.

"I wasn't one bit of a risk-taker in those days. Lane was a no-risk choice. Plus he seemed like a nice person, and he had nice friends.

"Lane and I broke up for two months before we finally got engaged. He just said, 'I'm not ready to get married.' In those days, there was nowhere else for a relationship to go. You were either getting married or you weren't.

"Then one day, he called up, invited me to dinner.

"During the time I wasn't seeing him, I'd felt so rejected. When he reappeared, I was vindicated."

Pat knew in advance the agenda for the dinner: an act of contrition followed by a marriage proposal. She did what all of us did in those days to mark so momentous an occasion. She bought a new dress.

"And let me tell you, it was quite an outfit," Pat recalls. "It was the fanciest cocktail dress I'd ever owned—a gold brocade sheath, with a scoop neck.

"I was making about eighty dollars a week then and that dress cost more than a week's pay. I also had my hair 'done.' I don't think I've had my hair done in twenty years.

"A lot of thought and expense," Pat says, "went into that dinner date."

Intermarriage was not an obstacle for Pat and Lane. "If anything," Pat says, "my Catholicism was a source of reassurance. Lane hadn't been brought up with any religion at all. My faith gave him a sense of stability, he said. He liked the idea of his children having the security of a highly structured religion. Later on, when our marriage was falling apart, Lane said he was sure that my being Catholic meant I could never leave him.

"We never discussed personal problems. I had no idea that Lane had a really terrible childhood. Both his parents were alcoholics. His father had died of cirrhosis of the liver at forty-six. His grandmother, who lived with them, was a morphine addict.

"We had just become engaged," Pat recalls, "when we went to a performance of O'Neill's *Long Day's Journey Into Night*. Lane said afterwards that the family on stage was 'quite a bit' like his own. I was appalled. But I didn't pursue it. In those days, you just didn't talk about things like that."

If they had talked about it, Pat says, she would have revealed that her family were no strangers to alcoholism either. "They weren't totally incapacitated like Lane's parents, but I could certainly have understood all the problems."

Philip Catania didn't marry until he was thirty. "You would have thought I'd have done better, waiting that long," he says wryly.

"I liked her a lot," he says of his first wife. "Virginia matched the image I had in my mind of what I thought I wanted: attractive, bright, a doer. She was the top secretary in a big state agency. But it was obvious she had more ambition than that. And in fact, she's gone on to become a big success in private management. Even then, it was clear she wasn't just looking to find the right guy and give up everything."

Phil readily admits that he was also attracted by what he knew of his wife's family background. She was Irish Catholic, and her father, Phil gathered, was a successful neurologist. "For an Italian-American boy whose father was a dentist, that was already two giant steps up.

"I didn't discover until the engagement dinner when I went to Chicago to meet her family for the first time, that her father had to be wheeled in for the occasion. He hadn't lived at home for ten years. He hadn't supported the family—six sisters and a brother. God knows how they managed. By that point, he was barely supporting himself. He was too alcoholic to have much of a practice."

There have always been skeletons and dirty linen in family closets: alcoholic fathers, crazy mothers, siblings who were "a little off," "not all there." In the fifties climate of normalcy, we were bombarded as never before with images of happy, smiling families—busy consuming, in endless advertisements, or having good clean fun together, as in *Leave It to Beaver* or *Father Knows Best*. Families with problems became nightmares of shame.

In the thirties, the depression caused such massive social dislocation that individual family abnormalities were less private. Unemployment, abrupt changes in finance and status, alcoholism, and desertion were commonplaces of family life, reaching well up into the middle classes and causing less stigma than would be the case again until the therapeutic seventies.

Wartime provided still more plausible explanation for family troubles. With fathers commonly absent, women working in

nontraditional jobs, mothers and children moving "back home"
with grandparents, it became hard to remember what a "normal"
family looked like.

A friend once reflected that her mother's "melancholy," which
kept her parent in a darkened bedroom for most of her childhood,
was always explained by worry about Daddy, serving overseas.
A severely depressed woman, her incapacity as a mother was excused by "exceptional" circumstances. Individual pathology could
be projected on the wide screen of collective crisis.

With the "back to normalcy" movement, the abnormal was
atomized—once again a family affair to be disguised, hidden, or
denied. As college classmates became close friends, I heard sagas
of life at home that were Gothic horror stories. Behind the hedges
and driveways of upper-middle-class suburbia were tragedies of
madness, suicide, and—most prevalent of all—chronic and severe
alcoholism. In the last decades, the pathology in the lives of
"ordinary people" has become nightly television viewing. In 1954
"no one," as Pat Catania says, "talked about these things."

The real revelation for me was the role played by children in
the comedy of keeping up appearances. Many of my new friends
had been pressed into service early as happy smiling fronts, emis-
saries of family normalcy, cheerful proof that "nothing was really
wrong" at the Joneses.

Middle-class respectability has always required revised scripts
of family life. But with postwar mobility—geographic as well as
social—the nuclear family became the only actors on stage. In the
new communities to which many of our contemporaries moved in
their high-school years (most often, a change that signaled moving up), the burden of performance fell on them, the younger
members of the family, to act as ambassadors, bearing letters
patent of conformity to the outside world.

These overburdened adolescents went off to college with a
mixture of relief and guilt (the latter heaviest if younger siblings
were left at home). Dread surfaced as vacations approached. "It's

face-the-music-time again," a friend announced grimly, as she packed for a stressful and alcohol-soaked family Christmas.

Until the ring was on the finger, facing the music together would have been unthinkable. (Marriage, we thought, was going to be an escape from the "family romance"—as Freud called it— not its replication.)

It wasn't only, or even primarily, the outside world from whom family secrets had to be kept hidden. Any "serious" interest among the opposite sex would be the last to see any warts that didn't show.

"My friends all knew more about me than Tom ever did," Diane Weikert says. "Telling a boy anything negative was just too risky."

That was our saddest assumption: No one would want us without a Norman Rockwell family; with "troubles," personal or parental. It would never have occurred to most of us that the one we planned to spend our lives with should also be an ally, an advocate, a friend. (That might magically happen after the wedding ceremony; the marriage broker would tactfully disappear offstage, along with all our wariness and distrust.)

Meanwhile, before you got to the altar, before the ring was on the finger, Low Romantic was the style. With the intense fear of appearing ridiculous, of venturing too much too soon, the currency of exchange between lovers was the silvery coin of "cool"; playful irony, verbal games and puzzles.

Low Romantic style was send-ups and put-downs—the core of fifties humor. Long pointless stories and anecdotes were exchanged that functioned like Zen parables. (With close friends, much time was spent in deciphering these cryptograms—letters written in invisible ink between the lines, orphic utterances.)

Fifties men and women still recognize this style of discourse from a single phrase. We are likely to connect to one another in the wake of words, or through sounds inaudible to all but our own species, like the squeak of bats.

"Don't tip your mitt"—writer Helen Lawrenson's advice to an earlier generation of girls—would have been superfluous counsel to either sex among our contemporaies. Nobody I ever knew tipped his or her mitt.

"It was a beautiful Sunday, late in the spring of sophomore year," Carol Cornwell remembers. "I was sitting on the grass under a tree, across from my dorm.

"Don and I were still going out, but we were also dating other people. In the last few months, though, he had made it clear he wasn't happy with this arrangement. I wasn't seriously interested in anyone else. I was just having fun.

"But suddenly, I thought, I might as well go back to Don. Because otherwise I wouldn't get married. I wouldn't find anyone else. Nobody would want me."

In the fall, "as soon as Don got his fraternity pin, we were pinned. We announced our engagement the summer before senior year and we were married three weeks after graduation—the exact same schedule as everyone else.

"It was really sad," she says. "Because there were none of the wonderfully positive reasons for wanting to be together. It was all kind of negative."

"A flight from the negative"[5] was precisely the way one observer described the rush for the chapel on graduation. Defining "negative" as the vacuum he sensed in young people, William Graham Cole, Professor of Religion at Williams College, found the typical student at his New England men's college during the fifties has "no heroes, embraces no causes, professes no creeds, displays no great passions; he has no faith in yesterday's ideals or ideologies and no faith in the future either. Pursuit of success," Cole observed, "is apt to be called the rat race. Any remaining sense of meaningfulness is in marriage and a home."

Other observers were struck by the anxiety that shadowed ever-earlier marriages, nervous mergers that seemed fueled by fear rather than love.

Fear was the continuum between the Great Saturday Night Terror and the "exact same schedule" followed by millions of young people: going steady, getting pinned, engaged, and married in that "inevitable" sequence. And fear turned us into cautious marriage brokers, experts at "risk avoidance," armed with models, "types," C.V.'s of our prospective mates.

Once out of college (even if that meant graduate school), real solitude—not just the dread of being left out—threatened.

On our second date, over dessert in a Greek restaurant in Boston, a melancholy first-year law student proposed to me. Caught with a mouthful of baklava, I was able to parry my shock for a few moments by chewing vigorously.

"Why do you want to marry me?" I asked.

"I'm lonely," he said, with commendable lack of hypocrisy, adding, as a cautious afterthought, "and you *seem* to be a very nice person."

Marriage was the most practical and immediate solution to loneliness. As loss of the group loomed with the end of schooling, we sought urgently to fill the vacuum of companionship. As part of a couple (soon to be a family), we became an instant "us."

Advance word of the outside world, moreover, suggested that it wasn't a place where you would want to spend much time alone.

The only escape from the daily rat race, young men about to matriculate in real life were informed, was the evening commuter train. Young working women found that if you had missed Mr. Right in college, the rats were harder to avoid. In *The Best of Everything*, Rona Jaffe follows the uneasy fortunes of Caroline Bender (Radcliffe, 1952) and her friends, roommates, and co-workers, as they negotiate the snares of sex and career in the big city. Married or not, the rogues' gallery of men in their lives would have any young single woman of sound mind on a fast train to Scarsdale.

A girl who doesn't settle for the real estate salesman back home in Colorado or the dull young lawyer who will never forget birthdays or anniversaries (the same seniors whose blueprinted futures so depressed David Riesman) can look forward to abandonment, abortion, alcoholism, madness, and suicide (in alphabetical order.) Mr. Right was certainly dead, as Jaffe tells us in a subsequent novel.

Good popular fiction, more than great art, gives us the texture of its time and place. The people are plastic, but the period—its values and style—lives. In Jaffe's world of New York City in the 1950s, we are centuries away from Yuppie couples, jogging along on an equal footing: successful, self-respecting young women and their fast-track "live-ins." Men in fifties novels—always richer, older, powerful, or socially prominent, cynical seducers, or married crybabies—hold all the chips; women have none. Women's jobs (like most of ours were) are so marginal they might as well have "office temporary" signs on their desks. Jaffe's heroines are all waiting for Lane Brewster III, Pat Carroll's onetime corporate Galahad, to rescue them from the sordid world of work. Those who survive the jungle are more than ready to trade in tuna fish on whole wheat (hidden in the sprigged Bonwit Teller shopping bag and munched at the desk) for peanut butter and jelly on Wonder Bread, eaten in the kitchen with the kids.

Just like all of us.

Few young people saw life experience as a prerequisite for becoming husbands, wives, and parents.

Steadily, through the fifties, the age of Americans at first marriage kept dropping, to reach the lowest point in our history. And for the first time, there was a dramatic rise in the number of teenagers getting married.[6]

Worrying the problem, "Why They Can't Wait To Wed" and "Marrying In Haste in College," anthropologist Margaret Mead went back to another generation's anxieties to explain the phenomenon.

"Parents," she declared, "fear that the present uneasy peace time will not last, that depression or war will overtake their children as it overtook them. They push their children at ever younger ages, in Little Leagues or Eighth Grade proms, to act out . . . the adult dreams that may be interrupted . . ." until finally, Mead concluded, in a sharp note of accusation, "they consent, connive, and plan toward the earliest marriages for both sons and daughters."[7]

Describing a "New Barbarism" that virtually "forced" young people to marry early, Mead charted a sinister progression that began with mothers who worried about kids not dating in high school and continued with spineless college administrators who apologized for not having enough housing for married students (instead of expelling them, as in the good old days). She added peer pressure that stamped a girl as a man's personal possession after a few dates, and ended with employers and their demonstrated preference for a trainee who came equipped with a wife and at least one child, along with a fresh B.A.[8]

A Masculine Mystique was abroad in the land. If its young male victims were not altogether prevented from attaining their "full human growth and maturity," as Friedan claimed the female version had done to women, the expectations were equally unyielding. Marriage separated the men from the boys. The role of husband, father, and provider combined to create the only acceptable definition of manhood in America. A normal clean-cut All-American adult male (the only kind any employer wanted) was synonomous with the "man of the family."

White, middle class, and mainstream, the Masculine Mystique had nothing to do with "macho"—that later borrowing from another culture and class. Before the Age of Aquarius, men's sexuality in America was as strictly linked to marriage and fatherhood as women's was defined by the role of wife and mother. Only "immature" men (that is, boys) were allowed to be creatures of swinish and uncontrollable lust, impulses that in most other cultures were ascribed to *all* men. Here, male as well as female sexual needs, it was assumed, could be contained by the conjugal bed. The sooner a young man settled into one, the better. Once wed, the marriage manuals promised, he became a happier, more productive employee. At the same time, he would avoid acquiring those "unconventional tastes" against which they warned.

Only in America in the early 1950s could the findings of the first Kinsey Report have created such shock waves, revealing that slightly more than one-half of American men had been unfaithful husbands.[9] In 1925, the college-educated public would have viewed Kinsey and his researchers as victims of cultural lag, just catching up with the changed mores of the Jazz Age. By 1950 the middle-class ethos had so enveloped public discourse that husbands who strayed (even once, like most of Kinsey's sample) were considered a danger to public morals.

Traditionally, concern had focused on the problem of "female" sexuality; either it didn't exist or, if it did, early domestication was the solution. Containment of male sexuality, in the form of social pressure for the transition from youth to manhood to take place within marriage, was something new. One historian has linked anxiety about nuclear attack to a vision of postatomic sexual anarchy.[10] If we couldn't contain the Communists or control the Bomb, at least we could yoke the libidinous impulses of the young to the establishment of peaceful family life.

In 1951 the *Journal of Social Hygiene* published an article on the dangers of atomic attack and what to do about them. The author, Dr. Charles Walter Clarke, a Harvard physician and executive director of the American Social Hygiene Association, described the "worst scenario" of nuclear holocaust: sexual chaos.

Once the constraints of "normal family and community life had broken down," he predicted, "there would develop among many people, especially youths . . . the reckless psychological state often seen following great disaster. Under such conditions, moral standards would relax and promiscuity would increase." And Dr. Clarke went on to urge "strict policing . . . vigorous repression of prostitution and measures to discourage promiscuity, drunkenness and disorder."[11]

Maiming, death, genetic suicide, destruction, and nuclear winter were nothing as compared to the untrammeled sexuality the Bomb would unleash.

More than a haven in a heartless world, the family was the only fortress against sexual anarchy, the Maginot Line protecting us from mass orgies and meaningless sex. The more illegal, immoral, or unobtainable unmarried sex became—for young men as well as women—the easier it was to encourage early family formation.

"There were always a couple of fraternity brothers who got married sophomore year," recalls Dick Robertson. "We used to sit around and think, my God, they can do it every night, *right in their own room*. We were so envious, we couldn't stand it."

Unmarried pledges also envied their wedded brothers for another kind of status.

"Being married gave them instant maturity even though they were the same age as the rest of us. That was *the* desirable thing in the fifties," Dick says, "the best anybody could say or think about you was that you were mature."

"When that clock started running down—just like a basketball game," as Dick said, "it was time to finish with that kid stuff and get married."

Engaged by the spring of senior year, along with his entire pledge class, married that summer, Dick Robertson found, in his first job as a management trainee in the fall of 1959, "there wasn't an unmarried male to be seen anywhere. All I was meeting was other guys in my same situation."

"The bachelor's freedom is a vanishing theme," David Riesman observed mournfully, comparing his own Harvard class of 1931 with their counterparts across the nation in 1955.[12] Indeed, postcollegiate bachelors were disappearing faster than the bald eagle, with the culture cheering on their extinction.

Escape from freedom,* fear, or solitude; a flight from the negative or rush down the aisle, we plighted our troths in millions and
millions of half-carat diamonds. Acting as our own brokers, we
cautiously invested in low-risk futures. Real love was for high
rollers, those with emotional capital to spare. Passionate love
stories, especially those that ended happily, seemed more romantic
than a movie.

One friend fell in love with his future wife watching her shop-
lift at the student coop in a Midwestern college town. Dutiful and
conscientious, the classic nice Jewish boy, he had never failed to
hand his homework in on time, to put in his two hours of practice
on the violin. The instant he saw the blonde cornfed madonna,
placidly slipping books and records under her voluminous poncho
—*stealing*—he was seized with passion.

I think of my friend's transfixing vision of his beloved (now
his wife of thirty years) as a peculiarly fifties scenario of love at
first sight. To one who accepted authority so unquestioningly, a
young woman shoplifting appeared an avenging angel of liberation. A decade later, one-third of the browsers in that store would
be given to the same activity, genially dubbed the "five finger
discount" by students of the sixties.

"Steal This Book," Abbie Hoffman enjoined potential readers in
1974.** His agenda of "culture to the people" is long since passé.
Today theft and murder, not revolution, are the stuff of everyday
life; criminal acts too trivial to trigger romantic passion.

"She was coming down a staircase, and the moment I saw her, I
got this feeling."

When Paul Michaelides describes the first time he saw his wife
Elaine, his normally fluent phrases fail him. He is recaptured by

---

* The title of humanist psychoanalyst Erich Fromm's best-selling analysis of contemporary malaise. First published in 1946, it was widely read on college campuses throughout the 1950s.

** Hoffman himself is snugly back in the system, earning large lecture fees to "tell
it like it was" to college audiences.

that moment thirty years ago when he was struck speechless with love.

"It was a school dance, sophomore year. I had brought another girl and she was with a boy I thought was a wimp. And I said, What's an attractive girl like her doing with that kind of guy? The girl I was with was not a serious thing, so I cut in, as we used to do in those days," Paul says.

"I talked to her and she was bright and sparkly, energetic and clever and funny. I thought, Wow, what a girl!

"But I felt very comfortable with her, too, with no need to hide anything or be anything other than myself. She seemed so undemanding and unpretentious and understanding. She was articulate, too, in a very down-to-earth way.

"Very early on, I felt I could tell her about my disappointments, about anything that went wrong at school or at home. I didn't have to pretend, put on the kind of false facade I always felt you needed with other girls, where you had to be entertaining and witty or strong.

"From the beginning, I felt as though I could show her my weaknesses and tell her my worries—without ever being concerned that she would be critical or misunderstand.

"And I did. Virtually from that first conversation while we were dancing, I revealed more to her than I ever usually reveal or have since then—to anyone."

9
GETTING STARTED

As soon as the engagement was announced, the household was christened. Showers—the name so perfectly suggestive—invited friends to inundate the bride-to-be with presents for her new home. Now it was official. The couple had become a new unit of consumption: the family.

With its miniature, umbrella-decorated invitation, the engagement shower was a uniquely American tradition that seems to have originated in the early years of the century. But as an occasion for gift giving by the bride's women friends and relations, its focus shifted significantly in post-war America.

In the 1920s the star of the shower was the bride, her trousseau the traditional theme of the event. My mother, her sisters, and their friends spent months stitching, appliquéing, and embroidering for each other nightgowns and peignoirs of satin and silk chiffon.

By the 1950s shower invitations specified "kitchen" or "bath." No more lolling about in maribou-trimmed bedjackets. Well before the wedding, the bride had already become a housewife. Madison Avenue troubadours turned "labor-saving devices" into the stuff of lyric poetry.

"For a wedding present, I'm getting you a deep freeze or an electric washer or any other major appliance you want," pledges Beauregard (Don Murray) the innocent rancher as he woos Chérie, the chanteuse with a past (Marilyn Monroe) in the film *Bus Stop* (1956).

Limiting shower presents to the kitchen (the most popular among my friends) or bath reflected the new bride's all-consuming concern for those areas of the house associated with the comfort, well-being, and health of her family. (The nursery had its own "blessed event." Stork-decorated invitations would shortly announce the baby shower.)

Whether a restaurant lunch given by coworkers or a tea, shower ritual dictated "women only." If the occasion was at the end of the afternoon, the finale featured a clothed version of the girl who leaps from a cake at the stag party—the bridegroom-to-be appeared! In fact, his presence was functional. A stalwart male— preferably with a car—was needed to bear away the loot.

Monogram madness, along with the mania for "sets" (not just the traditional silver, china, and crystal but everything else— Tupperware, Revereware, casseroles, and Dutch ovens—had to match) reached their frenzied height in fifties wedding presents.

From our obsession with initials, it was hard to avoid the suspicion that a generational identity crisis was under way. Every object in the new household that had space for three letters was monogrammed: ashtrays and table lighters, glasses and ice-buckets, silver photograph frames and leather ones, even disposables, like matchbook covers and paper cocktail napkins. Engaged friends often commented on the more—or less—pleasing monogram their new last initial would create.

In *Breakfast at Tiffany's* (1961) impoverished writer and kept man Paul Varjack (George Peppard) accompanies call girl Holly Golightly (Audrey Hepburn) to her favorite New York jeweler's. With only ten dollars to spend, he can find no present in the store to celebrate their budding romance. But wait! For well under that amount, the sympathetic salesman tells him, they will engrave

Holly's initials on Paul's prize ring from a Crackerjack box.
Tiffany's wasn't just playing Cupid. They knew that as soon as the
lovers stop selling their sexual favors to other people and opt for
middle-class marriage, they'll be back with wedding present lists,
ready for the monogramming orgy of all time.

When I ask the women who are my contemporaries about their
wedding presents, they usually disappear for a few moments.
Then, giggling, they return with white leather albums. Inside, the
lined pages are inscribed with the gift, the donor, and the date a
thank-you note was mailed.

What good girls we were! The "best little third graders in the
world," a friend says sourly.

Wedding gifts, as entered in those neat columns, reveal the
schizophrenia of middle-class domesticity in the fifties. All that
shiny silver mirrors us as a transitional generation, caught between
our parents' way of life and a new do-it-yourself ethos.

Even without the donors' column, the provenance of presents
is clear. Family friends and fathers' business associates sent gifts
that looked backward or in their own view, perhaps, forward to
our greater prosperity and the end of the "servant problem."
(Little did they know, we were to be a part of a new servant
problem: a horror of hired help, even when we could afford it.)

They gave us service plates in Spode or Wedgwood, designed
to be admired by dinner guests, then whisked away, replaced by
piping hot dishes waiting to receive food. Our shrimp cocktails
or melon balls, they hoped, would keep nicely chilled in footed
bowls with room for cracked ice. They sent julep glasses; silver
iced-tea spoons with heart-shaped bowls and handles that were
also straws; sterling or pewter candlesnuffers (I received four,
two from contemporaries).

Some of us wrote thank-you notes on our new monogrammed
"informals," then rushed back to the store to exchange the julep
glasses and candlesnuffers for double boilers and blankets. But
thousands of women used and enjoyed these reminders of a more
leisured past. If "gracious living" hadn't been part of their families'

style, they had fond memories of sorority teas and candlelight dinners. Service plates were icons of aspiration, of the way "things should be done."

After her husband's military service in the East, Sue and Bob Hodges moved "back home," into a Cape Cod colonial house in a Chicago suburb. "As soon as I got settled in," Sue says, "I gave several sit-down dinners every month. There would be four or five couples. The husbands were usually other young lawyers.

"One time I invited a younger colleague and his wife. He was just out of law school. The girl looked around my dining room and said: 'I don't believe this! It's just the way my mother entertains, the silver candlabra, the crystal, the damask, the beautiful china. I love it!'

"I couldn't have been more than four years older than she was, but those four years between the Class of Sixty-one and Sixty-five were the Big Divide. The way I did things told her I was part of our mothers' generation. And I am."

The ideal, if not the reality, of our mothers' generation was expressed by the most popular style of home furnishings for millions of young marrieds in postwar America: colonial Williamsburg.

Between 1946 and 1956, one economist calculated, the increase in single-family home ownership was greater than that in the entire previous century and a half of our history.[1] New householders needed a style of furnishing that could create out of still newer tract houses in raw subdivisions an instant all-American home. And John D. Rockefeller's recreation of an eighteenth-century Virginia town stood ready to provide it.

"This epoch of gracious living," promised the catalog of "authentic" Williamsburg reproductions, "is one of our richest heritages from our colonial past. Besides existing to see and enjoy in Colonial Williamsburg today, its objects serve also as an inspiration in planning our future homes."[2]

As inspiration, artifacts of our common past found an eager market. An American eagle on the door, a Queen Anne wing chair in the living room, and particularly the warm colors—"Raleigh Tavern Peach," "Kings Arms' Rose"—and cozy patterns of the licensed paint and fabrics created the feeling of historical roots for uprooted young families.

By the mid-1950s, countless American housewives, notes one historian, "had painstakingly reproduced the Brush-Everard House of Williamsburg on small self-contained lots twenty-seven miles from Times Square or the Loop."[3]

Unlike dinner in the Brush-Everard House in 1756, when the Tidewater planters were waited on by slaves or indentured servants, gracious living 1950s-style involved only one domestic—the "wife-servant," as John Kenneth Galbraith described us.

Manufacturers lost no time in supplying the needs created by home entertainment with a staff of one, wives who were going to be doing quick-change acts: from cook, butler, maid, busboy back to gracious hostess—"Lady Bellamy one minute, Ruby the scullery maid the next,"[4] as one woman subsequently described herself.

As fifties and early sixties brides, we received at least one appliance to keep food hot. There were plate warmers and bun warmers, hot trays and tables, along with the traditional chafing dish for our favored buffet suppers. (My chafing dish was used only once. I overfilled the heater with kerosene, causing it to overflow and set the tablecloth on fire.) Especially welcome was the oven-to-tableware that replaced silver serving dishes once handed round by help.

The do-it-yourself ethos of the fifties did not exclude men. Electric carving knives aided the new head of the house in flawless public performances of slicing. Hosts played bartender, sometimes in finished basements, at real bars complete with matching stools and elaborate equipment for shaving ice and making exotic drinks. (When asked what she wanted for a wedding gift, one friend confided that her husband needed a glass froster for his frozen daiquiris.) In the film *Diner*, set in Baltimore in 1961, one of the young protagonists' fathers proudly tends a particularly lavish basement bar. High on the list of coveted fifties "collectibles" today are all the accessories of serious drinking at home, from chrome-trimmed bar and chairs to ice buckets and glamorously streamlined cocktail shakers and martini pitchers.*

Behind the scenes, the man of the house played a role analogous to the "wife-servant"; he was "Mr. Fix-it."

In the fifties, home improvement, with the owner doing the improving, was the prescribed weekend "relaxation" for millions of American men. Suspect was the male householder who did not boast a basement "shop" with workbench and imposing array of tools and hardware. Overnight, manufacturers who had once supplied "to the trade" only, added kits of prefabricated parts with instructions for the amateur contractor, plumber, and electrician. In 1954 statistics gatherers reported that "70 percent of all wallpaper was hung by novices, while some 11 million carpenters drilled, sawed or sanded 180 square miles of plywood with their 25 million power tools."[5]

While sipping the host's famous frozen daiquiris, guests were invited to admire his latest addition to the house, which might be as ambitious as an extra room or, at the least, bunk beds for the kids or a pair of lamps made from old vases.

Less utilitarian hobbies also flourished, especially when they were home-centered. Amateur photographers proliferated, and the householder who did not display the latest in lathes was likely to have built his own basement darkroom. Inspired by world leaders Winston Churchill and President Eisenhower, who were also Sunday painters, once doubtful artistic pursuits became acceptable for men. Nor were the less gifted left out. In 1952 the first painting-by-numbers kit was marketed—with enormous success.[6] Do-it-yourself had become a way of life.

"The most important signs of the way a society lives," historian

---

* As any viewer of the *Late Late Show* knows, most fifties cocktail accessories, like much of the furniture and even automobile chromework of the period, reflects 1940s designs that couldn't be manufactured during World War II.

Warren I. Susman observes, "are often the simplest, most ordinary artifacts of its culture."[7]

In a "system of signs," the barbecue grill is most significant to the culture of the fifties for what it has to tell us about the way millions of young families would live, about the way they would divide household chores by gender, separate "togetherness"—the new family credo—into rigidly assigned functions around the house, basement, patio, and yard.

"Doing his grill work," is Paul Michaelides' approving reaction to the vacationing father in our picture. Like Paul, he is automatically in charge of all outdoor cooking, seen as an extension of yard work. By the same token, the kitchen (with the exception of Sunday pancakes or other "specialties") is emphatically not Daddy's domain.

For most Americans married during our decade, wedding present lists included accessories for backyard or patio meals—sets of grilling implements, corn-on-the-cob holders, aluminum or plastic glasses and plates, divided into compartments to segregate potato chips from oozing catsup. And just as surely, this type of meal—the menu, setting, early hour, and conveniently unbreakable tableware—tells us that children—even very young children—were included.

The November after her graduation from the state university in 1961, Betts Cassill, then an assistant kindergarten teacher, met Sam Saunders, a fourth-year medical student. They were married in June, heading for California right after the wedding, where Sam's internship began two weeks later.

"As soon as we came back home from San Francisco," Betts recalls, "we moved into a development with mostly other young residents." And like most of their new neighbors, the Saunderses now had two children: eighteen-month-old Sam Jr. and Laura, five months old.

"We did lots of entertaining," Betts says, "because as young medical families, we didn't have the money to go out. The salaries were pitiful.

"But a mistake that we all made was to have babies right away," Betts says. "So you had to entertain in a way that allowed for bringing children. Nobody could afford sitters. We had potluck suppers. The hostess would do the main course—lasagna, chili, or something else very inexpensive. Someone else would bring chips and dips and dessert. And in warm weather, it was always backyard barbecue."

An urban equivalent of barbecue informality (but without toddlers) was the fondue supper. Most brides of the later fifties unwrapped at least one fondue set.

Like the barbecue, the fondue supper was a favored early Sunday evening form of entertainment, and it enjoyed some of the casual "icebreaker" appeal of the porch or patio meal, including come-as-you-are dress. One of my first friends to marry always invited singles for fondue. Retrieving a fellow guest's toast triangle from the depths of bubbling cheese had been the start of several big romances, she claimed. (An untidy eater as well as an intense talker, I rather dreaded fondue suppers. More than once, I had been enjoyably immersed in conversation, only to realize from my neighbor's agonized expression that I had dripped scalding Gruyère on his knee while flourishing my fork.)

It was in Cambridge, Massachusetts, in 1958 that I first encountered "young marrieds." In their freshly painted apartments or houses, the bright colors of the fondue pot, with its teak-handled forks, often coordinated with the other furnishings, whose sharp-edged look John Updike characterized as "half Door Store, half Design Research."

Invariably, there was an oiled teak dining room table and chairs. A matching storage unit housed books, records, and the hi-fi components, the relative merits of whose speakers and turntables and whose woofer and tweeter problems were a staple of Cambridge dinner table conversation.

It was the Design Research half of Updike's equation that fascinated me. My family's preferred style was haphazard High Victorian, heavy on the horsehair sofas and tufted chairs. The furnished Cambridge apartment that I shared with two friends— my first living quarters away from home that wasn't a dormitory —featured Depression Overstuffed, sagging and dun-colored with age. Our landlady's one concession to Fifties Contemporary was a kidney-shaped coffee table of laminated plastic. (Only an age as relentlessly rectilinear as this decade could use the terms *kidney-shaped* and *free-form* interchangeably.)

My introduction to the D/R Shop, located in a homey painted frame house on Brattle Street was, quite literally, a revelation. Furnishings and housewares—including the lowliest mixing bowl or colander—did not merely provide attractive amenities or tools for meal preparation, they prescribed a way of life whose philosophy was laid out by the architect-founder of Design Research, Benjamin Thompson, in 1953. Thompson had been the partner of German emigré architect Walter Gropius and Design Research had begun as a home furnishings outlet for the Architects' Collaborative, Gropius' Cambridge outpost.

"Art," Thompson said, "is *not* for particular people, but should be in everything you do—in cooking, and God knows, in the bread on the table, in the way everything is *done*."[8] Indeed, the furniture and housewares so invitingly displayed proclaimed that the owners—home-centered and sophisticated at the same time— did everything with art, using objects that were uniquely austere and colorful, amusing and "natural," practical and pleasing to the eye.

Despite their democratic, proudly machine-made image, all D/R wares were expensive. In keeping with the art-and-architecture aesthetic promulgated by Thompson, young marrieds "collected" these artifacts. Of still greater significance, they did so collaboratively. In Cambridge in the 1950s, couples, noted Jane Davison, "shopped together in D/R on snowy Saturday afternoons."

By replacing interior *decoration* with *design*, adding a dash of high tech spin with the word *research*, D/R rescued the inside of the house from the realm of the feminine. As an Americanized, off-the-peg version of Corbusier's "machine for living," its look was both rugged, suggestive of saunas and northern forests, and sleekly professional: The clean lines, "nubby" fabrics, and natural colors were closer to offices and boardroom than to parlor or boudoir. Indeed, the masculinization of "quality contemporary" design that began in the fifties and holds firm today was responsible for making home and office furnishings indistinguishable. Williamsburg reproductions continued to be bought by women. Real men felt at home browsing on Brattle Street.*

To the limits of their budget, couples tried for a total D/R look, summed up for me by a dinner party where the napkins, placemats, throw cushions, and hostess' dress were all made from the same Marimekko fabric.

Nothing expressed the philosophy of the D/R household—in all its contradictions—as eloquently as this tent-like garment. *Marimekko* (in Finnish, a "little girl's dress for Mary") was the label on smocks or loose coatdresses whose prints conveyed a child's vision of wildflowers, rocks, or fried eggs. On grown-up women, though, these dresses cut for big kindergartners hinted at eternal pregnancy, seen as a condition so "natural" and constant that the wearer would continue to bake her own bread, with all the art that Thompson urged, until the moment of each delivery. (In keeping with the implied fecundity of the household goddess, the aluminum flatware found on D/R tables, especially the forcepslike serving pieces, suggested obstetrical instruments that could be pressed into service for an emergency home delivery.)

Here was the heart of the paradox, located in those innocent Marimekko frocks and matching cushions; the chirpy, poppy-red casseroles; the commonsense coffee mugs.

* D/R sales, like those of all "contemporary" home furnishings,[9] were concentrated in the Northeast: Cambridge, New York, and California. Middle America—geographically as well as aesthetically—was Williamsburg country.

On the one hand, the D/R ethos implied a "rejection of feminine conservatism," noted architectural historian Jane Davison, "all those hope chests filled with damask, embroidered tea cloths, gold-rimmed floral china."[10] The inclusion of men in choices of all home furnishings promised an end to the segregation of women in an area once deemed beneath male interest. Thanks to Design Research, young middle-class husbands now pondered the relative merits of glass or wooden salad bowls. At the same time, for the perfectly integrated cook-mother-hostess-housekeeper, "full of art in everything she did," there was no escape.

"Slipcovered in the same fabric as my sofa pillow," Davison wrote of her Marimekko-shrouded years as a Cambridge home-maker, "was it any wonder that I found it increasingly difficult to distinguish between my house and myself?"

Pleasure was the heaviest burden of all. The joy these artifacts were supposed to confer on the tasks at hand was the best prescription for guilt since mother love. Wearing the most popular smock, a style the D/R catalogue christened "Gay Kitchen," a woman had better whistle while she worked.

And work she did. The young wives who now fed me were my college friends, newly married to law or B-school students, young architects or editors. My classmates worked as secretaries for the university or at publishing jobs in Boston. Women a few years older whom I visited, "brought round" by dates, had retired to motherhood. Drinks in hand, we tiptoed in to admire an infant sleeping under his D/R mobile, then to jolly a grumpy toddler sibling, allowed to socialize over cocktails before being stashed (Daddy's job) just before dinner was served.

Fondue suppers were the least of it. Most dinner parties were banquets, highly competitive displays of skill and particularly, of effort. For these gourmet cook-offs, no dish could be respectably served that required fewer than two days of preparation. Each meal involved a sequence of elaborate courses, marinated, poached, stuffed, and skewered. Eggplants were eviscerated to reappear as moussaka; quenelles began with a predawn trip to the

North End fishmarket. (Even husbands helped in the labor of boning, crushing, and pounding required by the sauce.) Ladyfingers for the charlotte had been made from scratch. There were silent agonies of suspense: would the aspic unmold, the soufflé rise?

Compliments to the cook factored in time devoted to the meal. ("Why, Liz, you must have spent days on this incredible [daube] [cassoulet] [galantine].") At which the wan and tottering young wife would croak: "Oh, I do it in stages over several nights, after the baby's asleep."

While the hostess wearily accepted tributes to her culinary prowess and stamina, the young husband displayed his newly acquired wine connoisseurship. Bargains were debated along with the merits of laying down a case of a local find. The fifties were the first era to see wine snobbery—a favored target of cartoonists of the period—trickle down to the middle classes. Next to the D/R wine rack, the Bordeaux breathed.

Immolation on the altar of gourmet cooking, as a preferred fifties form of martyrdom, owed little to the feminine mystique. Great chefs were as traditionally masculine as board chairmen. Virtuoso performances in the kitchen, moreover, turned loving wives and nurturing mothers into hollow-eyed ascetics or hysterical divas, shrieking over curdled hollandaise. (Some of my friends seemed close to the unhappy fate of Vatel, chef to Louis XIV, who committed suicide when he ruined the royal fish.)

"We can't go home yet, Douglas," I once heard a father explain to his querulous little boy, as both shivered in the park on a late Saturday afternoon in February. "Mommy's cooking."

Fathers who chose an untimely return over freezing to death or taking a toddler to an X-rated movie, risked an explosion of long-simmering wrath. The first arrivals at dinner parties were often greeted by quivers of static from the Big Fight, interrupted by the doorbell.

Why did so many nursing mothers and rush-hour wage slaves stand over stockpots until 2:00 A.M.? Display of cultural advan-

tages was one answer. We were the first generation since the 1920s
to be "exposed" (as the phrase of the period went) to travel and
study abroad. Like the posters we hung on our walls of the Matisse
chapel or the running of the bulls at Pamplona, the creation or
re-creation of foreign dishes was an exercise in nostalgia. As fifties
adolescents, our parents had been pleased to see us redeem the
isolation of the depression and war years. In record numbers we
took part in the Experiment in International Living and American
Field Service exchanges. Later, as college and graduate students,
we benefited from junior year abroad programs and Fulbright
grants. (Participants in government-sponsored programs also
functioned as Exhibit A in Democracy. Friendly, attractive, well-
fed American students were a Cold War message to countries "at
risk" of going Communist. If they stuck with Uncle Sam, their
kids might turn out like us!)

Those who felt confined by the sandbox or routine secretarial
jobs could express a stifled creativity in the kitchen. Motivational
psychologists, led by Dr. Ernst Dichter,[11] advised advertisers on
how to exploit the discontents of the overeducated housewife.
Creative and *professional* were the watchwords of campaigns to
sell household products to women who were to be addressed as
efficient managers and creative homemakers. The more demanding
and time-consuming the chore, the more "satisfaction" was
guaranteed.

Unlike diapering, vacuuming, or oven cleaning, however, classic
cuisine *is* an art as well as a highly rewarded profession, the
apprenticeship as arduous as dance or opera. We just happened to
be its first acolytes to hold other, full-time jobs. No advertiser or
Dr. Strangelove of motivational psychology would have dared
propose the "overtime" that so many of us volunteered in the
production of extraordinary meals.

After a grueling day as a buyer-trainee in Macy's, newly married
Kay Strong, Vassar '33, one of the heroines of Mary McCarthy's
novel *The Group* (1954), can't wait to try her husband's "company" recipe for chili con carne: "made with canned kidney beans,

Campbell's tomato soup, onions, and a half pound of hamburger; you served it over rice and it stretched for six people."

By 1961, the year I was married, it would have been hard to find a contemporary who admitted even to recognizing a bouillon cube. The quick-and-dirty approach was beyond disgrace, its banishment made official by one book published that same year: *Mastering the Art of French Cooking*, by Julia Child. High on our list for shower and wedding presents, my college generation made Mrs. Child an instant best-seller, soon providing her as well with a devoted television following.

Cookbooks have always been a staple requirement of the bride. Edwardian standbys, like the famed Mrs. Beeton, assumed that there would be someone "downstairs" to "do" for the young wife. Nonetheless, as middle-class matrons, her readers should know how to do it themselves, if only to train and evaluate the help.

Earlier American classics like Fannie Farmer, and then Irma S. Rombauer and Marion Rombauer Becker's *Joy of Cooking*, dealt with the reality of the servantless household. These writers took it for granted that, besides learning to make delicious, attractive meals, their readers both needed and wanted to save time and simplify food preparation.

Rombauer's commonsense manual, first published in 1943 (with ten million copies sold in the half-century since) never sinks to canned kidney beans and tomato soup expedients. Still, her recipes often include "Version II," a timesaving shortcut based on the original.

By the end of the next decade, however, gourmet cooking psychology assumed that the young urban working wife or suburban mother, alone at the range, would not want to skip a single step followed by four-star European restaurants employing large kitchen staffs.

She would also require similarly professional equipment. The *batterie de cuisine* in costly French cookware—stockpots to *bains-marie*—required by these recipes was another heavy entry on wedding present lists. Our new inventory also expanded and up-

graded in stylishness the housewares floor of every American
department store from the late 1950s on.

Julia Child and I were destined to part ways early. Late one
Friday night, I was removing some half-poached veal from a heavy
casserole. The next step as specified? Both the veal and casserole
were to be rinsed, the meat then returned to the casserole with the
strained stock.

Why, I asked myself suddenly, does it have to be rinsed? (Once
you start asking questions like that, you're halfway back to hamburger.) Inexorably, another question followed: Why am I doing
this? The ritualistic rinsing of the veal was my revelation. I
decided that ostracism was preferable to fetishism; no friends and
the *Late Late Show* to social life that found me sullenly swabbing
pots at 1:00 A.M.

Gradually all of us, we who gave "Julia" and Michael Field and
the *Larousse Gastronomique* to each other as wedding and shower
presents, abandoned fancy cooking. Couples divorced, women
went back to school or juggled demanding jobs and the needs of
still-young children. The very successful splurged on a caterer for
a flossy once-a-year dinner party. Mostly, we went to the movies
followed by a hamburger—eaten out.

For many of us, "Julia" figures as a relic of rueful fifties
nostalgia, one of the last pieces of evidence describing the way
we were. Laughing, my friends recall the long day spent making
the ladyfingers for charlotte Malakoff the way we remember the
bilious green bridesmaid dresses with matching cartwheel hats
(the *one* dress we'd wear again and again, the bride's mother
promised) and the evenings devoted to washing white gloves (and
the fresh pair we always kept in our desk drawer at the office—in
case of an unexpected invitation for a drink after work.)

Sometimes we still feed each other, but these occasions are no
longer carefully orchestrated evenings with "dinner partners" and
elaborate menus. "If you *promise* you won't cook," is a frequent

reply to invitations from friends who seem in danger of back-sliding.

Why did we do it, all that crazy cooking? is a question we still ponder. Guilt, I think, is one answer to the haute cuisine madness. Food is love. We would compensate for our deficiencies in the one by a pound of flesh mixed with the other.

Were we unloving mothers? Those who disliked being with young children could legitimately take refuge in the monastic isolation imposed by the creation of gastronomic marvels.

Or unlovable wives? To the marriage broker's list of attributes, we could add: "Superb cook: her puff pastry is famed the length of the Northeast corridor." Being proud of us should be enough. It was a shock to discover that food as a substitute for love didn't always work. When her husband leaves her for another woman, Rachael Samstat, heroine of Nora Ephron's novel *Heartburn* and a classic fifties compensatory cook, is more stunned than sad-dened: How could any man give up a woman whose peach pie is "infallible" (recipe follows)?

Guilt was also social—not as it would be in the later sixties, when having been born white and middle class made us part of every problem. Ours was the more diffuse guilt of having it too easy. Everything had been "handed" to us by parents and fellow-ships and plentiful jobs. By the late 1950s the rumbles of feminism already in the air were beginning to devalue the housewife's "unpaid" labor—as, indeed, all voluntarism came to be dis-paraged. Those who didn't work "outside the home" had the easy life of "kept" women. How could it be made harder?

Design Research and its art-of-living ethos was no more respon-sible for "displays of culinary emulation" (to paraphrase Thorsten Veblen), than was the culture at large. Compensatory over-cooking, moreover, afflicted a particular segment of the population vulnerable to its challenge: young wives living on either coast, in communities clustered around large urban centers. D/R merely followed the market. Still, "gracious living," colonial style, imposed fewer burdens on the overburdened 1950s homemaker than the modern art of living demanded by Design Research. There was no Williamsburg equivalent to Marimekko's "Gay Kitchen" smock; a housewife in Oak Park or Mission Hills who donned hoop skirt and mob cap to churn butter in her kitchen would have been deemed certifiably insane.

Without the charge that there be "art in everything you do—in cooking and God knows in the bread on the table," an authentic reproduction of a Georgian silver breadbasket might, with no shame to the hostess, hold Pepperidge Farm rolls.

PAYING BILLS AND HAVING BABIES

When Margaret Mead made the case against parents that they "consent, connive and plan toward the earliest marriages for both sons and daughters," her accusation was based on economics. Parental connivance in youthful marriages created an unprecedented phenomenon of the fifties: family subsidy of student households.

Traditionally, a young man waited to wed until he could afford to support a wife and children. Becoming a head of household was based on paying the bills. A wife's dowry or even income might help, but the bride's means did not absolve the bridegroom from establishing himself before he established a family.

In the America of the late 1940s, veterans who returned to marry and start families, with the help of federally guaranteed housing loans and the GI bill, set an example of "mature" student marriages. Families of the next college generation proved eager to take up the slack—they would subsidize "immature" ones. By the mid-1950s, "both sets of parents," noted Amherst College president Charles Cole, "were expected to help,"[1] first to establish, then to maintain undergraduate households, soon to expand from a couple to a family.

In the view of Mead and others, these inducements to play house corrupted the meaning of marriage as an adult responsibility. At the same time, they robbed young men and women of their "right" to a period of intellectual growth without domestic distractions. Past rules forbidding undergraduates to marry, Mead thought, were only in small part a legacy from the monastic tradition. Their real function was to protect that short-lived freedom from adult family cares—seen as inimical to the life of the mind.

Among my early-marrying friends, unions of undergraduate couples were rare. Girls either dropped out or transferred to their husbands' school or an institution nearby. The bridegroom, though, had usually graduated from college and was about to start work or professional school. Parental subsidy of these households was also an incentive for the young wife to complete her degree. Like Sue Hodges' parents, most of our families would have been unhappy to see us drop out of school—*not* because they expected for a moment that we would become another Dr. Margaret Mead. In case of another depression, in the event of divorce or widowhood, they wanted us to have the "insurance" of that piece of paper—the B.A. that by the late 1950s was already a minimum requirement for any kind of work.

"Don't have a baby right away!" was maternal advice friends often found enclosed with their monthly allowance check. When daughters listened, both parents continued to pay tuition, contributing room and board to the young household instead of the college bursar's office. When this counsel went unheeded, grandparental subsidies underwrote the baby boom.

Without help from home, few couples could afford the wife's "foregone income" as either student or mother. Babies were postponed only because young wives' wages were essential to maintain households where husbands studied instead of worked.

Thus came into being another economic phenomenon of fifties marriages. The elders of the tribe told a youth barely past adolescence that he became a man upon marriage. He was now encouraged to hasten this coming of age by doing what no self-respecting, able-bodied American male had ever been allowed to do before—be supported by his wife's paid labor.

In his depression Class of 1931, David Riesman recalls, most of his contemporaries married late for reason "of economic hazard"; many simply "did not want to be tied down; nor would it have occurred to us," he notes disapprovingly, "to have our wives support us through graduate school."[2]

Between wives and parents, the financial base of many fifties marriages was the altogether novel—indeed revolutionary— economic dependency of the male, whose "maturity" as head of the household might be underwritten by either or both his family and his bride.

When Paul Michaelides and Elaine Donald were married in June 1952, she had just turned twenty and had a brand-new A.A. in Child Psychology from the local junior college. Due to a "few years of floundering, helping to run the family hardware store, taking a few courses here and there," at twenty-one Paul was just starting his junior year at the state university.

A full-time student, majoring in business and economics, Paul was head of the student council and president of his fraternity.

"Elaine was working, and I was working. Ours was one of those self-supporting student marriages: no help from home and no scholarship money at this point.

"We had a little apartment—and I mean little," Paul says. "It was on the third floor, behind a dry cleaner. Really one room and a corridor that led to a bathroom that only had a toilet, not even a shower. That was basic living. Thirty-five dollars a month with our own furniture."

Through the windows of a comfortable book-lined study and TV room come summer sounds of splashing and laughter. Two of the Michaelides' visiting "middle kids"—Janet, a law student, and Rick, a chemical engineer—are having a predinner swim in the pool.

The sofa where he and I sit, Paul points out, was "our first real possession," a Hide-a-Bed that's been recovered too many times for him to remember. "That was our living room and our bedroom and our dining room.

"Elaine was a secretary. I did everything from selling suits in Robert Hall to reconditioning soda crates and working the night shift in a brewery.

"Through these piecemeal jobs, we managed to do OK. We lived on a very tight budget and a very tight schedule.

"It was quite a mix, having to study, work, and provide. Elaine was working and providing in a substantial way. She made more money than I did and enjoyed it. We were all over the lot as far as the calendar and time together went: there was very little.

"My parents never suggested that we wait. They saw marriage as a settling influence. And they liked Elaine very much. Her parents didn't really like me. My kind-of mixed heritage bothered them: the Greek and the Russian-Jewish. They were Scotch Presbyterians. They thought I was taking her away from the world she should be in. But as the kids started coming along, they decided we were a good family and a good example."

Elaine worked until their first child was born. Paul Jr. was planned to coincide with the end of his father's first year at the business school. By that time, "I had a grant-in-aid, and we had a real apartment in subsidized housing for married graduate students. It wasn't luxurious—not by today's standards—but at least it meant that Elaine could stop working."

In 1958 almost every typewriter in Cambridge was activated by a recent bride. After her regular office job ended for the day, she would more than likely be moonlighting, typing theses and term papers through the evening hours.

Whether she had dropped out of college to marry or rendered her English major of use in the real world by a stint at "Katie

Gibbs," women's wages helped pay the bills while husbands acquired degrees in business, law, and medicine.

I recall an evening during which a law student (male, of course) lamented the present debasement of his liberal arts degree: "Last spring at this time," he said tragically, "I was writing an honors thesis on T. S. Eliot. Now I have to think about a case where a guy is suing a radiator company."

A young wife commented that at least he got to think about the case. After her final semester of college, writing a thesis on Dostoevsky (in Russian) she was now typing letters for the law school dean.

We all laughed.

Starting out married, for most couples, was inseparable from beginning life as parents. High on the list of "lasts" for our generation: we were to be the last brides and grooms in "shotgun weddings."

As a high-school senior in the early 1980s, my daughter had never heard the term before. She found the concept to be as quaint a cultural artifact as the buttonhook or virginity before marriage. Since her birth, access to contraception and abortion ended unions based on irreversible pregnancy. Still harder to recapture are the attitudes of another era. The notion that, for a young man, any obligation attaches to paternity has something of the endearing sentimentality of a Victorian valentine. "They had to get married"—a phrase that to our generation was literally pregnant with meaning—requires considerable and detailed explanation today.

All of Cass Hunnicutt's fraternity brothers and his friends from home were marrying right after college. "I just didn't want to do that," Cass says. "I had a real desire to go and see and do. I've been called unusual in that way—then and now."

After his graduation in 1961, "there was a lost period in there," Cass recalls. "I just wandered. Spent a dull six months serving my country" and another six months, as he had agreed, working for his father, "being the worst boss's son you can imagine: chasin' girls, drinking, coming to work late, taking three-hour lunches." Then Cass decided to "strike out for the West—which included hanging out in New York, working for the World's Fair in Seattle, buying a wreck there for forty-five dollars and driving it down through Mexico to Nicaragua. After a year of wandering around, I went to Aspen, where I lived on a guy's sofa and skiied all winter."

"What was I looking for?" Cass ponders. "All the usual things: happiness, peace of mind, myself . . ."

"I came home that spring to find my future had been decided for me. Betsey, now my darling wife of twenty-two years, was expecting our first child."

Betsey was then "a girl I had dated on and off for two years when I was home. But our story goes way back. Her grandmother and mine had been in each other's wedding. My grandma had wet-nursed her uncle. In that generation there were several kids who thought they might get married. But it was the two of us who finally did.

"We had slept together, on and off, for a couple of years. There had never been an opportunity for her to conceive. But the one time it was possible for her to do it, she did.

"We had a crash three-week engagement. And as beautiful a wedding as our families could arrange with so little time.

"I don't see this as coincidence," Cass says. "It was something that was intended to be. My friends had even told me that Betsey was probably the person I was going to marry. She was someone who really understood me. She listened to my soul."

But he still wonders whether he would have married Betsey if she hadn't told him that night, driving back from a dance, that she was pregnant. "I'm not sure what would have moved me in that direction," he says. "I sure was afraid of everything about marriage—the responsibility but, even more, the kind of closeness where I could be hurt. I'd always looked on women as challenges or adversaries; I'd never had a woman as a friend. It was always so separate—boys and girls, parties and sex. I couldn't imagine it being any other way."

As soon as Cass and Betsey were married, they moved to San Francisco.

"We both have such huge families here, we felt very little in the way of individuality. We knew we had to get away. That was the deepest thing we had in common," Cass says. "Because, like millions of other couples, we got married to find out that we really didn't know each other at all. And suddenly it was just the two of us, with a third one on the way."

In 1956, the summer between her junior and senior years in college, Carol Cornwell worked in New York as an editorial assistant on a chemical trade magazine.

"It was the perfect job for me," Carol recalls. "As a Chemistry major with a minor in English, I loved rewriting and editing science articles, learning about the chemical industry, plus the excitement of getting out a weekly magazine.

"Then, in the middle of January, they wrote to me at college offering me the job of assistant editor. I was just thrilled. Everyone else was just starting to look for jobs, and I had the one job I wanted looking for me."

But Carol had to say no. "Because, in those days, of course, you went where the man's job was. The irony for me, though," Carol observes, "was that Don didn't even have a job offer yet. Still, when the editor in chief wrote to me, I couldn't very well write back, asking them to hold the job until we found out where we were going to be. As it happened, Don's corporate employers sent us to the wilds of upper New York State, so, I couldn't have taken the job, anyway."

Even if Don's first assignment with his company had left them in the New York area, Carol questions how long she would have remained a science editor. Adam was born thirteen months after their wedding, and "he was very much a planned baby.

"We discussed having children constantly before we were married. We each had just one sibling. Don's sister was ten years older, so he always felt like an only child.

"We wanted five children, and we had gone together for so long before we were married that we wanted to start a family fairly soon.

"But I think it was really me," Carol reflects. "I couldn't wait to have a baby."

"We were both interested in a large family," Paul Michaelides says. "All of our six kids were pretty much planned to happen within a period of eight years."

Nothing in Paul Michaelides' childhood—with all the vulnerability to hard times of his father, a laid-off printer who just managed to feed his family—would be conducive to an expansive view of the breadwinner role. Yet Paul claims he never worried about the "financial side" of clothing, feeding, and educating six children.

"Mostly, it was a general feeling of optimism," he says. "Then I had these early successes that told me: 'You're bound to do OK, and you might do very well.' So I said, 'This is all going to fit. We'll be able to support however many kids we have, in whatever they want to do.' "

In conversations with men and women who married in the early or middle years of the fifties, the phrases "wanting or planning to have lots of kids" is a constant refrain. Many of them point to the one brother or sister, typical of depression families, as a privation for them and, they assume, for their parents. The desire for large families, a desire in which husbands and wives united, resonates still with Paul Michaelides' optimistic view of the future. The confidence, for men, that—with their college education, willingness to work hard, and the evidence that an expanding economy needed them—providing for many children would be well within their power.

For the young women who become their wives, many of whom

had been Psychology or Education majors in college (specializing in Early Childhood) large families had been part of the plan since adolescence. Even when women worked before marriage, their chosen fields, like Rowan Walsh's career of pediatric nurse, reflected their future role: "Anything that would make me a better mother, I was all for it!" she says.

These large, planned families of the early fifties are not the peep through the picture window we get from Friedan's *Feminine Mystique* or from later books like Marilyn French's novel *The Women's Room.* As implied or explicitly stated in most feminist writing, children are either accidents or conceived in a despairing, "What the hell. I'm so miserable and trapped with one, two, three, I might as well have another.* A milder but equally deterministic premise portrayed fifties mothers as mindless protoplasm, prisoners of the "culture." In this scenario, women who would have stopped at two—as later ZPG (zero population growth) buttons would urge—have four and five because "society told them to." Large families, to be sure, were "in style," but the extent to which individuals are seen as patterned by the culture is always greater when the critics happen to disapprove of what they are doing. The same writers who see wives of the fifties, in their desire for large families, as victims of "cultural norms," are less likely to see today's young women who "want it all"—the law partnership and the two perfect children—in the same passive light. In fact, the culture cues all of us. We tend to see an "autonomous" individual when we approve his or her script.

Demographer Richard Easterlin explains classic baby boom parents like Paul and Elaine Michaelides by a cyclical theory of prosperity and depression: Periods of expanding economy create confidence in the future that finds expression in large families.[3]

Sociologist Glen H. Elder, Jr. interviewed men and women

---

* British novelist Penelope Mortimer's *The Pumpkin Eaters* (1962) is about a woman whose response to periodic bouts of depression is to have another baby. By the book's end, she has seven children.

who, like Paul Michaelides, were adolescents in families hard-hit
by the depression. Hard times had forced these young people
to assume adult roles earlier. Boys often worked when fathers
were unemployed; girls helped more with housework and child
care. In effect, they "skipped" youth and were ready sooner to
become parents and breadwinners in their own households.
Marrying earlier, they had more children.[4]

But Harvard demographer Andrew Cherlin insists that we still
don't know why young Americans in the postwar period married
earlier and started larger-than-average families.[5] All the reasons
advanced to account for the phenomenon could just as well
explain the reverse. One classic explanation is a retreat from the
devastation of World War II and the anxiety of the Atomic Age
into the manageable microcosm of the family. This theory sounds
plausible until we recall that, twenty years later, a similarly bleak
world view rationalized the "irresponsibility" of creating new
life on earth.

Journalism has been held accountable for the outbreak of wars
but perhaps insufficiently responsible for peacetime phenomena
like escalating fertility. One document explains more about the
fervid nest-building of the fifties than the expanding economy
or the contractions of the Cold War.

"Togetherness" was the subject of the editorial in the May
1954 issue of *McCall's* magazine. Its smarmy suffix made the
term an instant joke among the cynical, but the sentiments
launched nothing less than a new domestic policy for the second
half of the decade. "Today women are not a sheltered sex," the
editors began.

> Men and women in ever increasing numbers are marrying at
> an earlier age, having children at an earlier age and rearing
> larger families. For the first time in our history the majority
> of men and women own their own homes and millions of these
> people gain their deepest satisfaction from making them their
> very own.
>
> We travel more. We earn more, spend more, save more. We
> listen to finer music, read more and better books. We worship

more. And in ever greater numbers we enjoy the advantages of a higher education. . . . But the most impressive and the most heartening feature of this change is that men, women and children are achieving it together. They are creating this new and warmer way of life not as women alone or men alone, isolated from one another, but as a family sharing a common experience.[6]

In the eighties, this description seems nothing more than a bland statement of the obvious. Thirty years ago the promise that "modern" family life would end the rigid separation by sex roles—in household chores, child rearing, and shared pleasures— had a revolutionary ring.

McCall's manifesto proclaimed another fifties phenomenon— the middle classing of America. The way of life the magazine held up as the norm had nothing to do with traditional marriage as experienced by young people who weren't white or who hadn't yet "enjoyed the advantages of a higher education."

When Steve Ortiz was married at twenty-one, he had just left construction work, determined to give college one more try. Like the other working-class students at the university, "I was always out hustling a buck," he recalls, "working nights at Monty Ward and cleaning garages." His wife Rita had a job as a medical secretary. She continued working when their first child arrived, leaving the baby with her mother.

"We had totally separate lives," he says of his first marriage. "Women were supposed to be smart on the job but not when they got home. Saturday nights, we would get together at somebody's house with beer and potato chips. Wives would talk and gripe in the bedroom. We'd talk and gripe in the living room."

For Steve and Rita Ortiz, the suburban New Jersey family chosen to illustrate "togetherness" in *McCall's* would have seemed as exotic as Martians.

In *McCall's*, Ed Richtscheidt, a paper mill executive, not only shares the household chores with his wife Carol, but, like the young husbands shopping in Design Research, he participates in all decorating decisions, helping "select furniture, rugs, draperies and paint colors."[7] As a father he is as much involved in the day-to-day aspects of caring for their three young children as his commuting schedule permits, including non–"quality time"* activities like bathing and feeding (as opposed to storytelling and "teaching").

Reading of the Richtscheidts' happy and fulfilling family life, with no one ever griping in the bedroom or living room, it's easy to see why Togetherness, instantly blessed by media and clergy, became the key to the expectations of millions of young people. Its central article of faith, the shared joys of child rearing, assured young women especially that, no matter the number of children, the burden would never be theirs alone.**

From the outset, the big family scenario, whose theme was Togetherness, failed to provide some fairly crucial stage directions. However willing they might be to assume the care of small children, fathers were away all day—just as they had always been.

The new plot outline called for spacing three and four children very close together. Thirteen months was the magic number.

"Getting it over with" was the description of this belief, as put into practice by most young families. "It" referred to that period when, as a friend said, "you just stopped living." If you survived "it"—five years of four children under eight, no help, and the real possibility of losing one's sanity—they would all then be "out of diapers" or "in school"—whichever happened to be the individual mother's vision of the light at the end of the tunnel.

Other arguments were advanced for planning children thirteen

---

* "Quality time," a phrase invented to soothe the consciences of later working mothers, suggested that twenty minutes of "meaningful interaction" with a child was "better" than having Mom at home all day and unhappy.

** The birthrate kept climbing until it peaked in 1957, three years after the *McCall's* editorial.

months apart. They would be "company" for one another, requiring neither little friends nor Big Mama for entertainment. This fairy-tale illustration projected the image of a trio of preschool siblings happily building a block city, while keeping a weather eye on a slumbering infant—instead of trying to destroy the house and kill each other.

Earlier, the ideal large family spaced children far enough apart so that the next older sib could tie shoelaces and mind the baby. The four years between each of her six children suggests that women like my grandmother preferred frequent respite from babies to the far-off goal of future freedom. Nothing in my grandmother's "life plan" made a sixth child at forty-four a calamity.

For our generation of housewives and mothers, "getting it over with" was our promise to a future deferred. We would "do something" with our college education (or finish it) when we "got out from under" diapers, formulas, car pools.

Steeped in the article of faith that preschoolers needed a mother's attention, we were emphatically *not* ready to leave young children with "significant others." By the time all the kids were in school, we would be set to return to the work force.

Neither experience or example, however, had prepared young women for the realities of the "multiplier effect" created by the presence of more than one small human who has not yet reached the age of reason. "Getting it over with" sounded good, but few were aware of the toll "it" would exact on mental and physical health—and on marriages.

Whether we grew up in two-child households, as many of us did, or with more siblings, young women just out of college who found themselves alone in brand-new ranch houses in just-built subdivisions were overwhelmed, unprepared for the drudgery and dangerous exhaustion created by four preschoolers and no household help.

HELP! was the cry heard by the *Ladies' Home Journal* in 1956, when the magazine convened a roundtable discussion on "The

Plight of the Young Mother." Bannered by the cover copy, "The Problem of the 84 Hour a Week Worker/No Help" demanded "*National Attention.*"[8] Participants were four "typical" middle-class women with a total of four single-family houses, four resident husbands, fifteen children, and not a single hour of paid help. Among other experts summoned to find solutions to the problem (seen as particularly harmful to the "next generation"), were anthropologist Ashley Montagu and family relations counselor Paul Popenoe.

Much of what emerges from these women's descriptions of an average day is all-too familiar—if not from our own experience, then certainly from our readings of the last twenty years, detailing the full-time housewives' day: the two-generation suburb with no older women or even teenagers close by for baby-sitting; virtual imprisonment at home in the event of a sick child (one woman noted that her only moments out-of-doors were spent hanging laundry); evening hours devoted to household chores like floor waxing, which can't be done with toddlers underfoot; and, finally, the lack of adult companionship or even time alone.

Solutions proposed by the male experts were not impressive. ("Certainly, a young mother should not, in most cases, assume all household duties a week after giving birth," suggests Dr. Popenoe.) Other proposals included community activities such as Cub Scout den mother or "getting out" more with Daddy.

There were no "accidents" in these large families. From each woman's testimony we learn that her four children (only the intern's wife is behind schedule with three) were all planned—spacing included. After telling us that "there aren't enough hours of the day to get my work done" and "no time set apart that I can call my own," the wife of a department store manager and mother of four adds that she wants "at least two more children."

More surprising, though, is the evidence that help—in the form of relief from child care—would be unwelcome. The young doctor's wife sees parental attention as a substitute for not-yet-affordable consumer goods. "Living as we do," she says, "on an intern-resident's salary, we cannot give our children as much as we would like to. The main thing we can give them is ourselves. Consequently, our life centers around them." With the exception of her husband, who spent most weekends and evenings at the hospital, fathers helped with chores. One woman noted that the only time she paid someone to clean the house was when "it was just impossible for my husband to do it." But the only mention of men and child care was in the realm of disaster. A father who had agreed to take charge of the children one evening a week found "he just couldn't cope."

Yet, typically, none of the women wanted "outside" child care. Even when available, teenagers were dismissed as "immature." The surgeon's wife seemed to sum up the feelings of all four panelists: "Someday, I'd like to have somebody to do the cooking and help with housework," she said. "So I could spend more time with the children."

With six children and a husband whose work always involved traveling, Elaine Michaelides never wanted help at home.

"I went through a period of insisting," Paul recalls. "In fact, I would arrange for housecleaning, not child care. There Elaine always resisted—and always won.

"Part of it was: No one can do it like I can," Paul explains. "Part of it was: I don't want the invasion of privacy, and the other part was that she hadn't had that kind of example herself. Her mother ran her home without any help, in terms of what the woman does. Elaine agreed on help only because I was adamant."

"I just couldn't afford any baby-sitting," Carol Cornwell recalls, adding that she "really enjoyed" being with her three little ones—the magic thirteen months apart. "Everyone in the community had kids the same age; I made terrific friends right away through the children." Still, she admits that by the time Matthew, her third, had arrived, "I would have enjoyed getting out more, going into the city, being more involved in adult activities."

There was no question of Don Cornwell ever taking charge of the children. "Even if they were in bed for the night, he flatly refused to spend an hour with them alone in the house."

Carol Cornwell also recalls that most of their friends seemed to have more discretionary income than they did, even though "our husbands were pretty much at the same place on the organization chart.

"In fact, Don's corporation matched executive contributions to a savings plan. He used to invest much more of our income than we could really afford. Any extras like baby-sitters or cleaning help just weren't available to me."

Lack of money is often the first reason given by women for having no help. It's rarely the "real" one, however. The issue is usually how money got spent and who decided. By the time the third child arrived, husbands were moving up the corporation or out of residencies and into private practices.

Betts Saunders is one housewife and mother who never claims poverty had anything to do with lack of help.

Her husband returned from Vietnam early in the war with his residency completed. A partnership practice and a professorship in orthopedic surgery were waiting for him. Another son, Chris, and daughter, Caroline, soon joined Sam Jr. and Laura.

In Betts's view, child rearing is just too important to be entrusted to "people you pay." Only parents can produce the perfect children that she dreamed of as a psychology major at the university: happy, well adjusted, beautifully behaved (because they only saw civilized, mannerly adults); and unselfish and cooperative (because they had "learned to share with and care for each other from infancy").

With the exception of two hours every Friday afternoon, when

Betts did her Junior League work, she never left her four children until they went to school.

"We raised our children 'so 1950s,'" is Betts's synonym for "perfectly." "Since they were babies, they've gone everywhere with us. We've taken them to fine restaurants. We've flown with them. We've never gone on a trip," Betts says, "without the kids in the back of the car."

When Betts Saunders talks about raising her children "so 1950s," she is describing an American ideal that goes back thirty years earlier: *raising the perfect child.* Beginning in the 1920s, when the U.S. Government Childrens' Bureau distributed pamphlets asking *Are You Training Your Child to be Happy?*[9] experts had begun to suggest that parents—even middle-class, college-educated parents who wanted and loved their children—were helpless bunglers in meeting the needs of their young. In his most famous and widely selling book, *The Psychological Care of Infant and Child* (1928), behaviorist John Watson decried the ignorance of parents (doing nothing to dispel this unhappy state) as he warned: "No one today knows enough to raise a child."[10] Child study associations and new university-based centers for research on children all agreed. Professional intervention was required to rescue a child from familial incompetence. Bedwetting or thumb sucking, shyness or aggression—parents exacerbated every problem. The nursery school movement gained momentum, historian Sheila Rothman points out, as a strategy of "removing" the child from the environment of amateurism at home, at least for a few hours each day.[11]

Had it not been for the depression and World War II, our families, the target of all this abuse, might have allayed their anxieties about us with more professional help. They had other things to worry about. We didn't.

By the time we became parents, in an era of peace and prosperity, the ideal of the perfect child was still more pervasive. Now, however, this goal had few unhappy distractions and a new twist. *We could do it all ourselves.*

The function of the modern family, sociologist Talcott Parsons observed, is the "production of personality." The function of the fifties family was the production of the most perfect specimens of childhood ever seen. For our generation, producing larger numbers of children sooner may also have been a matter of scope. Like the scientist who needs the biggest, best-equipped laboratory, we required plenty of raw material for trial and error. True to the do-it-yourself ethos of the postwar period, we would become the experts our children deserved.

Enter the great mediator between the professional and the amateur—Dr. Benjamin Spock—ready to assure us that Dr. Watson was wrong. Parental instinct and common sense, joined with love, affection, and the enjoyment of babies, couldn't help but produce the happiest, healthiest, best-adjusted child in history.[12]

Far from being fatal influences on our children's perfectability, parents were indispensable.

It was certainly good news to hear that only we could do the job. But the new parental contract had some fine print. Indispensability also meant total availability. And although *parent* was the "operative word" in all this encouraging advice, the reality behind the rhetoric left no doubt as to which parent was to be indispensable and totally available: Mother.

The Spockian assumption of availability* had unintended consequences. Like compensatory overcooking, the hidden agenda of many "total mothers" was guilt. Women who had not even wanted one child would punish themselves. They would not get a single undeserved hour off.

"The crazy thing was," Diane Weikert says, "neither of us ever intended to have babies. We even talked about it—which is

---

* Almost as influential for fifties parents were the series of studies by Dr. Arnold Gesell and his colleagues of the Yale Child Guidance Center. In these reassuring descriptions of the "normal" child's developmental stages (including problems), the same assumptions prevailed: Mother would be there to observe and anticipate these behavioral changes on a round-the-clock basis.

probably more than most engaged couples in middle America in 1955 did."

Diane and Tom Weikert were married at the end of her junior year. "Of course, I got pregnant immediately. Peter was born three weeks after I got my B.A."

In their apartment complex in off-campus university housing for married students, everybody was on the same schedule. The week of graduation, Diane recalls, "I was standing at the backyard barbecue, bulging out to here. My husband came outside, laughing. A lady from town had just accosted him, when she saw me from the street. Why did they let all these pregnant women go to college, she wanted to know?

"Being a mother," Diane says, "was probably the most frightening thing that ever happened to me in my whole life. The commitment was very depressing. Coming back from the hospital, I held that baby in the car and I thought, I have an obligation here for the next twenty years. And I didn't want it.

"I felt awful about the way I was really feeling. I kept saying to myself, You shouldn't feel this way. But it was overwhelming."

When Peter was a few months old, Diane's high-school principal called to ask if she could step in as an emergency substitute teacher. She taught English and Social Studies for two years, moving back to her mother's farm with her new family.

"I was so relieved," Diane says, "to be able to go to work almost immediately. My Mom was terrific with the baby. It was almost like I didn't have to be a mother for a while."

Two years later, Tom Weikert was on the first rung of the executive ladder at a new job. The commute back and forth to the farm was too long. It was time to buy a house.

"I loved teaching," Diane says. "I loved the kids and the school. But in the new subdivision where we lived, everybody in the neighborhood was having coffee together. I didn't have any friends at all. I wanted to become a part of the community.

"That's when I decided to quit teaching, which is probably

the biggest mistake I ever made. Because I never fit into that neighborhood. I was as miserable there as I've ever been in my life."

"Peter was then about twenty-six months old. I said, 'Well, if we have one baby, we should have another.' Thirteen months later Joanna was born." Within the same year, we ended up with a third. When my sister and her husband were killed in an automobile accident, we adopted my two-year-old niece.

Diane gives the usual reason for having no household help: money. But after the excuse of poverty, she admits, "I'm a nickel nose; I couldn't deal out four dollars—which is what a cleaning woman cost in those days."

When she talks about child care, though, she no longer bothers with budgetary arguments.

"With the children, I felt I should be doing it myself. When my niece Barbara came to live with us, I went through a very difficult adjustment," she says carefully. "But anytime my mother would say, 'I'll take her' or even 'Let me take all of them for a week,' I kept saying: 'No, I have to handle this myself.'

"I couldn't let anybody else do it. You have a child that's suddenly yours. And you say, 'I don't love her.' Then you say, 'You should.' These were the same feelings I had when Peter was born—but this was even worse," Diane says, "because here was this kid who was impossible to love. All I wanted to do was belt her. I felt so bad about it. Why don't I love her? There's something wrong with me.

"I felt too guilty to get help with the children. I had to handle the situation alone."

In *The Unnatural History of the Nanny*, nanny-raised British author Jonathan Gathorne-Hardy describes his wonder at the "remarkable phenomenon" that gave impulse to his book. "How was it," he marvels, that

> hundreds of thousands of mothers apparently normal, could
> simply abandon all loving and disciplining and company of

their little children, sometimes almost from birth, to the absolute care of other women, total strangers, nearly always
uneducated, about whose characters they must usually have
had no real idea at all. It was a practice, as far as I knew, unparalleled . . . in any other culture which had ever existed.[13]

The opposite of this practice in the America of the 1950s was
equally unparalleled. Never before had hundreds of thousands
of college-educated women, wives of the professional middle
classes, refused to share even the most menial duties of childcare
with paid help.

Among my contemporaries whose second, third, and fourth
children came along in the early sixties, a compromise was
reluctantly adopted—the *au pair*. Despite its French name, the
au pair, like the nanny, was a British discovery. Shortly after
World War II, English housewives found that middle-class
young women from the continent were willing to become
"mothers' helpers" in exchange for room and board, along with
free time to pursue their studies and any available young men.
    As a domestic arrangement, the *au pair* was a solution that
was designed to fail. With her unspecified duties and murky
status, she was a perfect reflection of the ambivalence of her
employer (who, of course, wasn't *really* an employer) on every
front—reluctance to share responsibility for household and
children and discomfort with the idea of domestic help. As the
civil rights movement gained momentum from the mid-fifties
on, the *au pair* appeared to solve yet another difficulty involving
paid servants: the unacceptability of being served by minority
women.
    Young mothers made haste to explain to visitors that Waltraut
or Véronique was a student here to learn English, *not* a servant.
Further complications arose when the *au pair's* social standing
turned out to be superior to that of her . . . uh . . . host family.
At one dinner party I recall, the new *au pair*, it was whispered
to arrivals, was a baroness! Certainly her demeanor did not

promise less work for mother. She sat watching stonily as guests and hosts scraped plates and relayed casseroles back and forth between kitchen and dining room.

If she wasn't too aristocratic for KP, her other problems— linguistic, emotional, or sexual—demanded the attention of her already beleaguered sponsor. Far from providing relief from domestic burdens, having an *au pair*, she soon learned, was a dismal preview of life with an adolescent daughter. One of my first friends to return to work full time spent most evenings and weekends on the telephone with Church youth groups and Irish social clubs. Homesick and dateless, the *au pair* wept; Bridget's nocturnal sobs were giving the children nightmares.

By the end of the fifties, something was happening to the big family scenario. Data on births, intended and actual, weren't sufficiently refined twenty-five years ago to test out my own hypothesis. Paul and Elaine Michaelides' confident stake in the future—in his career, their marriage, in life itself as infinite in possibilities—characteristic of the early fifties, was weakening by the end of the decade. The birthrate itself was still up there, but it was the fourth, fifth, and sixth children of the Michaelides' (and people like them) who were keeping the numbers at a steady high.

Some informal statistical observations: my husband's class-mates, vintage 1952, have no fewer than four children; six is by no means unusual. Three was the maximum number produced by most of my college cohort, c. 1958.

By the time those of us who graduated in the late fifties were married, with one or two children, it was the early sixties. Change was in the air. Few of us could have named it, but whatever was happening was creating uncertainties that hadn't existed eight years earlier. We were enjoying ever more prosperity, but we were overpopulating the earth. The Cold War was heating up, both in Asia and at our doorstep. There was "another America" at home—the millions who had never benefited from the consumer society we had taken for granted since adolescence.

Within our own walls—painted Raleigh Tavern Peach or stark Contemporary White—all was not well. What John Updike called the "hedged bets" of late fifties marriages was revealed in the downward revision in numbers of children. Couples who had happily talked about five were now wondering about two. (A friend once asked me guiltily how I "got away" with having one?) A sense of "traveling light" was in the air.

Right after college in 1959, Dick and Barbara Robertson moved to a small city of about 30,000 in the Southwest, where Dick went into the retail business with his father-in-law. Their son, Laurence, was born that same year, followed thirteen months later by daughter Nancy.

"Then I pretty much decided that was it," Dick says.

Life wasn't quite as wonderful as we expected. Or maybe, it was what we feared we deserved.

"All I did was go out and work all day. All she did was stay home and clean house. Every Friday night somebody had a party," Dick says. "Every Friday night it was exactly the same people and exactly the same conversations. Everything was the same, just a different location.

"It was really very stifling, but I sort of assumed that was marriage."

Going steady in high school and through college had given Carol Cornwell happier assumptions about marriage.

"The one thing I did not expect was violence," she says. "Early on, Don's temper really surfaced. He would shove me around, slap me, and sometimes lock me out of the apartment. This was before Mat was born, when I was pregnant. Then, when he was an infant, it continued.

"Don just couldn't control his anger. His father was like that, too. I found out that his dad used to throw dishes and hit his mother constantly. Don never discussed troubles at home. For the longest time, I had no inkling they weren't a perfect, picture-book family.

"As with any family," Carol reflects, "there was lots of bad stuff going on. But when you were dating, everything had to look good."

Pat Carroll Brewster would have "preferred to have waited." Instead, she became pregnant three months after she and Lane were married.

"I didn't use contraception then. That was still part of my Roman Catholic belief—one of many articles of faith I've changed my mind about since those days," Pat says.

Just before she was married, Pat had been promoted to researcher at the national news magazine where she worked. "I loved my job, and I was determined to keep it." When her son Daniel was six weeks old, she went back to work. "They didn't have any maternity leave in those days; if I'd stayed out any longer, I would have lost my job.

"It was very tough," she says, "rushing to get to work, rushing to get back to let the sitter go. I couldn't afford a full-time housekeeper on my salary, and Lane was not about to pay for me to work.

"By the time I got home, the baby was already asleep. I hadn't seen him all day."

After a month, Pat decided that she "just couldn't do it." She arranged with the magazine to work one week out of six. "I could get up for that. In fact," Pat recalls, "a week felt like a vacation from daily child rearing."

More than the stimulation of change, Pat was already convinced of the importance of "keeping my hand in."

"When I went back to work, fourteen months after my wedding, I realized how failed my marriage was. None of it was working. We never talked about anything. Sex was terrible.

After so many years of thinking the earth was going to move, that was a big disappointment.

"I tried discussing this with the doctor at the time I got pregnant. He said: 'It'll be better after the baby is born.' But he looked up at the ceiling while he said it."

Pat thought of asking her husband for a "brief separation at this point. Just so I could get my own self together. But where was I going to go?

"Instead, I went into neutral. And I stayed that way for ten years. Ian was born two years after Daniel. And Eleanor two years later. Then it was 1961. I went on the pill. That was the beginning of liberation."

The beginning of liberation was the official end of Togetherness. Unofficially, the canonized version of fifties family life had immediately come under attack. Men, especially journalists most likely to write of such matters (and even likelier to prefer a few drinks after work to going home and putting the kiddies to bed) lost no time in equating the new ethos with the emasculation of the American male.

Intellectual adversaries saw togetherness as imposing the lowest common denominator of family activity on individual members. Instead of Mom writing that report on Reinhold Niebuhr for her Great Books Club, Dad practicing a Mozart quartet with his amateur chamber music group, Junior working on the peaceful use of the atom with his new chemistry set, they would all be watching *Romper Room* "together" with Baby Sue.

But the real backlash against togetherness came from the erosion of an ideal: the cynicism created by expectations betrayed. It came from the discovery of how "stifling" or sexually terrible or physically violent marriage could be; of how exhausted husbands and wives were at the end of a day that had been separately grueling for each. Far from sharing the pleasures and problems of children and household, many couples never shared a single thought of importance to either partner.

Disillusionment hit women harder. They had no "other life": no office allowed them to forget failure at home. From adolescence girls had taken it for granted that the family would be central to the existence of the young men they wed. Together—from high-school or college courtship days—they had planned the numbers of children they would have, along with a way of life where friends, neighbors, and community would cushion them against the pressures and temptations of striving and competition. The rat race—that fearful fifties image—and its dubious rewards would be held at bay.

11

SUCCESS BREEDS SUCCESS

Success Breeds Success, the Cadillac ad of 1956 announced, while the accompanying image showed an Eldorado whose length required a double page spread in magazines like *Life* and *The New Yorker*. This summa of automotive status was parked in the driveway of a palatial home or possibly a country club (the distinction between the two was deliberately blurred).

Loftier than appeals to mere sex ("Buick makes you feel like the man you are"), General Motors' soft sell had a moral edge. The glamour, luxury, comfort, and prestige of their top-of-the-line car was the visible reward of the American male's own "drive," the fruits of his ambition and hard work. Moreover, as the copywriter's fertile image suggested, the Eldorado owner wasn't going to stop there. This year a Cadillac, next year the corporate suite. Tomorrow, the world.

Still, the fact that Detroit had to remind automobile buyers that success was the worthiest of all goals and Americans should strive for it, gives us the clue that something was wrong. In the America of the 1950s, success seemed to be suffering from an image problem. Among the young, ambition itself was in disrepute.

Eavesdropping on college seniors, about to march meekly into corporate training programs, hearing them ask recruiters about pension plans, observers wondered what had happened to that all-American "go" and "drive"; the big dreams and large ambitions that "had made this country great." Had the ruthlessness of the robber barons, the competitive juices of earlier business buccaneers run aground, to end with these anemic robots in droop-shouldered suits?

Reading of the modest claims on the future of the Class of 1955, David Riesman described their goals as "low-ceilinged, like the rooms of the new ranch houses where they would live"[1] (and unlike the lofty Victorian rooms of their fathers' houses). "Contentment" and the "good life" had replaced conquistador fantasies, even the hope of making a mark on the world in one's chosen field.

What had lowered the sights and reset the goals of the young American male, causing him to "dream in second gear?"[2]

The young American woman.

Going steady in high school had given girls an early "softening" influence on the career choices of boys, deflecting them from lonely and demanding long-range goals involving deferred rewards.

Margaret Mead and fellow researchers found that in schools where girls perceived scientists to be "poor husband material," characterized as "sexless" or "too wrapped up in the laboratory,"[3] boys stayed away from the Bunsen burners in droves. Noting the decline in medical school applications in the mid-fifties, Riesman repeated the hypotheses of his faculty colleagues: influenced by girl friends, fiancées, or brides, young men appeared to prefer professions that were "compatible with decent domesticity" over "arduous careers" requiring sacrifices of time and effort.[4]

In 1954, critic Russell Lynes sifted through the answers to four hundred questionnaires sent to subscribers of *Mademoiselle* magazine, seeking to discover "what young women consider success to be—in college, in jobs, in marriage." Lynes disposed quickly of what the magazine's readers wanted for themselves (an "interesting" job where one met "interesting" people, all of which would make one an "interesting" wife). His astonishment came from what his respondents did *not* seek in their husbands, the findings conveyed in the title of his article, "What Has Succeeded Success?"

Few young women, Lynes discovered, were interested in marrying a man who was headed for the top of his profession. From the answers to *Mademoiselle's* questions emerged "a constant identification of achievement with ruined health and lost friends."

Pursuit of success in the marketplace, moreover, suffered from a still more negative image than the white jacket of the scientist or overworked doctor. The corporate climb was "associated with trampling other people on the ladder, with having no time for the children and working incessantly over weekends." A business career was synonymous with "breaking necks and hearts trying to get rich."[5]

What *had* succeeded success? The four hundred young women who returned their questionnaires sounded a chorus of agreement: the family—its solidarity, community of interests, and first among those, the well-being of the children.

Reading the evidence of these critics—marshaled from high-school girls, female undergraduates, and young wives—that women were blunting the traditional male pursuits of achievement and success, I was puzzled. How to reconcile these findings with the unhesitating answers given by dozens of my contemporaries—answers that placed them in a far-from-flattering light? Their attraction to the man they married was his "drive" and "ambition." He was "head of everything on campus," "most likely to succeed," obviously a "guy who was going places," a vice president at thirty. These were the same middle-class, college-educated young women who in 1954 were telling interviewers that their ideal mate was a "family man," one who would spurn demanding

careers, high pressure jobs, the "ulcer belt,"* who had displayed
no desire to become rich or famous. Thirty years later, they sat in
$100,000 kitchens or even their own sleek offices, telling me that
they had known back in high school or college that Bob, Mike,
Dan was the man for them because he was headed straight for
the top.

What did they really want? (If Freud never found out, could
I?) Both. What all of us—men and women—always "really" want.
And our troubles with each other almost always derive from the
unhappy truism that "both" tend to be in clashing opposition. Like
Dan Ross, we wanted an artistic and "creative" yet "traditional"
woman who would be a wonderful mother and serve all our needs.
Or we wanted the ambitious, admired, successful lad who would
leap from BMOC to CEO, while remaining a totally involved
husband and father.

But there may be another explanation for the apparent discrepancy expressed by my contemporaries about the men and
the kinds of lives they wanted, as articulated in 1954 and 1984.

Thirty years ago no middle-class American was allowed the
frankness about success that has become a commonplace today.
(Only Madison Avenue hucksters could be so "tasteless.") In the
genteel fifties, ambition and lust for money or power—even if we
were aware of such impulses in ourselves or attracted to them in
others—were "unmentionable," like alcoholic parents.

When Diane Weikert says that her husband's desire to go into
business and make a lot of money was the "most intimate thing I
know about him," she is right. As Tom Weikert's fiancée, she had
been entrusted with classified information.

The first time a young man told me he "only wanted to get rich,"
I was at once shocked by his admission and admiring of his
"honesty." How daring of him to confess to such an unseemly goal,
all the more titillating because he "certainly didn't act that way."

* One of David Riesman's respondents' phrases for big-city jobs.

(It was like discovering a white-collar child molester or drug addict among one's acquaintances.) No one did. Acting that way was "unattractive" in the extreme.

Hunger for success—for money, fame, power—was the "dirty little secret" of the fifties that Norman Podhoretz discovers in his autobiography, *Making It*. Growing up in a Jewish immigrant culture, the author tells us, the "gospel of success" reigned supreme in the world of his childhood. But as a student at Columbia College in the early 1950s he learns that "the word 'successful' glided automatically into the judgment 'corrupt.'" He continues:

> The books all said that Americans regarded ambition as a major virtue, and yet a system of manners existed at Columbia which prohibited any expression of worldly ambitiousness. It was thought contemptible to dream of the rewards contemporary society had to offer, and altogether despicable to admit to so low a hunger, except in tones of irony that revealed one's consciousness of how naughty a thing one was doing. . . . Ambition (itself a species of lustful hunger) seems to be replacing erotic lust as the prime dirty little secret of the well-educated American soul.[6]

Ambition, as Podhoretz soon learns, equals "brash" and "pushy" and other synonyms for "Jewish."

"A real Sammy Glick" was the first anti-Semitic remark I ever heard. By the mid-1950s, the antihero of Budd Schulberg's 1941 novel *What Makes Sammy Run?* had become a term of generic opprobrium. An anti-folk hero, Glick was the antithesis of what every nice young man, "regardless of race, religion or national origin," should be.

Clearly, the researchers who were blaming young women for tempering the keen ambitions of American men didn't spend much time at the movies. In the dark of the local Rialto or under starry skies at the drive-in, they would have enjoyed a delicious historical irony: The "pushiest," "brashest" Jews ever to claw their way out of big city tenements into Beverly Hills palaces were busy making movies showing how striving for success caused coronaries, corrupted morals, destroyed families and even corporations.

"I'm not going to die young at the top of the tower," says "hands-on" engineer Don Walling (William Holden), explaining why he isn't in the race for president of Tredway Furniture Corporation (not yet). In *Executive Suite* (1957), the tower is synonymous with death; the most recent occupant has just died of a heart attack. Before him, the founder's life was cut short by terminal power lust.

Walling changes his mind about wanting to be Number One when he realizes that his fellow VPs have nothing but greed and ambition to recommend them for the job. All he has to offer is talent and his determination that the company "live not die."

Ambition has been replaced by vocation. Only a sense of calling justifies the will to occupy the tower suite. But every mission requires sacrifice: the vocation of women.

"It'll make you very lonely sometimes, when he shuts you out of his life," corporate widow and orphan Julia Tredway (Barbara Stanwyck) warns Mary Walling (June Allyson). "But he'll always come back to you and you'll know how fortunate you are to be his wife."

The inverse ratio between talent and reward is the running joke of *Will Success Spoil Rock Hunter?* (1955), one of many Hollywood satires on Madison Avenue and its television commercials. About to be fired from his ad agency, Rockwell Hunter (Tony Randall) sees his fortunes dramatically reversed when Marilyn Monroe look- and sound-alike Rita Marlow (Jayne Mansfield) barters his consort services for a lipstick endorsement. After years of trying hard, of "wearing sincere knitted ties until they became insincere," Rock Hunter becomes president of the agency by walking into a star's bathroom at the right moment.

"Success will fit you like a shroud," sneers his ex-boss, echoing Hollywood's favorite death image. The former chief has retired from the rat race to grow prize roses. Rock Hunter will find happiness when he follows this sage example—giving up the CEO's private bathroom to raise chickens with his bride.

In Sunrise Hills Estates, the new California subdivision in *No Down Payment* (1956), ambition and striving are at the root of all ills afflicting the couples who bought into the postwar American dream.

"Nobody in this development owns a home they can afford," announces alcoholic used-car salesman and get-rich-quick fantasizer Joe Flagg (Tony Randall).*

The marriage of atomic physicist-engineer David Martin (Jeff Hunter) and his glamorous bride—the toniest couple on the block —is headed for disaster because of her ambition. She wants him to get out of research and into sales, the first rung on the management ladder.

"I'm a good engineer. Next year I'll be a better one. But that's not enough for you," he complains.

"There's nothing *wrong* with being an engineer,"** she says, wrinkling her upturned nose in disdain. "I just think you could be so much more . . . important."

But she soon learns the wages of wifely ambition. If her husband hadn't gone to his first overnight sales conference, she wouldn't have been raped by a neighbor. Wanting to be rich, famous, important, or powerful was an invitation to disaster. In Hollywood's antisuccess scenarios, good but misguided people see the light at the eleventh hour, learning from tragedies like rape, alcoholism—or children who watch TV all the time.

Dating couples who watched these black-and-white morality tales on the screen got the message together. He might harbor

---

* Beamish and crew-cut, Randall was often cast as a young man on the make, either in comedies or dramas, where his air of jaunty hustle would be revealed as self-deception.

** Engineering was the favored profession for fifties white-collar movie heroes. Combining specialized and advanced education (so he could get to be president) with populist craft skills (anything they can do on the assembly line, he can do better), the engineer was the perfect college-educated "ordinary guy."

dreams of empire building, complete with trembling minions addressing him as "Chief" or "Boss," knowing in his heart that he was prepared to kill for the "title on the door and the Bigelow on the floor." She can easily admit—thirty years later—that such were the qualities she admired, wanted, and needed, along with the goodies they were sure to provide. But neither was likely to confess this even under ether in 1955. Naked ambition and the lust for success had gone underground. In less than a decade, these qualities would surface in a more congenial climate.

In the 1970s, Sammy Glicks, including many who had enjoyed "all the advantages," popped out of every closet, joined by corporate "killers" and "gamesmen." Former members of the A-team had become Type A personalities: "workaholics" who drove themselves and subordinates, husbands and fathers who were never at home.

Meanwhile, it was easy to see why observers equated the soft-pedaling of hard-edged male competitiveness with the softening influence of young women. Traditionally, the feminine embraced the expressive and affective side of life: the nurture of children, the comfort and care of older relatives. Even in play, girls were socialized to cooperate, not compete. If young men in the fifties appeared to be withdrawing from the fray, the bugle of retreat could only have been sounded by the young women to whom they "committed" at ever earlier ages.

Our youth was the wild card in calling our attitudes toward success. Fifties critics who decided that American men had rejected individual achievement and its sacrifices were basing their judgment on very young people, scarcely past adolescence— college seniors and just-married couples—those most likely (especially in that most conformist decade) to parrot the cultural norms. Listening to their obliging duets about the good life, one might well see only a "picture of thoroughly barbecued bliss," the text provided by McCall's doctrine of togetherness.

Somehow, now that they were wives and mothers, young women forgot about those "other" qualities they had noted so

approvingly only a few years before—the "drive" and "ambition,"
the indications that he was a "real go-getter." They had bet on
winners who suddenly, it appeared, were intent only on winning.
Or without placing bets at all, they ended as losers.

When she wed her high-school sweetheart in 1955, one year
after graduation, Rita Ortiz could never have predicted how far
her husband would go and how changed he would be from the
boy she married.

In 1965 Steve Ortiz left the high school where he had been a
shop teacher for a job with the Migrant Worker Program near
Tucson. In less than twelve months, he was promoted from clerk
to area director.

"My goal had been to double my salary in one year," he says,
"and I made it."

"I was starting to read *Forbes* magazine, *The Wall Street
Journal*," he recalls. "I was thinking, there's got to be a way to be
more successful. I was teaching with people who'd gone to Notre
Dame and to Ivy League schools. They had a larger view of
things. I was starting to think about my own life differently."

His new job also turned Steve into a weekend husband and
father. The ten-hour drive between work and family he made
every Friday and Sunday afternoon, crossing the state, seemed
longer every week.

"The philosophical difference between us was getting bigger all
the time," he says. "Our life expectations—about the kids, about
money—were changing, along with our ability to communicate.

"I have to admit I felt she was holding me back. She would
have been happy to stay in that first little house, to go out to a
night club once a month."

For other men, thirty minutes on the expressway became farther
from home each night.

"He just disappeared into his career" is the way Sue Hodges
describes her seventeen-year marriage.

Divorced now for five years, she still looks reflexively through the arched doorway of her formal living room to the chandeliered foyer and front door beyond.

For fifteen years before that, from the time they returned to Chicago after Bob Hodges' military service, "he wasn't around much," she recalls. "He was always busy. Always working. First getting himself established," Sue says, "then becoming a big success."

By the time the Hodgeses adopted their second baby, the rising young attorney had three jobs. "He had his own small law practice. He was assistant city counsel, and in the evenings he was working on a master's degree."

Then, in the mid-1960s, came "the Big Coup." With two partners, Bob Hodges started a bank. "It was a lot of work. There were endless meetings with the legislature, with other lawyers. A ton of paperwork.

"At that point, things were still OK. I really did try to support him in all of that. Even though he was hardly home at all.

"He wanted to be a millionaire before he was thirty," Sue says. "That was his secret obsession. He was really into making a lot of money."

In millions of American households, the same drama began to unfold. Five years and three children after the wedding, a newly emergent success ethic and a firmly entrenched togetherness ideal came into head-on collision.

By the early 1960s, the fifties American male had discovered *work*.

"I was totally self-oriented in terms of achievement," Mike DiStefano says. "I wanted to be successful. For me success meant being a doctor, but also being a good doctor. In addition, I made an early decision that being a doctor and treating patients wasn't enough. I had to teach, because I saw how important teachers had been for me. I also had to find some administrative position where I was the boss. Finally, I was very concerned about financial security: earning, saving, and investing. In the early years of the sixties, I was hell-bent on those goals.

"Rowan always wanted to have lots of children," Mike says. He sees his wife's vocation and skills in this area as the reason why having four babies "back to back" was no problem for her.

"She's a wonderful mother. That was her role. Mine was the breadwinner. We were both so busy in those days, I'm not sure we got to know each other very well. We each had separate lives."

Hearing himself describe his marriage in this way, he qualifies, only to grasp another image of separateness.

"It wasn't really a problem," he says. "We were just on different tracks."

Rowan Walsh DiStefano never expected that marriage would be a matter of parallel lines that never met. What she had expected, though, didn't happen.

"Mike never participated in the rearing of the children the way I'd assumed he would," Rowan says. "He'd come home, say hello to the kids, and that was it. He never fed a child or changed a diaper or even played with them when they were little."

Somehow, the refusal to have fun with the kids is the most hurtful by every woman's account. They, the mothers, would have gladly done the scut work, for the vicarious pleasure of seeing children and fathers enjoy themselves together.

"He never wanted to see his kids being born, never wanted to wait in the hospital with me," Rowan says. "It was like I was the wife and I did all these things alone. He just went to work and brought home the money. I was terribly disappointed.

"He'd come home from the office, and I'd say: 'David's got a fever of 104.' Mike would say: 'Why are you telling *me*? Call the pediatrician. I'm tired. I don't want to hear about it!'"

Whatever the sixties may have portended in the larger scheme of things, for young middle-class families, the early years of the decade were a time of total exhaustion. Young wives were overwhelmed by several tiny children. More and more, men's energies were siphoned off by the demands of making it. Togetherness became a grim and bitter joke. Many couples, in their separate lives, on different tracks, hardly ever saw each other. When they did, tempers were short. Grievances were stockpiling on both sides.

What had happened to the ideal of the family? More to the point, where was Daddy? But most perplexing of all, where did the expectation arise that fathers were going to share in the dailiness of child rearing?

Hearing this same assumption and its frustration described again and again, it became clear to me that women's utopian view of marriage predated *McCall's* happy sloganeering. The magazine —like all media—had simply described a belief already in place for large numbers of readers. What was its origin?

Certainly, few of the men and women of my generation had ever seen a man "involved" in child care (or indoor household chores, for that matter).

The only time my father ever fed me, as a young child, dinner, the occasion proved so dramatic, he immortalized it with his Kodak. One night, at the beginning of the war, my mother went off unexpectedly to an air raid wardens' meeting. An hour of fruitless foraging revealed that my father was lost in the kitchen. He hadn't the faintest idea where anything was kept or what to do with whatever he might have found there. Feeling abandoned to male incompetence, I was immortalized sobbing over my sparse supper—an apple and a glass of milk.

Where were our male contemporaries supposed to have learned to do better? How had we come to expect a coparent at home?

Rising expectations of fathers began with an increasingly negative image of American mothers.

Although he took a dim view of parents generally, behaviorist John Watson reserved his special loathing for the poisonous maternal influence.

"Most mothers," he insisted, in a book influential through the thirties and forties, "should be indicted for psychological murder. I know hundreds . . . who have slain their young. They want to possess their children's soul."[7]

Even the slaughter of the innocents did not move Dr. Watson to propose that fathers should actually stoop to hands-on child care. But the psychologist could still be admired by social radicals like philosopher Bertrand Russell because "he was not afraid to suggest that a real man should spend plenty of time in the nursery observing his young."[8]

American misogyny directed against mothers found its most vehement expression in Philip Wylie's 1942 best seller, *Generation of Vipers*, which made "Momism" the buzzword of the period. And although children of both sexes were the ostensible victims in the crime of "smother love," there was no doubt about which child was the real concern of male critics. Dr. Watson's "overkissed" little boy was not apt to shine on the Gough Femininity Scale when he got to kindergarten.

As women were forcibly retired from the workplace to the home following World War II, hysterical fear of maternal dominance could be expressed in more objective terms. As infantilized consumers, housewives' had become so limited they were no longer competent to deal with the professional requirements of educated child care.

Now to fears of Momism and the know-nothing amateur mother were added a positive argument for fathers' expanding role. Freudian doctrine insisted on the importance of the pre-oedipal years. "The analytic emphasis on the need for young children's early contact with the male parent," notes psychoanalyst Henriette Klein, "became absorbed by the culture."

"Some fathers have been brought up to think that the care of babies and children is the mother's job entirely," Dr. Benjamin Spock pointed out in the first edition of his famous book in 1946. "This is the wrong idea. You can be a warm father and a real man at the same time." The soothing doctor went on to stress that the "father's closeness and friendliness to his children will have a vital effect on their spirits and characters for the rest of their lives. So the time for him to begin being a real father is right at the start."[9]

A few years earlier Dr. Arnold Gesell, the pioneer of child development, underlined the importance to the preschooler of time alone with the male parent:

> Excursions and times with father are highly prized by the four-year-old. Saturday and Sunday take on new meaning because father is home and special things are planned with him. The father realizes that these excursions are still best taken alone with the child, who can adjust to a larger group . . . but who is most relaxed and happy when alone with one adult.[10]

Still, neither fear of our own unskilled or sinister influence nor Freudian trickle-down, via Drs. Spock and Gesell, really explains the tenacity with which a belief had taken root: middle-class fathers were to share the work and the pleasure of parenthood. *

The intensity of this expectation was only matched by the bitterness of the disappointment that followed. As to its source, the cliché seems to be the only explanation: the man's role in child rearing was an idea whose time had come. But for only one parent.

In 1963 marriage and life seemed to be improving for Pat and Lane Brewster. Eleanor, their third and last child, was a year old. "I could see the end of the trail," Pat says. "It wasn't going to be long before everybody was out of diapers and I could really begin to grow up."

Pat discussed the pill with a young Jesuit. Since using it, she told him, the marriage was "somewhat better, mainly because I

---

* Until Spock revised Spock in the late 1960s, the pediatrician did not envision fathers' having an equal role in child care. Indeed, just after insisting on their importance, Spock seems alarmed by his own temerity. "Of course, I don't mean that the father has to give just as many bottles, or change just as many diapers as the mother. But it's fine for him to do these things occasionally. He might make the formula on Sunday."[11]

was no longer terrified of getting pregnant." If she had to give up the pill, she said, "everything would slide back down again."

"Pat," Father Forché had said, "if the pill makes the marriage better, it's no longer a matter for confession."

Then, just when life at home seemed to be happier, Lane Brewster left the food products company where he had worked since graduation from college in 1953, moving swiftly from trainee to vice president, to become director of marketing for a multinational drug manufacturer.

"It was a very, very tough job," Pat says. "The office was only a short commute. But Lane was never home. He worked punishingly long days. He'd take Saturdays off—sleep until noon—because the poor guy was exhausted. Then he'd go into the office all day Sunday.

"I never saw him," Pat says. "The children were very small and the entire responsibility for them was mine—and I mean 'entire.' Lane was totally uninvolved.

"One evening when he got home, I asked him if he would go down to the basement of our apartment building and get the clothes out of the dryer. I had Eleanor on my hip. Ian was two and Daniel, who was four, was in bed with flu." He said no. He didn't know where the laundry machines were. If he found out, I'd ask him to do it again, and he really didn't want to be asked again.

"So, you just put on a hair shirt and you did it," Pat says.

The collision of togetherness and the "self-oriented" work ethic created epic psychodramas at twilight across the land, with a cast of thousands: hair-shirted, martyred housewives; exhausted, resentful bread-winners; cranky, tired toddlers.

Who could go downstairs to fetch the laundry if there was nobody upstairs but an infant and two preschoolers? The finger pointed at fathers. They were getting off lightly. How could a reasonable man expect to waltz into a tidy house and have a peaceful martini with his well-groomed and smiling wife—behaving as though there were a cook in the kitchen and a nanny to bathe and bed the children? With the "no help wanted" injunction in effect,* fathers began to be seen as the failure in the system of household management. It was apparent that overburdened young wives and mothers could literally do no more.

By the late 1950s, women, including mothers of young children, were starting to return to the labor force. Questions were beginning to be raised about child care that went beyond family squabbles. Attitudes as well as schedules had to become more flexible.

For the first time in American history, men were being expected to share what had traditionally been "women's work." When they became angry, refused, forgot, "pulled rank" (you expect *me*, president of Astral Communications, to run out to the market because *you* forgot the milk?), many wives, in turn, decided they had married egocentric, infantile monsters who "expected women to do everything." But women had *always* done everything. The difference was: these women had not always been wives. They had been paid help. Suddenly men, in what had come to be known as the professional-managerial class, were expected to assume both the nurturing roles of mothers and the physical labor of housewives, "hired girls," and nursemaids. And they were expected to do this at just the same moment, in the early 1960s, when attitudes toward work, career, and success were undergoing radical change.

In 1953 William H. Whyte had issued a warning to his fledgling Organization Man: "The old employer," he said, "was content with your sweat; the new man wants your soul."

A decade later, the man in the gray flannel suit had repossessed his soul, to be laid on the altar of achievement and success—his own. The company loyalty and groupthink of the primitive postwar model had yielded to a new individualism. The work itself—

---

* One father theorized that rejection of professional child care was a way of punishing husbands—"don't think you can buy your way out of your responsibilities."

its perks, power, and rewards—was what counted, not the organization. The bureaucratic role of the executive, seen as lifelong member of a corporate family, shifted to work as an individual vocation, a sacred calling that required sacrifice.

By the early sixties, wives could no longer complain about the impossible demands the "company" placed on "Charlie." Charlie had internalized both the carrot and the stick. The new male professional, flogging himself to ever greater effort and productivity, was now described by a new form of pathology: he was a "workaholic."*

He was Dr. Michael DiStefano, with two medical practices, one in his suburban community, the other in the city; a dean's office and a teaching post. Or he was a lawyer like Bob Hodges, who "disappeared into his career" merging banks and "doing deals" over dinner and far into the night. Or Lane Brewster, for whom working those long, long days and spending Sundays in the office paid off. In two years, he moved from marketing director of one multinational drug company to the presidency of another.

"Achieving effortlessly"—the gentlemanly gentility of the fifties ideal—gave way to proud huffing and puffing. Among many men, the ninety-hour week was a boast, a badge of merit.

The new workaholism was well rewarded. With a commitment to his own career, not to the company or to any one product, the Organization Man had become a "professional manager." Whether his "production people" canned carrots or manufactured helicopter parts made no difference to this flexible flyer. Carrying his skills and reputation with him, he was free to go with the highest bidder. No more waiting for the gold watch. Mobility was more often out, not just up. The new zigzag, however, created greater strains and pressure to outwork the universe. The mobile executive no longer competed only with those in his own corporation. The

---

* Significantly, the term is credited to a "pastoral counselor," Dr. Wilson Oates, who first used it in print in 1971.

talent pool had expanded to include "peers" at his level of age and experience within an entire profession: academe, government, industry, law, or finance. Any man who expected to be on the shortlist for the top job might not know who he was running against. With all the unknown competition out there, he could never slow down.

Meanwhile, on-the-job mobility had added another crucial requirement: willingness to travel.

Starting in the fifties, the successful executive and his family had to be prepared to relocate—as far and as frequently as his company (or succession of companies) found necessary. In 1951 *Life* magazine noted a "new American phenomenon, the migration of hundreds of thousands of families of men who have found that the way to move up in corporate life is to keep moving around." A map of the continental United States, crisscrossed with lines, represented the 210 moves made in one month by executive families in four corporations: 60,000 miles of travel for 688 people, "plus a sizeable number of dogs, cats, parakeets and guppies."[12] One of the corporations, IBM, built relocation into the structure of management training and promotion. One move every four years was the rule. In their philosophy, changing communities reinforced company loyalty. A family who put down roots ceased being an IBM family: they became a Greenwich or a Winnetka family. Wives like Carol Cornwell, who presided over the "average" four transfers in twenty years, might well have spoken of hair shirts. To them fell the burden of moving households, leaving friends, changing children's schools. By the late 1950s there was every likelihood that the head of the family would be away when the movers showed up. The age of the business trip had arrived.

Before World War II, business travel, almost exclusively domestic, was delegated to lower-echelon employees—as in traveling salesmen. The boss stayed in the home office, at his rolltop desk.

With the postwar jet age, business went international. In the process, the business trip itself enjoyed dramatic upward mobility, conferring new status and perks, and even creating new kinds of work. A man's career might take place largely on the road or, more realistically, in the air. Getting to the top added yet another requirement: willingness to be away from home for long periods of time.

When Paul Michaelides graduated from business school in 1956, he accepted the offer of two young faculty members to join their financial consulting firm.

"There weren't many people around then who were offering the kinds of services we were," Paul recalls. "We did fantastically well. Within a short time, we had a worldwide network of client corporations and other institutional investors, from Sydney to Düsseldorf." And in the division of labor among the partners, most of the client contact was delegated to chubby, smiling Paul, deemed least professorial and most personable of the three. "I did a lot of traveling," he says, of a period of his life only recently ended. "There were times when I was away for a couple of weeks, home for a weekend, then off again."

Paul readily admits that the brief stopovers at home created more problems than they solved:

"I would arrive with no 'history' of where we were on that weekend and just lark around." But the larking around had more profound explanations than the needed R and R. It was self-protection.

"I felt as though I couldn't really get involved, because I was only going to be there a brief time. I had my own stresses. I'd be going back into the fray. So, I deliberately stayed out of things. I would leave it all to Elaine. The absences and brief descents created definite strains. Because she was not only burdened but to some degree unsupported in her responsibilities. I really didn't know how to handle a full-parent role on a part-time and -place basis.

"She never complained directly," Paul recalls. "She'd say: 'I understand. It's part of the job.' But her anger would still come out. Sometimes she would use the phrase: 'Everything seems to wash over you.' And it did."

He notes that her accusation covered only the periods when he was physically present but not "there." It was only later, Paul says, that he could allow himself to realize what he had missed completely and irrevocably: most of his children's childhood.

"I didn't feel it so much then. I saw it afterwards. Because I had gaps; they told me of things that were *really* important that I had totally missed.

"Paul Jr., our oldest, got hurt wrestling. His nose was broken. There were complications. He came very close to major surgery for blood vessel blockage. I didn't appreciate the seriousness of it."

Although he called home every night—one of the ways Paul tried to keep in touch—on that particular night, Elaine said, "Paul had a little accident today." "She minimized it. I didn't realize until a couple of years later how serious it was, how much I was not in it, not able to provide any help at all."

Then, he missed the birth of his next-to-youngest child, Peggy, entirely. "I was in Seattle at a business meeting. I just couldn't get back for several days." Peggy still reminds him of that "in her charming way." But his daughter's teasing reminders also force Paul to confront the fact that "there's still resentment there. The five others remind me, too, in their own way. I wasn't there for them, when other fathers were."

A greater sadness for Paul, at least now, is missing "all those happy events: someone getting an award, someone in a dance recital. The kind of stuff that you really treasure later. I got some of that, but just enough to know the importance of all the moments I missed."

With the era of corporate travel, executive husbands and fathers became bit players in family life. Their walk-on roles often didn't allow time or attention for even a briefing. Many fathers' arrivals and departures were strictly fortuitous. They might or might not be there for a child's star turn, serious accident, or even the birth of a new baby. When Daddy did descend, expectation and excitement were apt to be dampened by the discrepancy between the remembered parent and the zombied out victim of jet lag, still on Zurich or Tokyo time.

"I just don't know how I could have done it any differently," Paul says. "The travel certainly wasn't voluntary." But he decided that something had to change. That was a prime motivation for his move to a client corporation, a European electronics firm offering him the position of vice president of marketing for North America.

The move was not only a big jump for Paul, but as promised, his new job allowed him more time at home. Yet even at this level, "travel was still significant, if not as unrelenting" as it had been when he was self-employed.

"It was still essential to get out there with clients," he says. "Whether it was selling or wrapping up, you just had to be there."

Travel had become a key article of faith in the mystique of work, its necessity—even in the age of the telex and the conference call—unquestioned.

Now that those at the top were doing it regularly, business travel required more comfortable, even luxurious conditions: more status, like the corporate jet that now waited on the tarmac to take Paul to meetings in Houston or Brussels, "even if I was the only passenger."

Once the mystique of work had declared travel compulsory, and the business trip a stressful and fatiguing part of the job, no tax-deductible expense was spared to make time away from home less wearing to body and spirit.

However many reminders of the miseries of life on the road or in the air, it was hard to avoid the conclusion that fathers were having a lot more fun than anybody at home. They missed not only major family dramas and "those happy events," but domestic crises, like broken boilers and kids throwing corn flakes at each other at 7 A.M. on a Monday morning.

For the middle management executive with a mortgage and three-plus children, the standard of living was a lot higher on the company's or client's nickel. While Mom was shoveling out the hamburgers with stretcher for herself and the kids, Daddy could well be having Chateaubriand for two—a meal that might or might not include a charming dinner companion to brighten the evening.

As "Salesman of the Year" for a manufacturer of prefabricated A-frame houses, Cass Hunnicutt spent half of each month on the road.

"I won't deny," he says, "that I took advantage of all the sexual opportunities available to a man alone. I was in my early forties, I was a big success. It seemed like I'd just discovered sex. I couldn't get enough of it, I went crazy. And away from home, it didn't seem to count."

Getting away from the grind of family life didn't even have to include sex. One executive admitted off-the-record to a (male) interviewer that whenever possible he left on Sunday morning for any scheduled Monday meeting, preferring a peaceful afternoon and dinner alone or with other adult companionship to the rigors of a day devoted to the entertainment of young children.

Yet the myth of the business trip was that it was lonely and boring. To find oneself in a luxury hotel in Düsseldorf or Rio on a Sunday morning, a banker once told me, was to experience the "death of the soul."

Many men realized they were getting off lightly on the family front and sought to compensate, if only symbolically. A friend spent an instructive half-hour at an airport gift shop one Friday evening, observing the brisk commerce in large and costly stuffed animals, purchased by prodigal fathers on their way home.

As children got older, vacations took on a compensatory catch-up function. In the many executive offices I visited in the course of interviewing for this book, photographs of the family on holiday are an interchangeable element of decor. From silver tryptichs or curved Lucite frames smile tanned youngsters, clutching ski poles or billowing spinnakers or self-consciously feeding giraffes at African wildlife preserves.

Sometimes Mom is in the lineup, too. (Daddy—absent in art as in life—is clicking the shutter.) These mementos of expensive holidays speak volumes. The way the family squeezes together to get everybody into the shot always suggests to me the burden of cramming both the unexpected and planned "fun for all ages" into that short week; making sure there are enough happy memories to last until next year. What parent doesn't recognize the obliging grins of teenagers, trying not to look as though they'd rather be with their friends. They know how much these intense interludes of togetherness mean to the "parentals."

The vacations Paul Michaelides has taken with his family, he says, are "part of an effort to make up by doing special things with everybody and getting reacquainted.

"I can remember coming back from one holiday feeling as though I'd discovered some people that had previously been just figures in another room, or even in the same room. Or even," he says, "at the same table. But never before feeling we were together."

These figures in another room were his three older children, whose childhood had been most marked by their father's absence. That memorable vacation, Paul says, was really a moment of revelation when he felt, for the first time, that "we really are in touch and that they are people I care a lot about."

That particular Italian holiday, not so long ago, forced Paul to confront the protective barriers he had erected.

"Sometimes, I would get so remote I would almost say to myself, 'Well, what's so special about that guy—*my own son*— that I should have to be home all the time?' On that trip, I came to the realization that he is very special and precious and dear. I really want to be with him."

As a realist, one not prone to invent fade-outs of teary reconciliation, Paul concludes, "You can't ever recapture those times that were lost." He can only hope that his children, now young adults who reappear only occasionally from law school and laboratory, have forgiven him. He would like to think that present friendship, the golf weekend with a twenty-three-year-old, makes up for the time not spent with a three-year-old. And he is prompt to produce other consoling evidence that this is so. In the poems and hand-made presents they give their parents for birthdays and anniversaries, his children, Paul feels, "go out of their way to let us know we've been a good example." That their example endures, Paul credits entirely to his wife.

"If Elaine had not been as sturdy a person, as strong and as resilient, I would have had a failed marriage—like all the others."

Still, Paul knows that the sturdiness and resilience were role-playing, an adaptation to his demands and refusals.

"She would minimize the problems, explain them away. She knew I was busy. She learned from all the times when she was telling me things that were important and I wasn't really listening. She must have said, 'That doesn't play, so I better not tell him everything I want him to know.'

"That became the pattern. No deep communication. I was only getting what she thought I wanted to hear." But he knows this was not Elaine's choice. "I wouldn't have listened to anything else. By not responding, I taught her to act that way."

Some of it, Paul insists, "was just plain consideration on Elaine's part. She knew I was involved with things that were traumatic in their own way: demanding, exhausting."

But in the familiar and sad irony of marriage, we resent the deformation we impose on the other. Paul sees his wife's "minimizing" as "going much beyond *my* limit" into martyrdom.

"Sometimes I would say 'Why are you being so noble?' So we would get into that *Games-People-Play*, Don't-be-noble, I'm-not-being-noble type of thing," as he describes it humorously. But he views the martyr role as "calculated to make me feel guilty."

As long as work was traumatic and exhausting, men, in turn, could resent being made to feel guilty—either by nagging wives or uncomplaining martyrs. Like surfers, they were riding the crest of a Big One that also happened to be a major cultural shift: from husband, father, and decent provider to success story hero. The genie was out of the bottle, ever more exigent, never to return. The missed baseball game, birthday party, or birth would have to be "made up" later: on the golf course, or in fancy restaurants, on special holidays; occasions to be immortalized by the new Instamatics. Daddy brought to you by Polaroid.

"In law school," Dan Ross recalls, "my idea of success was to create new legislation. Instead, I just made lots of money."

The early years of his marriage are a "blank spot in my mind. They went by so fast.

"I was really starting to get ahead. I was completely focused on the competition, who was doing what in the office.

"It was work, work, work. The young lawyer doing a job, keeping his nose clean, getting well known.

"In 1960, I was thirty. I'd been with the firm five years. I was determined to make partner before the end of the year. I made my goal."

But three years later, he was getting restless. He went out on his own with a colleague. "By then," Dan acknowledges, "I had a little bit of a reputation. I was known as a good tax and business lawyer."

Then, in the late 1960s, a law school classmate called on Dan. He had a cousin who was in a folk-rock group. They were coming to New York to make a record deal and they needed a lawyer.

"I met them on a Saturday. Three guys and a girl. They were the weirdest-looking people I'd ever seen, long hair and kooky clothes. That was before they made it and upside-downed my life."

Within three weeks of hearing them perform, Dan Ross had become their personal and business manager as well as their lawyer.

"They were like my children and my first love affair combined," he says. "I was enthralled by them, their art but especially their

lives. They got as much out of each day as they could, whether it
was beating on their bodies with drugs or making it with broads,
it was: 'tomorrow will only bring more.' My whole way of life had
always been 'put it away in the bank, dust it, don't let anyone get
near it. Get maturity. Get business. Do things in a normal way.'

"I was not a very good parent to my own kids, at this point.
They were very young then. I was bored with them. Just coming
home at night was the most painful thing in the world, whether
I was out screwing or just being with show business people. I was
running a very hot hand then," Dan says. Some nights he never
got home at all. "I figured, as long as I'm there as a father figure
in the morning, they'll know I haven't deserted."

The men who made togetherness into an American ideal turned
out to be the first to disappear from family life.[13] Admitting that
he "routinely worked a ninety hour week," the president of a large
advertising agency added, "my kids claim they never saw me until
they were twenty-five years old." Another Madison Avenue chief-
tain reported that for twenty years he "normally arrived home
after ten o'clock at night, with my children already asleep."

"I have been captured by what I chased," he said.

12
DEVIANTS AND DISSIDENTS

"I don't know where the sixties went," Dick Robertson says, still bemused. "Whatever was happening, I seem to have missed it all. Like the Beatles. I was trying to make a living, support my family, and here the whole world was changing!"

Millions of Americans of our generation would agree, especially the 96 percent of us who were married with young families. Even without the defense of domesticity or the claims of the bread-winner role, most of us were sideliners by vocation, spectators of the political and social upheavals of our times.

"I never went on any civil rights marches or sit-ins," Sue Hodges recalls, "although I was really tempted." In 1959, her Midwestern college town was still a "Southern-sympathizing place," she says, where restaurants didn't serve blacks. "I was mad about that. I *almost* went to a sit-in organized by the local Y." But finally, she never did go.

"In 1968 I remember being upset about what was happening in Chicago. And yet, it was like it didn't really affect me. I had my little baby, and I was just as happy as I could be. Here I was, a trained social worker, and I never got involved in any anti-poverty action.

"I'm ashamed when I look back."

Many of us point to "someone else" we knew and admired who was an activist, as though having a surrogate absolved us, the sympathizers invisible behind our protective coloration.

"My best friend went on the Selma March in 1965," Diane Weikert mentions proudly. "She was in my sorority. She was the only activist I knew. By then, she had little kids, too. I always meant to go to Washington with her later. Instead, I wrote letters to my congressman."

As an administrator and teacher in the Migrant Worker Program, Steve Ortiz made it a point, he says, never to get involved with civil rights: *La Raza*.

"I grew up with all that stuff. Why would I want to go back? My goal for the migrant worker kids was the opposite of radicalizing them. By god, I thought, I was going to make them all middle class. All of my kids were going to get into Harvard!"

"The liberal Anglos in the program were really down on me," Steve Ortiz recalls. "One guy said, 'There's nothing worse than one of them who comes back to teach his people.'

"They were advocates for the poor. I was an advocate for middle-class America.

In the mid-seventies, a former student activist asked me what I had been doing when he was occupying the administration buildings of the college of his choice.

"Pushing a swing," I told him. I added, lamely, that my husband, a pacifist since college, never missed a major peace march or antipoverty demonstration. He was still shocked. Were there really mothers sitting in playgrounds in those days of rage and confrontation? Even while cities burned, civil rights workers and national leaders were murdered; while a far-off war moved closer to home? You bet. Vast numbers of us peered at those events on television screens in disbelief and horror—tempered by distance.

To his astonishment, Cass Hunnicutt saw himself on that screen, a bit player on the evening news and on the stage of history.

1960 started out to be the "high point" of his life. After less than a year at the university, Cass, a transfer student, was so popular on campus he was elected president of his fraternity.

"It was the first time in my life I'd actually received an honor like that. I could hardly believe it."

From outsider and clown—with his crazy Elvis imitations, "forlorn" left-out feelings, a genius for getting into trouble and out of assorted schools—Cass was suddenly high on reciprocated love: the ultimate tribute from his fraternity brothers that assured him he was first among equals.

But a few months after his election, the university was integrated by federal court order. Cass's senior year, which would have been consecrated to giving the best parties and dances, celebrating Old South Week in the most memorably bibulous style, became, Cass says, "one of the most harrowing times I can remember.

"The campus was in constant turmoil. Were the black students going to stay, or weren't they? Crowds would gather in seconds on the strength of rumor."

For the first time, Cass Hunnicutt, like many other Southerners —black and white—became the focus of national news media attention. And he still marvels over that "mind-blowing experience" new to Americans living in the second half of this century: "to take part in an event, *be right there in person*, then watch the whole thing happen again on the evening news."

In the polite way of his part of the world, Cass describes his media baptism as "an awakening thing." But it has left him with a lifelong cynicism about the relation of people, events, and news.

"The TV reporters would interview two guys—a real bitter prejudiced country boy: 'aw-I-hate-those-damned-niggers-don't-want-them-comin-to-this-school'—that kind of stuff. Then they'd talk to a young man from the law school who'd say, 'What is really at stake here: Can the federal government tell the state what to do in all instances that involve federal money? He'd present his case in a coat and tie.

"Who do you think got on television? They just edited out any reasonable, moderate expression of opinion. Because they wanted to paint a scene of explosive antagonism.

"On one occasion, the news people actually asked two boys to stand there and shake their fists at the camera. I was witness to that."

Cass's fraternity, largely Southern, was founded just after the Civil War in reverential homage to Robert E. Lee. Its pillared house was distinguished by a mammoth twenty-by-forty-foot Confederate battle flag flying in front.

"Some of the real diehard guys," Cass recalls, put the flag at half-mast when the black students were on campus. As soon as they left, they would raise it back up again." When the newspapers ran a picture of the flag-lowering scene, Cass knew it was time to remove this emotional emblem of another South, the Stars and Bars that still flew on the state flag.

"I took a deep breath," Cass says, "I went upstairs and I took the flag down.

"To put it mildly, it wasn't a popular act with my fraternity brothers."

But Cass soon had more to contend with than his contemporaries. "Some of the boys in the house had fathers who were very influential around the state. They were using their sons as tools on campus to prevent integration at 'their' school. They were on the phone constantly, trying to get their boys to be campus politicians, fighting the old man's anti-integration cause."

Arguing with his friends revealed to Cass what he had begun to suspect: Their fathers' fight was no longer a deeply felt cause.

"I finally asked one of these 'last ditch guys,' 'What has the black man ever done to you that you should thwart him from getting an education, from bettering himself?' "Cass, I've never thought of it that way," his brother said, "and I'm ashamed that I haven't."

"These guys were just repeating what they heard around the kitchen table at home," he says.

Cass Hunnicutt's part in the high drama of his time and place was a small one. He would be the last to suggest that lowering the Rebel flag from the front of a fraternity house places him in the heroic company of Rosa Parks or the young black children who, accompanied by federal marshals, walked into schools in Little Rock and New Orleans five years earlier or in the ranks of those white officials and parents who placed their lives and the safety of their families on the line for months on end.

Still, the cherished acceptance of the former outsider, the popularity that, the fifties taught us, was the greatest glory we could ever win, was a considerable offering on the altar of conscience. To risk what we most highly prize is no small thing.

Yet Cass knows that in jeopardizing the "happiest time of his life," he stepped into the frame of something larger—as worthy of relating to his sons and grandchildren as the stories of the battles in which their great-great-grandfathers carried those Rebel flags.

"I was really part of a moment of history," Cass says, still astonished. And he wonders, "What are we doing right now that is changing the course of anything?" Nothing, he is sure. Not the way those events in the fifties "rewrote the history books, when the South changed forever."

Elsewhere in America, the new era did not announce itself so dramatically. The fifties limped to a close. But already subterraneans, underground men and women, were seeing signs and receiving messages. Rebellion and anger would soon be channeled into issues. The deformations of middle-class children would be judged as just one more crime committed by an oppressive society that created victims everywhere: rage toward mothers and fathers found larger foci—patriarchal authority, schools, the Establishment. By the middle of the sixties, there was no individual wound or failure that didn't have its corresponding social or political cause.

What the fifties had "done" to us demanded restitution. For some that meant drugs or sex. Men and women on the threshold of middle age huffed and puffed to keep up with the young. Acts of violence were explained as purgative, necessary exorcisms of the prohibitions of the past. Norman Mailer's stabbing of his second wife, Adele, seemed a fitting end to the repressive fifties, described by that writer as "the worst decade in the history of man."[1] Heroism lay in exploring the limits of every inhibition and fear.

Gail Feldstein, the rabbi's daughter, whose overpoliced childhood had imposed privation without protection, was possessed, she says, with a "craving for insecurity."

For Gail, the fifties ended in 1958, when she graduated from the women's college she hated, where she had always felt an outsider. As soon as she arrived, a graduate student in English, at Columbia, she discovered friendship with men and political activism. FOCUS, the group she founded with two male fellow students,* had a double agenda: to end racism and atomic testing.

"We had grandiose ambitions," Gail recalls nostalgically. "We wrote to Albert Camus, we organized colloquia, we put out endless pamphlets and white papers. I educated myself about the bomb. I read up on strontium 90 and cobalt."

More important, she discovered goals other than adult approval. "For the first time in my life, I turned in papers late. I stopped being a good little girl. My rebellion wasn't underground anymore."

---

* Both men went on to distinguished careers: one in politics, the other in economics.

After three years of teaching in a suburban high school, Gail applied for the Peace Corps. It was time to do something bigger, more important. But during the training program in Georgetown, she learned they would have servants in Ethiopia. "I immediately objected. 'I'm not going to have domestics,' I said, 'I believe in democracy.'" In spite of her high grades, she was "selected out" of the program.

Only weeks before, Gail met the fellow trainee who was to become her husband.

"I didn't even like him," she says. But after they had gone out a few times, "Enzo asked me 'more as a joke,' Would I marry him?"

"'Yes,' I shrieked instantly, taking him up on his offer. I think it terrified the shit out of him."

They spent a "miserable year-and-a-half married," which Gail ended by "cutting out" and going to Mississippi. It was Freedom Summer, 1964.

"God, it seems like a million years ago," Gail says, recalling the famous summer when students from all over the country came to Mississippi to register black voters and teach their children, excluded from schools that closed down rather than desegregate. At the end of that summer, almost every one went home, back to college and real life. Gail decided to stay, becoming statewide coordinator of freedom schools.

"I was a terrible martinet," she says, "a parody of all the macho stuff I've always hated. I started hating myself, so I resigned." She moved to a small town where, as the administrator of the only school, she lived with a succession of black families. But after a year, Gail decided that she didn't want to "sponge off people anymore, playing at being poor.

"I felt like such a phony. We all were. Because we could call SNCC headquarters in Seattle and get a money order instantly.

"I wanted to teach in a 'real' black school, but they wouldn't let me. They knew my politics.

"It was hard. Very hard. I felt very isolated. I made a lot of mistakes. I said a lot of rash things to people." But mostly, it was the way she talked to them, Gail reflects, "the old racist, contemptuous way.

"Here I was educated, moneyed—compared to them—coming down there like a missionary to try to save them. What arrogance!

"Black men went crazy over me. I was their first experience with a white woman. We were warned about doing that. Nobody listened.

"There was one man, Jonah. He was just eighteen. He was the first. There were many, many others. Some of them were SNCC workers. Some were white, some were black.

"Part of it was the atmosphere—the tension, the fear. People needed support. We needed to love and hold one another. But there was a lot of fooling around, too. Just conquest.

"At one time, I was sleeping with three different guys in one day—two white men and a black. I didn't feel good about myself when I was doing that, but it was so nice to be desired. After all those years of not being considered pretty enough or popular enough, not attractive. People never get over that. So when someone says, 'Marry me, sleep with me,' I immediately shriek 'Yes! Whoever you are, whatever you bring, I'll learn to love you.'

"I used a diaphragm when I was married, but I didn't take it down South with me. I never asked any guy down there to use anything. I couldn't have said that to a black man; I would have been afraid to hurt his feelings."

Observing the middle-class students who came South to work that summer, Dr. Robert Coles pondered the "frailty of some, the fearlessness of others." The "most tenacious," he concluded, "have frequently been those most aggrieved by background."[2]

Gail Feldstein spent two years in Mississippi. In those twenty-four months, she was arrested twice. The first time she was jailed along with other teachers in her freedom school. They were arrested when there was "trouble" after Martin Luther King was killed. The black woman principal of her school blamed Gail.

"Black women hated us," she says. The second time, Gail went to jail alone, for picketing to demand a compulsory school-attendance law in Mississippi. This time the charge was "corrupting the morals of minors."

Although she had no one to go home to, Gail felt too alone in the South. She packed quickly, said sad good-byes, and began hitchhiking her way to Seattle.

It was her first ride and still daylight. The white truckdriver turned off the state highway and onto a dirt road, where he tried to rape her.

"I talked my way out of it." Before he threw her out of the cab, he said, "Everybody pays, right?"

In Seattle she served as a VISTA volunteer, working with blanket Indians, then headed for New York City and a teaching job. But a few months into the 1967 school year, Gail left her classroom to become a "scab" in the Oceanhill-Brownsville strike in Brooklyn, where daily confrontations split the union, closed the schools, and pitted mostly Jewish teachers against the black community.

During this time, there was another man and another abortion. Then she became the lover of a black teacher and activist; their affair lasted for five years.

"We always kept separate places," she says, "which was fine until Junius started seeing other women. I just can't deal with that. I never could. I absolutely have to be the one-and-only." She wonders whether that isn't "part of our fifties baggage as women."

Gail paid for Junius to stop teaching and go to computer school.

"He must have had contempt for me for doing it, so he had to pull away."

One night Gail came back early from a dance class and found Junius in bed with a woman. "I just blew apart!" she says.

"I was very depressed with teaching." She quotes Gandhi: "The worst violence is poverty." The violence done to many of the children she taught seems to her to have locked their minds beyond reach. "It was classic burnout." She borrowed money from her family and, like thousands of sixties activists, sought refuge in the Berkshire hills.

"I came up here for the country, the way I remembered it from college."

To support herself, she did substitute teaching and cleaned houses—the same way she lives today. After six years of celibacy, she met Lou, who taught shop at Gail's school.

Louis Gerard was a working-class French-Canadian, unhappily married with four kids. "He desired me, he wanted to marry me, so after eleven years of knowing marriage was no cure for anything," Gail says wryly, "of course, I said yes."

"Nothing was really right with this marriage either, but I felt with a ring on my finger, people wouldn't just brush me aside. I'd be OK in this society. That was crucial. The only better thing," she says, "was to be pregnant. And after twenty years of desperately wanting a child, weeping when she saw babies in carriages, in the second and next-to-last year of her marriage, at the age of forty, "there I was walking around the streets of Springfield, pregnant.

"I was in. I'd made it. Finally, I'd paid my dues."

As soon as Maggie was born, Gail says, her chemistry changed. "I became a mother, a totally obsessed mother." By this time the marriage was over. "And that was really the end of men for me."

Emerging from motherhood, Gail became politically active again. Until 1979 she had never read a feminist book.

"I thought there were more important things than women's rights. I thought like a man, shook hands like a man, I always had orgasm."

Radical feminism was the central issue of the world she now inhabited. Most of the women she met "had chosen to live without men."

The political group she founded with two other teachers was focused on nuclear disarmament. But both her associates were gay women. "The one I felt closest to came out to me," she says.

It was becoming clear to Gail that she was preparing for this change. She was ready before she moved here, to this most beautiful country of bookstores with names like Womanfyre, dozens of women's soccer and softball teams, where bumper stickers urge *Take Back the Night* and those who read these words fill in what's missing: take back the night from men and their sexual violation of women.

Ari, Gail's present lover, is twenty-five and works in her family's bakery. She will not tell her parents about Gail and disappears for days at a time either to go home or elsewhere. As Gail falls prey to the familiar panic and possessiveness, Ari becomes sullen and distant.

"I don't want to suffocate her, drive her away," Gail says desperately.

I, too, feel suffocated by her pain and anger. My exact contemporary, she has done many things I am heartily ashamed not to have done. And I am humbled by the physical courage of this tiny woman, with the surprisingly awkward walk of a dancer. As she climbs into the cab of the immense pickup truck parked in her driveway, there is a poignant image of a small child pretending to drive.

She has rushed to embrace her deepest fears. I'm grateful when mine don't come stalking me.

Our deepest fears. Some are as purely human or animal as life itself—fear of physical danger and death. Other terrors have more to do with gender. The millennium will have come and gone before men can imagine the lingering dread of "seduced and abandoned." Perhaps not quite so long, though, until women know the horror of failure: the quick assessment men make of other men, especially in America, to which the women of our generation were merely accessory. (On learning that my husband was a teacher, one executive I interviewed inquired baldly, "Does he have tenure or a chair?" Success required the constant reassurance of being among "peers," even if by proxy.)

There are generational fears, too, by which I recognize my contemporaries as readily as though they still sported crew cuts or billowing crinolines—that fifties horror, noted earlier, of appearing ridiculous. But deeper still, you will know us by our dread of deviance: those symptoms or behavior causing an individual to be rejected by the group.

Stigma is the outward sign of this disfavor. And it's no accident that one of the most brilliant observers of American life at midcentury focused on the adaptations of the stigmatized as "the management of spoiled identity."[3] For our generation, stigma lurked most terrifyingly in the failure to become a man or woman —identifiable by a mate of complementary gender and a family.

How its "management lessons" were learned is described by an event that frames past and present for Martin Duberman.

"At Halloween, when I was a kid, in the days before people put razor blades in candy, we used to go out on the town. I would dress up to the nines in my mother's furs, looking like Theda Bara. Some of the others settled for greasepaint, but not me! I was a Hollywood glamor queen."

Now, every Halloween, there is a famous party attended by most of his friends, all people active in the gay political movement. "I've yet to make it," he says. "Because I've yet to have the courage to dress up. Some of my friends go as sexy vamps; others —the muscular, hairy ones—come as cleaning women, with aprons and mops. But I can neither put on a funny costume or a glamorous one. I cannot get up the courage in 1984 that I had in 1944."

Between 1944 and 1984 Martin Duberman achieved every professional distinction. In careers not easily joined in this specialized society, he is a prizewinning biographer, historian, playwright, and teacher. A man of compelling and glamorous presence, at fifty-three he is more graceful in his gray-blond good looks than he was as a stolid and cherubic undergraduate. His self-mocking humor—the stamp of our generation—points constantly to the ways he has exploited and suffered from being so favored and cursed.

Conflict and contradiction are at the core of his life. His dual career as a scholar and man of the theater reveals only the most visible—a craving for solitude and hunger for applause.

In 1963 his play *In White America* first exposed the history of black oppression and triumph to audiences throughout the country. A few years later he was one of the first teachers to act as mentor to the radical students of SDS. "But, in the seventies," he says, "I was one of the last of my generation to come out as a gay man.

"I can act on behalf of others, but not myself." Quick to disclaim the morally grandiose in such a declaration, he recalls that sex-as-politics was not an easy equation for any of "us," trained in secretiveness and duplicity, whatever our sexual orientation.

"I was ambitious and determined to distinguish myself," he says. The question was, where?

"I was not going to be a world-famous athlete. I was not going to be part of the fox-hunting set. I was not going to be a foreign service officer or elected official, because of my sexual orientation. Academic life seemed a natural resting place, congenial to my notions of success."

With its promise of individual freedom and social acceptability, the teaching profession attracted, in the 1950s, legions of new recruits. The image of the gentleman-scholar still obtained, even as universities became more hospitable to the children of immigrants. Both status and salaries of academics climbed in the course of the decade, as colleges and universities expanded to accommodate new students and new government financing. (In the wake of *Sputnik*, you could study Chinese Art or Old Church Slavonic, courtesy of the National Defense Education Act of 1957.)

As a graduate student at Harvard, Martin Duberman met his

first lover, Larry, at a gay bar in Boston. In the fifties, he recalls, there was an underground network called the "bird circuit"—those few gay bars in big cities that all had names like the Blue Parrot.

They became part of a small secret group—"five or six of us who saw each other constantly. Our open circle of hidden friends," he calls it.

"We were the models. As the only couple, we had succeeded in approximating the acceptable norm of the period—lifetime monogamy. But secretly we were not monogamous, which is important, because it shows how much we tried to do everything possible—without even knowing that we were trying—to meet the going standard of the day!"

There was no escaping the sanctions against "casual sex," "promiscuity." In every corner, however secret or hidden, the couple was the fifties ideal of health.

Within their group, it was safe to talk. But frankness was not self-acceptance. "What we said about ourselves wasn't very flattering."

Disease and pathology were the themes. "Clearly we are deficient. How do we make the best of this bad hand that's been dealt us by fate? Maybe we can still lead useful lives. But how?

"We never had much faith in our ability to sustain relationships," Martin Duberman says. "We believed—as everyone in the fifties did—in that capacity as *the* index of maturity and adulthood. We viewed gay promiscuity with at least as much horror as straight people did."

Today, when he talks on campuses to gay groups, "twenty-year-olds think I'm a creature from another planet. When I describe my guilt, my 'shame,' my horror at my promiscuity, or I use the phrase 'cheating' on my lover, they say: 'What the hell are you talking about? We all have lovers, but we openly, guiltlessly have sex with other people!'

"They really are a different generation. Because of what was done to me, I am and I always will be of the fifties."

Five years later, the small secret Cambridge group had dispersed, its members scattered to jobs and other lives elsewhere. The personal side of life stayed subterranean and guilty. But politically, the good patriotic American boy who believed his country to be the best of all possible worlds had begun to change radically.

In 1962, a few years before the brushfire of campus upheavals, Martin Duberman started teaching at Princeton. With its Southern tradition, reaching back to the days when young Virginia gentlemen arrived at the university with their slaves, combined with the austere Presbyterian legacy of Woodrow Wilson, Princeton was the most conservative of the Ivy League schools. But even here, on the cusp of the sixties, dissent was brewing.

Within a few years, the same student demands for change— expressed by sit-ins, demonstrations, and strikes—would be heard as clamorously here as elsewhere, insisting on an end to war and colonialism abroad, racism and poverty at home, beginning with the rejection of the authority closest to hand.

Most of his colleagues were outraged, threatened—morally if not physically—by the young raucously rejecting their elders' claims to superior wisdom and knowledge. Martin was exhilarated by their anger and eager to learn from their revolutionary agenda.

He rejects now, as he did then, the image of his students as spoiled rich kids, permissively reared children of the Spock generation, looking for bigger Daddies against whom to rebel. For him, the young radicals in SDS were direct heirs of the abolitionists.

"When William Lloyd Garrison started the protest against slavery in 1841," he says, "the words used to discredit him and his followers were the same adjectives used against SDS in the sixties: 'foolishly idealistic,' 'uninformed,' and 'self-indulgent.' "

Protest—his or theirs—cannot be dismissed with psychology. "The students didn't invent these problems: racism, colonialism, inequality in American life; they revealed them. Far from being wrong, the radicals in SDS were too right. The proof is that the problems are as profound now as they ever were. Nobody is doing anything about them anymore. The country has yet to find the stamina to face up to what SDS was exposing.

"I continue to believe that they were the best of their generation," he says of his students. "They showed us the possibilities of harmony, connectedness, affiliation. All of the things I value most received sanction and affirmation in the sixties."

The pied pipers of the sixties did more than release the life-affirming impulses of uptight elders. Suddenly "rebellion and defiance" were in.

"In the fifties I learned to sit on those feelings," he says. "Because to express them was a death sentence, almost literally." In their half-life underground, rebellion and defiance became the stubborn insistence on remaining a gay man. "In spite of everything," he says, "my middle-class values, my desire for approval, my presenting myself constantly for 'cure,' I never gave in.

"I took it for granted I would always be an outsider. Then, suddenly, I was plunged into a new social climate. Everybody wanted out. Suddenly, being an outsider had tremendous clout and status. I was swimming against the tide most of my life. Suddenly, I'm in the tide.

"It was an immense thrill. Like coming home."

Heirs of the abolitionists, the young were going to set us all free. Sworn to redeem the promise of our collective history, they held out the hope that we could rewrite our individual pasts as well.

It was hope doomed to betrayal. The sixties, in which Martin Duberman and thousands of others found a "temporary home and a real sanctuary," were not the Gates of Eden.[4] For the no-longer-innocent, entry did not restore sex without shame.

"The irony is," he says, "that the movement was *not ever* a sanctuary for my gayness. Even though we were all outsiders—me, my students, all my friends outside the university—being gay was never allowed as one of the attributes of outsider status.

"Here I was, 'Mad Martin Duberman,' SDS mentor, addressing a vast student rally, exhorting them not to knuckle under, not to crack under administration pressure. I was egging them on: 'Don't let them cow you! Don't lose ground!' While in my sexual life, I was closeted and terrified, confined to stealthy forays into New York."

"These were my 'roaring early thirties,' " Martin Duberman says bitterly. "Horny as hell. And I was still that much under wraps."

The most horrifying irony of all, to him now, is the reason why he could still "lead a life of such profound deception and self-deception.

"I bought in. I wanted to be accepted for the kind of image I was presenting; just as I did in the forties and fifties at Yale when I wanted to get into Fence Club and Skull and Bones."

"I was still hankering after legitimacy in the most traditional social sense, at the same time that I was fighting it tooth and nail on the political and educational barricade."

Rebellion, for many of us, was muffled and diffuse. Our political, sexual, and social selves met only by accident—long after we learned there are no accidents.

Dr. Camilla Carstairs, forty-eight, is an unmarried, heterosexual, and childless woman. For her, deviance is a daily public accusation. There is nowhere to hide from stigma. Her closet has glass walls.

How did it happen? How did this conventionally "attractive" woman, children's services administrator in city government, with her pleasing manner, cheerful smile, expensive accent, and matching tweed skirt, escape her predictable destiny? "That husband, those children," she says, with the practiced irony of one who has long lived with the expectations her style creates—the station wagon full of tents and sleeping bags or loaded with a week's marketing for six.

"By my middle teenage years," Camilla says, "the expectation was clear: Get married and have children. It was absolutely taken for granted. There was no other way."

"It was perfectly obvious to me that after college, I'd work for a year or two, meet a nice man, have a nice loving husband and some nice loving children. It never crossed my mind that I'd never marry." After commencement, Camilla put all her belongings into the second-hand car her parents gave her as a graduation present and drove straight to Washington. Life in the real world was happier. She loved her job as aide to the Republican senator from her state ("not that I was going after a career, of course"). But the men in the real world, like the boys in college, did not turn out to be husbands. The series of "serious sexual involvements" that began for Camilla cast men who were classically "unavailable." The first was a bisexual who, after several years, moved "definitely in the direction of homosexuality." Some were alcoholic. An affair with a married man went on for many years, at the same time that she was involved with others. "At that period, I was living several lives, because our relationship had to be secret."

Only very recently has she given serious thought to why her life turned out the way it did. Episodes of rebellion, she sees now, were part of a pattern of revolt.

"The ultimate rebelliousness in me was not to marry. At the time, I was devastated when these relationships didn't end at the altar. It's only in retrospect that I see I wasn't going to let them."

Stigma, Camilla Carstairs says, is the "really awful part of being single. People always think there's something wrong with you. Either I'm a lesbian or I'm a whore. The assumption is, if you're not married, you can't have a normal sex life. There must be something 'they' don't know about you. You like girls, groups, or you're totally asexual."

Consciousness of these questions eroded self-esteem in other areas of life. "It just didn't occur to me that I could become a professional or get a Ph.D. I was too scared. Lack of confidence in my intelligence and ability tied in with being single—feeling different, alone."

The small humiliations of the stigmatized, as Camilla calls them, are the worst. The headwaiter who looks past her shoulder for a male when the reservation says, "Dr. Carstairs"; the "defensive strategies"[5] as described by single writer Jane Howard that lead her and Camilla Carstairs to make sure their engagement book doesn't have a blank next Wednesday evening.

Stigma deforms most through the denial of the victim. In the fifties, Camilla says, "the single state just couldn't be. So I had this fantasy that around the next corner, Mr. Right was waiting. 'I am a decent caring human being; therefore, he will be there.' It was that simple. For much too long, I continued to delude myself that it was going to happen: 'that husband, those children.' The truth would have been just too devastating."

Like Martin Duberman, it's the wasted years that make her bitter. "All that time when I could have been looking for me, instead of for him.

"I have lots of anger about being a woman in the fifties mold," she says. "Mostly about the options we didn't have." The missed possibility that makes her angriest is parenthood. "Either having children myself or adopting. Married or not, if I had been born twenty years later, I would have a couple of kids now."

Beyond the stigma of singleness, the deviation from the norm of fifties family life holds a harsh future reality. "Aging alone," she says, "is just too horrible to think about." Her grandparents, aunts, and uncles all lived well into their nineties, knowing they would be looked after by an even larger younger generation.

"What do we do when we're eighty?" she asks. "Who will even know us?"

13
THE THERAPEUTIC SOLVENT

In 1949 *Death of a Salesman* opened on Broadway, a drama of middle-aged failure and defeat by thirty-four-year-old playwright Arthur Miller. Until that year, Miller recalls,[1] "I doubt that I was acquainted with more than two or three people who had seen a psychoanalyst face to face. Psychiatry was for the critically ill or the idle rich grown desperate for something to do."

One New York psychoanalyst, in practice since the late thirties, confirms that "the ones who came originally were the wealthy. Not only was it acceptable in these circles, it gave you status. It was Number One cocktail party conversation."[2]

By that last postwar year, as Miller calls 1949, everything changed. Whether because guilt—as defined by congressional committees, the press, or the FBI—had already marked many of Miller's friends for investigation or because the successful young playwright now moved in new social circles, suddenly everybody he knew was doing it. "A veritable horde of people," he noticed, "went searching out psychoanalysts, and with much the same motive as they had, a decade or two earlier, searched in sociology or Marx for certitudes." Collective ideals of social justice were beginning a long retreat into private concerns: solving individual problems, producing well-adjusted children and happy families. The fifties had arrived.

The "talking therapy" created a strange new self-consciousness. The woman who, Miller observed, used to ask, "What's the matter?" now said: "You aren't relating to me." The verbal vanguard of psychobabble was filtering into common parlance. Well-brought-up boys and girls, once rewarded for leaving ugly thoughts and angry feelings unexpressed, now manifested "hostility and repression."

Several years before Arthur Miller discovered "hordes" of analysands among his acquaintances, pop Freudianism had infiltrated Broadway and Hollywood. Films like Alfred Hitchcock's *Spellbound* (1945) showed psychiatrist heroine (Ingrid Bergman), rescuing amnesia victim (Gregory Peck), framed by the real killer—another shrink. From the forties on, criminal psychopaths and schizophrenics stalked the screen, "explained" at the end by a kindly, humane psychiatrist. In later fifties movies about juvenile delinquents, the same doctor would enlighten parents: there were no bad kids—just unloved ones.

Alternate modes of treatment were not ignored by Hollywood. In *Bedtime for Bonzo* (1951), young psychology instructor Ronald Reagan tries to coax a seemingly suicidal chimp from a building ledge. "Maybe he'll respond to Gestalt therapy," he advises his colleagues as he goes after the primate.

The inhibiting self-consciousness of the analyzed, along with their strange new vocabulary, soon became the subject of a new genre of humor.

In the Broadway musical *On the Town* (1947),* a lustful lady anthropologist laments the vanished instinctual sexuality of prehistoric man. With "no psychoanalysis/He never knew what made him tick/He never paid, it seems/For telling his dreams/Poor

---

* A major motion picture of 1950.

prehistoric hick." Too dumb to know better, her noble savage is also free of Freud's civilization and its discontents: "With no repression/He just believed in self-expression. . . ."

Shrink jokes also made the psychiatrist's couch a basic fixture of cartoons. Getting the point assumed a familiarity with psychoanalytic processes like transference—"My analyst can see through your analyst"—along with more inevitable objects of humor like penis envy. Even when psychoanalysis was not the specific subject, the concepts it popularized created characters unimaginable in a pre-Freudian era. *The Secret Life of Walter Mitty* (1942) exemplifies a constant theme of James Thurber's stories and cartoons: the sexy, heroic fantasies of a meek, henpecked husband.

For a student of literature in college in the mid-1950s, Freudian interpretations of classic texts were required reading. Like all freshmen of the period, I was stunned to learn, through the study of symbols, the "real" meaning of books once deemed suitable for schoolgirls: incest in George Eliot, homosexuality in *Huckleberry Finn*. We caught on fast. Before I had ever seen a phallus, I, too, was writing papers about phallic imagery in Yeats.

It was not until 1959, a decade after *Death of a Salesman* and a few months following college graduation, that I met my first psychoanalytic patient population. And population they were. By the late 1950s, it seemed, the only residents of Cambridge, Massachussetts, who weren't on the couch for several hours a week were the doctors listening to those who were.

Young men would invite you for coffee after class and begin the conversation by telling you how depressed they were. I had never heard this term before—or, indeed, any other clinical self-description.

At first, I was flattered by these confessions. I must be wise and mature, as well as sympathetic, to elicit such personal remarks from virtual strangers. It was soon apparent that these revelations were not to be construed as intimate. Emotional temperature-taking was the conversational coin of the realm: smaller than small talk.

In college, my friends and I were miserable much of the time, but our unhappiness, we believed, had an immediate cause—men. If "he" asked you down for the weekend or to marry him, or if you weren't pregnant, everything was wonderful. It would never have occurred to us to link our total vulnerability to such larger or deeper causes as society or the family. Neither Marx or Freud applied to us.

My only experience of contemporaries "under psychiatric care" were friends who had ceased to function or whose cries for help took obvious "textbook" form.

"What's wrong with you?" I blurted to the first young man who announced that he was off to see his analyst.

"That's the most naïve question I've ever heard," he said huffily, disappearing into the drizzle of late autumn Cambridge. But in fact, most of the people I now met who were "seeing someone" suffered from more specific dysfunctions than generalized depression or anxiety. One friend was immobilized for days by severe colitis attacks that could be traced to no physical cause. The reputations of local therapists were based on highly specialized skills. A Viennese woman psychoanalyst was famous not merely for getting graduate student patients over "thesis block." Her forte was historians and political scientists.

Whatever the symptoms or the therapist's "school," the cure was "adjustment" to the prevailing social norms. No Cambridge analyst ever wondered whether "thesis block" wasn't nature's way of telling its victims to sell insurance, write advertising jingles, or hit the open road. Indeed, the ideal graduate of "successful" analysis looked suspiciously like the ideal fifties citizen: a mature, responsible professional who, if male, was also a husband and father and, if female, recognized that a fulfilling life required being a wife and mother.

In Cambridge in the early 1950s, Martin Duberman presented himself for the first of many "cures."

"Therapy did only negative things for me in the fifties and

through the sixties," he says. "It made me more self-hating. Therapists were so convinced that homosexuality was a character disorder, they managed to persuade me I was diseased—something less than human."

As soon as his sexual orientation came up, he says, the therapist immediately saw it as symptomatic of his "condition" about which something had to be *done*. Various suggestions were made.

"My first doctor insisted that I give up my lover. The next, that I abstain from all sexual contact for a year and a half. Another therapist suggested that I practice up my heterosexual 'techniques' on female prostitutes.

"Suggestions like these," he says, "were standard twenty years ago."

One of the phrases of the period that speaks volumes was "getting straightened out." Merging the moral and psychological, deviants, whether in reform school or therapy, could become "useful members of society." Even straight arrows.

In the fifties it was easy to mistake the part of America that turned to psychiatry for the whole. But, in fact, the "hordes" of fearful ex-radicals-turned-patients that Arthur Miller mentioned in 1949; the anxious and depressed population of Cambridge, Massachusetts, in 1959; the single professional young men and women worried about "normalcy" in the early sixties were, demographically speaking, as representatives of the rest of our generation as a tribe of Berber herdsmen.*

As close to Cambridge as Quincy and Somerville—and as far away as Joplin, Missouri—stronger traditions prevailed. There was immigrant separatism: "We don't tell our troubles to strangers." There was pioneer stoicism: You "got points" for enduring

---

* Betty Friedan's Rockland County, New Jersey, housewives, as described in *The Feminine Mystique*, were atypical in seeking psychiatric help for "the problem that had no name." In the mid-1950s, their counterparts in Bloomfield Hills, Michigan, or Oak Park, Illinois, wouldn't have sought help for problems that *did* have a name.

pain without complaint. And finally the Puritan legacy held guilt (precisely what psychoanalysis pledged to diminish) to be both proof that you had sinned and the first step toward redemption.

"'You made your bed, you have to lie in it'; that was my family's philosophy," Sue Hodges recalls.

Not even collective disaster let most Americans off the hook.

In the depths of the depression, one psychiatrist told Studs Terkel, everybody accepted his role, including

> responsibility for his own fate. Everybody, more or less, blamed himself for his delinquency or lack of talent or bad luck. There was an acceptance that it was your own fault, your own indolence, your own lack of ability. You took it and you kept quiet.[3]

Especially men. The phrase "take it like a man" is just one of many Americanisms that equate masculinity with a stoical and solitary acceptance of suffering.

Most American males, brought up with the definition of manhood as self-reliance, had not changed as young adults. If their fathers could blame themselves for the disaster of the depression, the sons' "personal" troubles, twenty years later, could hardly justify sympathy or help.

"If I have a problem, I try to solve it myself," an Irish-American Boston lawyer said, after telling me of his wife's alcoholism and suicide and the difficulties of being the single parent of a troubled young son. "I don't believe in whining to other people."

"I've never had a problem I couldn't deal with alone," Dick Robertson says of his career changes, divorce, and lesser "life crises." "My decisions always seem to have been the right ones. I guess my own counsel has proved the only one I'll ever need," he says.

Beyond the shame of "washing dirty linen in public" or of "whining," there was another rationale for men keeping their troubles to themselves: the importance of a successful image. The gospel of the cheerful, confident winner as propagated by self-help best-sellers like Dale Carnegie.* *How to Win Friends and Influence People* (1936) warned against being seen as a sad sack. The message—role-play your troubles away—was going strong in the fifties, carried by pastors of positive thinking like Dr. Norman Vincent Peale, and *his* best-selling sermons, along with every article in the *Readers' Digest.* To reveal troubles, real or feared, was not just unmanly, it was damaging to chances of success. To appear worried or defeated was to become, in fact, a loser. Keep smiling. Act confident and successful and you soon will be. Echoing everywhere was the same hollow and self-deluding optimism that destroys Willy Loman in Arthur Miller's *Death of a Salesman.***

In the booming economy of the fifties, with its unprecedented opportunities for the college-educated, there were few excuses for personal failure of any kind. "Everybody felt shame and defeat in having to get help," recalls psychoanalyst Dr. John Weber.[4]

Even in those urban centers where two decades of resident European refugee analysts had made psychiatry more acceptable, "fifties' patients came in on all fours," another psychoanalyst reported.

"By the time we saw them, they were really sick," notes a Midwestern clinician who began his psychoanaltyic practice after military service in Korea, and they came "with discrete symptoms, like medical illness."

"They were obsessive compulsives who, if they touched a book on venereal disease, wouldn't touch the one next to it," recalls Dr. Henriette Klein. "They came with severe migraine. They had stomach disorders. You don't see those symptoms anymore. Start-

---

* Dale Carnegie Schools proliferated throughout the country, promising to transform the anxious or gloomy into Salesman of the Year.

** Despite disclaimers "framing" the film, emphasizing that Willy Loman's fate was *not* to be construed as an indictment of capitalism or "the American way of life," the movie version of *Death of a Salesman* was picketed by pro-McCarthy groups in every theater where it played.

ing in the sixties, patients changed. They were generally unhappy, dissatisfied, lost. 'I'm miserable. Fix me up!' And mainly, that's the current patient population," she says.

In 1956 it took more than stomach cramps, diarrhea, and violent headaches to bring Mike DiStefano, then a second-year dentistry student, to the university psychiatrist He was suffering acute anxiety attacks in the middle of seeing clinic patients, "complete with blackouts and the shakes."

It started on that Valentine's Day in 1955 when he arrived at his girlfriend's apartment with his bunch of violets and found the roses with the card from her long-time married lover.

"My whole world started falling apart," he says. "It was the first period of my life when I didn't know what I was going through.

"I was very depressed. I had trouble finishing course work. I dropped from the top of my class to below the middle. I was ready to leave school."

He tried telling his oldest friend, Phil Catania, what was happening. But at that time, Mike recalls, "if you tried talking to Phil—or for that matter to most guys I knew about anything serious—they made a joke out of it."

"Everyone else knew she was screwing around but you," Phil said, by way of consolation.

As a student in the health area, Mike says, it was easier than it otherwise would have been for someone from his background to move from seeking medical treatment for his symptoms to seeing one of the university psychiatrists in the same building. But the help he expected wasn't forthcoming.

"He kept telling me I'd get over it. Meanwhile, I should 'stick with it,' not drop out of school, and keep seeing him, for 'support.' There was no suggestion of treatment or psychotherapy, as there would be now.

"We never even talked about my depression or anxiety attacks, even though I had come in with very severe symptoms."

Besides physical pain, there was another salient "presenting" symptom of fifties patients: "The marriage wasn't working," notes Dr. John Weber.

"Most people whose marriages were falling apart," recalls Dr. Klein, "came too late. They were no wiser than our own parents about getting help when they should have. When it hit them, they came. Because they were floored; they didn't know what to do."

The ones who came were mostly women. Because in the fifties, Dr. Klein observes, more men left women than women left men. Women were not leaving their husbands and coming for help as they would do a decade later. They were being discarded or abandoned, with no skills and no jobs.

Men came, she says, "who could afford to do the abandoning, and so they felt tremendous guilt. Others were miserable because they couldn't afford to leave."

If marriages hadn't collapsed, Dr. Klein is convinced, men and women of our generation would never have sought help. "They were not part of that next phase—self-improvement."

Between New York and Boston on one side of America and San Francisco and Los Angeles on the other, marriages were also unraveling, with bewildered partners wondering what had happened. Mainstream Americans, though, were not ready for psychiatry with its connotations of "mental illness." Psychoanalysis, "terminable or interminable," as Freud titled a famous paper, was intellectually forbidding and financially prohibitive.

Counseling was the form of help most middle-class Americans sought when marriages were in trouble. Through counseling, many fifties men and women backed into psychotherapy.

Historically, seeking specific solutions to specific problems is part of American pragmatism. There was less shame and blame attached to "solving" the problem marriage than for either spouse to admit there was "something wrong with me"—and certainly less opprobrium than attached to divorce. (That troubled marriages "masked" the ills of disturbed spouses, as Dr. Klein observed, would only emerge later.)

"Since the 1930s," one historian notes, Americans have been prompt to admit that they "needed professional help in playing individual roles *crucial to maintaining institutions*" [italics mine].[5] Whether because "experts" undermined our confidence in our instinctual abilities, as critics like Christopher Lasch maintain, or for other reasons, "doing what comes naturally" as husbands, wives, lovers or parents, began to seem more difficult, dangerous, or impossible.

Marriage counseling combined the promise of professional help with a reassuring "cover." Until the late 1960s, most counselors were professionals in other fields, who only incidentally advised couples about marital difficulties. They were clergymen; priests, rabbis, and ministers, whose training traditionally included "pastoral counseling" to troubled parishioners. Or they were social workers, lawyers, and especially doctors.

"As late as 1950," report two historians of professional marriage and family therapy, "over one-quarter of the members of the American Association of Marriage Counselors were gynecologists and an almost equal proportion were in other medical specialties."[6] The gynecologist who, while looking at the ceiling, assured Pat Carroll Brewster that sexual relations with her husband would improve after the birth of her child would probably have also described himself as a marriage counselor.

As the American divorce rate began its climb immediately following World War II, agencies and experts proliferated whose goal was "keeping the family together." Dr. Paul Popenoe,* a biologist by training and founder of the social hygiene movement, became the best-known practitioner and publicist of professional marriage counseling through "Can This Marriage be Saved?"—

---

* One of the panel of "experts" summoned by the *Ladies Home Journal* to advise on "The Plight of the Young Mother" in 1956.

his enormously popular column of monthly advice in the *Ladies Home Journal*—and on early television, where he provided the case histories for *Divorce Court*, a "semidocumentary" of the 1940s and 1950s that is still going strong.

Soon the natural fit between marriage counseling and the training of psychologists and even psychiatrists created a growing army of practitioners dedicated to helping men and women remain husbands and wives. For those imbued with the expectations of the fifties, the stigma and guilt attached to "seeking help," failing to solve your own problems, was outweighed by "the worst scenario": getting divorced.

Don Cornwell would have been the last man in the continental United States to agree to counseling—with his wife or alone. He would never talk to Carol about any of the problems that led to their two separations and eventual divorce, his anger about her increasingly radical views and political activism, her arguments with his corporate colleagues, her unhappiness about their sexual relations, and his ever-more-frequent physical expressions of rage.

Then, in 1969, a few months after his company had moved them for the fourth and last time, Carol Cornwell told her husband she was deeply involved with another man and asked him for a divorce.

"As soon as we separated, we both started counseling," she recalls. "Don started seeing a psychiatrist. I was seeing a psychologist. In a way, I was astounded that he would see anyone. But he desperately wanted the marriage to survive. The idea of divorce just appalled him. Part of it was his parents. They were so horrified, they wouldn't tell anyone that we were separated."

Neither would Don. "It was supposed to be a secret. When people called the house for him, I wasn't supposed to say he was no longer living here. I was just to say he wasn't home and take the message."

Nine months later, Don Cornwell had moved back into their brick colonial house in a picture-book New England suburb.

"I admit it, I just caved in," Carol says. "I panicked about money. The man I was in love with just dissolved as soon as I was separated."

For the next year, the Cornwells were in "couple counseling" with the psychiatrist Don had been seeing. "He saw us together and occasionally separately." But there were crucial areas of the marriage that the therapist never mentioned. "Sex, for example. He never brought it up. Not once. Yet that was a major area of dissension between us.

"He kept telling us that we had to communicate better, but he obviously never saw the sexual as part of that process. It just staggers me, when I think about it now."

We were not the therapeutic consumers we would become, knowledgeably weighing the gender, ideology and training of potential therapists; long-term or situational, behavioral or Gestalt, group or individual treatment.

Nervously, couples crept into counseling. In the safe presence of a third party, some were prepared to say the unsayable for the first time. "His" and "her" versions of family life poured forth. Blame was amortized, "owned" by each spouse. Fifties husbands and wives who had never had anything to say to one another were going to learn to "communicate," by God.

However primitive or incompetent the counseling—or doomed the marriage—it was the first crucial experience for many of our generation of expressing and hearing "forbidden" feelings. The referee's inadequacy or "Band-Aid" approach was often the first step in sending clients into more sophisticated therapy. From Band-Aids, many husbands and wives moved to surgery. With help, they were able to "cut out" of an unhappy marriage, at the same time severing their ties to traditional religious beliefs.

On the grueling drive each Friday, over the Arizona mountains, Steve Ortiz felt confusion, guilt, and anger. He dreaded going home. He would be exhausted and yell at his kids. He had no

desire to see his wife. He wished he could spend the two days
of leisure drinking and arguing politics with his new friends. But
the way Steve Ortiz had been brought up, these were no reasons
for a man to leave his family. He and Rita needed advice, he
decided.

"First, we went to a priest for help with the marriage. He
punched me on the shoulder. When he found out how long it
had been since I'd been to confession, he said, 'You're not in a
state of grace.' Then we went to a marriage counselor. His view
was we should work together more. Rita should wash the dishes,
I should dry. That would solve all our problems. It was completely mechanistic, completely idiotic. Then I saw a psychiatrist.
He helped me to end the marriage."

Not all marriage counseling prescribed togetherness at the sink
as the solution to drifting apart in other areas of life. But like Dr.
Paul Popenoe, who could point proudly at the number of families he had helped to stay together, counselors were counted
successful when marriages remained intact. As a symbolic act of
good faith, the refusal of "professional" help—a refusal most
often voiced by men—almost always announced that the marriage was over.

In the spring of 1974, after flying for what felt like days, Sue
Hodges found herself alone in La Paz, Bolivia, signing adoption
papers for their third child. At the last minute, Bob Hodges hadn't
been able to get away.

There had been months of discussion about this child. After
two adopted daughters, Bob badly wanted a son. Sue, already
troubled by his lack of involvement with the children, was reluctant to start all over again as an unofficial single parent.

"He was absent even when he was there," she says. "I felt
abandoned and alone most of the time."

She tried to talk him into marriage counseling before making
the final decision about another child. "Absolutely out of the

question," he declared. "Our problems are nobody's business." In fact, there *wasn't* a problem, Sue says he insisted, "except that I was always bitching."

Sue gave in. If having a son meant so much to Bob, she reasoned, maybe this new baby would change things.

During the five days in Bolivia, she realized for the first time in her life that "I was very angry. I was still mad when I came back. And I've never gotten over it."

A few months after her return, "we had gotten to the point where there wasn't anything happening," Sue says. "We were just so distant."

It was 1975. They had been married for seventeen years, since Sue's junior year in college and Bob's first year at law school.

In the last year of their marriage, they did get help. "It was really divorce counseling, though," she says, "family therapy to help make it through the separation with as little pain as possible —especially for the kids."

Among many ironies: the counseling that eased the end of their marriage accommodated Bob Hodges to professional intervention in his personal life. When their oldest daughter, then eleven, began having problems in school following the divorce, a child psychiatrist told Bob Hodges that he had to spend more time with Nancy.

"I could ask him to spend time with the kids; it was like talking to the wall. When the doctor said he had to do it, he did it. The paid expert had spoken!"

Diane Weikert, beauty queen and sorority star, had too many secrets to ever risk telling a single one. She couldn't have told anyone about her sexual relations with her boyfriend in ninth grade, her fear of getting pregnant, her terror of having V.D. She would not have confided in anyone—not even her best friend— of her cold calculations in wanting to marry Tom Weikert, leader of everything on campus and likeliest to succeed. She could not have articulated to herself her guilt in surviving the death of her only sister, killed in an automobile accident in which Diane was not even present; or how much worse she felt about not wanting to care for her sister's child.

With so many secrets, so much to feel bad about, it was easier to numb out and play dead; to play corporate wife over candlelit dinner tables, or doting mother dying Easter eggs; to decorate three houses, go bowling with the girls and later, learn to play golf and fly a plane. And read all the time.

"That was how I had always escaped. Besides what I learned from books, what did I know? I knew that children sometimes drive you crazy. I knew that I didn't like the people in my neighborhood. I knew that Tom never paid any attention to me."

If anyone were to have asked her, "Are you happy?" she would have felt guilty saying no. "I had everything to be happy for. What more could I want? Just ask any man," she says, laughing.

Two years ago, Diane Weikert, who never told her secrets to anyone, appeared in a psychotherapist's office.

"I had a crisis in my life," she says cautiously. "I lost someone very dear to me. I lost her and I felt that I didn't want to live anymore. She was a neighbor. We became very good friends. We became more than friends. We were lovers."

For the first time in her life, at the age of thirty-two, Diane Weikert was close to another human being. She had emerged from the "emotional hibernation" one writer has described as characteristic of many of our generation.

"We talked for hours. We talked all the time. We talked when we were making love and when we were hiking, or paddling down rivers. Sex was just part of it. It was the totality of the love that made the sex so marvelous."

"She thought I was wonderful," she says shyly. "No one had ever thought that before."

Her husband knew how much she loved her friend, but to what degree or in what way she isn't sure to this day.

"He didn't seem to mind that I'd found her.

"But then he was getting more successful and rewarded in his career, both in the office and out. He was on government commissions. He traveled constantly."

Her lover chose to end their relations. She had become bored. Or irritated. Or guilty. "She removed herself from my life, slowly and painfully.

"That was when I wanted to die."

Once, those who were saved from suicide and thus, mortal sin, might have consecrated their lives to God. Diane Weikert's life is devoted to therapeutic salvation. Besides her own continuing treatment, she is a counselor in an adolescent drug program. She will do for others' children what she could not do for her own adopted daughter.

Since leaving her marriage, she lived briefly and unhappily with another woman. Alone now, she hovers uneasily on the margins of her city's lesbian community.

She is full of regret and afflicted by memories: of her own failures of love and the loss of the one passion she might ever know.

In another era, she would have become a holy woman; her guilt and suffering a mark of election. With her tragedies commuted to problems, she is condemned to seek cures.

From the middle of the 1960s on, the sexual revolution and its "liberation" of women seized the headlines. The effects of feminism, of women returning to the work force; the consequences of the pill and the evidence of limitless female orgasmic capacity were worried by media and scholars. The separation of female sexuality and conjugal love was, it appeared, the psychosocial transformation of our time. Upheavals though these might be to the social order; women of our generation adapted to changes in the sexual climate with ease and enthusiasm. Feminine "restraint" and "natural" monogamy were revealed as fear of pregnancy or a "bad" reputation. "If the Mother Superior could see me now!" a friend crowed, detailing her latest sexual adventure. Protected by nearly foolproof contraception, many of the most conventional women, including those brought up within the confines of religious orthodoxy, discovered that guilt was an invention of mothers' sons.

"Welcome to the post-pill paradise," coos Georgene, one of John Updike's proper suburban matrons in *Couples* (1966) as, naked, she welcomes the hero for "elevenses" on her sun porch. Unlike his neighbors' wives, Piet Hanema is a guilty adulterer, wrestling in nightmares with his Dutch Calvinist God. Most satire of the sixties derives from the conflicts of traditional fifties men: Philip Roth's Neil Portnoy, Peter de Vries' tweedy suburbanites, all of Woody Allen's heroes, still dragging the chains of Jewish or Protestant sexual taboos, as they sink in the moral and psychological quicksand of loosened mores. Given permission to do it, with women available as never before, there wasn't a fig leaf left. A man who failed to take advantage of this sexual cornucopia, or one who felt terrible when he did, "needed help."

As the father figure to his folk rock group, Dan Ross had all the paternal conflicts that came with the job, added to his split-level commuting life. Half the week he was in his Park Avenue law office, a telephone clamped to each ear, and checking in at home in Great Neck; then it was on the plane to San Francisco.

"We were right in the middle of Haight-Ashbury when it was a hot scene," he recalls. "The group had just had their first big hit; the mayor was coming to our parties. We lived on two houseboats in Sausalito—the band, the singers; the girlfriends, the groupies."

"At first," Dan says, "I wouldn't even go to parties because everyone was smoking dope. I kept thinking I was going to get busted and go to jail for the rest of my life. My diploma's going to go out the window."

There were other temptations that he wanted to act on, but he didn't. "I was nervous about getting V.D. About who knows what? I put crosses up in front of myself. If the gal was too easy, she was easy for ten guys before me. My father used to have an adage: any woman you can sleep with the first night is a trashcan and everybody's been trashing her.

"I used all these icons to protect myself."

One night, after a sold-out concert, there was a party on the houseboat. Dan Ross celebrated by smoking his first joint.

"I remember this gal sitting cross-legged, at the end of my bed, facing me. She had on one of those miniskirts that came up to her hips. I thought the group was going to leave her there for me. But since I didn't put any move on her," he recalls, "she left with the others for another party.

"A few months later, we got a letter from a V.D. clinic out there. They gave us a list of people who were contacts of hers. She apparently had such a bad case, they were trying to track down everyone she'd ever been with," he says, still sighing with relief. "This was one opportunity I passed up that wouldn't have been worthwhile."

Shortly after, Dan Ross went into analysis, "classical Freudian, with a woman doctor," he says. "I went to get rid of my uptightness, my secretive ways," hoping finally, that he could break with the past. He was determined to escape sexual guilt, the path "patrolled" by his parents.

Delivering on the implicit promise of orthodox Freudian analysis, greater achievement and success, Dan Ross started making millions. He had, it turned out, a "golden ear" for picking musical talent. The second rock group he took on, as manager and lawyer, became even bigger than the first. They were at the top of the charts in weeks, followed by a sold-out concert tour. He discovered a beautiful folksinger and composer. He took her career and life in hand. She became a star in months.

Meanwhile, Dan recalls, "I was making a lot of money as a bread-and-butter lawyer in taxes and real estate. I bought an insurance company, a medical consulting firm, and a small outfit that produced musical education tapes. I had the Midas touch."

He also had a beautiful blonde Gentile mistress, "just what every novel and movie said that every Jewish boy wanted," he notes, "plus a wonderful wife who loved me very deeply and two nice children."

"I had it all," Dan Ross says, "and I wasn't happy.

"At one point, I thought I had an infection. It turned out that I didn't," he recalls. "But I was fucking more women than I wanted and I thought, This is crazy. Why am I out to seduce every woman that I meet? Why am I obsessed with sex? I would get into bed with these women and say: What am I doing here?

"I asked my internist for another shrink. I said, 'This is failing. There's something wrong with my system.'"

Analysis never yielded to Dan Ross the secrets of his psyche, of what was wrong with his system. Instead, he says, he found out something much more important—that "it doesn't matter"— a discovery that still makes him roar with laughter.

What mattered was revealed to him on a mountaintop in the Smokies. Mysterious are the ways of the Lord and of the varieties of therapy in the seventies.

It happened when he decided to merge his medical consulting firm with his small recording business to produce mood-altering tapes. Music had influenced him so deeply that he became convinced its psychological and especially its therapeutic potential had never been explored. To learn about the process, he joined an intensive five-day retreat in the Carolinas. The leader, a noted music therapist and LSD researcher, had shown, Dan says, "how music helped break through the blockades built with words and thoughts."

His original motive was profit. "My idea," he says, "was to go to the major manufacturer of Valium, and tell them we have tapes to enhance the value of their tranquilizer for the housewife; one tape for anxiety, another for depression. Ultimately," he explains, "she would be weaned from the pills and just use our tapes. But, of course, I wouldn't tell that to the drug people."

"It took me a day and a half to wash Freud and New York out of my system. The group on the mountain was very unsophisticated—sweet, gentle people.

"We practiced the therapy on each other: first you counted down to an alpha state; your partner told you when to go with the music. Then you described to your therapist the images or fantasies in your head.

"I had a rebirth experience. It was incredible. I felt myself dropping through a system of gates, like a water chute. I came out into the light of day, into a new, bright world. I knew I had traveled through time and space. I felt timid and loving and gentle for the first time in my life.

"In imperceptible ways, my personality changed, permanently. The last night, on the mountaintop, I looked through the trees at a full moon. I thought of my father. I had a revelation: I love my father and I never told him: That was the message of those five days. I better get home and tell my father I love him before he dies.

"I went home. I told my father all I had been feeling. I told him how much I loved him. How grateful to him I was. He immediately deflected it. He said, 'Tell your mother; she needs it more than me.'

"But that was the turning point of my life, and the beginning of my break with the past."

After three years of psychoanalysis, Cass Hunnicutt returned from California to the Southern city of his birth. At forty-four, he was finally able to say it:

"Mother, I hate your guts," he told her.

Twenty years before, in June 1965, he had arrived in San Francisco, just married, with a child on the way. Like millions of Americans before them, Cass and Betsey Hunnicutt had gone west, knowing more about what they fled than what they sought. Still, flight from family had put Cass in possession of a truth that most young men of his generation had yet to discover. He was arrested in adolescence.

"I knew I lacked self-discipline and willpower. I didn't seem to have much control over myself; I had just gone pell-mell along. I felt as though I was always in motion. I just couldn't seem to settle down to anything."

Now, he decided, was the time he had to do it, "the time to begin to act grown up."

Young men of every period and culture experience this "great divide," when youth yields to becoming a man. Peculiar to our generation, though, was the conviction that if we can just "act the part," "becoming" will follow naturally.

He began with hypnosis. From the most mechanized form of control and direction, Cass moved through the full spectrum of the human potential movement, trying to seize and expand those fleeting moments—"glimpses," he calls them—"when I surprised myself in physical or mental capacity." There was PACE; there was est, there was Lifespring. There were other courses, programs, and seminars—all of which he calls "growth experiences"; each of them seeming to "explain a piece of the puzzle that was me." Together, they also provided the reassuring continuum of the group, the fraternity.

The transitional men of the late fifties who emerged into reluctant adulthood on the cusp of the sixties were made-to-order candidates for the new psychotherapies. Imprinted with fifties values, they wanted "that straight and true track" Cass Hunnicutt sought, whose destination was known and laid out in advance. At the same time, change was potently in the air, including the impulse to jump that same track.

"What I was looking for," Cass says, "was something to be released in me that was buried."

One program, defining man as a "goal-seeking mechanism," seemed to work so well for Cass, "it was spooky," he says. "I thought I was magic. I thought I'd found the key."

At the time, he was selling prefabricated A-frame weekend

houses. Within six months, he became number one salesman in the United States.

"I thought I could handle anything," he recalls.

He borrowed a "ton of money" and bought a competitor's business. But all he had done, he discovered, was "build a house of cards." The reality of failure was devastating.

"I got to this low point," Cass Hunnicutt says of his depression. "It was like living at the bottom of a black cave where you eat the moss off the walls."

Then, when it was supposed to happen, Cass says, he found "a very large, strong and gentle man" who was also a psychoanalyst. In three years of treatment, he confronted the "unfinished business" of his life. While he parents were still alive, he decided, there was only one place where he could complete the work of growing up.

Cass Hunnicutt measures the distance he has come in the year since his return home by a visit with his mother a few days ago. In the same garden where he played as a child, he was laughing and talking with his mother about loving and hating her.

"I told her that you can't hate someone unless you love them. You have to have the same energy. You have to care enough to hate."

A tiny population, consisting of the intelligentsia and the rich, who were clients of psychoanalysis in the fifties, had become a critical mass of Americans learning to speak of love and hate, to scream like infants, or simply to "communicate." From puritans we had become a generation of patients.*

In their lifetime, our grandparents experienced the technological revolution—from horsedrawn buggies to airplanes. Our generation lived through another extraordinary change: the transition from shame in seeking treatment for personal problems to a

---

* But not, I believe, the patients described by Christopher Lasch in the *Culture of Narcissism.* In any case, it is unclear about whom Lasch is writing: his— and my—contemporaries, converted to these "new" symptoms, or our juniors.

sense of entitlement. Alleviating emotional pain no longer needed to be justified as "crisis intervention" or excused as frivolous cosmetic surgery. We had a right to all the help we could get. Increasingly, our fellow taxpayers and employers would have the obligation to pay the bill.*

From the puritanical attitudes of our upbringing—the virtues of solving our own problems, of not complaining, of lying in the beds we had made—we were suddenly, as adults, enjoined to view life as a no-fault accident against which all prudent parties should be insured.

The burden of this change fell on fifties men. Although women outnumber males as clients of psychotherapy, it is the growing numbers of men who illustrate, most dramatically, the shift from the early 1950s to the present.

Besides becoming guiltless—if not tireless—sexual performers, the fifties male, that last holdout of the silent generation, was enjoined to find his tongue. Between the extremes of love and hate, he was now expected to express the entire spectrum of emotions "appropriate to the roles" of father, husband, lover, and friend. But, as the authors of a recent study ask,

> Who [was] resocializing them with the skills needed to realize such relationships—skills in openness to feelings and fantasy, skills in self-disclosure and emotional sharing?[7]

Skills, we should add, that women were always expected to develop.

Just as the transitional male of our generation had never seen men take on the physical tasks of housekeeping and child care, still less had he had occasion to observe adult males in the act of conveying love, tenderness, and intimacy. Quite the reverse. If he learned what it meant to be a man from his own father, the lessons were apt to be those of emotional restraint and authoritarian style.

* The most incontrovertible proof of this shift to entitlement: "third party" payments for psychotherapy.

When Lane Brewster was fired as president of a multinational food products corporation, he was given a year to find another job. Along with an office and a secretary, "outplacement support" in the 1970s also provided executives with psychotherapy.

To his surprise, he liked the psychiatrist chosen by the company. So he was agreeable when the doctor asked him whether Pat would be willing to come and talk to him.

"I'll tell her to call you in the morning," Lane said.

"Why don't you try asking her?" the doctor suggested.

To his credit, Pat says, Lane came home, stricken, as he described the exchange. "That was the first time," she says, "he realized the way he talked and treated—all of us."

"I never knew," he said. "I didn't hear those kinds of things because I'd always heard them."

Were fifties males, as psychoanalyst Dr. Henriette Klein suggests, "hopeless"? Or, through effort and therapy, was there hope? One thing was certain: whether they remained in first marriages or tried again with the statistically probable younger woman, both the contract and the life script would be revised.

For women, the process of unlearning through therapy involved two phases. First came a veritable potlatch of fifties definitions of femininity: submissive, conciliatory, dependent behavior; seductiveness and "making nice" to men—at home, in bed, on the job—were all to be jettisoned. The sacrificial role, especially, was the sign of ill health. No more putting everyone else's needs before our own—including children and aged parents. The Good Housekeeping seal of approval was the brand of the slave.

Saying no was the easy part. The busiest therapists were ministering to women struggling with Phase II. After Nora slams the door, how does she earn a living, while accepting herself as a less than perfect mother, daughter and friend? And where is the man who will love her, stripped of her lovable fifties self?

14
GROWING UP—SEPARATELY

Carol Cornwell has an "imaginary Polaroid" of what she calls the turning point in her life.

It is December 1964. Late afternoon in her cheerful kitchen, where drawings by a six- and an eight-year-old cover two cork bulletin boards and one refrigerator door. She is directing the artists, Mattie and Chris, who are now creaming butter for Christmas cookies while she nurses the baby.

At the same time, she recalls, "I've got the telephone crooked between my ear and shoulder advising another nursing mother in my job as volunteer La Leche counselor.

"I was telling her to hang in there," she says. "That I was breastfeeding my third child, even though my husband was angry and jealous, my gynecologist was embarrassed, my mother thought it was lower class, and my Junior League friends teased me for being a hippie.

"Suddenly, I looked at my typical suburban kitchen, my happy kids making cookies, the baby in my arms. I heard what I was saying to this stranger and I thought: I'm a traditional woman, and I'm a radical."

Breastfeeding—as an issue, an ethos, a way of life—sums up the conflicts and continuities of the fifties and sixties. What, after all, could be more traditional, more maternal, than the Madonna-and-child image of the nursing mother. Wasn't Princess Grace of Monaco* herself a prime mover of La Leche?

At the same time, though, breastfeeding ran counter to both the image and roles of the antiseptic suburban wife and mother, striding from her stainless steel kitchen of labor-saving appliances to the station wagon. Her schedule was dictated by commuter trains, car pools, Cub Scouts, and the cocktail hour. The return to the organic rhythms of mother and child were, in fact, a monkey wrench thrown into the smoothly running gears of family and social life, fifties style.

The new pediatric wisdom told us that breastfed babies were healthier, with proven immunity to most childhood diseases—including the common cold. Anyone (which meant everyone) of our generation who wanted to be a better mother with a healthier child would breastfeed.** Beyond physical health, nursing held the promise of greater intimacy and emotional closeness between mother and child—a bond many of us felt had been lacking in our relations with our mothers. (A less exalted reason was the convenience, which I appreciated most: dispensing with nasty plastic bags of Enfamil on outings; being able to read and telephone while nursing—activities impossible to manage holding a bottle.)

Yet the fifties marriage "partnership" imposed an ethos of wife-companion. A woman was supposed to be emotionally, sexually, socially, and professionally available to her husband.

---

* Grace Kelly's credibility as a La Leche patroness was enhanced by her life story, as retold in endless interviews and articles: the ultimate fifties woman who had sacrificed a career for the joys of marriage and family.

** When Priss Hartshorn Crockett, Vassar '33, insists on breastfeeding her new baby, her classmates, in Mary McCarthy's novel *The Group*, ascribe such exotic behavior to her husband, "a budding pediatrician" anxious to try out his theories of infant care.

In particular, the wife's roles as hostess and consort were seen to be crucial—as never before—to a man's success.

Breastfeeding became a prime example of two conflicting "goods."

Wives of professionals and executives who were also nursing mothers agonized: What to do about the missed feeding on evenings when they were summoned into the city for a dinner with clients?

In the early sixties, one friend described emptying her painfully engorged breasts into a pink marble sink in the ladies room of the Waldorf-Astoria, during a black-tie dinner of the American Bar Association.

"It was one of those moments," she said, "when you look in the mirror and see yourself as a vignette in the satirical novel of our times."

For Carol Cornwell, La Leche counseling was the beginning: "It got me thinking. I started to see men's opposition to breastfeeding as part of a pattern of controlling women. From there, I began moving out, doing things independently."

If she had had extra money for baby sitters, Carol says, she would still have chosen "fairly conventional volunteer work, like Meals on Wheels or the local thrift shop. But I was limited to the telephone."

One evening, a lawyer and new neighbor asked Carol if she would help on a fair housing committee. She could do phone canvassing and clerical work from home.

Rezoning their community for public housing added another topic to the agenda of political arguments at the Cornwells'.

"Do you want a bunch of poor blacks on welfare living here?" Don Cornwell demanded.

"I realized," Carol says, "that was just what I did want. I didn't see how you could call yourself a Christian and vote to keep poor minority families out of your neighborhood."

Don Cornwell didn't see why Christianity should result in bringing both property values and the neighbors' wrath down on their heads. But he did feel strongly, when the fourth and last of their corporate moves took them to Massachusetts, that it was time the children had a religious education. Carol could choose the denomination.

"We joined the Unitarian Church," she says, "and that became my life." But like so many of our lives, the particular events seem "accidental."

"I went to a meeting of the Social Responsibility Committee: I misread the announcement. I thought it was Sunday School Night." A few weeks later, she was in the forefront of antiwar activity. She opened the church's peace office, which put Vietnam draft resisters in the area in touch with counseling. "I went on all the peace marches, taking the kids with me."

Because of her experience, she was asked to head the committee on fair housing. From the church committee, Carol got involved with a group in town.

"Our community had a sizable black population who were being discriminated against at every level—from middle-class professionals to welfare families."

Then, through the children, she found herself in the heat of a still more incendiary local issue: busing. The parents' group she joined as class mother "were not your usual PTA. They were determined to integrate the suburban schools. I really got out there and worked for probusing candidates. I rang doorbells in very hostile ethnic neighborhoods in the city, trying to talk to people."

What changed fifties sideliners into sixties activists? Or didn't they change?

"I think I was always a radical," Carol Cornwell says. "In the fifties, there was nowhere to go with it."

By the middle of the sixties, there was no doubt about where to go and what was at stake: America's moral survival.

"These were life and death issues: Vietnam. Poverty. Racism," Carol says. Issues to engage the moral indignation and religious beliefs of Cold War children for whom immorality and sin once meant "going all the way."

Another life-and-death issue pried Pat Brewster from a decade spent in neutral.

One winter day in 1973, she found herself on a bus headed for Albany, along with the rest of a delegation from *Catholic Women for Abortion.*

Only a few days earlier, another mother in her son's catechism class had telephoned. "It was just after the Supreme Court decision: *Roe* v. *Wade.*" The state legislature's bill was pending.

"This woman whom I didn't even know said: 'Pat, the Right-to-Lifers are running up and down the halls, with foetuses in jars, screaming. Will you go to Albany with us?'

"She warned me that I had to be willing to interrupt the legislative proceedings, and that we ran the risk of going to jail.

"I thought about it for a minute. Then, I said, 'Yes, I'll go.' "

"Ten years before," Pat says, "I wouldn't use the pill. Now I was ready to go to jail for abortion rights. That's how far I had come."

Going quietly to jail, for most of us, would have been easier than noisily interrupting a session of the legislature. One historian saw the new lack of deference to institutions, public figures, or social occasions as the most profound rift in values that came to separate young sixties radicals and their parents.

"For any generation born before World War Two," writes Philip Slater, "rituals, ceremonies and social institutions have an inherent validity that makes them intimidating—a validity that has priority over human feelings."[1]

Slater recalls a sketch by comedian Shelley Berman satirizing attitudes of passengers about to board an aircraft rumored to be unsafe at any altitude. "Most people," Berman observed, "would die quietly, rather than 'make a scene.' "

Especially most fifties people. Far more dramatic than differences between parents and children is the 180-degree turn made by Americans of our generation in their middle thirties. Taught by our elders that there was but one unforgivable sin, we nonetheless risked eternity in the inferno: *We made a spectacle of ourselves.*

Carol Cornwell and Pat Brewster were not exceptions. The most traditional wives and mothers became community organizers; antiwar activists, and regular participants in sit-ins, marches, and demonstrations.

Despite women's statistical record of being more conservative than men, my own observation of the gender gap among college-educated urban Easterners is that wives moved to the left while husbands stayed put. Women traveled light. We had less invested in the status quo (or so many believed until divorce dispelled this illusion) than professional men. As fifties full-time wives and mothers, we were the last generation to be "unproductive" drones in the hives of corporate capitalism. As marginal members of society, we were entrusted with such unprofitable areas as the care of children; charity, religion, and culture.

When all institutions came under siege, in the late sixties, it was often women with the strongest ties to those traditional areas of "feminine" concern who became fifth columnists of the Establishment.

La Leche League counselors like Carol Cornwell began to see husbands and doctors as part of a system of "patriarchal oppression." Middle-class playground mothers picketed city hall for after-school programs for poor children. From making brownies for the class bake sale to lobbying for school integration wasn't such an enormous leap. For "liberal" wives and mothers of my generation, the traditional social gospel easily became a radical agenda.

"Once I got into abortion rights," Pat Brewster Catania says, "I started to see how the oppression of women and minorities went together. How the same kind of people were responsible for

Vietnam, Kent State, and the murder of the three civil rights workers in Mississippi."

The "same kind of people" were men. Not so different, in fact, from the men they had married.

Even as marriages were unraveling for all the usual reasons, divorce, for many women of our generation, was still too shameful to be considered for "personal" reasons alone. A larger moral rationale was needed to justify escalating hostilities at home. You couldn't just say you had come to hate your mate for faults affecting only nearest and dearest.

"He" had become an "enemy of the people," "part of the problem," a "corporate fascist," as another friend venomously described her spouse—a harmless fellow whose sin was to believe in 1965 exactly what he had believed in 1955: that the interests of Mobil and mankind were identical.* "My opinions hadn't changed any since we met," he said, still bemused by his former wife's militant turn to the left. "Hers did. Suddenly, I was responsible for everything that was wrong with America."

"Political arguments at home became really ugly," Carol Cornwell recalls. "Don had always been a registered Republican. I was a Democrat since college. We used to joke that we canceled out each other's vote. But there were no more jokes. We couldn't discuss any issue without a fight. Just as these quarrels masked a lot of personal anger, they also reflected a shift in the balance of power at home.

"Once I was frightened of Don," Carol says. "Now the tide turned. He was scared of me."

Politics and sex became ever more fused and confused. An early form of "liberation theology" appeared to be lifting adultery from the index of proscribed behavior. Not because married men and

---

* Charles Wilson, then chairman of General Motors, achieved considerable notoriety when he voiced this view in 1957; in fact, he was only expressing the beliefs of all his peers.

women hadn't always strayed. But they hadn't done it with a sense of entitlement, especially not middle-class churchgoing wives and mothers.

Before she fell in love with a younger man she met through her draft counseling, Carol Cornwell had other lovers. "Quite a few," she says evenly.

"I never felt the slightest bit guilty. I'm a very sensual person; sex was so perfunctory at home."

When she learned her lover was going to be in the city for a four-day conference, there came an "incredible moment" in her marriage.

"There was no way I could spend several nights away from home and lie about it. Not right in town. So I told Don.

"Of course, he was very upset. But then we went right along as though nothing had happened."

It was saying it—not doing it—that was incredible.

However unbelievable it sounded to Carol Cornwell to hear herself announce that she was going to spend four nights with her lover, the "real changes" in her life—as for so many women— came from her first paid work since summer jobs in college. It was an important administrative position in the church.

"I knew I could do it better than the two male candidates. But they were men, and I applied late." To her amazement, she got the job.

That fall, when Carol started work, Susanna, the youngest, began kindergarten. The arrangement was that the little girl would stay with a next-door neighbor until her mother arrived home.

"Talk about guilt and anxiety," she says. "Not being home for a five-year-old! I felt awful!"

For fifties women, that was the moral watershed. Not being there when your child came home from school was the day the image in the mirror started to crack. Our presence in the house at that moment was necessary reassurance that we were perfect mothers. More important than any meal, the after-school milk and cookies were akin to Eucharistic substance, symbolic of maternal nurture and love.

Like all working women who are also parents, Carol tried harder.

"I still did the Supermom thing," she says. "I got to all Matthew's 'home' soccer games. I did my duty as a PTA parent. And, of course, I still shopped, cooked, and cleaned."

Besides being Supermom, business-as-usual wife, and hostess, there was now a hidden agenda.

"I knew I had to be self-supporting if I was going to leave the marriage."

Thinking the unthinkable required the Plan. For a middle-class fifties wife schooled in prudence, in looking before she leaped, it was a time of taking stock, of weighing assets and liabilities.

Knowing that she would "never be accepted in the church as a serious professional" unless she became an ordained minister, Carol decided on divinity school. The Plan involved a well-orchestrated sequence of steps: saving as much as possible toward tuition from her full-time job, then moving to part-time consulting work, which would pay enough to cover expenses while allowing the time for demanding course work and her homemaker-mother responsibilities.

Graduate and professional schools of the late sixties and seventies were full of women armed with the Plan, in various stages of completion. The places that younger men had vacated to pursue countercultural activities—making stained glass, becoming carpenters, or just "dropping out"—began to fill with women in their late thirties, commuters from suburbia like Carol Cornwell or refugees, like the ex-wives in Marilyn French's novel *The Women's Room*.

For Pat Brewster, the Plan took shape on a Sunday afternoon and in a soothingly familiar form—making lists.

"I'll never forget the moment," she says. "We'd been married sixteen years. I sat down in the living room and wrote down all the steps which would get me from A, where I was, to B—out of the marriage."

"It was just like running a race or studying for a final exam. I knew I had to be prepared."

The first step was to become financially independent.

"My parents were both dead. I had no money. Lane was probably earning over two hundred thousand a year. I had two thousand dollars in my checking account. That was it!"

First on the list was a new résumé, followed by names—and more names. All the "contacts" she could think of, from editors at her old magazine to clients, advertisers, and other "useful" people Lane had insisted they invite to dinner over the years.

Eight weeks later she had a job and a new career. The payoff of all those dinner parties was an entry-level offer from a public relations executive, the competitor of the firm where she is now vice president.

To her surprise, Lane was encouraging about her going back to work. In four years the kids would all be away. "He saw a job as preventing 'empty nest' depression," Pat explains, "not as preliminary to divorce." The Plan did not include enlightening husbands.

One evening, a few weeks after Pat's first promotion, Lane's youth services board had its annual benefit. Instead of accompanying him or staying home to catch up on paperwork, Pat went to a cocktail party. After some mildly flirtatious conversation, an attractive unattached man invited her to dinner and a movie.

Pat remembers the movie, *Marathon Man*, because it was the sort of gruesome film she avoided in her "neutral" days. But more shocking than Laurence Olivier as a torturer-dentist, Pat recalls, was the sudden realization of how she happened to be sitting in this movie theater.

"I went to that party *looking* for a man. It wasn't sex. By that time, we all had reason to know sex was better outside of marriage. It was the premeditated act of looking." Like telephoning a man, you couldn't chalk it up to impulse or accident.

When she arrived home a few minutes after her husband, she told Lane: "I should have said this ages ago, but it's taken me a long time to grow up and be able to articulate it. This marriage is over."

The next day, he was fired.

At that point Pat dropped the separation plan. "With my upbringing, it would have been out of the question: Kicking someone when they were down."

"My prayer was that adversity might somehow be mending," she says. "That we would all pull together in a way we hadn't needed to do before."

Her optimism seemed vindicated when Lane was offered another corporate presidency within the year. A new city promised a new life. But not—as it turned out—a new marriage. "We just brought all our problems with us," she says.

As a final good-faith effort, Pat went to a marriage counselor, a priest who also happened to be director of family relations for the diocese.

"Throw in the towel, Pat," Father Conlon told her. "This marriage can't be saved."

"He was really great," she says. "He removed any lingering guilt I felt about divorce."

On the Richter scale of fifties values, the most jolting seismic shifts came from religious institutions, those that had taught us— the last generation of American children to be so instructed— that faith, family, and duty came before individual happiness. After Vatican II, the great liberal awakening that swept through the Catholic Church in the sixties, a highly placed member of the Church no longer spoke of Christian marriage as a sacrament. Like any secular psychotherapist, he was there to remove "any lingering guilt" about divorce, to reassure his congregant that "in a marriage where neither person helps the other, there was nothing left to give up."

By one of those coincidences that do happen, even outside the pages of Charles Dickens, Philip Catania, Pat's husband of one year, had gone to see the same priest following his divorce.

After ten years of marriage and six months of screaming and shouting at each other, Philip Catania says, "I finally got the idea: Virginia wanted out."

"It was like a death in the immediate family," says the tall, boyish fifty-year-old.

"For that entire next year, I was no good to anyone; least of all to myself. I dropped down to 180 pounds—which I hadn't weighed since Marine boot camp. My business acumen was way off; any interest in other women or sex—forget it!

"And the guilt! If you were reared a Roman Catholic—whether you believed it or not—the feelings that hit you. What have I done wrong?"

Guilt was reinforced by four-year-old Marian who, her father learned, "was feeling the same thing as both her parents, that she was the cause of the divorce."

By the standards of the fifties, Phil Catania wasn't just a later marrier. In waiting until he was thirty-six, he qualified in 1969 as a "confirmed bachelor"—an ambiguous category in those days. Yet, by another measure, the mind-set of the upwardly mobile, first-generation American male,[2] his caution is not unusual.

Finally, when he met Virginia Dane, ten years younger: "smart, attractive, a real doer," Phil says, "not just looking for a man to take care of her" (unlike the women who were his contemporaries), it seemed like the combination that couldn't fail: Handsome, successful, eligible entrepreneur meets glamorous "new woman."

What no one had foreseen was the way this particular generation gap could torpedo a marriage. Somehow, in Philip's mind, Mary Cunningham was going to turn into June Allyson as soon as the honeymoon was over.

Phil Catania's version of domestic life was based on his parents and the other families he knew when he was growing up: where men did not choose to be with women—especially not wives—for companionship and fun.

"My typical day would end at six-thirty or seven at night," he recalls. "Then I'd want to go somewhere and have a beer with my political pals. Her idea was that at five o'clock, I should be home having cocktails with her.

"We were at loggerheads right from the beginning."

The conjugal martini at home versus beer with the boys was only the first round.

At forty, the ten-year difference in age between Philip Catania and his wife was the longest decade in American history, the Great Divide separating the fifties from the sixties generation.

One evening, five years after they were married, when Virginia was three months pregnant, the Catanias went to their first childbirth class.

"Except for Ginny, I was fifteen years older than the oldest person there," Phil recalls. "There were six unmarried black women and a dippy twenty-year-old nurse who was our instructor. First she told us, everyone had to squat on the floor," he says, his face wrinkling in distaste at the memory.

"Then she said, 'I know what you're all dying to ask me about, sex with your husband or *partner.*'"

When Philip Catania recalls his first—and last—childbirth class, he underlines the word *partner* with heavy irony. Somehow, this term sums up everything that he found alien and painful about the whole experience: the sex-manual lingo of the "dippy" nurse, the differences in age, race, and class that separated him from the others—the majority unmarried black women.

He has wandered into the wrong era of history, into a room where mothers-to-be are not assumed to have husbands, where "partners" are not necessarily the fathers of the unborn children, where men in business suits are expected to feel comfortable squatting on the floor, in couvade-like imitation of their gestating companions; where all of those present, it's assumed, will want to "share" their questions about sex during pregnancy. His beautiful statuesque wife, in leotard and turtleneck, is perfectly comfortable. She squats and listens intently as hands go up around the room. Then, sensing his unease, Virginia gives him her "Oh, loosen-up" look.

But it's too late for him to loosen up. Or he was born too early.

"I said: What the fuck am I doing here? I got up at intermission and left. That was the end of my childbirth training course."

Virginia worked "right up until the moment Marian was born." Afterwards, Phil recalls, she began what was supposed to be a part-time, three-hours-a-day, three-days-a-week type of thing, as he describes it, for a foundation.

But within a year and a half, Virginia Catania had her boss's job. "She was flying around the country, raising a bundle of money, giving speeches. I was at home with our daughter.

"No way did she want to stay home and be a full-time mother. She was on her own track to success. She's proved it already by what she's doing now." His former wife is president of a scientific management consulting firm, specializing in medical technology. "I don't even understand what they do."

When Phil speaks of Virginia, he still slips reflexively into a tone of pride in her achievements and attributes. At the same time, in the words of the Rolling Stones (whose music he wouldn't willingly have listened to with Ginny and "her pot-smoking friends") he may have gotten what he needed, but not what he wanted. And he has learned something about the difference between the two.

"Her innate ability was one of the attractions to me," he says, "but when it came down to it, I wanted her at home with our child. Just waiting for me—with smiles and open arms—when I got home at eight o'clock."

Five years of marriage left Virginia a complete mystery to Philip. Her ambitions, her needs, her frustrations were as unknowable in their substance as the complex work she now directs.

Even more, the ways in which she was a child of her period elude him.

He makes no connection between her decision to leave the convent the night before she was to take her final vows, her involvement in the women's movement, and her dazzling career success. These experiences in Virginia's life, like the politics of the period, seem remote to him. He insists that there was nothing about the changing times that touched him directly.

"The sixties weren't very meaningful to me," Phil says. "I missed it."

"Like a lot of men," Dick Robertson recalls, "the seventies started me thinking: *What have I missed?* When we were in college, they had curfews. Now these same students were sharing dorm rooms."

He often compares himself to other men, seeing himself as typical, representative. "Like a lot of guys I know," "like most of my divorced friends," are phrases that introduce many of his reflections on his own past.

And indeed, like many fifties men and women, Dick Robertson describes his "first" life—first marriage and first career—with a curious detachment, as if describing a life lived by another.

When he speaks of that earlier self, it is in images of a helpless insect or small animal. Glued. Trapped. Caught. In those days, he says, "You stuck with your job. You stuck with your wife. You stuck with everything."

The culture decreed that decisions made by twenty-year-old college seniors were irreversible. Herded into early marriage, headed for the gold watch after signing on with the campus corporate recruiter, they missed out on life, not just sex. In the fifties, impermeability to experience passed for adulthood. By the sixties, boredom and curiosity had become an unstable compound, waiting to be ignited by the new permissiveness of the seventies.

Among his friends, Dick Robertson saw two waves of divorce. Early fifties marriages were the first to go. After fifteen years, he explains, there was this "drab little housewife sitting at home. Out in the corporate world, the husband has had a few promotions. He's making some money. Suddenly, he's an expert on everything, and he's 'outgrown' his wife."

It was different, he says, for couples who married in the late fifties.* Like Dick and Barbara Robertson. Twelve years after their wedding, it was the early seventies. By that time, "most women were more aware. There weren't many drudgey housewives among our contemporaries." Trouble came from outside the home. In the office, on the streets, in bars—"there were all these girls walking around without bras." Gorgeous, smart, college-educated girls. Girls who wanted to have fun.

"That's what we all missed," Dick Robertson says. "It wasn't another woman who ended my marriage. It was other women."

Meaningless sex was leering at millions of Dick Robertsons from every office watercooler and after-work "watering hole": reminding him of the motels that had terrified him as a student, of his envy of married fraternity brothers. Married! Not even love was a requirement. And if he had said to any of the adventurous young women he now met, "I promise that I'll still respect you," they would have laughed. Respect was what you didn't even show your dad anymore.

"It started to become very clear to me," he says. "I would like to get to know other women. I don't just want to go to bed with them." In his late thirties, he was attractive to women. Women had never noticed him before, he says. Now they did. A few years before his divorce, women had started looking at him with that unmistakable stare. Invitation and possibility warmed every encounter. Thoughts and feelings surfaced, he says, that he'd never

---

* Dick Robertson's comparison between early- and late-fifties marriages accurately reflects a larger statistical picture: the steady shrinkage in the number of years before divorce. While 29 percent of couples married in 1952 were divorced by their twenty-fifth anniversary, couples married in 1967 reached that percentage after only ten years.[3]

had before. "Am I living with the person I want to be with?" And finally, the question that signals the end of every marriage: "Is this all there is?"

"Once you ask that question," Dick Robertson says, "you're on a downhill slant. You start by feeling bored, then trapped. You think, 'I can't get out of this; I can't get a divorce because of my wife, because of the kids, because of money. Because of what my parents will think, or our friends.

"Then," he says, "you start thinking how you can do it."

During their seventeen-year marriage, Barbara and Dick Robertson never had a fight. "It was just kind of a slow withdrawal on my part. Barbara would have been happy to stay married had I been a different way. But the only way I could have been different was to have been in love with her. And you can't change that."

Dick Robertson's slow withdrawal from his marriage took almost three years.

"I started staying away from home a lot. After work, I'd hang out at a bar, go play cards until seven or eight o'clock. Or I'd stay away overnight, sometimes for two or three days. Business trips were one excuse. Golf tournaments were another.

"I'm not sure I even wanted to go, but they gave me a week away from home."

He finally said to his wife, "We should end this." She was very upset, very bitter. He is still surprised.

"It wasn't like I just came home one night and said, 'I'm leaving,'" he explains.

If he had stayed in construction work, Steve Ortiz thinks, "I'd still be married to my first wife." But when he went back to school, "there were lots of younger women. You interacted with them in a totally different way. There was an easy flow, an equality, right from the beginning. You'd get friendly after class. It turned out she needed a potter's wheel. So I made her one, in return for having a paper typed.

"We would get together over these exchanges, and sometimes, it wasn't just friendship anymore.

"It was all so different. Nobody talked about sex in the fifties. Nobody talked about anything. You'd speak to each other. But you never said anything."

"We were getting rid of all those other selves. The people we thought we were. We'd grown and changed. We all had money. Girls had money. Maybe they'd buy the beers. We'd go to girls' apartments. There was real friendship. There was sex. That was when couples started splitting."

Making up his mind to get divorced, Dick Robertson says, was the best decision he ever made. "I didn't have one bad minute. The instant I was free, I was happy." Inseparable from leaving the marriage, in his memory, was the decision to leave corporate life, to start his own brokerage business. Both choices paid off handsomely.

In his first week of bachelorhood—the first of his adult life— he found out how much the world had changed. As soon as he left home, Dick Robertson moved into a new "adults only" apartment complex with a swimming pool. Late one Saturday afternoon, minutes after he came upstairs from a swim, there was a knock on his door. "It was the nineteen-year-old lifeguard. She just walked into my apartment and peeled off her bathing suit.

"I was just stunned. Here I was, forty years old. I'd never turned on any women that I'd ever noticed. Suddenly, I was attractive to young girls.* I thought, My God, what have I been missing?!"

---

* Changes in clothes and hairstyles, along with cross-generational dressing, had a lot to do with more youthful middle-aged males. A look through the family album will reveal that our fathers, at forty-five, dressed like elderly men. In the sixties, a man who could cut a decent figure in jeans, body shirts, and torso-molding turtlenecks, who could grow a boyish head of hair, adopted these styles with enthusiasm —enjoying social approval and envy.

Even his conservative Midwestern city, in the "most Republican state in the nation," now boasted a swinging singles scene—bars, clubs, apartment complexes, an in-crowd that lived for parties. Like college, but with notable differences.

"Temperamentally, I wasn't cut out for that kind of thing," he says. But sometimes, curiosity prevailed over prudence.

He discovered the secondary sexual characteristic of success.

"The combination of hair on your head and money to spend," he says, "is irresistible." Glamorous young women were prepared, on the briefest possible acquaintance, to accept invitations for safaris in Africa or a weekend in Palm Springs. The higher up you go, he noticed, the greater the freedom and opportunities. It wasn't that he deliberately sought out women fifteen or twenty years his junior. "I just didn't meet single ones of my age. They were all home with kids, worrying about how to pay the bills," Dick says.

"Socially, the world had changed, too. Women were ready to be friends as well as lovers. I'd never had a woman friend before. For that matter, I'd never had men friends either." Women no longer waited meekly for invitations. They called him—for movies, dinner, to arrange weekend outings.

Other experiences caused him to realize that his first life had been oddly sheltered.

"I'd never lived alone. I'd moved from my parents' house to a dormitory, to a barracks, to marriage."

He discovered that he liked to cook and to give dinner parties. Even doing the laundry—which all his divorced men friends complained was "the worst part of being single"—wasn't "as bad as I'd heard."

Some might find Dick Robertson's detachment chilling; his freedom from guilt, a sign of shallowness; failure to mourn his marriage, evidence of moral deficiency.

Like many men he knows—to use his favorite opener—his keen intelligence is not often placed in the service of introspection.

The peaks and depths of his feelings, one suspects, are further flattened by the style of his region's speech, as planed as the prairie views from his office windows.

His perspective on the curious conjunction of his life and times is equally straight. He sees himself as a "pretty conservative" fellow, saved by social change from a lifetime of unhappy marriage. When the culture permitted him the choice, he could choose to divorce. Born ten years earlier, he would have echoed the resigned explanation given me by another executive for staying married: "We decided," he said, "that we might as well stick it out."

In their comprehensive study of shifting American attitudes between 1957 (the year of the Robertsons' marriage) and 1976 (one year before their divorce), authors Joseph Veroff, Elizabeth Douvan, and Richard Kulka report the greatest change to have been the image of divorce: elevated from "grave personal stigma" to a "viable alternative."[4]

No-fault divorce laws, adopted by most states beginning in the early 1970s, both reflected and reshaped the changed values of most Americans.* Marital dissolution no longer implied sin or error, emotional instability or a flawed character.

You got no points for "sticking it out." Whether we accept explanations summed up in phrases like the "me generation" or "culture of narcissism," the more than doubling of the divorce rate between 1960 and 1970 underlines another profound change. The dissatisfaction of one spouse no longer required dereliction by the other.

Boredom—sexual or intellectual; a sense of "something missing," feeling stifled by family life, changing social or political values—all of these became valid reasons why even thoughtful, responsible, "mature" people might decide to divorce.

Unlike many of his contemporaries, Dick Robertson doesn't justify divorce as just another "passage" in the wonderful process

---

* Demographer Andrew J. Cherlin resolves the chicken-and-egg dilemma by suggesting that more divorces stimulated a change in values.[5]

of "growth and change." He has never been a consumer of the new therapies of the human potential movement or a patient of traditional psychoanalysis. He never suggests he was morally entitled to the "more" in life missing from his marriage. He is straightforward in acknowledging the biological and economic injustice of his "second life"—an attractive, highly successful man in his early forties, companion of beautiful twenty-five-year-olds, while women his age were home with kids, worrying about how to pay the bills. But it's precisely his second chance, with all its choices, that defines him as a fifties male: recognizable as a short-haired domestic animal.

Like "most of his friends" and almost all divorced males of his generation, like all of the men in this book (including "off-stage" husbands), Dick Robertson remarried within four years.

15
THE MARRYING KIND

From his own description of life as a born-again bachelor, Dick Robertson sounds suspiciously like the heartless males lurking behind a recent study. In *The Hearts of Men: American Dreams and the Flight From Commitment*, Barbara Ehrenreich portrays a new easy rider. Exploiting feminism, male liberation, self-actualizing therapies, the fifties husband (if he hadn't been felled by a coronary or rendered impotent and bankrupt by his demanding wife) was home free. Once *Playboy*'s message got through, he tore off his gray flannel suit, tossed his attaché case from the window of his commuter train, and put the down payment on the bachelor pad with heart-shaped bed and mirrored ceiling.

Men of every generation have indulged in this fantasy. For some few of our male contemporaries, these daydreams were, indeed, dress rehearsals. They are the men who became successful enough to underwrite "second lives," in Hugh Hefner's image, while providing for their "first" families. Others simply abandoned their wives and children. The American West was won by just such "liberated" men. The impulse to cut and run has just gone by different names at different times.

For men imprinted with the fifties ethos, the flight from commitment was a brief detour. They were day-trippers, as the Beatles sang; sexual utopia was a nice place to visit, but you wouldn't want to live there. Domesticity was all they knew. They were as defined by the roles of husband and father as by the mothering they had received from wives.

"Nobody cares," one divorced executive wailed to a sympathetic listener, "whether I took my pills this morning."

He would not long remain uncared-for. Divorced men of our generation who failed to remarry—or settle down with a mate—are rarer than egrets.*

One year after his separation, Dick Robertson's sixteen-year-old son decided to live with his father. At that point, Dick recalls, "I kind of snapped to. I bought a house. I made sure to be home for dinner." Within another two years, he had merged family life with the ultimate fifties male fantasy. He married Megan Wilson, a flight attendant, divorced, with a five-year-old daughter.

There are many differences between Dick Robertson's first and second marriages. Most of them are summed up by his declaration that he is finally "living with the right person for the right reasons."

But as a realistic businessman, he is also quick to note another happy change: money.

"It was no fun to be married with three little kids and not an extra dime to spare. That was the way it was for everyone back then." Getting married immediately following fraternity life, Dick Robertson notes drily, was "not the best preparation for the sacrifices you have to make as parents."

Still, if money and love differentiate his present union from his "first life," there is an important constant:

---

* I can attest to the statistical probability of fifties men re-marrying, or settling down with a mate within a few years of divorce. With the exception of those presumed to have changed sexual orientation, no one I asked could think of a single *single* divorced man.

He is still the sole provider and breadwinner, happy to have rescued Megan from a "terrible life." She had been flying for thirteen years, three of them as a single mother who hardly ever saw her young daughter. Now "she really enjoys being a housewife.

"I'm old-fashioned," Dick Robertson explains. "I like the fact that she depends on me. A lot of people do. I need that. I feed on it. I've always been someone that people can depend on. I like responsibility."

Among the people that he is happy to have depend on him are his three children. Although their mother remarried before he did, "without any lawyers leaning on me," Dick says, "I assumed their support all through college, until they were twenty-one."

A man is not a man, in Dick Robertson's view, if he is unwilling or unable to support his family.

"That's what my father did for us," he says.

At the same time that Steve Ortiz was separated from his wife, funding for the migrant worker program dried up. He was out of a job.

"I knew I had to make the really tough decisions. What do I want to do? Where do I want to be? Who do I want to be with?"

He still had his old construction workers' union card to tide him over, while he pondered his future. But after a few weeks' work on a site, he was fired "on the same day my divorce was final."

Together, the events seemed a sign. He left the Southwest for good, heading for Chicago. From his year of college in Illinois in 1953, Steve says, "I picked up a lot of mainstream middle-class attitudes. Enough to know that if I stayed in Arizona, I'd be stuck in my own ethnic group for life."

Soon after he arrived in the city, he found a job as assistant school administrator. Evenings, he took advantage of free adult classes at the Jewish Community Center. The courses carried titles like "How to Fight Fair," "Love Is What It's All About," "Honesty in Relationships."

"I was like a sponge, soaking it all in. I felt I had to redo myself completely."

Steve Ortiz met his second wife, Carrie Parker, a high-school Spanish teacher, through a colleague. Carrie grew up on a ranch in Oklahoma. She had long honey-colored hair and pale skin with a dusting of freckles. She had her own apartment and a brand-new car.

"At first, I thought, 'Oh, shit. Another one of these Anglos who's into Hispanic culture.' But it turned out she wasn't that way at all."

He warned her that he was a pretty direct guy. To prove it, he pulled out his list of forty questions from his transactional analysis class. The list began with "How do you feel about Roman Catholics?" and ended with questions about her relationship with her father. "A woman who is close to her father," Steve says, "will probably have a better understanding of men."

Carrie passed the interview with flying colors. "She could handle anything," Steve says proudly. "I knew then she was the sort of middle-class all-American girl I should marry."

Sex was just a part of it, he says. "It wasn't like the fifties, when that was why you got married. This time it was our values—what we both feel is important—that meshed."

With their new family of three children added to Steve's first three, Carrie Ortiz-Parker's salary is essential. Other than maternity leaves, she has never stopped working. Although he "does what he can" for his older kids, Steve admits "there's a lot of resentment. We seem like millionaires to them, because we have a lot of *things*.

"My kid brother calls me a typical fifties money grubber," Steve says. "He dropped out to smoke pot and do a heavy radical scene. Now César has a Ph.D and coaches college athletics in California. But he's still pretty laid back. Not like me, with my nose always to the grindstone."

Steve and Carrie Ortiz-Parker work as hard as they do, including frequent moonlighting for Steve, to buy more than the gadgets he loves. He has already started investing in real estate; later, he hopes to invest in a small business.

"You can't build up any equity in education. It was good for status. That was the big thing for me, as a Hispanic in the fifties. Not any more."

Both the gadgets and the equity, Steve admits—"and some status, too"—depend on his wife. Carrie, an all-American middle-class young woman of the seventies, expects to work for her entire life. The two-income couple, a phenomenon unknown in Steve Ortiz's youth, makes possible the way he lives now.

A crystalline Saturday morning. By a seeming miracle, the leaden New England winter sky has disappeared in the night. The entire city looks deserted. Everyone has headed for ski slopes or a country inn.

Not another human being is to be found on the floor of the glittering skyscraper occupied by Pat Brewster's public relations firm. "I'm playing catch-up," she says apologetically. After a week in London, the contents of her in-basket overflow onto the immaculate desk.

I remind her of that "first life," her description of Lane Brewster sleeping Saturdays, working Sundays, never seeing his family. Could she ever have imagined herself alone in a corner office at 8 A.M. on a beautiful weekend morning?

Never, not in a million years. Any more than she could have imagined, in the days just before her divorce, when she had two thousand dollars to her name, that she would be writing a check to the IRS in the amount of forty thousand dollars, representing federal income tax on one year of her earnings.

Another reason that she feels free to devote weekends to work? There are no children at home anymore. She glances at the college and prep school commencement photographs on the cabinet facing her. Still, she admits that her husband Philip would never be in his office on a glorious Saturday morning.

Even on those alternate weekends when his daughter Marian is with her mother, Phil is off at dawn to putter on their Berkshire farm.

This is the big divide for us. New marriages are not necessarily families with resident children. They are "something else"— especially for our generation, programmed to believe that being a spouse is synonymous with being a parent.

"We're elderly Yuppies," said a friend of her second marriage. "We have no more baby-sitters or school bills. We both work long days, eat out a lot, and spend Saturday shopping."

Pat and Philip Catania would suggest second marriage as a professional merger—if this image didn't convey a dispiriting calculation that would be all wrong. Still, what they share and admire about each other has more to do with professional than domestic virtues. And their praise is also a measure of how far each has come in order to appreciate the other.

"Phil's fantastic!" Pat says of her husband. "He built up that enormous operation entirely by himself. He didn't have a dime when he started. And no blue-chip connections either," she says proudly. (She does not add that these were her first husband's attractions.)

Now that we are self-made women with careers of our own, the qualities we value in men are different, too.

"One night when we had been going out casually for a short time," Pat recalls, "I was feeling very down about work. It was time for a raise and promotion. I had really nailed some big ones. I was just too scared to ask. Every way I formulated my case sounded wrong. On top of that I was full of the self-hatred you feel when you know you're being exploited.

"We were on our way to a very fancy black-tie Christmas party given by Phil's friends. I told Philip why I wasn't feeling too festive. Instead of going to the party, we went to a very quiet restaurant where he spent the whole dinner coaching me, what to say and how to say it. When to talk money, when to talk title. Then we rehearsed.

"I went in the next morning and made an appointment with the president for the afternoon. The next day I had the promotion and the salary that went with it."

"How can you not love a man who can do that for you?" Pat asks, laughing. How, indeed.

Pat works until 7 P.M. most evenings. She spends one night a week in Chicago, doing more business traveling than her husband. If he wants to have a couple of beers with his old friends, watch the game from their favorite bar, his wife is not waiting home alone—frostier than her solitary martini. Among the many advantages of second marriages: Time is on their side. Sources of friction for the young families we were twenty years ago—small children and the endless labor they create, the monomania involved in "making it"—have been outgrown by the older couples we are today.

If his workaholism paid off, the young father who barely looked at his family while keeping his eye on the ball is apt to own or manage the team by now. (If not, he's gone as far as he's going to go.) His children and stepchildren grown, he's flattered if they deign to descend for a country weekend (and entirely at their disposal now—as he never was in their childhood). He's a father emeritus.

His second wife—whether she is his contemporary or, more probably, a "younger professional woman"—is just as likely to be the one whose working day ends at 8 P.M.

High-powered executive couples like the Catanias count on weekends for intimacy—or even socializing. Some weeks' schedules are so hectic "we hardly exchange two words," Pat says. The importance of their Berkshire farm as a place to "unwind and catch up with each other" is very different from country weekends with young children and their friends. Knowing how easy it is for people living together to disappear into separate lives, they are protective of time alone.

Failed first marriages also taught other lessons—some of them elementary.

"I learned that women are people too," Philip Catania says. "Dumb as that sounds," he adds sheepishly. "But I hadn't gotten there yet the first time. I thought I knew myself. I thought at thirty-six that I was a mature person. Neither of the above were true.

"I learned the hard way. I really should have spent a hell of a lot more time thinking about Virginia's personality and her needs. The second time around, I've made that effort."

Whether through effort or the natural process of change—including signals from the culture that have seeped in—second marriage for the Catanias is a union of equals. Neither *McCall's* togetherness or Hollywood high romance, Phil Catania describes the compatibility he enjoys with his present wife in images of a successful partnership.

"Everything is on the table between us." Just as Pat underlines the importance of her husband's mentor role in her career, Phil Catania speaks appreciatively of Pat's "immensely helpful counsels." Even her "intelligent listening" often points him toward the right business decision.

When he looks back on the resentment and anger aroused by his first wife's ambition, by her refusal to be a full-time wife and mother, he sees the changes wrung in his new vision of happiness. "That kind of woman would no longer interest me."

Spoiled by success, reborn as radicals, lost to the joys of meaningless sex—these marital casualties are still the minority report.

Most fifties men and women stayed married.

Not only did we wed earlier and have more children; we divorced less, proportionately, than any other generation since 1870. Despite the anecdotal evidence, despite our sense that everywhere, all our contemporaries were uncoupling (certainly, my own impression in the early 1970s), the larger picture tells us otherwise.

Based on the long-term trends of the twentieth century, in which divorce has shown an unsteady but inexorable upward climb, "couples who wed in the decade or so after the Second World War," notes Andrew Cherlin, "were the only cohorts in the last hundred years to show a substantial sustained shortfall in their lifetime levels of divorce."[1]

On both sides of us, the news was worse. Although the annual divorce rates were temporarily low in the early 1930s, Cherlin observes, as soon as the economy improved, unhappy couples dissolved marriages in record numbers. Streaming into this tide were marriages contracted during World War II, whose immediate aftermath witnessed an epidemic of marital breakup. Less surprising to us (because heavily reported by the media) were the volatile unions of our juniors. By 1977—only seven years after marriage—one-quarter of the couples wed in 1970 had already divorced. (Now, as our young-adult children already know, one out of two first marriages will not survive.)

Astonishing as it seems, our generation is a plateau of stability in a century whose divorce rates are still climbing.

Why did so many more of us stay married in the face of fewer sanctions and more temptations than any husbands and wives had ever encountered before?

For most, the new "permissive society" came too late. In Freudian terms, our superegos were always on duty. Like the police in any banana republic, they had spies everywhere, threatening the tortures of eternal guilt and public censure if we acted to please ourselves.

Like the citizens of any police state, we could act covertly—as long as we didn't have to announce irresponsible self-indulgence to the world.

Suddenly, in our mid-thirties, we were informed the revolution had taken place yesterday. We must stop behaving like the craven

conformists of our youth. Now, we were "free to be you and me."
But, like newly ,emancipated slaves, most of us were too fearful
for any mass rush to freedom. (Even if we knew who "you and
me" were, would we recognize ourselves without name tags
designating us as husbands and wives, mothers and fathers?) Our
social radar had been permanently set to oscillate to the opinion of
others, even when those others were too busy tearing their own
lives apart to notice us.

Topping any list of high anxiety items for our generation was
money. The real privation of our parents, children of the depression, filtered down to many of us as irrational, free-floating anxiety
about finances—an anxiety that prosperity did little to assuage.

At the same time, the rapidly rising standard of living for many
fifties families made worrying about money a rational response to
the over-mortgaged life. Greater success meant ever-larger commitments: second homes; school bills; cars, boats, and country
clubs; orthodontia and psychiatry.

The men of our generation who appeared in Dr. Henriette
Klein's office "miserable because they couldn't afford to end unhappy marriages" were not atypical; psychotherapy was a bargain
compared to supporting two households.

Happy families, Tolstoi wrote, are all alike; every unhappy
family is unhappy in its own way.

We wouldn't know about the happy ones. Among our contemporaries, they aren't the people we read or hear about. They
do not appear in "women's" novels or the coming-of-age fiction of
male writers. They are absent from case studies of psychologists
and sociologists, pop or academic.

We hardly see them anymore on television. Gone are the
squeaky-clean suburbanites whose wholesome presence dominated the small screen in our innocent fifties youth: understanding
if bemused parents like the Nelsons in *Ozzie and Harriet* or
"Beaver" Cleaver's swell folks. They were replaced in the late
sixties by a clinical population of "problem families." In docu-

dramas or "specials," we watch husbands and wives cope with alcoholism or Alzheimer's disease or blame each other for pregnant, addicted, or runaway children. For escape, we enjoy watching families corrupted by money and power, the deliciously vicious denizens of *Dallas* and *Dynasty*. Or guiltily, we see the faces of our fellow citizens, as they tell of the damages visited on them and their children by unemployment, single motherhood or homelessness.

Unlike Tolstoi, most of us have met too few happy families to compare them to one another. More likely, we have been too well briefed by our post-Freudian, postfifties culture. We now know that the "family romance" was Grand Guignol all along, gruesome goings-on behind the facade of "ordinary people." Or else we have learned to see through the neurotic satisfaction procured by role-playing: "she" is Wendy to "his" Peter Pan; the children abandoned by parents flash-frozen in their infantile selves; marriage as "games people play," where everybody loses.

Those who remembered their own parents as happy have mostly been disabused of such naiveté. Doubly victims, we were first damaged by what they "did" to us. Then, our self-deception in failing to see their marriage "as it really was," caused us to replay the parental roles when we became husbands and wives. But even worse is the guilt we feel as ill-paired children of those rare parents who were exemplary husbands and wives.

"My father and mother seemed so happy together," Carol Cornwell recalls. "They were always loving and affectionate with each other. I feel so badly that we couldn't give our kids an example like theirs. I wonder. How did they do it?"

We all wonder. Because there's no mistaking the real thing— then or now.

Sunday. The four museum guides who volunteer on the busiest day are closing their office. Outside, the rain is torrential, the entire city seems about to sink into the prairie. Sam Saunders has managed to catch the last Sunday of a loan exhibition of Chinese art. But he has also come to the museum to pick up Betts. He does not like her to drive in the pouring rain.

Betts Saunders relates this proof of solicitude with an air of surprise. After twenty years of marriage, she takes none of her good fortune for granted. Not the opulence of her material life— her "dream house and garden," the stylish clothes and sports car, the travel abroad. And certainly not the loving presence in his family's life of Sam Saunders.

One of the most successful specialists in his field, orthopedic surgery, he has every excuse, Betts knows, to be less than the involved parent he has chosen to be.

"He's an incredible father. He's always taken fifty percent care of the children. He drives half the car pools. He takes them shopping. He practices tennis with them. He's head timer for the swim team, and he takes two days off for the meet. He's never missed one."

As a small-town general practitioner, Betts says, "Sam's father was always gone so much, it was his choice to be there for his kids. I've never asked him to do anything."

Most of her friends complain that their husbands are only interested in medicine and sports. "They come home from the hospital, sink in front of the tube, and that's it." Since he was in college, Sam has always been passionately interested in art. "It used to astound me," Betts says, "that Sam would get on a plane to Chicago to see a Paul Klee exhibit. Now it's an interest we share. We prepare for visiting European museums by reading up together on what we're going to see."

If Betts Saunders has one complaint about her husband, it is only that his virtues sometimes seem those of principle more than partiality.

A few years ago, Betts had a long bout of flu. For two weeks afterwards, "I just lay around the house in my flannel nightie, groaning. As usual, Sam was wonderful. He made dinner for the kids or took them out. He did all the urgent chores. But one morning, when Betts looked in the mirror, she said to her husband, "I don't know how you stand it. You work like a dog all day. You come home and I look awful. The house is a mess. There's no food in the fridge. I wouldn't blame you for taking up with one of those cute nurses who are always all over you."

"He was appalled," Betts says, "that I could think he'd do such a thing." What "deeply offended" Sam Saunders was that his wife questioned his morality. She would have liked him to say, "Darling, I love you so much, I don't care how awful you look. I would never do that, because you're number one in my life."

Like every woman of our generation who is a wife, Betts laments the inability of men to share intimate feelings, to "communicate," which includes the "stroking" she sometimes misses—compliments and words of appreciation for the care she takes of everything and everyone in her life.

There is no question of the depth of his feelings for her, sexually and emotionally, Betts says. He just hasn't learned to put them into words. Even his Valentine's Day roses to his wife come with a card signed, "Your secret admirer."

Still, Betts Saunders' most moving tribute to her husband comes in her unhesitating reply to my question:

"He's the first person I turn to with any problems."

Of the many wives who have given me as many answers, Sam Saunders is the only husband to be so named.

Regional differences, we're often told, are fast disappearing in this country. But it's hard to believe that the strengths of Betts and Sam Saunders' marriage don't derive in large measure from the values of small-town Midwestern America they both share— beliefs that have withstood their transformation, in other ways, into an affluent, sophisticated, professional family.

Raised as Methodists, there was a decade of "drifting away from religion" after they were married. They now go as a family every Sunday to a nearby congregation, Disciples of Christ. Among other shared aspects of their lives, "Sam and I are just about equal

in our uncertainty on theological issues," Betts says. They both
wish they could have the "childlike faith and conviction of fundamentalist friends." Instead, the importance of church has become,
for them, "a medium for reminding us of our Christian values";
significant among them, counting your blessings.

Last year, Betts Saunders went back for the twenty-fifth class
reunion at her "wrong-side-of-the-tracks high school," a hundred
miles away. The Class of 1955 celebrated in a Quonset hut, now
the local country club. "The food was roast beef and ham, totally
dried out, boxed mashed potatoes, and white bread. They were
so thrilled with the meal; that's what made me want to cry."

"If I'd stayed in Silver Falls," Betts says matter-of-factly, "I'd
still be eating dry roast beef."

When Betts Saunders was homecoming queen and the prettiest
girl in her senior class, she could have clearly described her
present life. She could have pictured her four handsome, polite,
smart children; her gracious cream-color brick house, with its
sloping lawn and English garden; and the handsome doctor she
would marry.

If Betts Saunders were a fictional heroine, her planned future
would have had cruel ironies in store, her "answered prayers"
haunting her with a ghastly mockery of teenage fantasies.

Or, like most of my friends, she would have changed, "outgrown" the constricting roles the fifties had in store for all of us.
She would have experienced the "housewife's moment of truth"[2]
or Carol Cornwell's "kitchen Polaroid"—the flash that led to a
life of lonely independence. But for Betts Saunders, neither
the abrasions of family life nor the revolutions "out there" in
the sixties and seventies have caused her to revise her notions
of the desirable.

Indeed, "out there" is a remote place to her and many of her
friends.* Unlike many of us, her expectations of life and of herself didn't "rise" in the course of the past twenty years. Her

* Among their old friends who are also contemporaries, only one couple has
divorced.

sources of fulfillment and self-esteem remain rooted in being the wife of a successful man; a perfect mother, a devoted friend, and a hardworking volunteer; a homemaker and hostess who still "does it all herself."

In her community these attributes are still admired and valued. To be sure, news from the front lines of social change arrives— from books, television, and magazines. She has read all the writing of popular feminists, watched them on "Donahue" and the "Today Show."

She is not the enemy my feminist friends envision, neither "total woman" nor Phyllis Schafly. She is the Trojan horse of our generation—hundreds of thousands of Betts Saunders who do not consider being wives and mothers as roles but as what they are. The system worked for them. But smart women like Betts Saunders know it worked because the men they married did not leave them holding the bag, turning them into a front for happy family life. But mainly, she knows it worked because of the part that no one can write in; the reason why she describes her life as even better than she thought it would be, the reason why Tolstoi found all happy families to be all the same: alike in the accidental grace of enduring love.

On the gold chain that Rowan DiStefano wears around her neck, there is a tiny gold cross and a dime-size gold medallion. Engraved on one side of the disc is the date, June 12, 1980, when Rowan was graduated summa cum laude and first in her class with a B.S. in nursing; on the reverse, "Love always, Mike."

"I was always telling her how dumb she was," Mike DiStefano says, "but when they read her name out at commencement, I was crying. I've never been so proud in my life!"

The tears, pride, put-downs, and set-ups are only a sampling of scenes from the longest-running passion play in town: the marriage of Rowan and Michael DiStefano. Twenty-five years of four children, two separations, several other women, one marriage counselor, three psychiatrists, thousands of tranquilizers and antidepressants, and a chorus of in-laws, friends, neighbors, and colleagues.

Mike DiStefano moved out for the first time in 1969, a month after their tenth wedding anniversary.

"There may have been one gal—or several," Rowan DiStefano says. "But that wasn't the main reason he left. He just wasn't happy with me, with the way I was. He said he wanted somebody different—less passive, less accepting, more aggressive."

"I used to compare Rowan to more assertive women we both knew—who came on stronger. It just enraged her," Mike says. "I don't even know why I did it. These type of women turn me off completely."

When he left home, Mike DiStefano sublet a furnished apartment near the city hospital. "It had roaches," Rowan recalls. "He got hysterical. He'd call up every night and just talk. He was very depressed. It really scared me."

"My practice had become very successful. I had lots of patients," Mike says. "I started to think I was some special guy. And that my wife who was raising the children was doing nothing except staying at home."

"Until this time," he says, "I was one of these men who was never interested in other women. The most attractive patients came into my office. I was so wrapped up in what I was doing, I wouldn't even notice them. Suddenly, I got these terrible uncontrollable feelings. All I could think about was sex and other women.

"I hadn't really sowed any wild oats. Rowan and I were out of sync. I hated the whole feeling because I didn't even understand it. I wouldn't even want to come home. I used to play tennis—anything to keep myself busy—just to suppress those kinds of desires. I became distant from my wife. We argued more. It was as though I was angry at her for these desires.

"I felt so guilty. I couldn't stay married. The only way I could deal with it was to leave home."

But after four months of roaches, depression, seeing other women, but mostly "fantasizing," he was home again.

"Marriage counseling kept us together for three or four months," Rowan recalls. "But Mike just wasn't happy.

"He moved out again, this time to a really nice apartment. He said maybe that's why he wasn't happier the last time. He bought new furniture. I realized then that all this sixties stuff had gotten to him, plus turning forty. He still called me all the time. He missed me. But I think he missed the kids more."

"I was getting bored with work," Mike says. "Within five years of starting my practice I was earning a hundred thousand. That's where you level off. You can't continue to grow because you don't have people working for you.

"Boredom made me realize that I was getting older. I was only forty but I started to think about death. Every time a twenty-eight-year-old woman would come on to me, I'd think, This may be the last time in your life it's going to happen!"

"There I was, alone with three little kids," Rowan says. "I was hysterical. I hadn't worked for years. I didn't have a college degree, just an R.N. Having all these marital problems forced me into the real world. I went back to school. I got my degree. I really enjoyed it. The courses didn't seem like any work at all. Mike's mother did all the baby-sitting. I went out and got myself a good job—teaching nursing."

"We saw several psychiatrists separately and together," Mike says. "I was starting to see things I hadn't seen before. I was finding out that other women had their problems. When you got to know them, they didn't look as good as they did in magazines or in my dental chair.

"I found out that I wasn't a very good father. When I was with the children by myself, I didn't know what to do with them. I had been working all the time. Rowan had been the one taking care of them. When they came to visit me in the apartment, they were uncomfortable. They were angry at me because I made their mother unhappy. They saw her crying. They didn't see their father crying. It was tough for them.

"That whole experience changed me. It was so painful. I'm still not too expressive. I'm not the kind of person who can tell people I care for them. I'm better at it than I used to be," Mike says. "But I'm still not very good."

"He moved back home. On our first visit to the marriage counselor, we decided to get a divorce. Boom. I called my lawyer. I can't tell you how relieved I was," Rowan says. "To think this thing was finally going to be over. Thank God! The next day Mike called and said, 'I changed my mind. We're going to work on it. We're going to do it.' That was it, he's been home ever since."

"When Mike came back home," Rowan says, "I had a part-time job, teaching nursing at a local hospital. He was happy I was working, he said, but it also used to drive him crazy. I had to do a lot of catch-up reading. It drove him insane to see me with my head in a book. Just like he can't stand to see me knitting. He can't stand for me to hold the cat. I don't know why. He doesn't know why, either. So I quit working."

Passion or pathology. Love as a disease or a state of grace.

"You can't understand me without talking to him," she said. He says the exact same thing about her. They're both right. They are so intertwined, totally dependent on each other, they're not separate enough to even use the word *love*—or *jealousy*. He can't mention another woman; she can't pet the cat. After twenty-five years, the intensity of their feelings vibrates through the house: a nightly opera in 3-D with wraparound sound.

"Both of us feel that marriage is the important thing," he says, "Rowan in particular. She's driven to stay married because of her parents being divorced. For me," Mike says, "I have an image of myself, and marriage is a part of it. Not being married is failure and rejection."

Staying married—the ultimate fifties value—for Michael and Rowan DiStefano is an excuse to stay together. The domestic virtues allow them to rationalize the irrational; literally to domesticate their overwhelming need and passion for each other. "He's always been a good provider and very generous about money." "She's a fantastic mother; you should see her with kids." Marriage, as a "good" in itself, allows them to explain why they tear each other to pieces, threaten to separate, call each other's bluff, become enraged by jealousy, guilt, blame. Together, they have made a fascinating discovery: Marriage is the perfect cover for mad, crazy love.

It's "the deal." The "arrangement," the "unwritten contract." Sometimes, it's "out in the open," as in "open marriage." More typically, it's tacit, in the original meaning of silent: understood, accepted—more or less willingly—by both spouses.

"It" is sexual infidelity, the issue that most reveals us, men and women of the fifties, as a transitional generation. Ambivalent on that score as on so many others, looking back, we see the imprint of the scarlet letter—like a razored-off appliqué. We try the double standard with a nonjudgmental twist ("Rowan couldn't do it without getting emotionally involved; men are different," insists Mike DiStefano). Applying the same rules to both is uncharted territory. Safety is sought in the language of the interoffice memo.

"We have a policy of non-embarrassment," one executive told me. Equal opportunity in his marriage means that he is not expected to spend the night alone on his frequent business trips. Nor does he inquire what his wife does in her after-work hours, while he is away. But they both "draw the line," he says, at involvements that would "threaten the marriage."

That line is a high-wire act for many fifties men and women who have remained husbands and wives.

In the old days, Dan Ross explains, it was called the "secret service." It was what the culture allowed all men to do. Everybody knew about it. Nobody discussed it unless there was a scandal. It wasn't a social problem.

"Now, it's beyond the single standard," he says. "We have awareness, self-awareness. There are trade-offs, changes in expectations, role reversals. If marriage survived, the contract got rewritten."

The first rewrite for Dan Ross came with the success of his wife, an executive who loves work. Business is her major pleasure, he says.

"That's always been a problem in our marriage. I wasn't prepared to be a spouse. My training is: I want attention. I want to be the male focus. I married a woman who played that role when I found her," he says. "That was the role I was attuned to. Intellectually, I could deal with the new ideas. Emotionally, it was another ball game."

When his wife's career took off, Dan Ross fell in love, "for the first time," he says.

His lover was "incredibly beautiful." She was also dependent, tender, and sexy. She'd never been to college. She was a born-again Christian. Her conversation, Dan recalls, was one part quotes from Chairman Mao, one part Christian Fundamentalist stuff, and the third part was her husband.

"She'd actually quote the schmuck," Dan says.

"Her marriage was falling apart. That was the problem. I was in love, but I wasn't 'mad.' I kept my sanity. I didn't want to be involved in the middle of their breakup. She had this crazy husband who was out to shoot us both. I had to hire detectives. All these gauche things! And this guy was fucking around himself. It was all nuts!"

With his wife's absorption in work, plus "the normal attritions of marriage, I thought I wanted another kind of spouse, a nonprofessional," he says. But he didn't.

"What I really wanted," Dan learned, "was a great affair. She was moving it from a great affair to I-want-another-husband-to-take-care-of-me.

"I found every reason I could not to go further. I said to myself,

I can't leave my wife, I can't leave my kids. They all care too much about me. I cannot put my selfish desires ahead of their happiness.

"All right," Dan admits, "I really didn't *want* to leave my family. I thought to myself, What I've got is tested. It's stable and comfortable and manageable and controllable. That's the important thing. Even if it isn't emotionally satisfying, I can control it.

"Something else I learned about myself was even more important. I'm limited in my ability to commit."

"I'll go in up to my knees," Dan says, "but not over my head."

Needlepoint it on the cushions. Monogram it on the towels. The lessons of our adolescence spring to mind unbidden—don't go off the deep end.

"Dip your foot in," he says. "Play with it, enjoy it. But don't go in all the way. Because there's a shark out there somewhere. Or you might drown."

The secret service was over. This time, Joan Ross knew—if she hadn't always known. "The crazy husband had called up, giving her the whole song and dance," Dan says.

Everyone's bluff has been called.

"You want to walk out on me? You want me to walk out on you? Let's stop playing the game," he said.

She knows that he will never leave. That fear of his own feelings and terror of women will have him scurrying back home when the going gets heavy. She also knows that the price of her success is his illusion of freedom.

He knows that she wants and needs to stay married, that she's still uneasy about the negative image of the "high-powered woman executive." She requires the "halo effect" of her lovely family. He is not wrong when he says that "deep down, it really doesn't bother her if I fuck around occasionally. She wants to be sure that I'm there when she's sixty-five."

He will be.

The threat of abandonment, Germaine Greer claims, "is at the heart of marriage always, for man or woman and it is the main reason we all put up with indignities and even hate."[3]

There are other reasons. For our generation, being a husband or wife is still a mainspring of identity. No matter how miserably wed—in past or present lives—or how successful, most of my women contemporaries still feel that they are "nothing without a man."[4]

Without a wife, men of our generation fear confronting a dismal truth: They are what they do—and nothing else. By providing them with social life, their wives have allowed them the illusion that they have friends. Cut off from companionship that requires no effort, they will be reduced to self-help manuals like *The Lonely Guy's Book of Life*.[5]

Once upon a time, in the memory of some of us, divorce was attended by social ostracism, religious sanction, professional "black marks." "Broken families" were blamed for every individual and social ill from homosexuality to juvenile delinquency to Soviet space superiority. Whether it was "for the sake of the children," "his career," or "what the neighbors will think," middle-class men and women had a host of excuses to stay married.

We are the first generation with no place to hide. Being married is important only to us. Nobody else cares.

Those of us who, for good reasons and bad, are still together, have become uneasy icons. To our contemporaries, we stand for something. We are the representatives of a failed ideal.

16
MYTHS AND MARTYRS

The ancient Greeks gave us the word. *Martyr*: one who bears witness. Throughout history, the martyr has accused the blindness, folly, or evil of his or her contemporaries. More eloquent in death than in life, martyrs require disciples—first, other witnesses to tell of their lives; then younger followers to remind the world of their redeeming sacrifice.

In secular societies, political martyrs replaced saints. Rosa Luxemburg, Leon Trotsky, Robert Emmet provided the state with enemies and dissenting factions with heroes and heroines. In the United States, anarchists Sacco and Vanzetti, executed for murder in 1927, and Julius and Ethel Rosenberg, electrocuted as Soviet spies in 1953, fulfilled both functions, becoming symbols as well of the paranoia that lies close to the surface of American life. In our two periods of greatest peace and prosperity, we were haunted by "the enemy within." As scapegoats of political hysteria, the Rosenbergs are part of a long historical tradition.

The fifties left behind a book of martyrs who could have lived and died in no other time and place. They are men and women who bear witness to the myths and taboos of our coming of age: the fear of youth and sex and women; the sanctification of the

335

family; the violence behind the liberal pieties; and finally, the curse that celebrity—the new religion of the sixties—would lay upon the celebrated.

By our dead—James Dean, Marilyn Monroe, Montgomery Clift, Elvis, Lenny Bruce, Anne Sexton, Sylvia Plath—will you know us, the survivors.

They are all deaths by suicide—swift, slow, or "accidental"— with one possible murder. These tabloid endings, whose victims were possessed of uncommon talent, beauty, brilliance, or celebrity, cast long shadows on the lives that were wasted. God-fearing Christian or unchurched atheist, we are great moralists all, our generation. We are always ready to find sermons in the stoned.

The pun on Emerson is not just wordplay. Fifties casualties were the first wave in the drug-related deaths that would proliferate in the next two decades, claiming—along with the celebrated—thousands of ordinary young people.

Our heroes and heroines specialized in lethal cocktails of alcohol and sleeping pills.*

More cautionary than the causes of death, though, are the lessons to be drawn from the lives. Our dead have become mythographied; human sacrifices on the altar of fifties culture. Like the heads stuck on the fencepost of Kurtz's jungle fortress in Conrad's *Heart of Darkness*, victims of a madman's fantasy, our slain (in the martyrology of the following decades) were propitiatory offerings, casualties of the craziness of their period. James Dean (at one with his screen persona) raced from adult indifference or persecution to the death-on-wheels of a teen idol. An anxious macho culture exacted poisonous self-hatred from homosexual Montgomery Clift. Comedian Lenny Bruce was driven into drugs and madness by a rage of truth-telling; his obscence humor, scatty and racist, revealed the obsessions beneath the genteel hypocrisies

---

* Were we the first generation to suffer insomnia in such numbers? Or are we aware of a collective sleep disorder only because of the proliferation of drugs to cure it—the Nembutal, Seconal, and Tuinal that, along with the tranquilizers Miltown and Valium first began to be manufactured in the fifties?

of the day. Women's talents were wasted, their lives deformed, in roles ordained and policed by a patriarchal culture: Marilyn Monroe trapped in male sex fantasies; Sylvia Plath, the poet, suffocated by domesticity. Truth or apocrypha, these are the legends of martyrdom.

Not all homilies on the death of heroes absolve the fallen. Cass Hunnicutt sees the life of Elvis as a parable of the talents. Cut off from his roots, the man's gifts were unnourished, his soul corrupted. "He forgot who he was, who his friends were, where he came from," says Cass, the returned prodigal son. When Elvis became inaccessible to ordinary people, when he lost physical touch with "his own kind"—the fans who lived in mobile homes and listened to him in honkytonk roadhouses—Elvis was a dead man.

It was then that he met his idol for the first time, when Cass was an extra in one of Elvis' cornball specials, *It Happened at the World's Fair*. By then, the local boy, clowning for photographers, had all but disappeared.

"He was flanked by his Memphis mafia. He had bodyguards around him all the time. His manager, Colonel Parker, dictated his every move," Cass says.

False to his past, to his region, to himself, Elvis could only become an amnesiac, other people's creature, kept under control by a steady supply of pills, prepubescent girls, and cheeseburgers.

It wasn't stardom, fame, or money that destroyed Elvis, nor the doctor who gave him all the uppers and downers he wanted. What killed him, Cass says, was that "he lost track of who he was."

"A Faustian scenario of sell-out and corruption" is the way critic Greil Marcus describes one gloss on the Elvis gospel.[1] Cass Hunnicutt has another frame. He points to the way the rhythm of Elvis's life accelerated dangerously. Once he left sleepy Southern local time to go national, he was on fast forward all the way.

In America, this version of the Fall had long been part of

folklore, creating the morality tale of the small-town boy and girl, changed forever by the big city. By the end of the fifties, though, that process—like all the others in our collective life—had speeded up. Success. Stardom. Oblivion. It was all "instant"—like instant coffee and TV dinners. From being a " 'good ol' boy,' a regular guy—*vrooom!*—all of a sudden, he was a major star. I don't think he ever knew what hit him," Cass says.

Even today, in the South, on country roads a few minutes from interstate highways and large cosmopolitan cities, there are signs reminding drivers that speed and distance will not deliver them to where they should go: I Am the Resurrection and the Life. He Died for our Sins.

"I look on Elvis as a modern day sacrifice," says Cass Hunnicutt. "If you want to see the emptiness of fame and wealth, if you want to see the false gods of success, if you want to see how forgetting who you are and where you came from delivers you into the forces of darkness—Elvis died to prove that to us again."

Even in death, the King has it all ways. His fans, now middle-aged, come to Graceland to gawk at the wages of sin: Golgotha with gold drapes.

Before Elvis there was Jimmy Dean, "our first teen martyr."[2] Strip away the creepy necrophiliac goings on, the stuff of slumber-party shivers (did he really rise from his coffin?), and this sullen, androgynous adolescent promised what the seventies and eighties delivered—the canonization of youth.

Central to the myth are Dean's wholesome all-American beginnings. A high-school basketball star from Indiana, he might have been a Booth Tarkington hero, courting his girl on the porch glider. Instead, reported director Joshua Logan, Dean "likes racing cars, waitresses and waiters."[3]

He died in 1955 in a high-tech Wagnerian style, crumpled in a brand-new $7,000 silver Porsche Spyder. Driving at eighty-six miles an hour to get to an auto race, Dean collided with another car at an intersection near Salinas, California.

With only three major movie roles, James Dean managed to speak straight to the soul of a new population: "alienated" middle-class teenagers, the bored and ignored causeless rebels of prosperous fifties' America.

French filmmaker François Truffaut, creator of the postwar masterpiece of injured adolescence, *The Four Hundred Blows*, claimed that in James Dean, "today's youth discovers itself."[4] And he denied that Dean's persona confirmed the worst fears of adult society in the fifties—violence, sadism, hysteria, pessimism. Rather, Truffaut insisted, Dean as rebel revealed the best: "moral purity without relation to everyday morality, but all the more rigorous; eternal adolescent love of tests and trial . . . pride and regret at feeling oneself 'outside' society."

His outsider status was Dean's real bond with his audience. The bad boy stuff, he seemed to suggest, was a forlorn substitute for love. "When he got hooked on speed" (the Porsche kind, not the chemical kind), his biographer notes, "he hoped, as he had with all the other things and people he tried, that it would give him some relief from the ache of abandonment."

Like all martyrs, his fame as an actor was obscured by his death and rebirth as a cult figure. There was a brisk business in Dean relics (including such items as a ring said to contain shavings from the aluminum paint of his wrecked car). Fan clubs and newsletters proliferated. Innumerable tabloid articles proclaimed him alive, if not well, in places ranging from an Orange County nursing home to the South Seas.

Dean was a made-to-order martyr for the America of the fifties —the last period when youth was feared and loathed, not worshiped and emulated. He was the Saint Sebastian of speed freaks, too pained and pure to slow down and join the grown-ups.

On the night before his fatal accident, reports his biographer, Venable Herndon, James Dean went to a gay party at Malibu. Toward dawn, according to Herndon's source, "one of Jimmy's lovers put him up against the wall" about his sexual identity and demanded that he "come out" once and for all, and stop pretending to be sexually interested in women "except," as his accuser put it scornfully, "for publicity purposes."

If Dean had lived, would he have managed that double life? His idol, Montgomery Clift, was destroyed by the frantic shuttle between the two.

With only Marlon Brando for competition, Clift was the most talented and compellingly handsome of the new male stars of the fifties—men who conveyed an inner life along with emotions never before included in the repertoire of screen heroes. He was also homosexual. "Trapped in a macho age," notes his biographer, Patricia Bosworth, "Clift believed he must keep his sexual identity concealed from the public; otherwise his career would be finished, his life discredited."[5]*

In a profession where box-office success was dependent on the approval of mainstream Americans, for Clift to have revealed his sexual preferences would have been death; he would never have made another movie. He did not lack evidence of the social ostracism that would follow if the mask dropped. During the filming of *From Here To Eternity*, Clift and co-star Frank Sinatra had become close friends. A gold cigarette lighter the singer had given him for Christmas was inscribed, "Merry merry buddy boy. I'm with you all the way. Maggio." But when Sinatra saw Clift coming on to another man sexually at a Hollywood party, he had a bodyguard throw him out.

At the beginning of his career, such lapses were rare. According to his biographer, Clift was cautious about cruising, avoided obvious homosexual hangouts, and in general took few risks where exposure, entrapment, or blackmail could have resulted. When he did go out with one of his rare lovers of any duration, they were accompanied by an attractive young woman for cover.

---

* We need only recall the fate of Ingrid Bergman when she left her husband to live openly with Italian film director Roberto Rossellini. Pilloried by gossip columnists and denounced from pulpits across America, her career virtually ended until her comeback as an older character actress on television in the 1970s.

His three lives—public, private, and the demanding one of screen roles—began to take their toll. Increasingly, he needed barbiturates to sleep and alcohol to get through the day. The carefully maintained distance between his various personas was breaking down. Once, "only intimates knew he cruised 42nd Street; suffered beatings at the hands of male hustlers, robberies in his brownstone whose key he had given to more young men than he could remember; about threats of blackmail handled discreetly through a lawyer."

Before he was found naked in his bed, on July 22, 1966, his death attributed to coronary arrest and massive drug overdose, Clift had stopped hiding his "dark side." He openly cruised Third Avenue or solicited young men from the ground-floor window of his townhouse, where life inside was a night-into-day drug party. A constant stream of kept boys, male hustlers, pimps, and dealers swirled around the fogged-out host—unknown to most of his "guests."

"He was totally split sexually, that was the core of his tragedy," said his longtime friend and drama coach. He never stopped being conflicted and he never stopped feeling guilty.

"Monty never accepted his homosexuality," one of his lovers told his biographer. "He hated it; he was horrified by it."

At the end of his life, he still spoke of getting married. Happiness remained enshrined in the one fifties-approved scenario.

"He wanted to love women," Deborah Kerr said, "but he was attracted to men, and he crucified himself for it."

He didn't do it alone. The guilt, the fear, the lies, and the subterfuge were tributes demanded by the culture. In the fifties, recalls producer Joel Schumacher, "No one told the truth. People lied. Society was a group of liars. People pretended they weren't unfaithful. They pretended that they weren't homosexual. They pretended that they weren't horrible."[6]

If you couldn't or wouldn't pretend anymore, you were a marked man: a costly liability, an accusation and a threat.

Like homosexuality, adult female sexuality was threatening to many men and to the domestic social order. Women were wives and mothers, sex kittens or harlots; wayward little girls of perverse purity, worthy of the male endearments, "baby," "doll," "angel."

"Our angel, the sweet angel of sex,"[7] Norman Mailer called her. Like the angels on Victorian tombstones, cast in the image of dead children who will suffer no more, Marilyn Monroe's death has recast her life. A "martyr to male chauvinism,"[8] feminist critic Molly Haskell said of her, but in a style peculiar to her decade.

Unlike the sultry sex idols of the thirties and forties—Harlow and Hayworth—or a grown-up woman of the world like her contemporary Ava Gardner—Monroe was female sexuality as arrested development. "Jailbait," she suggested that "sex might be dangerous and difficult with others," Mailer said, "but ice cream with her."

The ice-cream image is the clue to her "double-bind," as psychiatrist R. D. Laing would later call it: the schizophrenic's "correct" reading of conflicting signals.

One directive required that she remain fixed forever in her childlike innocence, impervious to experience. Screenwriter Nunnally Johnson described her as "ten feet under water [as though surrounded] "by a wall of thick cotton . . . she reminds me of a sloth. You stick a pin in her and eight days later it [sic] says 'Ouch.' "[9] Physically, she could never age. Flash-freezing at the point of perfect ripeness is a terrifying, inhuman task. She always wore a bra to bed at night so that her breasts wouldn't sag.

At the same time, she was endowed with the skill of a million sexual encounters: the living embodiment of "the ultimate Fifties fiction," defined as the "lie that a woman has no sexual needs; she is there only to cater to or enhance a man's needs."[10]

Marilyn as a male fantasy of total availability and compliance, trapped in eternal innocence, created a curiously plastic amalgam. Beyond the green door was—Barbie doll, with her tiny, whispery voice, vanilla-and-strawberry make-up, Dynel hair. It was easy to imagine even the famous wiggle to have been wound into her by Mattel. Polyurethane perverse.

Her punishments were all of a period, too. Like Jayne Mansfield's breasts, the wiggle was made to stand for the whole woman. Her talents as a comedian—even, according to some— a serious actress, were forced to atrophy in roles that came ever closer to parodying her established off-screen personality. Playing herself, she became a succession of dim-witted popsies. At a time when female sexuality was never more terrifying, it had to be seen as a joke: *vagina dentata* turned into an ice cream sundae.

In private life the ultimate fifties imprimatur of womanliness, motherhood, eluded her. Were the miscarriages, "tubal," or "hysterical" pregnancies seen as punishments for the twelve abortions she admitted having had as a contract starlet?[11] (The obstetrician who delivered my daughter was also Marilyn's doctor. He was an elderly and formal European. When I sent an unmarried friend to see him about a minor infection, she reported that he had "humiliated" her with lectures about the evils of promiscuity. I wondered what he had to say on hearing Marilyn's medical history? Had she felt she deserved his censure?)

In August 1962, she was found dead, lying naked in her bed like Montgomery Clift. Her bedroom door was locked from the inside. The circumstances of her death—still undetermined— linked her to the world of conspiracy and assassination: the America of the sixties. Rumor had involved her with both Kennedys—the President and his brother, the Attorney General. Inevitably, the FBI and the CIA were reputed to have had more than a passing interest in her activities. "By the end," Norman Mailer claims, "political stakes were riding on her life and even more on her death."

As a sexual icon, Marilyn moved the saucy pinups and sultry glamor queens of the forties into the troubled ambivalence of fifties sex: Lolita auditions for *Deep Throat*. Her dying was another announcement that the sixties were with us. Sex and death

—even without the friendship of politicians—had become political acts.

Far from Hollywood and Broadway, there lived two brilliant young women who were also poets. Precocious in their talent, their promise was recognized early. While they were still students, their poetry was published. Prizes, fellowships, were showered on both. But they were also young women of the fifties. Two years after graduating college, they each married promising young men, becoming mothers as soon as possible thereafter.

In Cambridge, Massachusetts, in 1958, Sylvia Plath, soon to leave for England with her husband, British poet Ted Hughes, surveyed the competition. Adrienne Rich, she noted in her journals, was "honest, frank, forthright and even opinionated."[12]

As feminist literary history is written, "the opinionated one survived."[13] And not by accident. Adrienne Rich survived as a woman and a poet because, in her own words, she "saw through the lie of happy marriage, of domesticity." She survived the drudgery, the hatred followed by guilt, of a young mother with three children under seven:

> the repetitious cycles of laundry, the night-walkings, the interrupted moments of peace or of engagement with ideas, the ludicrous dinner parties at which young wives, some with advanced degrees, all seriously and intelligently dedicated to their children's welfare and their husbands' careers, attempted to reproduce the amenities of Brahmin Boston, amid French recipes and the pretense of effortlessness—above all, the ultimate lack of seriousness with which women were regarded in that world.[14]

She knew that if her poetry was to survive her own "indifference and boredom," her sense of unworthiness, she had "to remake her life." She divorced and, with three young sons, endured the suicide of their father.

From *Lies, Secrets and Silence*—the title of one of her books—a new self emerged, to redeem the central falsehood of the old one: "the heterosexuality that has drowned in silence the erotic feeling between women. . . . I myself lived half a life in the lie of that denial."[15]

Reborn into truth, Adrienne Rich at fifty-six is a feminist leader, doyenne of a lesbian separatist community and creator of poetry and prose that celebrates women—herself, her lovers, women famous or nameless and lost to history.

"A Great Outlaw Mother,"[16] one critic recently called her. Among other ironies of surviving the fifties, *outlaw* is now at the farthest remove from *outcast*. Our romance with tablet-smashers, born of the sixties, lives on.

Outlaw or outsider, Rich is squarely within the mainstream of American poetry. Still winning prizes and fellowships, teacher of the poor and the aged, her audience is made larger by a sexual and political agenda that extends far beyond the confines of the literary enterprise. They come to be strengthened by this "honest, frank, forthright and even opinionated" one of their own.

Sylvia Plath began her career as a poet of hymns to male sexuality, motherhood, and the redeeming reality of household tasks. "I long to become anchored to life," she wrote, "by laundry and lilacs, daily bread and fried eggs."[17]

Weeks before she committed suicide, in the freezing London winter of 1963, alone with two tiny children, she wrote to her mother about her last and best poems. They were, she said, "terrific stuff . . . it is as if domesticity had choked me."[18]

In her public persona, she was the classic fifties "good girl," only more so. "A rabid teenage pragmatist," she described herself. Perfectly groomed, perfectly behaved, a perfect A-student, working the system for the rewards and approval adults conferred on the young who gave no trouble. At Smith College, a close friend reported, the consensus of her classmates was that "except for the intelligence and the poetry, Plath could have been an airline stewardess or the ingenuous heroine of a B-movie." Marriage seemed to reinforce her deference to powerful men. A few years

later Robert Lowell noted her "air of maddening docility."
A. Alvarez, her friend throughout the seven last years of her life
in England, recalled his first impression of Plath's made-in-
America fifties-style femininity; "that curious, advertisement-
trained, transatlantic air of anxious pleasantness."[19]

Behind the frozen Ipana smile was an arsenal waiting for the
match: rage, guilt, and despair; wild ambition, and the fear that
would periodically engulf and finally destroy her.

"I am afraid. I am not solid, but hollow," she wrote in the
journal she kept in college.

> I feel behind my eyes a numb paralyzed cavern, a pit of hell,
> a mimicking nothingness . . . There is nowhere to go—not
> home, where I would blubber and cry . . . into my mother's
> skirts—not to men, where I want more than ever now their
> stern, final paternal directive.[20]

She did go home. Not to blubber to her mother but to hide
in the crawl space beneath her family's house in Wellesley Hills,
Massachusetts, there to wrap herself in her black raincoat and
swallow, one after another, the contents of a bottle of sleeping
pills.

Saved from death by merest chance, she was subjected, she
notes, in the chirpy cheerleader style of her letters, to "a semester
of reconstruction," which included hospitalization, psychotherapy,
and electric shock treatments. In a suspiciously short time, she is
pronounced "cured." Then she is back in college, still smiling,
winning prizes, and assuring her elders that she "hadn't lost either
my repetitive or creative intellect."

She had also gained a new sense of vocation—shared, unlike
poetry, by all her classmates: finding the "one man whom I can
make into the best man the world has seen," the "dark-eyed
stranger" who would save her from her demons. Crucial to this
process of salvation was motherhood. When she did not conceive
after two years of marriage to Ted Hughes, she was despairing.
"If I could not have children," she wrote in her journals,

I would be dead. Dead to my woman's body. Intercourse would be dead. My pleasure, no pleasure, a mockery. My writing a hollow and failing substitute for real life, real feeling, instead of a pleasant extra, a bonus flowering and fruiting. Ted should be a patriarch, I a mother.[21]

For the last six years of her life, she would, indeed, be the adoring mother of a daughter and son ("One cry, and I stumble from bed, cow-heavy and floral"); keeping house (including bees) in rural Devon, with a rustic absence of labor-saving appliances, and trying—in odd hours—to tend "the bonus flowering and fruiting" that was her poetry.

As a bride, Plath's rapturous descriptions of what family life would be for them—the "perfect" children, decor, garden, meals, both parents working away at their poetry—was the intellectual version of *McCall's* togetherness.

When she discovered her husband's infidelity, her dream of domestic utopia disintegrated along with her fragile equilibrium. She had cast him as male perfection; she was pitiless and unforgiving of his betrayal.* From Godlike heights, he had, she wrote witheringly, become a "little man"; sordid, human.

Suffocated by domesticity, murdered by marriage and motherhood, Plath the artist was canonized as another feminist martyr of the fifties—a counterpoint to Marilyn Monroe's detached sexuality and atrophied talents.

The poet's need to be affirmed as a wife and mother, followed by her abandonment in both these roles, made of her life and death a still more cautionary tale. (Feminist poet Robin Morgan proposed that, for his part in Plath's suffering, Ted Hughes be castrated.)

Even less extreme versions of the Martyrdom of St. Sylvia dis-

---

* According to one biographer, Plath burned the contents of Hughes's study, leaving written curses on piles of the charred remains (she had become interested in witchcraft in this period) and cut the telephone lines, so that he would be unable to reach his lover.[22]

miss the evidence that she embraced, with an enthusiasm exceptional even for the period, the expectations of a male-dominated
culture.

In her poetry as in her life, Adrienne Rich writes of Plath, "Man
appears . . . as a fascination and a terror" whose inescapable
spell lies in "his power—to dominate, tyrannize, choose or reject
the woman."[23]

Critics have seen in her autobiographical novel, *The Bell Jar*,
published in 1963, a feminist awakening, Plath revising the "false
consciousness" of her fifties coming-of-age. Her heroine, Esther
Greenwood, recalls a college boyfriend

> saying in a sinister knowing way that after I had children I
> would feel differently, I wouldn't want to write poems any-
> more. So I began to think that maybe it was true that when
> you were married and had children it was like being brain-
> washed, and afterward you went about numb as a slave in
> some private totalitarian state.[24]

The private totalitarian state was within her. In the coldest
winter of the century in Europe, Sylvia Plath stuffed the doors
and windows with rags and newspaper, and with her children
sleeping upstairs, turned on the gas and placed her head in the
oven.

> Viciousness in the kitchen, the potatoes hiss. . . .
> The smile of iceboxes annihilates me.

There is evidence that she expected, once again, to be rescued
from death. Her psychiatrist's number was on a pad next to the
telephone. The painter downstairs, like Plath, a dawn worker,
ought to have smelled gas. The arrival of the new au pair was
delayed by the great cold.

THE WAY WE ARE

The poetry, letters, and journals of Sylvia Plath take up half a shelf in Carol Cornwell's book-lined living room, joining works on feminist theology and most of the well-known women novelists of the last decades. On other shelves, in worn paperback editions, lean Spock and Gesell. Less accessible but still legible are the sturdy spines of the Chemistry and Psychology texts of college days. We may be the last generation to scan each other's bookshelves for clues about who lives here. For many of us, our books are, indeed, the story of our lives. Increasingly, with our parents gone, we have no more attics or "old rooms" to welcome the books that represent our past selves. We wheel them off to the thrift shop or carry them with us, like the chambered nautilus.

As on many other bookshelves of women my age, Sylvia Plath is the only poet represented. It's her life more than her art that speaks to us. We identify, especially, with her beginnings: that set of expectations—like the matching Samsonite luggage Plath carried to Cambridge University, sneered at by a fellow student for being "so typically 'American girl.'" To many women, her

death seemed only the extreme expression of familiar disappointments.*

"I could easily imagine doing it," a friend once said of Plath's
suicide. "But not with my children in the bedroom upstairs."

Children for us come first—before even suicidal despair. The
right to die is not a mother's right. We're relieved that the circumstances of Plath's suicide keep her at a safe remove. We aren't
that crazy. Thank God!

It's hard to stop thinking of ourselves as mothers—for good
reasons or bad. We can't seem to kick the habit. Like those of
most divorced women of my age, Carol Cornwell's living space—
a floor-through apartment in one of the "triple deckers" unique to
New England working-class neighborhoods—seems an empty
husk. The large rooms wait for the return of children or the re-
appearance of a man.

Thinking of family needs is reflexive, a tic that doesn't go away.
When she moves, Carol says, she would like a washer and dryer.
"The kids use so many towels when they visit." (How often is
that?) We are first and always, it seems, mothers of children who
must have rooms of their own to come home to. Their fathers are
comfortable with bachelor apartments, where a convertible sofa
suffices for guests and kids alike. For us, unaffordable extra bedrooms are seen as a necessity. Carol Cornwell apologizes for her
small study. "It's really a luxury," she says. Professional women,
we still feel we should work at the kitchen table like school-
children.

My daughter often suggests I convert her bedroom into a study.
She no longer writes term papers on her Victorian library table,
tapping away late into the night. But when I've tried working
there, my concentration oozes away. I wander to her bookcases,
looking at the spines of randomly crammed volumes: Robert

---

* According to the twentieth reunion report of my Smith College class of 1958,
one-third of my classmates had "seriously considered" suicide in the late sixties.
The answer to a follow-up question, the class secretary noted, "gamely professed
our belief that the worst was over."

Lowell, *Life Studies*, next to *Heidi*. Between the books are little baskets and bowls with pots of discarded makeup. I try on bright blue iridescent eyeshadow, relic of a brief punk-glitter period in twelfth grade; a fire-engine red lipstick worn once by "Lois Lane" at a Halloween party. The image in her mirror is alarming. I tissue off the vivid paint, embarrassed by my reflection. Nostalgia is not a productive emotion. I gather up my papers and heave my typewriter back to my own desk in the bedroom.

Women's homes so often seem like house museums—"kept exactly the way they were when the family lived here"—the brochure would read, shrines to a past more real than the present.

But for all of us, men and women, our children are reference points. Through them, we take the measure of our success or failure with a self-awareness new to our generation. It is not as husbands and wives, lovers or citizens, that we differ from our own parents, but as mothers and fathers. Our hope—often translated into a conscious effort—is that we are better.

We take pride in "being there" for our children, as our parents (secure in the certainties of another era) were not for us. Especially those of us who were children of privilege, determined to create a closeness we never experienced.

Even though everyone else he knew was "brought up by servants," these parental surrogates left Cass Hunnicutt with the "definite feeling of not being cared about." He recalls a conversation he had recently with a cousin his own age, also a father of teenagers: "We both just took it for granted that we would never miss our kids' soccer games."

When Cass was a Little League player, "it wouldn't have occurred to my parents to come to a game. We were just not the focal point of the house the way children are today."

The remoteness of his parents fed into the sense he had that, from a child's point of view, they were not a happy couple.

"They were always out," he recalls, "at a party or on a trip. They never seemed to want to be alone together—and certainly not with us." His children, he feels, "get a charge out of walking in the kitchen and finding their parents hugging each other and laughing. It increases their stability, just as my parents increased my instability by never being there. I always wanted a mother and father I could count on to be home most nights, doing whatever we were doing."

First-generation Americans often recall a father as provider and disciplinarian, a man who neither inspired nor expressed affection for his children. To a son like Philip Catania, his own overwhelming feelings of love for his child came as a shock.

During his first wife's pregnancy, he says, "I had this typically macho expectation that it would be a boy. I kept talking about 'my son, my son.'" But he recalls the first sight of his daughter as "instant religion—a feeling that has only grown with the years." Although his first marriage was unhappy from the very beginning, he still says that his only regret is "that we weren't fortunate enough to have more children."

In contrast to his own father, "remote and respected" by Philip, his sister, and three brothers, he "enjoys every minute" of being with ten-year-old Marian, who lives with her mother a block away. "I walk her to school every morning. If I'm on a business trip, we talk on the phone every day. And of course, she stays with us alternate weekends or when her mother is traveling."

"I like to keep affirming that love is there," Philip says. "But the truth is, the reaffirmation is more for me than for her."

Praise for his former wife is unstinting. "Her mother has done a spectacular job," Phil says. But he measures success in child rearing in ways undreamed of by his parents.

"Marian is such a sensitive person," he says, "always concerned about other people's feelings. Even when she was very little," her father notes proudly, "she was generous. It was never 'my toy,' 'my way.'"

It is moving to hear men who know they will never change in

these ways, describe how their sons redeem the limitations of the fathers.

"He's an unusually caring and empathetic human being," Mike DiStefano says about sixteen-year-old Mitch. "And he's able to express these feelings. I'll never be able to do that." As a measure of the difference between father and son, "Mitch has all these *female* friends," Mike DiStefano notes, his voice still registering astonishment.

"When I was his age, guys were buddies through sports. Girls —even if you only held hands—were a romantic or sexual relationship. Even now," Mike says, "the closest I've come to a woman friend is my wife."

We are prompt to point out the ways our children are morally superior to their parents.

Betts Saunders recalls the time when she referred to popularity in conversation with her daughter.

"I wish you wouldn't use that word, Mom, its so *offensive*," fifteen-year-old Caroline said. Her daughter, Betts says, "admires people who are kind, honorable, bright. She doesn't care who else does or doesn't like them."

"She's just such a great human being. God, when I think of what 'our' values were like at her age!" How did we do it? How did we ever produce these marvelous children?

Betts Saunders makes a point of telling her kids how wonderful they are.

"When I was growing up," she says, "there were no compliments. Everything I did wrong was pointed out—and punished. But there was never a word said when I did anything right. That was expected. I was so strictly disciplined that one of my vows, from a very young age, was that I would have *fun* with my kids."

We have fun with our children. We count ourselves lucky when we are friends. We feel vindicated when they talk openly and intimately with us. Unlike our own parents, we worry and blame

ourselves when this closeness is missing. We buy books telling us
how to improve "communications," how to encourage our children
to like and trust us, how to be better parents than we are people.

Success as friends and confidants is not without its price. Giving
up our role as "authority figures" has made us all too aware that we
can no longer protect even young children from the world "out
there." This particular illusion was one of many harbored by our
"innocent" parents, a state of mind we helped perpetuate by never
telling them anything. (Often, I have had occasion to think, our
elders were lucky—or perhaps cannier and more self-protective
than we ever realized. They didn't really want to know the tough
stuff; the laugh was on us.)* As my daughter's intimate and
friend, I am vulnerable to pain her grandparents were spared.

We are the first parental generation to suffer guilt without
power. Too "enlightened" to believe we can police against mistakes or prevent unhappiness, we castigate ourselves all the more
for our children's every problem and failure.

Betts Saunders once asked her mother if "she had ever done
anything wrong."

"If it were wrong, I wouldn't do it," her mother replied.

"My mother," Betts says, "never entertained a doubt about anything. You washed on Monday, ironed on Tuesday, and stayed a
virgin until you were married."

Uncertainty about most areas of authority—from whether a
child should be forced to clean her room to parental influence
about sex—has replaced her mother's certitudes.

In the Saunders' affluent suburb, early sexual activity among
teenagers is taken for granted. But it's the casualness more than
the age, Betts says, that distresses her.

---

* A. R. Gurney's play *The Dining Room* (1982) satirizes the refusal of an upper-
class WASP family to confront the ugly realities of their adult children's lives. In
one scene, the father (our parents' vintage) insists that his daughter find his
favorite highball glass before he will listen to the circumstances of her divorce. As
Daddy obsessively describes the pheasant engraved on the glass, the audience
shrieks with laughter at his "avoidance strategy"; I wondered whether those of the
father's generation found his maneuver so hilarious.

Their neighbor, a gynecologist, told her of the recent visit, including a request for the pill, by one of his son's ninth-grade classmates. "Say 'hi' to Doug for me," trilled the unembarrassed lass on leaving his office.

For Betts, this story illustrates her own conflicting feelings about sex and young people. She acknowledges that the fourteen-year-old's lack of hypocrisy, her assumption that her male classmate knows about—and thinks no less of her for—her sexual activity, is preferable to the days when "promiscuous" girls, usually from the "wrong side of the tracks," were mocked and ostracized by their peers, when classmates left school or college under circumstances unmentioned except in whispers. Still, for her, the cruelty, fear, and denial that attended sexual initiation in the fifties has simply been exchanged for its opposite—a social pressure to conform to the "no-rules, anarchic sex," as Betts says, of today's youth.

She mourns the sheltered coming-of-age allowed young people growing up in a small Midwestern city thirty years ago, where, "in our crowd, it was just necking at the drive-in or parked by the lake. The heart beat just as fast," Betts says, "but it was so safe."

In *Blooming,* Susan Allen Toth's memoir of a 1950s adolescence in Ames, Iowa, she wonders, "Does any girl today have the chance to grow up as gradually and as quietly as we did? In our particular crucible, we were not seared by fierce poverty, racial tensions, drug abuse, street crime; we were cossetted, gently warmed, transmuted by slow degrees."

That safe cossetting is no longer possible for us, parents now ourselves, to give our children—wherever we live. We love them more "wisely" than we were loved, with more honesty, attentiveness, and respect. Yet we are able to protect them less well. (Is it "them," "us," or a "changed" society? This is the puzzlement that all our contemporaries articulate in different ways.)

Abdicating the authoritarian style in favor of an uneasy equality, we have a sense that something has backfired. We are all the more vulnerable when our kids, exercising the autonomy and independence we encouraged, disappoint our expectations—the ones we were so careful not to "impose" on them.

Ever fifties fence sitters, we are also sitting ducks for having our bluff called.

Out of our own feelings of privation or of being "programmed" by parents, many of us welcomed the lessons of the sixties and seventies. Our children were not us. They were not here to act or reenact *our* ambitions (failed or realized), reflect *our* success or status, adopt *our* values. Instead, we were instructed, we should help them to become themselves—whatever that might be.

Yet few of us have kicked the most "traditional" aspect of our own upbringing: the need for what a friend calls the "reportable" signs of children's success. When I say, "Tell me about your kids," no parent fails to mention first a youngster's distinction—academic, athletic or entrepreneurial. Most are equally forthcoming in their anxiety about "very bright kids who could be doing a lot better." (And invariably, I am asked where my daughter "fits" on this spectrum.)

Significantly, our acceptance of "professional" help for children can almost always be traced to problems at school. After drug or alcohol abuse, "underachievement" in our offspring most easily convinces us that something is "wrong." (Is there a parent in our generation with a dumb, happy kid?)

Bob Hodges would not seek help to salvage his marriage, but when his oldest child was having trouble with schoolwork, he readily agreed to therapy and followed the doctor's advice to spend more time with his daughter.

For Sue Hodges, the therapeutic legacy is the healthiest change wrung from our parents' unsophisticated child rearing.

"My children all see psychologists and I think it's wonderful," she says. "We were brought up to keep our troubles to ourselves. 'It's your problem; you have to solve it'." Even with her training as a social worker, when it came to "my marriage, my problems— I had almost as much difficulty talking about them as Bob did.

"When our kids get to be adults, they'll take it for granted that when you're hurting, you get help."

"Both of my sons are very bright and creative," Dan Ross says, "but neither has achieved much in school. Certainly not what their mother and I expected of them, given their abilities." When Adam, the oldest, dropped out of college after two years, "I got very traditional, very uptight about it," his father admits.

"He's a lazy bastard. If he can avoid work, he will. I got frustrated as hell, trying to motivate him and get him going."

But Dan Ross now agrees that Adam was lazy only when it came to school. Once out in the real world, he got a job right away.

"He's into saving lives," his father says, with the mixture of pride and incomprehension that characterizes so many parents. "He joined a road emergency squad. His car is rigged out like an ambulance, with fire extinguishers, first-aid kits, resuscitation equipment. He's taking life-support classes. He'll stay up for twenty-four hours if there's a call," his father says.

With the benefit of psychoanalysis, Dan Ross sees his son's sense of "life as a disaster area" to be something of an indictment. "A kid who needs a uniform and thinks in terms of constant emergency is not a secure kid. Obviously, we didn't give him what he needed. He's the one that wants to be rescued."

But when his father pointed out to Adam the "neurotic" implications of his career choice, "he just looked at me and said, 'If that's the way you want to see it, fine!' "

"He doesn't worry that I'm right," Dan says. "He doesn't get mad. He sees this interpretation as my problem, not his. It's 'Fuck you, Dad.' "

There is unmistakable admiration in Dan Ross's translation of his son's attitude. Unlike our own parents, we're not sure we're entitled to more respect than we get. It's the rare father, in our guilt-prone generation, who feels he got the terrific kid he deserves.

"He's a chip off the old block"—that prideful paternal common-place—is an exotic sentiment these days. Its assumption of satis-faction with ourselves and our lives sounds a note from simpler times.

When Dick Robertson says, "My son is just like me," he is drawing both of them into a family tradition of achievement he enjoys contemplating. "Everyone always used to say I was just like my dad," he recalls, "from my business sense to the way I pulled at my knees when I sit down. Now they say the same thing about Pete. It's all just moved down a notch."

The year following his parents' divorce, Peter Robertson de-cided to live with his father and to work in a gas station instead of going to college. "That was fine with me," Dick says. "I figured he'd get bored after a while and change his mind. That's exactly the way my father would have handled the situation."

Last January, Pete graduated from the university a semester early. He'd already lined up a "tremendous job" with an oil com-pany, at a starting salary "that just blew me away. At twenty-one, he's on the road to financial success. Now, I think that's pretty good!"

Carol Cornwell feels uneasy about her son's single-minded pursuit of success.

"He doesn't seem to have much of a social conscience," she says. "When I ask him why he works for a bank or where the bank's investments are, he says, 'Oh, Mom, lay off.' "

On the day that Carol's father replied to her doubts about the existence of God by saying, "As long as you live in this house, you will believe what I tell you to believe," she determined "very consciously to do things differently when I was a parent."

"There was always room for discussion and argument in our house," she says. In such a liberal atmosphere, she supposed, liberal ideas would prevail.

Twenty-six-year-old Matthew, his mother says, is "just the way we were in the late fifties. He married right out of college. He's completely concerned with a career and having *things*—first a bigger apartment, now with buying a house." The only difference between Matthew and his wife, a software designer, and their parents' generation, Carol thinks, is "the change in sex-role stereo-types."

They both take it for granted that Jennifer's job, needs, and desires carry equal weight in the household. "That makes me very happy," Carol says. "But I'm still waiting to see how things will be when they have children."

Dan Ross is convinced that his sons "won't be stuck with 'the nurturing female image,'" with their father's need as the male to be the "main focus of attention."

"Their image of a mother," he says, "is a high-powered woman executive, tough and smart, who knows how to move up in the corporate world. They're used to a mother who travels more than their father, who's out drinking and socializing evenings with her confrères, who never worried about saying, 'I'm coming home late; cook yourselves dinner.'"

At twenty, Dan Ross reports, his son Adam has a girlfriend four years older than he is. "She's a nice, sweet, sexy lady who wants nothing except to get laid as often as possible. He's already getting bored with her. So I kid him. I say, 'Wait! You'll find a nice Jewish doctor!'"

"I tell my girls all the time, 'Rowan DiStefano says, You make sure you get a career out there! You make sure when you get out of college, you've got something. Then if you get married and it doesn't work out, you have a life for yourself.'"

Rationally, her daughters accept this, Rowan says. The culture is so different now. They get the same message from school, from TV, from movies. But then, she says, laughing, "they see the way I live, and I wonder."

"Lisa, my oldest, is a terrific student, a hard worker and really aggressive—just like her father," Rowan says. "But she tells me all the time she just wants to get married and have kids. That's all she wants to do."

Rowan DiStefano didn't know Pat Catania in the old days, when her Tiffany-engraved "informals" identified her as Mrs. Lane Snowden Brewster III, to which those who knew her would have added: "perfect wife, hostess, volunteer, model Roman Catholic communicant, and mother." Rowan knows, though, that her new friend, from being a woman much like herself, has changed.

Pat Brewster Catania's earlier selves seem to have disappeared. The gold-lamé cocktail dress has been exchanged for a gold credit card. This fall, she will not be on a bus filled with other Catholic Women for Abortion Rights, heading for Washington. She will be in an airplane on her way to a business meeting. When she looks up from her report into the clouds, she will ponder the possibilities of leaving the large firm where she is feeling "stuck" as vice president. Like the list she once made, noting the steps needed before she could leave her marriage, she now jots down the names of smaller competitors whose presidency might be open to her, or clients, like the magazine she knows is looking for a publisher. The anger and energy activated by civil rights and feminism is now focused on success. In a real sense, Pat Catania has not changed. She has come full circle, back to the realm of the private that once defined us completely. Only the objectives have changed. Ambition, the desire for achievement and reward, has shifted from the domestic—the perfect children and dinner party—to the professional—the next promotion.

Our daughters, especially if they are still students, seem to belong to a postfeminist generation. The revolution is over and won. (There are just a few corpses left by the roadside.)

"This is unbelievable!" whoops Rachel, twenty, leafing through my twenty-fifth reunion yearbook. I rush to see the entry that has aroused her disbelief. I reread it.

"I'm still married to Harry Hoffmeister (Dartmouth, '54; Yale

Law, '57)" begins the autobiographical essay in the familiar chirpy tone of all class notes.

"Isn't it *pathetic*," my daughter insists, seeing my uncomprehending expression, "that a woman still defines herself by where her husband went to school?"

She and her friends watch re-runs of *I Love Lucy* with the gaze of anthropologists who have come upon natives practicing unspeakable rites in the jungle. Is it possible there was, thirty years ago in America, a culture in which the otherwise carefully concealed intelligence of a woman was directed only toward conning a fur coat or a vacation out of her lunk of a husband? The "fascination of the abomination," indeed.

I do not have much in common with "Lucy Ricardo" (starting with the fact that I am not as smart as her real-life counterpart, Lucille Ball). But I am more defensive about my classmate Mrs. Hoffmeister. True, it would not occur to me to present myself by the schools my husband attended or the work he does, even in the context of reunion news. But, I remind my child, rarely a week goes by when I do not find myself in social situations where my identity (and my reflexive response to being thus identified) is that of "his lovely wife"—as alumni magazines of once-male institutions still unfailingly refer to "us." More shameful though, when I am feeling down about my professional life, when my "brilliant career" is going badly (the self-deprecating irony with which we refer to work is another generational giveaway), I take psychological refuge at home base. Not only do I count on my spouse's support and sympathy—which men have always done— I lean gratefully on the social approval (still) claimed by a wife and mother in our society.

The more courageous members of our generation suffered most. Those for whom the sixties provided both the support for personal change and the faith that individual change would transform society were left with disillusionment and loneliness.

"The brave new world," Martin Duberman says, "the America

that was to come about through black liberation, gay liberation, feminism, the end of poverty—has collapsed around our ears."

From being one of the last of his generation to "come out" in the seventies, he was in the forefront of gay activism for a decade. But recently, he says, he has resigned all his organizational board memberships. The radical alliance that once informed the movement has dissolved. Its members have moved, along with the rest of America, toward a privatistic center.

Gay rights now means the right to buy the condo anywhere you want. "It's basically a consumer movement," he says. "Meanwhile, poverty and racism are worse than they ever were. But nobody's interested."

Like many who "still believe in the expansion of human possibilities," he is left with a sense of diminishment—personal, social, political. "Mired down," "grounded"—these are the images that thread his speech, weaving back and forth from self-description to social analysis.

He talks of the "everyday madness" that confronts so many people now as "shrinking the capacity for intimacy." The harassments of life have finally struck the middle classes: crime, unemployment, and kids on drugs. In the fifties "people like us," he says ironically, "were so beautifully cushioned against those things. We've learned too much—to our sorrow and skepticism —from Vietnam, economic depression, the death of the sixties."

A "hapless romantic in a nonromantic age," he sees a new siege mentality, along with a loss of faith in social change, as eroding our belief in the possibilities of love.

"Unless you have the belief in possibilities, at the very beginning," he says, "you're negating yourself. Even as I make a gesture forward, toward another, I'm telling myself, What crap! What horseshit! How impossible. Lower the expectations, kiddo. That's not the way the real world works.

"We used to think that's how the real world did, and should, work. In the fifties, we didn't have any social commitments. But

we had a heavy investment in our relationships working out—
that was the source, the entry to human happiness.

"Now we don't believe in either," he says.

In a recent study four social scientists take the measure of the
lives of thirty-six Americans as they negotiate the conflicting traditions of individualism and commitment.[1] Behind these grander
abstractions lurk the old mixed signals of our coming-of-age:
doing good and doing well, our need for self-fulfillment and
community.

A generation of outsiders, we expressed our yearning to belong,
first, by an unprecedented surge of family-building. Middle-aged
now, many the parents of grown children, the men and women
in this book often confided a sense of needing more than the
satisfactions of private lives or even individual success. They
described present happiness or sadness in terms of larger community, lost or found.

Since he returned to his native city a year ago, Cass Hunnicutt
jumped right in. "I've gotten on the Chamber of Commerce,
civic committees. Two people have asked me to run their political
campaigns. I didn't feel I could do that before," he says. "I didn't
have the interest, because California was never home."

The emptiness that he felt before was a symptom of particular
failure. None of his other achievements, success in business or
athletic triumphs, "made any contribution," he says. "Only the
things I've done that contributed to a group, to a community or
another individual, give me that pleasure, the satisfaction that
escapes you when you're just doing something for yourself."

Cass Hunnicutt knows that few Americans of his age can return
to a place where their family still lives, representing, in force
of numbers, several generations of a name that still resonates
with a tradition of responsibility. Acceptance of the name and its
privileges as an opportunity, not a burden, is a measure of the

way in which Cass has changed. His dream now, he says, is "to help form a community that works, one that would be able to solve its unemployment and crime and poor education, for blacks and whites." Cass wants to be part of such a unifying effort, but less for visionary reasons than for the pragmatic ones that have always motivated Americans. "I'm of a mind," he says, "that this can be done."

Eight years ago, Gail Feldstein, at forty, finally felt accepted, "OK by society," because she walked the main street of her western Massachusetts city, married and pregnant.

In the last three years, this same region has given her the first real community she has known: women free of the need for men.

Healed by the accident of her move here, Gail Feldstein's life feels integrated for the first time, the wrath of the rabbi's daughter transformed into positive energy by the "negative community"[2] of lesbian separatism.

Her insistence on work that furthers social change—teaching prisoners to read and write, keeping women's studies alive at the local community college—is a requirement shared by most of the women she knows. Like Gail, who cleans houses to subsidize her other part-time work, most of her friends have blue-collar jobs to support volunteer activities like counseling battered women.

Among the greatest pleasures of her new community are her friendships with young people, both the working-class students she teaches and the privileged undergraduates at the Ivy League college nearby.

"College-age activists give *me* the courage to keep going," she says. "They believe in me and they're inspired by me. I have to live up to their expectations. So I challenge myself to do more."

To most of her contemporaries, Gail says, "My energy seems adolescent, my urgency naive."

"People our age have generally given up. They're into things again. Or security. Benefits and tenure. Radical kids trust me because they know I don't want any of that."

Through a combination of hard work and the social changes of the past quarter century, Steve Ortiz is part of a larger community whose existence he barely suspected thirty years ago.

"I never thought I'd become a middle-class Republican," he says.

To a "hyphenated-American" as he calls himself, growing up in the Southwest in the 1950s, "outsider" was not a state of mind, but a fact of life.

"If you were Jewish or Irish, you could pass, but you had to be white, I thought, with a father who was a doctor, to succeed at anything. I never imagined that being a businessman was available to me."

Changes in his social thinking that began when he was administrator of the migrant worker program in the late sixties were completed by his recent entrepreneurial activities: investing in real estate and the stock market.

"Each of us can go as far as our abilities will take us," Steve Ortiz says. "Making money is open to anyone."

He has learned on his own what many Americans of our age were taught. Sin is the failure to make use of opportunity.

Everything that happened in the last thirty years of his life has served to confirm Paul Michaelides' early optimism. He has easily managed to provide for the six children he and his wife both wanted. In orderly seven-year cycles, he has enjoyed the challenges and rewards of successively higher rungs on the corporate ladder, until as president of the American subsidiary of a Japanese-owned electronics manufacturer, he could decide that "we had more than enough equity" for Paul to take the plunge and become his own boss.

Their youngest child, Karin, left for college this fall. Elaine Michaelides is finally going back to school for the degree she always planned—and always deferred. To his surprise, Paul is feeling nibbles of "empty nest" depression that not even the demands of his new business allow him to ignore.

Dissolution of their family community has activated other, long-buried feelings of loss. Recently he has begun to experience "a kind of religious conflict." Twenty-five years ago, bringing up the children as Presbyterians hadn't seemed like any momentous decision, he says.

"Suddenly, I realize I'm surrounded by Gentiles. And I get this funny feeling."

Buried for so long, the Jewish half of his background is neither dead nor alive.

"Part of the Wailing Wall is still at the core of me," he says. "But it's nothing I can pass onto my children. It's gone forever."

The surge that swept Carol Cornwell from her marriage into feminism, divorce, and the ministry has moved out to sea, leaving her . . . well, she's not quite sure. Beached? In limbo?

With the exception of the nuclear freeze and disinvestment in South Africa, the social activism that engaged her and her church has become muted. If not quite business as usual, pastoral and theological issues of a more traditional sort have come to the fore.

She is still concerned with patriarchal language in the Scriptures and sexism in the church hierarchy. But she knows that, once assigned to a congregation, her work will be helping parishioners wrestle with the "old" problems—ones that she also confronts— the nature of humanity and divinity; "God as relationship," she says, quoting Episcopal feminist theologian Carter Haywood. But she'll also be helping them to cope with troubled children, divorce, loneliness, aging, and the fear of death.

About her own needs, she echoes Martin Duberman's sense of regret. There is a terrible sadness in the realization that all she risked and learned—at considerable cost to herself and, she admits, to others—about sex, love, work, and independence may finally have to serve a stoical solitude.

"At my age, the reality is that I may have to live alone for the rest of my life."

"When it first hit me," she says, "there was no one in the world that really needed or cared about me anymore, I really did a nosedive. Living alone just isn't a way of life for which anything in our expectations or training prepared us. It's very, very hard, but I'm getting better at it."

Work, as many of us—most recently, women—have found, is the most dependable ally in this effort, especially Carol Cornwell's work: "I've always been searching religiously. That's probably one reason my life has ended up where it has. Not because, as a minister, I have to have answers. But because, as a minister, I can devote more time to the questions."

The first wave of the women's movement produced a shelf of conversion literature. (Once I was a sniveling, dependent doormat of a wife and mother. Now I am a free, divorced professional and single parent.) These books had brave, assertive titles, a mirror of the courage and hard-won gains of their authors.

In *The Girl I Left Behind Me*, Jane O'Reilly chronicles her journey from convent-educated St. Louis debutante, through two marriages, to her present life as a hard-working breadwinner and feminist. On the author's evidence, though, Ms. O'Reilly didn't leave that girl behind her. She is still there for her—and us—in our dread of telephoning a man, our compulsion to make the bed before leaving for the office or sitting down at the typewriter, our need—whatever our present circumstances—to re-create some version of "happy" fifties family life, along with our belief that it exists . . . somewhere.

Like an image in a hall of mirrors, my fifties self is still there, smiling brightly everywhere I turn—from the clothes I still prefer; from my sense that, as a woman, I am responsible for the success of every social occasion; from my feelings of discomfort in imposing offices that these are places where I do not belong; in a certain secretiveness; in the distance I put (most often with ironic humor) between myself and others—especially people I

like—often with the wistful hope that if they are perceptive or
interested, they will know who lives there. More tellingly, I am
a creature of my period in the telltale "overinvestment" in my
child—a state of mind that has nothing to do with lack of other
interests or even, I think, with there being only one of her. If I
won the Nobel Prize tomorrow, it couldn't compete with the
rush I get from news of her success.

Still, if I were either a Freudian hard-liner, believing that the
personality is fully formed by the age of five, or a historical de-
terminist, convinced that we are merely creatures of our formative
period, I would never get out of bed in the morning.

Like many women my age, and some men, I have changed in
significant ways since 1958—the date of our cover photograph
and the year I graduated from college. In part this is the inevitable
process of aging, growing up (a slow process for all of us), learning something—one hopes—from the accumulation of experience.
But in larger measure, the ways that we are different men and
women from the ones we were, arise from the transformation in
social attitudes of the last two decades.

The importance of work, of sex and gender, of money and
class, were not part of our early education. Having to learn these
basic truths forced us to be more honest with ourselves—and
sometimes even others.

I will never see "political activist" following my name. But
neither am I the indifferent sideliner of the old days. On my first
and only antiwar demonstration, I found myself fleeing clouds
of tear gas, sullenly stared down by a pimply teenage MP with
a bayonet attached to his rifle.

"You're breaking the law by trespassing on federal property,"
he told me.

"I know," I heard myself say, in a state of shock.

Like virginity, automatic respect for law and order can only be
lost once. Along with millions of Americans my age and older, I
no longer accept authority as inherently legitimate (if occasion-

ally inconvenient). We have seen too much illegitimate behavior from those duly constituted to lead us.

Compared to my "old" self, quaking in constant terror behind a lacquered social mask, "low-risk" and "approval-oriented," I have become a high roller. More spontaneous and confident, I am capable of acting openly for reasons of principle, profit, or even pleasure, with relative indifference to the "good opinion" of others. I have appeared ridiculous, choosing to say what was in my mind or heart.

Still, I'm forced to admit that I've changed least in my attitudes about men. My husband has occasionally been heard to remark that I am often critical of men for the same failings I forgive—or don't even notice—in a woman. I think, unhappily, he is right. But there is a particular flavor to the all-too-often ungenerous tone and substance of our remarks about the men we know.

In our mothers' phrase, you were supposed to be able to "look up to a man"—intellectually and morally, in competence and worldly wisdom. (Their economic and political power were so much taken for granted that these were never mentioned.) Men were stronger, smarter, sexier, and, of course, always more successful. We have often found it hard to forgive them for failing by these measures.

"I don't want a man who's my equal," another sandbox mother once said, only half in jest. "I want one who's my superior—in everything." Too often, women have ended by despising what they cannot unqualifiedly admire. And, of course, the ways in which the men who are our contemporaries have both exploited and been victimized by these same myths of male supremacy have, by now, a large literature. Just as often, men have ended by hating women for those very assumptions, for the fear and anxiety created by such expectations. Indeed, most so-called fifties humor, from the "suburbo-realism"[3] of TV sitcoms like *I Love Lucy* and *The Honeymooners*, to virtually every movie comedy, to the routines of stand-up comedians like Mort Sahl and Lenny

Bruce, derives from exposure of male vulnerability—as women's only weapon.

So ingrained in our psyche—collective and individual—is this seesaw of exaltation and fear, expectation and disappointment, that *equality* will never describe the relations between men and women of our generation. Whatever we want the Other to be for us, it has nothing to do with "equal": romantic and mysterious, god- and goddesslike, but also friends, housekeepers, mentors, lovers, parents, and nannies.

Starting out as a no-choice generation, we compensated for our stifled beginnings—and then some. For all of us—and there are many—who have remained "hugging the shore," to borrow John Updike's title (among whose ranks I count myself), or who "went in up to our knees, but not over our heads" in Dan Ross's formulation, there are scores (including several of the men and women in this book) who, to their own amazement, went off the deep end!

How hard it was for us is summed up in a phrase used, remarkably enough, by dozens of people I interviewed about very different events in their lives: leaving marriages, changing careers, marching for abortion rights, "coming out," even looking for a job or going back to school. It was first said to me by a psychiatrist describing his feelings when, in the early fifties, as a young medical student with a government scholarship, he refused to sign a loyalty oath. "I felt," he said, "like I was walking off the edge of the world."

Every generation is transitional, a social and genetic link between the past and future. Ours may be more transitional than any in our history—perhaps the one respect in which we are extreme.

We are the last men and women in America to have expected to live the way our parents lived, only to be cast into uncharted terrain, with neither compass nor maps.

Yet, unlike those generations whose coming-of-age was marked by the depression, World War II, or Vietnam, we lack a common crucible of social and economic upheaval or the dislocations of war. In talking with veterans of the Korean "conflict," I was surprised to learn how little effect—moral or psychological—their experiences seemed to have had on the rest of their lives. In marked difference to those who participated in the D-day invasion, or who were dropped by parachute into Vietnamese jungles, they expressed no feelings of continued community with fellow combatants.

In further contrast to our seniors and juniors, our lives were characterized by constant contradiction. We got the best and worst of everything in this century: the prosperity and political repression, the "sheltered and gradual coming-of-age" and the sexual hypocrisies, the plentiful jobs and the obsession with security, the dream of home ownership and the miseries of suburbia. And finally, after doing as we were told for most of our lives, we were exhorted to "get with it"—to find out who we were and what we *really* wanted!

Our generational bond is not to be found in breadlines, foxholes or sit ins, or in the broad experiences many of us share—college, early marriage and parenthood, and our steadily improved standard of living—or even in the ways feminism, divorce, psychotherapy, sex, or success did or did not change our lives.

Like former prisoners, we connect in the knowledge of our past constraints and in a cautious sense of new freedom. It's the veiled joke, the glint of triumph, or the rush of sympathy. Still silent, we connect most of all in the unspoken question (and answers) of underground men and women: And how was it for you? We trade survival tactics and even a few secrets. We hope that having rolled with too many punches doesn't show. Still putting "best foot forward" in our public selves, we're ready to role-play the part of tribal elders.

ACKNOWLEDGMENTS

Many men and women shared their memories of the fifties and beyond who do not appear in this book.

Among the most valuable sources were my friends. As we pondered together our part in the perplexing history of the last twenty-five years, they jogged my memory, reminded me of books I should reread, suggested people to interview, and regaled me with personal experiences.

For this and much more, I am grateful to Halcy Bohen, Wendy Gimbel, Sallie Bingham, Celia Eisenberg, and Yoma Ullman.

Other friends whose ideas and comments are reflected in these pages are Martha Schroeder O'Connor, Phyllis LaFarge, Florence Hammond Phillips, Joan Bamberger Goodheart, Katherine and Graham Finney, Renata and Edward Selig.

With characteristic generosity, Nora Sayre showed me sections of her forthcoming book on the fifties.

One of the happier changes in my life is the presence of friends who happen to be men: Frederick Brown, Andrew Hacker, Milton Horowitz, and Woodruff Price reminded me of how little "we" knew about "them."

I have profited from conversations with Barbara Jakobson, Eric Pace, and Janet Malcolm. Favors were generously forthcoming from Richard Beattie, Joseph Kanon, André Schiffrin, Kate Hill Strickler and Thomas Wright.

It is a pleasure to thank the trustees and fellows of the Macdowell Colony for a productive stay in the fall of 1984 and the New York Society Library, its staff, and director Mark Piel, for constant help.

The care and fidelity Judy Cohen and Claire Wagner brought to the typing of the manuscript was a constant source of reassurance. I am grateful to Susan Llewellyn for her painstaking copy editing. The pleasures of work are increased and its sufferings diminished in the loving collaboration of my editor, Ellen Joseph.

Agreeing with Norman Mailer that the fifties "were the worst decade in the history of man," my husband provided sympathy, diversion, and benign neglect in just the right measure.

SOURCE NOTES

Chapter 1

1. Douglas T. Miller and Marion Nowak, *The Fifties: The Way We Really Are* (New York: Doubleday & Co., Inc. 1977), p. 417.
2. John B. Rae, *The American Automobile: A Brief History* (Chicago: University of Chicago Press, 1965), p. 193.
3. Miller and Nowak, p. 414.
4. Andrew J. Cherlin, *Marriage, Divorce, Remarriage* (Cambridge, Mass., Harvard University Press, 1981), p. 35.
5. Quoted by David Riesman in "The Found Generation," *The American Scholar*, 25 Autumn 1956, pp. 421–436.
6. *The Fifties: Photographs of America*, Introduction by John Chancellor (New York: Pantheon Books, 1985), unpaged.
7. Susan Allen Toth, *Blooming: A Small-Town Girlhood* (Boston: Little-Brown, 1978, 1981), pp. 3–4.
8. Victor Fuchs, *How We Live* (Cambridge, Mass.: Harvard University Press, 1983), pp. 182–183.
9. Warren I. Susman, *Culture As History: The Transformation of American Society in the 20th Century* (New York: Pantheon Books, 1984), p. 192.

Chapter 2

1. Thomas S. Buechner, *Norman Rockwell* (New York: Harry N. Abrams, Inc. 1970), p. 16.
2. William H. Whyte, Jr., *The Organization Man* (New York: Simon and Schuster, 1956), p. 384.
3. Robert Paul Smith, *"Where Did You Go?" "'Out'." "What Did You Do?" "'Nothing'"* (New York: W.W. Norton & Co., Inc., 1957), p. 38.
4. Robert Lindner, *Must You Conform?* (New York: Holt, Rinehart & Winston, 1956), p. 6–7.
5. Robert Lindner, *Prescription for Rebellion* (New York: Grove Press, 1952), p. 67.

6. Miller and Nowak, p. 152.
7. Joseph Pleck, *The Myth of Masculinity* (Cambridge, Mass., London: The M.I.T. Press, 1981), p. 158.
8. Ibid., p. 31 ff. All tests designed to measure masculinity are cited in Pleck.
9. Ernest Havemann and Patricia Salter West, *They Went to College: The College Graduate in America Today*. Based on a survey of U.S. college graduates made by *Time* magazine and analyzed by the Columbia University Bureau of Applied Social Research (New York: Harcourt, Brace and Co., 1952), p. 54.

Chapter 3

1. Bob Thomas, *Golden Boy: The Untold Story of William Holden* (New York: St. Martin's Press, 1983), p. 126.
2. Peter Biskind, *Seeing is Believing: How Hollywood Taught Us to Stop Worrying and Love the Fifties* (New York: Pantheon Books, 1983), p. 306.
3. Charles Highham, *Audrey: The Life of Audrey Hepburn* (New York: Macmillan Publishing Company, 1984), p. 68, and Thomas, *op. cit.*
4. Nora Sayre, *Running Time* (New York: The Dial Press, 1982), p. 25.
5. Biskind, p. 271.
6. Michael Wood, *America in the Movies* (New York: Basic Books, 1975), p. 39.
7. David Riesman, Personal communication to the author. January, 1984.
8. Molly Haskell, *From Reverence to Rape: The Treatment of Women in the Movies* (New York: Holt, Rinehart & Winston, 1973), p. 45.
9. Betty Friedan, *The Feminine Mystique* (New York: Norton, 1983), p. 305.
10. Norman Mailer, "The White Negro" in *Advertisements for Myself* (New York: G. P. Putnam, 1959).
11. Joyce Johnson, *Minor Characters* (Boston: Houghton Mifflin, 1983), p. 216.
12. Albert Goldman, *Elvis* (New York: McGraw-Hill, 1981), p. 156.
13. Ibid., p. 304.
14. Pete Townshend, "My Generation."

Chapter 4

1. Susan Allen Toth, *Ivy Days* (Boston: Little-Brown, 1984), p. 28.
2. Norman Podhoretz, "The Young Generation" (1957) in *Doings and Undoings* (New York: Farrar, Straus, 1964), p. 110.
3. Paul Goodman, *Growing Up Absurd* (New York: Random House, 1960), p. 14.
4. Whyte, p. 63.
5. Van Doren's testimony was quoted in full by *Time* magazine, November 16, 1959.
6. Ibid. See also *Newsweek*, November 9, 1959.
7. *Time*, October 19, 1959. For a discussion of Van Doren's large and distinguished family, see *Life*, October 26, 1959.
8. William V. Shannon, in *The New York Post*, quoted in *Time*, November 16, 1959.

Chapter 5

1. Whyte, p. 405–410.
2. Goldman, p. 24.
3. Carson McCullers, *The Member of the Wedding* (Boston: Houghton Mifflin, 1946), p. 50.
4. "A New $10 Billion Power: the U.S. Teen-age Consumer," *Life*, August 31, 1959.
5. Ibid.

Chapter 6

1. David Riesman, "Permissiveness and Sex Roles," *Marriage and Family Living*, XXI, August 1959, 211–217.
2. Samuel Harman Lowrie, "Dating Theories and Student Responses" (1951). Quoted in Hyman Rodman, ed., *Marriage Family and Society* (New York: Random House), p. 9.
3. Miller and Nowak, p. 47.
4. Charles W. Cole, "American Youth Goes Monogamous," *Harper's Magazine*, March 1957, p. 32.
5. George Gilder, *The Naked Nomads: Unmarried Men in America* (New York Quadrangle/New York Times Co., 1974).
6. Sheila Rothman, *Woman's Proper Place* (New York: Basic Books, 1978), p. 182 ff.
7. Willie Morris, *North Toward Home* (Boston: Houghton Mifflin, 1967), p. 172.
8. Nora Johnson, "Sex and the College Girl," *Atlantic*, November 1959, pp. 57–58.

Chapter 7

1. Grace Metalious, *Peyton Place* (New York: Julian Messner, 1956), p. 363.
2. Philip Roth, *Goodbye, Columbus* (Boston: Houghton Mifflin, 1955), p. 82.
3. Herman Wouk, *Marjorie Morningstar* (New York: Doubleday and Co., Inc., 1955), p. 417.
4. Eustace Chesser, *Love Without Fear: How to Achieve Sex Happiness* (New York: Roy Publisher, 1947), p. 82 ff.
5. L. Berg and R. Street, *Sex: Methods and Manners* (New York: Archer House, 1953), p. 14.
6. Fred Brown and R.R. Kempton, *Sex Questions and Answers* (New York: Whittlesey House, 1950), p. 48.
7. Chesser, p. 83.
8. Brown and Kempton, p. 51.
9. Berg and Street, p. 26 ff.
10. G. Lombard Kelly, *Sexual Feeling in Married Men and Women* (New York: Greystone Press, 1951) Figure 9.
11. *The Kama Sutra of Vatsyayana* (London: Unwin Paperbacks, 1963), p. 177.
12. Chesser, p. 81.
13. Leslie H. Farber, "I'm Sorry, Dear:, *Commentary Magazine*, November 1964, 47–64.
14. The phrase of literary critic Philip Rahv.
15. Alex Comfort, *The Joy of Sex, A Gourmet Guide to Lovemaking* (New York: A Fireside Book, Simon & Schuster, 1972), p. 159.

Detours

1. Paul Zweig, *Three Journeys: An Automythology* (New York: Basic Books, 1976), p. 57.
2. Helen Deutsch, "Certain Emotional Disturbances ("As If")" in *Neurosis and Character Types: Classical Psychoanalytic Studies* (New York: International Universities Press, 1965), p. 262–281.

Chapter 8

1. Sloan Wilson, *The Man in the Grey Flannel Suit* (New York: Simon and Schuster, 1955), p. 188–89.
2. David Riesman, see note 5, Chapter 1. The identical attitudes emerge from Otto Butz, *The Unquiet Generation* (New York: Rinehart, 1958), an anthology

of autobiographical essays Professor Butz solicited from his Princeton students, Class of 1957.
3. J.D. Salinger, *The Catcher in the Rye* (Boston: Little Brown & Co., Inc., 1945), p. 160.
4. Riesman cites a 25th anniversary report on Skidmore College. For a sample of *Mademoiselle* magazine readers in 1954, see Chapter 10.
5. Quoted in Mildred Gilman, "Why They Can't Wait to Wed," *Parents Magazine*, November 1958, p. 47.
6. Cherlin, p. 35.
7. Margaret Mead, quoted by Gilman; also Mead, "Marrying in Haste in College," *Columbia University Forum*, Spring, 1960, p. 31.
8. Mead, p. 31.
9. Alfred Kinsey, Wardell B. Pomeroy and Clyde E. Martin, *Sexual Behavior in the Human Male* (Philadelphia: 1948), *passim*.
10. Elaine Tyler May, Explosive Issues: Sex, Women and the Bomb in Post-War America. A paper presented at the annual meeting of the American Historical Association, December 29, 1982. Quoted with the kind permission of the author.
11. Ibid., p. 1.
12. Riesman, p. 435.

Chapter 9

1. Quoted by Martin Mayer, *The Builders* (New York: Norton, 1978), p. 132.
2. *Williamsburg Restoration Reproductions*, a selection from *The Craft House* (Williamsburg, Virginia, 195), p. 43.
3. Jane Davison, *The Fall of a Doll's House* (New York: Holt, Rinehart & Winston, 1980), p. 30.
4. Ibid., p. 185.
5. Miller and Nowak, p. 9.
6. Ibid., p. 405.
7. Warren I. Susman, p. 32.
8. Quoted in Davison, p. 178.
9. Cara Greenberg, *Mid-Century Modern* (New York: Harmony Books, 1984), p. 80.
10. Davison, p. 179.
11. Ernest Dichter, quoted in Betty Friedan, *The Feminine Mystique* (New York: Norton, 1963), p. 206–232.

Chapter 10

1. Charles Cole, quoted by Gilman.
2. Riesman, in "The Found Generation."
3. Richard Easterlin, "Relative Economic Status and the American Fertility Swing," in *Social Structure, Family Life Styles and Economic Behavior*, edited by Eleanor B. Sheldon (Philadelphia: J.B. Lippincott, 1973).
4. Glen H. Elder, Jr., *Children of the Great Depression* (Chicago: University of Chicago Press, 1974).
5. Cherlin, p. 43.
6. Otis L. Wiese, "Live the Life of *McCall's*," *McCall's Magazine*, May, 1954.
7. "Ed and His Family Live Together and Love It," *McCall's Magazine*, May 1954.
8. "The Plight of the Young Mother," *Ladies' Home Journal*, February 1956.
9. Quoted in Sheila Rothman, p. 211.
10. Ibid., p. 210.
11. Ibid., p. 214.

12. Benjamin Spock, *The Common Sense Book of Baby and Child Care* (New York: Duell, Sloan and Pearce, 1946), p. 15.
13. Jonathan Gathorne-Hardy, *The Unnatural History of the Nanny* (New York: The Dial Press, 1973), p. 61.

Chapter 11

1. Riesman, "The Found Generation," p. 433.
2. Russel Lynes, "What Has Succeeded Success?" *Mademoiselle* magazine, September 1954, p. 163.
3. Quoted in Riesman, "Permissiveness and Sex Roles," p. 211.
4. Ibid.
5. Lynes, p. 162.
6. Norman Podhoretz, *Making It* (New York: Random House, 1967), p. xv ff.
7. John Watson, *The Psychological Care of Infant and Child* (New York: W.W. Norton, 1928), p. 75.
8. David Cohen, *J.B. Watson* (London: Routledge & Kegan Press, 1979), p. 112.
9. Spock, p. 15.
10. Arnold Gesell, et al., *Infant and Child in the Culture of Today* (New York: Harper & Row, 1943), p. 210.
11. Spock, p. 15.
12. "Americans on the Move to New Jobs, New Places," *Life Magazine*, February 3, 1951.
13. Stephen Fox, *The Mirror Makers: A History of American Advertising and Its Creators* (New York: William Morrow & Co., Inc.), p. 209.

Chapter 12

1. Norman Mailer, "David Riesman Reconsidered," *Dissent* (Autumn 1954), pp. 358–359.
2. Robert Coles, *Children of Crisis* (Boston: Little Brown, 1967), p. 35.
3. Erving Goffman, *Stigma: Notes on the Management of Spoiled Identity* (Englewood Cliffs, N.J.: Prentice-Hall, 1963).
4. Morris Dickstein, *The Gates of Eden* (New York: Basic Books, 1977).
5. Jane Howard, *Different Woman* (New York: E.P. Dutton, 1973), p. 128.

Chapter 13

1. Arthur Miller, "1949: The Year It Came Apart," *New York Magazine*, December 30, 1974.
2. Dr. Henriette Klein. Interview with the author. November 25, 1984.
3. Studs Terkel, *Hard Times: An Oral History of the Great Depression* (New York: Pantheon Books, 1970), p. 80.
4. Dr. John Weber, Interview with the author. January 6, 1985.
5. Susman, p. 201.
6. Alan S. Gurman and David P. Gniskern, eds., "The History of Professional Marriage and Family Therapy" in *A Handbook of Family Therapy* (New York: Brunner/Mazel, 1981), pp. 11–12.
7. Joseph Veroff, Elizabeth Douvan, Richard A. Kulka, *The Inner American* (New York: Basic Books, 1981), p. 23.

Chapter 14

1. Veroff, et al., p. 15.
2. Many studies have documented the later marriages of young men who leave ethnic or minority communities for college; earlier, Philip Catania noted the avoidance of steady dating in his high school on the part of college-bound boys.

3. "The Changing American Family," Population Reference Bureau, Vol. 38, No. 4, October 1983, p. 7.
4. Veroff, et al., p. 16.
5. Cherlin, p. 48.

Chapter 15

1. Cherlin, pp. 24–25.
2. Jane O'Reilly, "Click! The Housewife's Moment of Truth," in *The Girl I Left Behind* (New York: Macmillan Publishing Co., Inc., 1980).
3. Quoted in Kathryn Perutz, *Marriage Is Hell* (New York: Morrow, 1972), p. 39.
4. Penelope Russianoff, *Why Do I Think I Am Nothing Without a Man* (New York: Bantam Books, 1982).
5. Bruce Jay Friedman, *The Lonely Guy's Book of Life* (New York: McGraw-Hill, 1978).

Chapter 16

1. Greil Marcus, *Mystery Train: Images of America in Rock and Roll Music* (New York: E.P. Dutton, paperback, 1982), p. 189.
2. Albert Goldman, *Elvis* (New York: McGraw-Hill, 1981), p. 206.
3. Patricia Bosworth, *Montgomery Clift* (New York: Harcourt Brace Jovanovich, 1978), p. 25.
4. Venable Herndon, *James Dean: A Short Life* (Garden City, New York: Doubleday, 1984). This quotation and the following biographical material are found in Herndon.
5. Bosworth, op. cit., and following quotations.
6. Joel Schumacher, quoted in George Plimpton, *Edie* (New York: Knopf, 1982), p. 182.
7. Norman Mailer, *Marilyn, a Biography* (New York: Grosset and Dunlap, 1973), p. 15.
8. Haskell, p. 254.
9. Mailer, p. 27.
10. Haskell, p. 255.
11. Monroe's abortions are cited in Fred Lawrence Guiles, *Norma Jean; The Life of Marilyn Monroe* (New York: McGraw-Hill, 1969) and Anthony Summers, *Goddess* (New York: Macmillan, 1985).
12. Frances McCullough, ed., *Journals of Sylvia Plath* (New York: Dial Press, New York, 1982), p. 49.
13. Carol Muske, "Lingua Materna: The Speech of Female History," *The New York Times Book Review*, January 20, 1985, p. 5.
14. Adrienne Rich, *Of Woman Born: Motherhood as Experience and Institution* (New York: Norton, 1976), p. 27.
15. Adrienne Rich, *On Lies, Secrets and Silence* (New York: Norton, 1979), p. 190.
16. Muske, p. 5.
17. Sylvia Plath, *Johnny Panic and the Bible of Dreams and Other Prose Writings* (London: Faber and Faber, 1977), p. 213.
18. Sylvia Plath, *Letters Home:* correspondence, 1950–1963. Selected and edited with commentary by Aurelia Schober Plath (New York: Harper and Row, 1975), p. 466.
19. The preceding descriptions of Plath are from George Stade's introduction to Nancy Hunter Steiner, *A Closer Look at Ariel: A Memory of Sylvia Plath* (New York: Harper's Magazine Press, 1973), pp. 19–20.
20. *Journals*, pp. 60–61.
21. Ibid., p. 308.

22. Clarissa Roche, quoted in Edward Butscher, Ed., *Sylvia Plath: The Woman and the Work* (New York: Dodd, Mead, 1977), pp. 85, 105.
23. Rich, *On Lies, Secrets and Silence*, p. 36.
24. Sylvia Plath, *The Bell Jar* (New York: Harper and Row, 1971), p. 94.

Chapter 17

1. Robert N. Bellah, Richard Madsen, William M. Sullivan, Ann Swidler and Steven M. Tipton, *Habits of the Heart: Individualism and Commitment in American Life* (Berkeley: University of California Press, 1985).
2. "Negative community" is Philip Rieff's phrase for the population of analysands. In the sense of a rejection of other social institutions, his description seems still more applicable to the lesbian separatist movement.
3. David Mare, "Say 'Explication de Texte, Gracie,'" *The Village Voice*, June 25, 1985.

SELECTED BIBLIOGRAPHY

Bosworth, Patricia. *Montgomery Clift*. New York: Harcourt Brace Jovanovich, 1978.

Butz, Otto. *The Unquiet Generation*. New York: Holt, Rinehart and Winston, 1958.

Cherlin, Andrew J. *Marriage, Divorce and Remarriage*. Cambridge, Mass.: Harvard University Press, 1981.

Chesser, Eustace. *Love without Fear*. New York: Roy Publications, 1947.

Davison, Jane. *The Fall of a Doll's House*. Holt, Rinehart and Winston, 1980.

Dickstein, Morris. *The Gates of Eden*. New York: Basic Books, 1977.

Ehrenreich, Barbara. *The Hearts of Men: American Men and the Flight from Commitment*. New York: Anchor Press: Doubleday, 1983.

Ellison, Ralph. *Invisible Man*. New York: Random House, 1952.

Fox, Stephen. *The Mirror Makers: A History of American Advertising and its Creators*. New York: William Morrow, 1984.

Friedan, Betty. *The Feminine Mystique*. New York: W.W. Norton, 1963.

Fromm, Eric. *The Art of Loving*. New York: Harper and Row, 1956.

Fuchs, Victor. *How We Live*. Cambridge, Mass.: Harvard University Press, 1983.

Gesell, Arnold, Ilg, Frances, Bates, Louise Ames. *The Infant and Child in the Culture of Today*. New York: Harper and Row, 1943; re-issued, 1974.

Goffman, Erving. *Stigma: The Management of Spoiled Identity.* Englewood Cliffs, N.J.: Prentice-Hall, 1963.

Goldman, Albert. *Elvis.* New York: McGraw-Hill, 1981.

Goodman, Paul. *Growing Up Absurd.* New York: Random House, 1960.

Haskell, Molly. *From Reverence to Rape: The Treatment of Women in the Movies.* New York: Holt, Rinehart and Winston, 1973.

Herndon, Venable. *James Dean: A Short Life.* Garden City, New York: Doubleday and Co., 1981.

Jaffe, Rona. *The Best of Everything.* New York: Simon and Schuster, 1958.

Lasch, Christopher. *The Culture of Narcissism: American Life in an Age of Diminishing Expectations.* New York: W.W. Norton, 1978.

———. *The Minimal Self.* New York/London: W.W. Norton & Co., 1984.

Lindner, Robert. *Must You Conform?* New York: Holt Rinehart and Winston, 1956.

———. *Prescription for Rebellion.* New York: Grove Press, 1952.

McCullers, Carson. *The Member of the Wedding.* Boston: Houghton Mifflin, 1946.

Mailer, Norman. *Advertisements for Myself.* New York: G.P. Putnam, 1981.

———. *Marilyn, A Biography.* New York: Grosset and Dunlap, 1973.

Marcus, Greil. *Mystery Train: Images of America in Rock and Roll Music.* New York: E.P. Dutton & Co., 1976.

Metalious, Grace. *Peyton Place.* New York: Julian Messner, 1956.

Miller, Douglas T. and Nowak, Marion. *The Fifties: The Way We Really Were.* Garden City, New York: Doubleday and Co., 1977.

Morris, Willie. *North Towards Home.* Boston: Houghton Mifflin, 1967.

Plath, Sylvia. *The Bell Jar.* New York: Harper and Row, 1971.

———. *Journals.* Edited by Frances McCullough. Foreword by Ted Hughes. New York: Dial Press, 1982.

Pleck, Joseph. *The Myth of Masculinity.* Cambridge, Mass., London: The M.I.T. Press, 1981.

Podhoretz, Norman. *Doings and Undoings: The Fifties and After in American Writing.* New York: Farrar, Straus, 1964.

———. *Making It.* New York: Random House, 1967.

Rae, John B. *The American Automobile.* Chicago: University of Chicago Press, 1965.

Riesman, David. *The Lonely Crowd: A Study of the Changing American Character.* In collaboration with Reuel Denny and Nathan Glazer. New Haven: Yale University Press, 1958.

Rich, Adrienne. *Of Woman Born: Motherhood as Experience and Institution.* New York: W.W. Norton, 1976.

———. *On Lies, Secrets and Silence.* New York: W.W. Norton, 1979.

Roth, Philip. *Goodbye, Columbus.* Boston: Houghton Mifflin, 1955.

Rothman, Ellen K. *Hands and Hearts: A Study of Courtship in America.* New York: Basic Books, 1984.

Rothman, Sheila M. *Woman's Proper Place.* New York: Basic Books, 1978.

Salinger, J.D. *The Catcher in the Rye.* Boston: Little Brown and Company, Inc., 1945.

Sayre, Nora. *Running Time.* New York: The Dial Press, 1982.

Smith, Robert Paul. *Where Did You Go? 'Out'. What Did You Do? 'Nothing'.* New York: W.W. Norton and Co., Inc., 1957.

Spock, Benjamin. *The Common Sense Book of Baby and Child Care.* New York: Duell, Sloane and Pearce, 1946, E.P. Dutton, 1974.

Toth, Susan Allen. *Blooming: A Small-Town Girlhood.* Boston: Little-Brown, 1982.

———. *Ivy Days: Making My Way Out East.* Boston: Little-Brown, 1984.

Veroff, Joseph, Douvan, Elizabeth, Kulka, Richard A. *The Inner American: A Self-Portrait from 1957 to 1976.* New York: Basic Books, 1981.

Watson, John. *The Psychological Care of Infant and Child.* New York: W.W. Norton, 1928.

Wilson, Sloan. *The Man in the Grey Flannel Suit.* New York: Simon and Schuster, 1955.

Wouk, Herman. *Marjorie Morningstar.* New York: Doubleday and Company, 1955.

INDEX